A Guide to Prayer

A Guide to Prayer

Rueben P. Job
Norman Shawchuck

Sunday Scripture Readings from the New Common Lectionary

UPPER
ROOM BOOKS®
NASHVILLE

A Guide to Prayer
  for Ministers and Other Servants
Copyright © 1983 by The Upper Room®
All rights reserved.

The Upper Room® Web site: www.upperroom.org

Scripture quotations not otherwise identified are from the Revised Standard Version of the Bible, copyright 1952 [2nd edition, 1971] by the Division of Christian Education of the National Council of the Churches of Christ in the United States of America. Used by permission. All rights reserved.

Scripture quotations designated (GNT) are from the Good News Translation in Today's English Version-Second Edition Copyright © 1992 by American Bible Society. Used by Permission. from the *Good News Bible, The Bible in Today's English Version*, copyright by American Bible Society, 1966, 1971, 1976, and are used by permission.

Book Design: Harriette Bateman
Library of Congress Catalog Card Number: 83-80411
ISBN 978-0-8358-0559-9
Printed in the United States of America

*For every pilgrim
who yearns
for God*

I sit down alone,
    Only God is here;
In his presence I open,
    I read his books;
And what I thus learn,
    I teach.

—John Wesley

Contents

MONTHLY RETREAT MODELS 347

Including Order of Retreat Model and Readings for Reflection

INDEX

Preface

This book was prepared out of our own desperation and search: desperation to find forgiveness for sin, release from guilt, the living God as a companion in our lives and ministries; and a search for resources and disciplines to help keep our relationship with God alive and vital every day. This book, therefore, is not a treatise written by experts; rather, it is a collection of resources by two pilgrims.

Every scripture, prayer, and writing in this book has been used for our own journey. We each have pondered the scriptures and writings and prayed the prayers; we have given ourselves to the daily discipline and the monthly private retreats.

In recent years, we each have been with persons in hundreds of private and group settings. Everywhere, we have discovered other pilgrims in desperate search and eager quest. Everywhere, the questions put to us are, "Now that I have begun the search, what can I do to keep my experience with God alive?" "How should I read the Bible for my own spiritual nurture?" "What can I do when I simply can't pray?" and "What books should I be reading?"

Finally, after much serious prayer, we decided to prepare a book in response to those questions. These are the scriptures, formal prayers, and readings that are feeding us. The daily discipline and monthly retreats are proving a vital key. The disciplines are not easy. Often we go to them not wanting to. The accumulated results to our own lives, however, seem ever to be a larger reward than we might expect from the (sometime reluctant) efforts we are investing in this journey—our great experiment with God.

We are not alone on this journey. Several years ago, the two of us entered into covenant to provide support and to call for accountability of each other in our lives and ministries. Over the years, our covenant community has grown to five persons. The five of us follow the daily discipline of scripture, prayer, and meditation. We all read the same material each day. This has created a "connectedness" among us even when we are separated by many miles and days. We gather for retreat five or six times a year.

There are high moments as we search, dream, and call for accountability to the covenants we have made. As weak and desperate as we are, we could hardly imagine trying to keep the disciplines and to carry on our ministries without the support and accountability of such a community.

This book is for you as an individual and for covenant communities. It is dedicated to the use of each and every pilgrim who may today be yearning for "a word of salvation for my soul."

Rueben P. Job
Norman Shawchuck

Acknowledgments

The first thought of this book originated in the authors' minds more than twenty years ago in their own personal search for spiritual growth and development. In the intervening years we have benefited greatly from the resources of other pilgrims provided to assist us on our journey. As we developed the disciplines that seemed most helpful to us and as we talked with and taught thousands of others who were in search of vital piety, the book in your hands began to take shape. And so it is that we express our sincere gratitude to each one who has offered assistance, guidance, counsel, and has pointed us Godward.

We are especially grateful to Maxie Dunnam, Janice Grana, Charla Honea, and Jill Reddig, who believed enough in the project to encourage us and who gave wise counsel and careful work throughout the process. We give thanks to and for family and friends who helped us hear and respond to the voice of God.

Our deep gratitude goes to each of the following people who offered a resource for the Readings for Reflection:

Bishop James Armstrong, Harrell F. Beck, Boyd Blumer, Bishop Edwin C. Boulton, Calvin L. Bremer, Ron Crews, John D. Crocker, John C. Dickau, William D. Ellington, Duane A. Ewers, Persis Flint, Roger Heuser, Mary Ann Hopkins, Beth Kelsey, Judy Kerr, DuWayne Lee, Nick Mager, Jim McKinney, C. Ray Miller, Danny E. Morris, Bruce Ough, Robert Paul, Lloyd M. Perry, Margaret A. Piderman, Glenn C. Smith, Kip Stratton, Sister Rita Thier, Dick Ward, John E. Weeks, Gwen White, Robert R. Wood.

How to Use This Book

This book contains materials for daily prayer and meditation and for monthly private retreats. The daily helps are clustered under weekly themes which basically follow the themes established by the New Common Lectionary. We deviated from the ecumenical lectionary themes only when we felt other themes might be more helpful.

To support daily prayer and meditation, we have adopted the following daily office:

Invocation. A call to enter into the presence of the Lord in faith that the Lord is waiting to meet with us. We have used ancient and modern prayers and encourage you to supplement them with the prayers most helpful to you.

Psalm. The Psalms are Christianity's most universal prayers. They speak to everyone's need and experience. Make the psalm your personal prayer—pray the psalm.

Some people are disturbed by the "bloodthirstiness" of many of the psalms and have rejected them to their own spiritual deprivation. In fact, the Psalms can (and should) be used to remind us of the "enemies" that seek our destruction, that we should hate, and then to guide us into prayer that God may destroy them before they destroy us.

In earlier times and places, the enemies were physical and concrete. This was the case in the experience of the writers of the psalms. David did have a death warrant hanging over his head; an army was dogging his every step; he and his companions did have reason to fear the "arrow that flies by day" and the "pestilence that stalks in darkness" (Psalm 91:5-6).

Those who first heard the psalms knew there were real lions, tigers, and serpents "out there," and the tents they called home were slim protection from such enemies.

But what about us? Are our lives free of "arrows" and "terrors" and "enemies" which threaten to destroy us? No,the "enemies" are just as many and as deadly, but they are now "in here," inside us, and they are more subtle and harder to escape—enemies such as the lust for power, worry, fear, laziness, spiritual boredom, unrelenting anger, extramarital relationships, pride, coveting another pastor's parish.

If we see the "bloodthirsty" psalms as the expression of frustration and helplessness every Christian experiences as he or she struggles against the enemies unique to himself or herself and a desperate plea for God's justice and deliverance, then the psalms can become some of our most powerfull prayers.

Spiritual growth requires that we do battle, not that we pretend the enemy is not there. The journey into the wilderness by the children of Israel—there to confront enemies, terrors, hardships and to discover the guardian care of God's angels—is a true picture of our own journey. In these struggles, the word of God is one of our greatest resources of prayers, hope, and direction—resources that may be wasted if we do not define our own wilderness and the enemies lurking there.

We list only one psalm for each week, suggesting you live with that psalm throughout the week. You may also want to read one or more other psalms each day.

Daily Scripture Readings. The daily scripture readings are intended to support the theme for the week. One scripture passage is given for each weekday. The three-cycle Sunday scriptures follow the ecumenical lectionary. If you wish to follow the ecumenical lectionary for the Sunday readings, please follow the notations at the beginning of each week.

We selected the weekday passages to be more specifically related to the spirituality and life experience of a person engaged in ministry. The Sunday scriptures are targeted more toward the life experience of the entire church community.

We suggest you read two passages each day—the one listed for that particular day and one selected from the Sunday passages. In addition, you may be led to a different passage which, for you, speaks powerfully to the theme in your own experience. When this happens, we urge you to record that scripture along with our selections in order that you may return to it in succeeding years of using these scriptures. That which sets scripture apart from all other writing is its universal and its singular appeal. It speaks to persons of every tribe and generation as though it were written for each individual alone. In order to accomplish this it was written in symbolic language.

A symbol is a representation of a greater reality. The symbol is not the reality but points to it. In order to grasp the truth of a symbol one must not look "at" it but through it to the greater reality that awaits discovery by the one who has eyes to see and ears to hear (Matt. 11:15).

Jesus wanted his teaching to have universal and singular appeal, and for that reason he taught through parables (Mark 4:33-34). To the person who carefully searches each Bible story it will reveal hidden truth suited for that person's situation-in-life. For the person who does not dig deeply, the symbols will remain nontransparent.

To help you to see through the story we suggest a two-step process for reading the scripture. First, read the passage with an open mind and heart, letting words flow into your being. Then respond to the scripture. Be aware of the scripture in relation to your own history, actions, and desires. Enter into dialogue with the scripture with your heart, mind, and emotions. Read it not as a portion of a book written for everyone, but as a letter written just to you—the message of one thinking only of you when writing.

Through the analogies, metaphors, parables, and "plain talk," enter into a personal dialogue with God-as-author. Then, it will help to make the passage uniquely yours if you search for insight into certain questions: (1) What is this passage telling me about God? (2) What is this scripture telling me about myself? What is God trying to say to me right now? (3) What does this scripture have to say to me about my ministry at this time?

It may be that you will want to read only one verse or a few verses, and that you will want to stay with those few words for several days. You can do this, knowing the Holy Spirit has still more to say to you out of the passage.

The point is to stay with each passage for a day or longer, until it builds for itself a nest in your heart from which it may speak to you all day long.

What we are suggesting is that you prayerfully ponder the passage—that you meditate upon it in such a way that it may flow into and through your life like oil through a sieve that leaves its essence upon every fine part of the sieve long after the last visible drop is gone. This is meditation.

There is, of course, another way to come to the scripture. That is to come to it not as a personal word but as a resource entrusted to us for ministry. In this manner, we study the passage to gain insights for preaching and programming; we read and teach it to others to comfort or instruct them. This is a vital aspect of your scripture reading, but we urge you to do this type of reading/study outside of your daily personal prayer times.

Readings for Reflection. In addition to the daily scripture, we suggest you reflect on one or more of the readings. There is great value in immersing ourselves in another's experiences of God. As we listen to another person's story, we come to see more clearly the movement of God in our own lives. This has always been so. Whenever the Israelites became discouraged or frightened or forgetful, their leaders would get them together to tell them "the story" one more time. They would always find God hidden in the story. And in finding God within another's experience they were able to interpret the movement of God within their own. We think it will be that way for you also.

The readings were selected to provide a variety of approaches to the theme for the week. All readings were chosen to speak to your life and ministry.

Wherever possible, we have changed generic male references to more inclusive language. Unfortunately, this was not always possible. We encourage you to mentally change these masculine terms as you read the passages.

Prayers. All that increases our awareness of God is prayer; therefore, all that you do in your daily prayer time is prayer. You will pray the psalm, pray the scripture, pray your personal and intercessory prayers. Your journal time will become a time of writing prayers. The hymn will become a time of poetic praying.

However, the daily office also includes a time for you to talk to God in your own way. There are various ways to pray; and each of us, while using several methods, generally will find one method that best fits our personality.

The desert mothers and fathers often spoke of three methods of prayer: verbal, silent thought, and contemplation, a type of prayer in which active thought is suspended as the person focuses attention on a simple word or a brief prayer. One method is not better than the others. We should feel free to utilize the method that best fits our mood of the moment or our basic personality type.

Two conditions are important to nurture a consistent prayer discipline, solitude and silence. Solitude is being by oneself. Silence is the quality of stillness within and around oneself. It will also help your praying to select one place to which you can go daily. You will soon find God is waiting for you in that place.

The time set apart for "prayers" may include adoration, confession, intercession (praying for others), and praying for yourself and your ministry.

Our prayers are often crippled because we do not support them by fasting. In Matthew 6, Jesus clearly taught an inexorable relationship between the two. Indeed, the "closet" in which effective praying is done must often be the "inner room" of fasting.

Fasting, perhaps as much as anything else, helps us to go into our "inner room," the space within ourselves. Fasting helps us shut the door of our inner selves to the outside attractions that crowd in and dissipate our prayer times and energies.

Fasting is the act of temporarily giving up something that is very important to us in order that we may use the time normally given to that thing for prayer and reflect upon the pain of the temporary "sacrifice" to better understand the mystery and meaning of Christ's passion and sacrifice for us.

Intercessory prayer can be greatly strengthened by fasting. In our retreats, for example, we often meet persons who struggle with their weight but feel helpless against their desire to overeat. We collect their names, and in our own periods of fasting (when we are feeling the pain of going without food), we pray for our friends who cannot yet bring themselves to eat less. And we pray for those who are hungry every day, for those who never know the privilege of a fast because they are forced to starve.

Reflection. At this point, we invite you to reflect on all the words, thoughts, and emotions you have experienced during the daily office and to record new insights, new commitments, a prayer. At other times, you will write about dullness, your struggle to pray at all, discouragement.

Be entirely honest in your writing. Write for yourself and God alone! Resist every temptation to quote from your journal or to allow anyone else to read any part of it. Your journal is to become a private log of your spiritual journey. The only exception to this may be when you share something in your journal with a spiritual guide.

Your journal is to become a personal record of your journey with God. It will enable you to reflect on the events and impulses of your life, to interpret their meanings, and to discover where God is leading you through those circumstances. Your journal will become a "travel log" and "road map" to help you recall and reflect on where you have been and to identify indicators of where you are going.

To do this, we suggest you use your journal daily, although you may find that writing weekly or at those times when an emotion or insight prompts you to do so is more suited to your needs. We also urge you to review your journal once a month, preferably at your monthly one-day private retreat. Over time, this will allow you to discern the movements and directions of God's leading in your life.

For several years we have made it a practice to devote a week each January to assessing our life and ministry of the year past and to setting directions and goals for the new year. We begin this week of reflection by reading through our entire journal of the past year. Each time we are able to celebrate problems that have been solved, changes that have occurred—and we are brought face-to-face with covenants unkept, disciplines not developed.

For your journal we recommend an inexpensive eight and one-half by eleven-inch spiral bound notebook. Generally, write about one-half page a day, although at certain times you may find yourself writing much more. The point is to focus your writing. Do not ramble; be specific.

Occasionally during your private prayer time you will discover insights, have a sermon idea or thought that you will want to share with others. Rather than putting these in your journal, we suggest you keep another notebook for this purpose.

Hymn. One hymn related to the stated theme is recommended for each week. When you are unable to formulate your own prayer, you can let the hymn be your prayer. Pray the hymn. The words of the hymn are included as the final entry in the Readings for Reflection for each week.

A Special Word Regarding the Monthly One-Day Retreats. We recommend that you spend one day a month in private retreat. To assist you in this we have included in this book a schedule of themes, a design to follow, and supporting resources.

The retreat models are designed for individual use although they can be utilized by two or more persons. Each retreat is planned for a twenty-four-hour period of time. Maximum benefit may be gained in a setting away from everyday routines. A retreat center, a camp, a motel room, a room in a church, or an unused room in the home can provide the necessary space. Only as a last resort use your office, study, or living room for your retreat.

Adjust the hours to fit your schedule, but try to give the necessary time to each segment of the retreat experience. Remember it is God who meets you and who provides for you. Have confidence that God's provision is adequate for your need. It is natural to wonder, what will I do? Have no fear. Countless numbers of persons have discovered that God is able to provide more than enough to sustain them in such a setting. Do not fear the solitude and silence of retreat. They can be the friends that reveal the presence of God. Resist the temptation to do your regular work during this retreat. However, many have discovered that the personal retreat setting is a good time to explore a spiritual formation book or resource in a more concentrated manner.

Some persons find that a day of fasting provides excellent preparation for a day of retreat. You may wish to try fasting during or following your retreat. Be sure to check with your health care specialist before embarking on a long fast for the first time.

If you wish to spend a week in retreat you may use two or more of the daily models to provide guidance for your reflection and response. Some have found that any one of the models is adequate for a week's retreat. To intentionally place oneself in God's presence and to ask, Lord, what do you think of me? Lord, what changes do you desire in my life and ministry? To have these questions in mind as one reflects on the scriptures, covenants made, the writings of the saints, and the events of our time is to provide opportunity for the Lord to draw us toward greater faithfulness. To reflect on the meaning of one's calling and to offer life totally to God again is to gain insight and strength for ministry.

Feel at liberty to adjust the retreat to meet your needs. Remember, God is your leader and spiritual director. The simplicity of the retreat models is intentional. The opportunity for quiet reflection, relaxation, and response to God is a great gift. Be attentive, open, listening, and receptive. You will not be disappointed.

Conclusion. In the journey of spirituality and faith, God will sometimes lead us into times when prayer is easy, spontaneous, and exciting; then after a while, we may be led into times when prayer is dull, prayer-thoughts become jumbled, words do not come, the heavens seem like barriers. God leads us into these times in order to keep us from spiritual pride—to remind us that even prayer is possible only through God's initiative. Prayer is a grace, a gift from God.

Nonetheless, we are to learn how to pray. What a dilemma! On the one hand, prayer is a gift. It is something we receive, and we are to wait in silent expectation for the gift. On the other hand, we can learn how to pray, and we are to give ourselves to the discipline of learning how to pray.

Our own personal commitment to solitude and prayer includes at least one hour each day, one day each month, one week each year. We give ourselves to this, knowing that without consistent prayer and meditation upon scripture there can be no spiritual growth. We invite you to undertake this intentional journey for the next twelve months. You will discover God near as you journey. You will also discover that during the next twelve months your life will be transformed.

Weekly
Devotional
Themes

1: *The Lord Is Coming*

I. Invocation
Almighty God, who came to us long ago in the birth of Jesus Christ, be born in us anew today by the power of your Holy Spirit. We offer our lives as home to you and ask for grace and strength to live as your faithful, joyful children always. Through Jesus Christ our Lord. Amen.

II. Psalm 95

III. Daily Scripture Readings

Monday		Matthew 3
Tuesday		Colossians 1:9-23
Wednesday		John 18:33-37
Thursday		Isaiah 43:1-21
Friday		Hebrews 10:11-25
Saturday		Zephaniah 3:14-20
Sunday	A.	Isaiah 2:1-5; Psalm 122; Romans 13:11-14; Matthew 24:36-44
	B.	Isaiah 63:16–64:8; Psalm 80:1-7; 1 Corinthians 1:3-9; Mark 13:32-37
	C.	Jeremiah 33:14-16; Psalm 25:1-10; 1 Thessalonians 3:9-13; Luke 21:25-36

IV. Readings for Reflection

V. Prayers: for the church, for others, for myself

VI. Reflection: silent and written

VII. Hymn: "Lift Up Your Heads, Ye Mighty Gates"

VIII. Benediction
You have been reminded that Jesus Christ is your Lord and that you are God's servant. You are loved; you are forgiven; you are empowered; and now you are sent to live as God's faithful one. Amen.

Readings for Reflection

✤ To have found God, to have experienced him in the intimacy of our being, to have lived even for one hour in the fire of his Trinity and the bliss of his Unity clearly makes us say: "Now I understand. You alone are enough for me."
—From *The God Who Comes* by Carlo Carretto

✤ Personal prayer is the meeting place between the Eternal One and me; the Blessed Sacrament is the visible sign of my covenant with him.

That is why I believe in personal prayer, and why every day I wait to meet him in the Eucharist. To pray means to wait for the God who comes.

Every prayer-filled day sees a meeting with the God who comes; every night which we faithfully put at his disposal is full of his presence.

And his coming and his presence are not only the result of our waiting or a prize for our efforts: they are his decision, based on his love freely poured out.

His coming is bound to his promise, not to our works or virtue. We have not earned the meeting with God because we have served him faithfully in our brethren, or because we have heaped up such a pile of virtue as to shine before Heaven.

God is thrust onward by his love, not attracted by our beauty. He comes even in moments when we have done everything wrong, when we have done nothing . . . when we have sinned.
—From *The God Who Comes* by Carlo Carretto

✤ You will find the living God in the pages of the Bible. You will find him also just exactly where you are. When Jesus knew that he would not have much longer with his disciples he knew that they were sad at heart and he said to them: "It is for your own good that I am going because unless I go, the Advocate will not come to you; but if I do go, I will send him to you . . . I still have many things to say to you, but they would be too much for you now. But when the Spirit of truth comes he will lead you to the complete truth." (John 16:7,12,13) Jesus does not break his promise.

God has sent the Spirit of truth, he dwells in your heart. You have only to listen, to follow, and he will lead you to the complete truth. He leads through all the events, all the circumstances of your life. Nothing in your life is so insignificant, so small, that God cannot be found at its centre. We think of God in the dramatic things, the glorious sunsets, the majestic mountains, the tempestuous seas; but he is in the little things too, in the smile of a passerby or the gnarled hands of an old man, in a daisy, a tiny insect, falling leaves. God is in the music, in laughter and in sorrow too. And the grey times, when monotony stretches out ahead, these can be the times of steady, solid growth into God.

God may make himself known to you through the life of someone who, for you, is an ambassador for God, in whom you can see the beauty and truth and the love of God; anyone from St. Paul and the apostles through all the centuries to the present day, the great assembly of the saints and lovers of God. It may be that there is someone who loves you so deeply that you dare to believe that you are worth loving and so you can believe that God's love for you could be possible after all. Sometimes it is through tragedy or serious illness that God speaks to our hearts and we know him for the first time. There is no limit to the ways in which God may make himself known. At every turn in our lives there can be a meeting place with God. How our hearts should sing with joy and thanksgiving! We have only to want him now at this moment—and at any moment in our lives—and he is there, wanting us, longing to welcome us, to forgive us all that has gone before that has separated us from him. "If anyone loves me he will keep my word, and my Father will love him, *and we shall come to him and make our home with him.*" (John 14:23) God makes his home in you. They are not empty words. It is true. "Make your home in me, as I make mine in you." This is prayer. Isn't this the answer to all our yearning, our searching, our anguish, to all the longing, the incompleteness of our lives and of our loving? Until we dwell in him and allow him to dwell in us we shall be strangers to peace.

—From *Prayer* by Mother Frances Dominica

ᨆ *Behold, I stand at the door and knock: if any man hear my voice and open the door, I will come in to him, and will sup with him, and he with me.*—Revelation 3:20.

I doubt that I know of a passage in the whole Bible which throws greater light upon prayer than this one does. It is, it seems to me, the key which opens the door into the holy and blessed realm of prayer.

To pray is to let Jesus come into our hearts.

This teaches us, in the first place, that it is not our prayer which moves the Lord Jesus. It is Jesus who moves us to pray. He knocks. Thereby he makes known his desire to come in to us. Our prayers are always a result of Jesus knocking at our hearts' doors.

This throws new light upon the old prophetic passages: "Before they call, I will answer; and while they are yet speaking, I will hear" (Isaiah 65:24). Yea, verily, before we call, he graciously makes known to us what gift he has decided to impart to us. He knocks in order to move us by prayer to open the door and accept the gift which he has already appointed for us.

From time immemorial prayer has been spoken of as the breath of the soul. And the figure is an excellent one indeed.

The air which our body requires envelops us on every hand. The air of itself seeks to enter our bodies and, for this reason, exerts pressure upon us. It is well known that it is more difficult to hold one's breath than it is to breathe. We need but exercise our organs of respiration, and air will enter forthwith into our lungs and perform its life-giving function to the entire body.

The air which our souls need also envelopes all of us at all times and on all sides. God is round about us in Christ on every hand, with his many-sided and all-sufficient grace. All we need to do is to open our hearts.

Prayer is the breath of the soul, the organ by which we receive Christ into our parched and withered hearts.

He says, "If any man open the door, I will come in to him."

Notice carefully every word here. It is not our prayer which draws Jesus into our hearts. Nor is it our prayer which moves Jesus to come in to us.

All he needs is access. He enters in of his own accord, because he desires to come in. And he enters in wherever he is not denied admittance.

As air enters in quietly when we breathe, and does its normal work in our lungs, so Jesus enters quietly into our hearts and does his blessed work there.

He calls it to "sup with us."

In Biblical language the common meal is symbolical of intimate and joyous fellowship. This affords a new glimpse into the nature of prayer, showing us that God has designed prayer as a means of intimate and joyous fellowship between God and ourselves.

—From *Prayer* by O. Hallesby

❧ The best metaphor for our world of today is astronauts speeding through the cosmos, but with their life-supporting capsule pierced by a meteorite fragment. But the Church resembles Mary and Joseph traveling from Egypt to Nazareth on a donkey, holding in their arms the weakness and poverty of the Child Jesus: God incarnate.

—From *The God Who Comes* by Carlo Carretto

❧ When her husband is near and does not let her want for anything she expects, hopes for and enjoys, a wife says she loves her husband, says it easily and normally. But when the husband is far away, when the waiting is prolonged for months and years, when doubt grows that he will ever return, oh, then the true test of love begins!

What light, what splendors in the possibilities this wife has to resist, while she fixes her eyes on the anonymous crowd and tries to pick out him, only him!

What power of real, living, strong testimony emanates from the faithful vigilance, the unquenchable hope, which this woman lives behind the bitter doorway of waiting!

Oh, how each one of us would like to be the bridegroom who returns disguised as a poor stranger, whom she does not recognize, but to whom she repeats, again and again, her certainty of his return and the sweetness of his love!

Well, every evening, when the darkness wraps itself round my prayer, he, God, is there, disguised as a poor man watching me.

When I endure, in the darkness of faith, the prolonged wait for the God who comes, he has already come to me and is embracing me silently, with the same embrace with which I, in faith, embrace him.
—From *The God Who Comes* by Carlo Carretto

All things are shadows of the shining true:
Sun, sea, and air—close, potent, hurtless fire—
Flowers from their mother's prison—dove, and dew—
Every thing holds a slender guiding clue
Back to the mighty oneness: hearts of faith
Know thee than light, than heat, endlessly nigher,
Our life's life, carpenter of Nazareth.
—From *Diary of an Old Soul* by George MacDonald

Thou far! That word the holy truth doth blur.
Doth the great ocean from the small fish run
When it sleeps fast in its low weedy bower?
Is the sun far from any smallest flower,
That lives by his dear presence every hour?
Are they not one in oneness without stir—
The flower the flower because the sun the sun?
—From *Diary of an Old Soul* by George MacDonald

Hymn: Lift Up Your Heads, Ye Mighty Gates

Lift up your heads, ye mighty gates;
Behold the King of glory waits;
The King of kings is drawing near;
The Savior of the world is here!

Fling wide the portals of your heart;
Make it a temple, set apart
From earthly use for heaven's employ,
Adorned with prayer and love and joy.

Redeemer, come, with us abide;
Our hearts to thee we open wide;
Let us thy inner presence feel;
Thy grace and love in us reveal. Amen.
—Georg Weissel

2: Preparing the Way

    I.   Invocation

        O God our Father, who didst send forth thy Son to be King of kings and Prince of Peace: Grant that all the kingdoms of this world may become the kingdom of Christ, and learn of him the way of peace. Send forth among all people the spirit of good will and reconciliation. In the name of Jesus Christ. Amen. —From *The Book of Worship*

    II.   Psalm 138

    III.   Daily Scripture Readings

Monday	Luke 1:5-25, 57-80
Tuesday	Matthew 4:1-6; 28:18-20
Wednesday	Matthew 3:1-12
Thursday	Isaiah 62
Friday	John 1:6-34
Saturday	Mark 1:1-8
Sunday	A. Isaiah 11:1-10; Psalm 72:1-8; Romans 15:4-13; Matthew 3:1-12
	B. Isaiah 40:1-11; Psalm 85:8-13; 2 Peter 3:8-15a; Mark 1:1-8
	C. Malachi 3:1-4; Psalm 126; Philippians 1:3-11; Luke 3:1-6

    IV.   Readings for Reflection

    V.   Prayers: for the church, for others, for myself

    VI.   Reflection: silent and written

    VII.   Hymn: "There's a Voice in the Wilderness Crying"

    VIII.   Benediction

        The Lord bless you and keep you: the Lord make his face shine upon you, and be gracious to you: the Lord lift up his countenance upon you, and give you peace. Amen. —Numbers 6:24-26

Readings For Reflection

⁊❧ It is a primary truth of Christianity that God reaches us directly. No person is insulated. As ocean floods the inlets, as sunlight environs the plant, so God enfolds and enwreathes the finite spirit. There is this difference, however, inlet and plant are penetrated whether they will or not. Sea and sunshine crowd themselves in *a tergo*. Not so with God. He can be received only through appreciation and conscious appropriation. He comes only through doors that are *purposely* opened for him. A person may live as near God as the bubble is to the ocean and yet not find him. He may be "closer than breathing, nearer than hands or feet," and still be missed. Historical Christianity is dry and formal when it lacks the immediate and inward response to our Great Companion; but our spirits are trained to know him, to appreciate him, by the mediation of historical revelation. A person's spiritual life is always dwarfed when cut apart from history. Mysticism is empty unless it is enriched by outward and historical revelation. The supreme education of the soul comes through an intimate acquaintance with Jesus Christ of history.

—From *The Double Search* by Rufus M. Jones

⁊❧ While I was beseeching Our Lord to-day that he would speak through me, since I could find nothing to say and had no idea how to begin to carry out the obligation laid upon me by obedience, a thought occurred to me which I will now set down, in order to have some foundation on which to build. I began to think of the soul as if it were a castle made of a single diamond or of very clear crystal, in which there are many rooms, just as in Heaven there are many mansions. Now if we think carefully over this, sisters, the soul of the righteous person is nothing but a paradise, in which, as God tells us, he takes his delight. For what do you think a room will be like which is the delight of a King so mighty, so wise, so pure and so full of all that is good? I can find nothing with which to compare the great beauty of a soul and its great capacity.

—From *Interior Castle* by Saint Teresa of Avila

ఠ Accompany me to-day, O Spirit invisible, in all my goings, but stay with me also when I am in my own home and among my kindred. Forbid that I should fail to show to those nearest to me the sympathy and consideration which thy grace enables me to show to others with whom I have to do. Forbid that I should refuse to my own household the courtesy and politeness which I think proper to show to strangers. Let charity to-day begin at home.

Leave me not, O gracious Presence, in such hours as I may to-day devote to the reading of books or of newspapers. Guide my mind to choose the right books and, having chosen them, to read them in the right way. When I read for profit, grant that all I read may lead me nearer to thyself. When I read for recreation, grant that what I read may not lead me away from thee. Let all my reading so refresh my mind that I may the more eagerly seek after whatsoever things are pure and fair and true.

Let me have a special sense of thy nearness to me, O God, in such times as I may be able to devote to prayer, to any public exercise of worship, or to the receiving of the Blessed Sacrament; through Jesus Christ my Lord. Amen.

—From *A Diary of Private Prayer* by John Baillie

ఠ We live at a time when holders of power are suspect and actions that stem from authority are questioned. *Legitimize power* has become an ethical imperative. Can discriminating people be helped to find the means for legitimizing power?

There are legions of persons of good will who could sharpen and clarify their view of the more serving society they would like to live in and help build—if in no other way than by holding a deepened interest and concern about it and speaking to the condition of others. Is not such widespread action necessary if the climate that favors service, and supports servants, is to be maintained?

—From *Servant Leadership* by Robert K. Greenleaf

ఠ Christ has
   No body now on earth but yours;
   No hands but yours;
   No feet but yours;
   Yours are the eyes

Through which is to look out
Christ's compassion to the world;
Yours are the feet
With which he is to go about
Doing good;
Yours are the hands
With which he is to bless now.
—Saint Teresa of Avila

❧ Having said all this, I realize that I have done nothing more than rephrase the fact that the Christian leader must be in the future what he has always had to be in the past: a man of prayer, a man who has to pray, and who has to pray always. That I bring up this simple fact at this point may be surprising, but I hope I have succeeded in taking away all the sweet, pietistic, and churchy aura attached to this often misused word.

For a man of prayer is, in the final analysis, the man who is able to recognize in others the face of the Messiah and make visible what was hidden, make touchable what was unreachable. The man of prayer is a leader precisely because through his articulation of God's work within himself he can lead others out of confusion to clarification; through his compassion he can guide them out of the closed circuits of their in-groups to the wide world of humanity; and through his critical contemplation he can convert their convulsive destructiveness into creative work for the new world to come.

—From *The Wounded Healer* by Henri J. M. Nouwen

❧ O Holy Spirit of God, visit now this soul of mine, and tarry within it until eventide. Inspire all my thoughts. Pervade all my imaginations. Suggest all my decisions. Lodge in my will's most inward citadel and order all my doings. Be with me in my silence and in my speech, in my haste and in my leisure, in company and in solitude, in the freshness of the morning and in the weariness of the evening; and give me grace at all times to rejoice in thy mysterious companionship.

—From *A Diary of Private Prayer* by John Baillie

ॐ Yes, Jesus reveals the Father and gives witness to him. He is the One who knows everything about him.

He speaks about him as though he saw him, as though he were in continuous communion with him, as someone with whom he has always lived and whose character, tastes, habits, and way of life he knows.

This is what is so marvelous about the gospels—nothing could have replaced Jesus in this mission. Through his words we come to know God himself, his exact will, his way of looking at things, his most intimate desires, his holy countenance.

But what is even more marvelous—in fact, divine—is that throughout the accounts of the precise words and the detailed experiences of Jesus, the mystery of God's face remains total, the night of divine Transcendence is as thick as it was in the temple of the first covenant. We are obliged to live on faith, hope and love, just as we always were.

Jesus does not shift the balance in the relationship between creature and Creator. This balance rests only on the human's act of abandonment and God's act of gratuitous love.

I should say that, although Jesus has given us the "photograph" of the Father in the gospels, the mystery, the "unknowing" of God remains. We see, and yet we do not see; we become acquainted, and yet we still need to become further acquainted; we know, but we are still very ignorant. It is a photograph that we are able and unable to see.

It depends on you. You are the camera, able to fix inside yourself what you see and what you don't see in the gospels and thus to make a photograph of your own. You know that the power of fixing an image in the soul depends on the Holy Spirit, who is love, who alone is able to make that photograph in proportion to your intimacy with him.

—From *The God Who Comes* by Carlo Carretto

Hymn: There's a Voice in the Wilderness Crying

There's a voice in the wilderness crying,
A call from the ways untrod;
Prepare in the desert a highway,
A highway for our God!
The valleys shall be exalted,
The lofty hills brought low;
Make straight all the crooked places,
Where the Lord our God may go!

O Zion, that bringest good tidings,
Get thee up to the heights and sing!
Proclaim to a desolate people
The coming of their King.
Like the flowers of the field they perish,
The works of all decay,
The power and pomp of nations
Shall pass like a dream away.

But the word of our God endureth,
The arm of the Lord is strong;
He stands in the midst of nations,
And he will right the wrong.
He shall feed his flock like a shepherd,
And fold the lambs to his breast;
In his pastures of peace he'll lead them,
And give to the weary rest.

There's a voice in the wilderness crying,
A call from the ways untrod;
Prepare in the desert a highway,
A highway for our God!
The valleys shall be exalted,
The lofty hills brought low;
Make straight all the crooked places,
Where the Lord our God may go! Amen.
—James L. Milligan

3: *The Coming of Christ*

I. Invocation

O Lord God, whose chosen dwelling is the heart of the lowly: We give thee thanks that thou didst reveal thyself in the holy child Jesus, thereby sanctifying all childhood in him. We beseech thee to make us humble in faith and love, that we may know the joy of the Gospel that is hidden from the wise and prudent and revealed unto babes. Amen.

—From *The Book of Worship*

II. Psalm 85

III. Daily Scripture Readings

Monday		Mark 13:1-13, 24-37
Tuesday		Luke 21:25-36
Wednesday		Revelation 1:1-8
Thursday		Ezekiel 34:1-10
Friday		Luke 12:35-48
Saturday		Acts 1:1-11
Sunday	A.	Isaiah 35:1-10; Psalm 146:5-10; James 5:7-10; Matthew 11:2-11
	B.	Isaiah 61:1-4, 8-11; Luke 1:46b-55; 1 Thessalonians 5:16-24; John 1:6-8, 19-28
	C.	Zephaniah 3:14-20; Isaiah 12:2-6; Philippians 4:4-9; Luke 3:7-18

IV. Readings for Reflection

V. Prayers: for the church, for others, for myself

VI. Reflection: silent and written

VII. Hymn: "Come, Thou Long-Expected Jesus"

VIII. Benediction

Lord, allow me, your servant, to go in peace. I have experienced your salvation that you have prepared for everyone. Uphold me as I seek to serve in your name. Amen.

Readings For Reflection

❧ These souls, then, can understand the Lord when he calls them; for, as they gradually get nearer to the place where his Majesty dwells, he becomes a very good Neighbour to them. And such are his mercy and goodness that, even when we are engaged in our worldly pastimes and businesses and pleasures and hagglings, when we are falling into sins and rising from them again (because these creatures are at once so venomous and so active and it is so dangerous for us to be among them that it will be a miracle if we escape stumbling over them and falling)—in spite of all that, this Lord of ours is so anxious that we should desire him and strive after his companionship that he calls us ceaselessly, time after time, to approach him; and this voice of his is so sweet that the poor soul is consumed with grief at being unable to do his bidding immediately; and thus, as I say, it suffers more than if it could not hear him.

I do not mean by this that he speaks to us and calls us in the precise way which I shall describe later; his appeals come through the conversations of good people, or from sermons, or through the reading of good books; and there are many other ways, of which you have heard, in which God calls us. Or they come through sicknesses and trials, or by means of truths which God teaches us at times when we are engaged in prayer; however feeble such prayers may be, God values them highly. You must not despise this first favour, sisters, nor be disconsolate, even though you have not responded immediately to the Lord's call; for his Majesty is quite prepared to wait for many days, and even years, especially when he sees we are persevering and have good desires.

—From *Interior Castle* by Saint Teresa of Avila

❧ God presents himself to us little by little. The whole story of salvation is the story of God who comes.

It is always he who comes, even if he has not yet come in his fullness. But there is indeed one unique moment in his coming; the others were only preparations and announcement.

The hour of his coming is the Incarnation.

The Incarnation brings the world his presence. It is a presence so complete that it overshadows every presence before it.

God is made human in Christ. God makes himself present to us with such a special presence, such an obvious presence, as to overthrow all the complicated calculations made about him in the past.

"The invisible, intangible God has made himself visible and tangible in Christ."

If Jesus is truly God, everything is clear; if I cannot believe this, everything darkens again.

—From *The God Who Comes* by Carlo Carretto

John says something that touches us deeply at the distance of centuries. In unparalleled words he writes with rousing witness:

> This is what we proclaim to you:
> what was from the beginning,
> what we have heard,
> what we have seen with our eyes,
> what we have looked upon
> and our hands have touched—
> we speak of the word of life.
> (1 John 1:1)

How existential is this beautiful sentence of John's: "What . . . our hands have touched."

Yes, Jesus, God on earth, was touched by human beings, handled, gazed on.

—From *The God Who Comes* by Carlo Carretto

The contemplation of God is not effected by sight and hearing, nor is it comprehended by any of the customary perceptions of the mind. For *no eye has seen, and no ear has heard,* nor does it belong to those things which usually enter *into the heart.* One who would approach the knowledge of things sublime must first purify one's manner of life from all sensual and irrational emotion. That person must wash from his or her understanding every opinion derived from some preconception and withdraw from customary inter-course with companions, that is, with sense perceptions, which are, as it were, wedded to our nature as its companion. When so purified, then one assaults the mountain.

The knowledge of God is a mountain steep indeed and difficult to climb—the majority of people scarcely reach its base. If one were a Moses, he would ascend higher and hear the sound of trumpets which, as the text of the history says, becomes louder as one advances. For the preaching of the divine nature is truly a trumpet blast, which strikes the hearing, being already loud at the beginning but becoming yet louder at the end.

—From *Gregory of Nyssa*

⁊ Our repose is to rejoice in the infinite happiness of God and, on a lower scale, in our own crosses and to desire still more of them, for in them we have the privilege of imitating him and proving our love, and there is nothing dearer to the heart that loves. We shall never lack either this happiness, nor God nor the Cross.

—From *Meditations of a Hermit* by Charles de Foucauld

⁊ How can one pity anyone who is doing the will of Our Lord? Is there anything sweeter on earth than to do the will of him one loves? And if it gives one some trouble to carry it out, the sweetness is all the greater.

—From *Meditations of a Hermit* by Charles de Foucauld

⁊ God is no longer the Friend I meet, the Father with whom I hold converse, the Lover in whom I delight, the King before whom I bow in reverence, the Divine Being I worship and adore. In my experience of prayer God ceases to be any of these things because he ceases to be anything at all. He is absent when I pray. I am there alone. There is no other.

If this experience persists—and is not the effect of 'flu coming on or tiredness—it means that something of the greatest importance is happening. It means that God is inviting me to discover him no longer as another alongside me but as my own deepest and truest self. He is calling me from the experience of meeting him to the experience of finding my identity in him. I cannot see him because he is my eyes. I cannot hear him because he is my ears. I cannot walk to him because he is my feet. And if apparently I am alone and he is not there that is because he will not separate his presence from my own. If he is not anything at all, if he is nothing, that is because he is no longer another. I must find him in what I am or not at all.

—From *Tensions* by H. A. Williams

❧ Being questioned by one of his own society (to whom he was obliged to open himself) by what means he had attained such an habitual sense of God, [Brother Lawrence] told him that, since his first coming to the monastery, he had considered God as the end of all his thoughts and desires, as the mark to which they should tend, and in which they should terminate.

That in the beginning of his novitiate he spent the hours appointed for private prayer in thinking of God, so as to convince his mind of, and to impress deeply upon his heart, the divine existence, rather by devout sentiments, and submission to the lights of faith, than by studied reasonings and elaborate meditations. That by this short and sure method he exercised himself in the knowledge and love of God, resolving to use his utmost endeavor to live in a continual sense of his presence, and, if possible never to forget him more.

That when he had thus in prayer filled his mind with great sentiments of that infinite Being, he went to his work appointed in the kitchen (for he was cook to the society). There having first considered severally the things his office required, and when and how each thing was to be done, he spent all the intervals of his time, as well before as after his work, in prayer.

That when he began his business, he said to God, with a filial trust in him: *O my God, since thou art with me, and I must now, in obedience to thy commands, apply my mind to these outward things, I beseech thee to grant me the grace to continue in thy presence; and to this end do thou prosper me with thy assistance, receive all my works, and possess all my affections.*

As he proceeded in his work he continued his familiar conversation with his Maker, imploring his grace, and offering to him all his actions.

When he had finished he examined himself how he had discharged his duty; if he found *well*, he returned thanks to God; if otherwise, he asked pardon, and, without being discouraged, he set his mind right again, and continued his exercise of the *presence* of God as if he had never deviated from it. "Thus," said he, "by rising after my falls, and by frequently renewed acts of faith and love, I am come to a state wherein it would be as difficult for me not to think of God as it was at first to accustom myself to it."

—From *The Practice of the Presence of God* by Brother Lawrence

&. And, O Lord, grant unto me that am now about to return to the common comforts and business of the world, such moderation in all enjoyments, such diligence in honest labour, and such purity of mind that amidst the changes, miseries, or pleasures of life I may keep my mind fixed upon thee, and improve every day in grace till I shall be received into thy kingdom of eternal happiness.

—From *Doctor Johnson's Prayers* edited by Elton Trueblood

Hymn: Come, Thou Long-Expected Jesus

Come, thou long-expected Jesus,
Born to set thy people free;
From our fears and sins release us;
Let us find our rest in thee.
Israel's strength and consolation,
Hope of all the earth thou art;
Dear desire of every nation,
Joy of every longing heart.

Born thy people to deliver,
Born a child and yet a King,
Born to reign in us forever,
Now thy gracious kingdom bring.
By thine own eternal spirit
Rule in all our hearts alone,
By thine all sufficient merit,
Raise us to thy glorious throne. Amen.
—Charles Wesley

4: *God Is with Us*

I. Invocation
O almighty God, who by the birth of thy holy child Jesus hast given us a great light to dawn upon our darkness: Grant, we pray thee, that in this light we may see light. Bestow upon us, we beseech thee, that most excellent Christmas gift of charity to all, that so the likeness of thy Son may be formed in us, and that we may have the ever brightening hope of everlasting life; through Jesus Christ our Lord. Amen.
—From *The Book of Worship*

II. Psalm 77

III. Daily Scripture Readings

Monday		Isaiah 7:10-17
Tuesday		Matthew 1:18-25
Wednesday		Isaiah 40:1-11, 28-31
Thursday		Ezekiel 34:11-16
Friday		Isaiah 9:1-7
Saturday		Philippians 4:4-9
Sunday	A.	Isaiah 7:10-16; Psalm 24; Romans 1:1-7; Matthew 1:18-25
	B.	2 Samuel 7:8-16; Psalm 89:1-4, 19-24; Romans 16:25-27; Luke 1:26-38
	C.	Micah 5:2-5a, (5:1-4a); Psalm 80:1-7; Hebrews 10:5-10; Luke 1:39-55

IV. Readings for Reflection

V. Prayers: for the church, for others, for myself

VI. Reflection: silent and written

VII. Hymn: "O Little Town of Bethlehem"

VIII. Benediction
I commend you to God and to the word of his grace which is able to build you up and to give you the inheritance among all those who are sanctified. Amen. —Acts 20:32

Readings For Reflection

❧ But God is present in reality no matter what unreality our practices and our ponderings imply. He is forever trying to establish communication; forever aware of the wrong directions we are taking and wishing to warn us; forever offering solutions for the problems that baffle us; forever standing at the door of our loneliness, eager to bring us such comradeship as the most intelligent living mortal could not supply; forever clinging to our indifference in the hope that someday our needs, or at least our tragedies will waken us to respond to his advances. The Real Presence is just that, real and life-transforming. Nor are the conditions for the manifestation of his splendors out of the reach of any of us! Here they are; otherness, openness, obedience, obsession.
—From *The Captivating Presence* by Albert Edward Day

❧ Father God,

Why is it that I think I must get somewhere, assume some position, be gathered together, or separated apart in the quiet of my study to pray?

Why is it that I feel that I have to go somewhere or do some particular act to find you, reach you, and talk with you?

Your presence is here
> In the city—on the busy bus, in the factory, in the cockpit of the airplane; in the hospital—in the patients' rooms, in the intensive care unit, in the waiting room; in the home—at dinner, in the bedroom, in the family room, at my workbench; in the car—in the parking lot, at the stoplight.

Lord, reveal your presence to me everywhere, and help me become aware of your presence each moment of the day.

May your presence fill the nonanswers, empty glances, and lonely times of my life. Amen.

—From *A Thirty-Day Experiment in Prayer* by Robert Wood

❧ Let us thank God a thousand times if in the sadness which invades us it seems to us as if we are rejected by the world. The depression and suffering, the bitterness with which we seem sometimes to be soaked, were the lot of

Our Lord on earth. Are we not fortunate to share them? We should pity the happy people. Pity those whose happiness, even though it be quite legitimate and innocent, keeps them attached to the world. God is good that he has so despoiled us of everything, that we can draw breath only by turning our heads towards him. How great is his mercy, how divine his goodness, for he has torn everything from us in order that we may be more completely his. So the sufferers are the happy ones through the goodness of God. In suffering I give thanks. May these days of Christmas festival bring you, in your suffering, I do not say consolation, but the blessing God intends for you. The Child Jesus will perhaps not give you any sweetness,—he reserves that for the weak ones,—but his hands will none the less be spread to bless you in these days of Christmastide, and whether you feel it or no, he will pour abundant grace into your soul.

—From *Meditations of a Hermit* by Charles de Foucauld

ֆ Later the soul will bring forth fruit exactly in the measure in which the inner life is developed in it. If there is no inner life, however great may be the zeal, the high intention, the hard work, no fruit will come forth; it is like a spring that would give out sanctity to others but cannot, having none to give; one can only give that which one has. It is in solitude, in that lonely life alone with God, in profound recollection of soul, in forgetfulness of all created things, that God gives himself to the soul that thus gives itself whole and entire to him.

—From *Meditations of a Hermit* by Charles de Foucauld

ֆ I am a creature of a day, passing through life as an arrow through the air. I am a spirit come from God and returning to God; just hovering over the great gulf, till, a few moments hence, I am no more seen; I drop into an unchangeable eternity. I want to know one thing—the way to heaven; how to land safe on that happy shore. God himself has condescended to teach the way; for this very end he came from heaven. He hath written it down in a book. O give me that book! At any price, give me the book of God! I have it; here is knowledge enough for me. Let me be *homo unius libri*.

—John Wesley

&. The divine quality of the Bible is not on display, it is not apparent to an inane, fatuous mind; just as the divine in the universe is not obvious to the debaucher. When we turn to the Bible with an empty spirit, moved by intellectual vanity, striving to show our superiority to the text; or as barren souls who go sight-seeing to the words of the prophets, we discover the shells but miss the core. It is easier to enjoy beauty than to sense the holy. To be able to encounter the spirit within the words, we must learn to crave for an affinity with the pathos of God.

To sense the presence of God in the Bible, one must learn *to be present* to God in the Bible. Presence is not a concept, but a situation. To understand love it is not enough to read tales about it. One must be involved in the prophets to understand the prophets. One must be inspired to understand inspiration. Just as we cannot test thinking without thinking, we cannot sense holiness without being holy. Presence is not disclosed to those who are unattached and try to judge, to those who have no power to go beyond the values they cherish; to those who sense the story, not the pathos; the idea, not the realness of God.

The Bible is the frontier of the spirit where we must move and live in order to discover and to explore. It is open to him who gives himself to it, who lives with it intimately.
—From *God in Search of Man* by Abraham Joshua Heschel

&. In my arguments about the insolubility of the problem of God I had never foreseen the possibility of that, of a real contact, person to person, here below, between a human being and God. I had vaguely heard tell of things of this kind, but I had never believed in them. In the *Fioretti* the accounts of apparitions rather put me off if anything, like the miracles in the Gospel. Moreover, in this sudden possession of me by Christ, neither my senses nor my imagination had any part; I only felt in the midst of my suffering the presence of a love, like that which one can read in the smile on a beloved face.

I had never read any mystical works because I had never felt any call to read them. In reading as in other things I have always striven to practice obedience. There is nothing more favorable to intellectual progress, for as far as possible I only read what I am hungry for at the moment when I have an appetite for it, and then I do not read, I *eat*. God in his mercy had prevented me from reading the mystics, so that it should be evident to me that I had not invented this absolutely unexpected contact.

Yet I still half refused, not my love but my intelligence. For it seemed to me certain, and I still think so today, that one can never wrestle enough with God if one does so out of pure regard for the truth. Christ likes us to prefer truth to him because, before being Christ, he is truth. If one turns aside from him to go toward the truth, one will not go far before falling into his arms.

—From *Waiting for God* by Simone Weil

ɤ God is not real to most of us because of the condition of our consciousness. He is closer to our minds every moment than our own thoughts. He is nearer to our hearts than our own feelings. He is more intimate with our wills than our most vigorous decisions. If we are not aware of him, it is not because he is not with us. It is, in part, because our consciousness is so under the sway of other interests that it cannot turn to him with the loving attention which might soon discern him.

Did you ever encounter, on the street, a friend whose physical eyes looked at you without seeing you? You walked right into him before the alien look on his face changed into one of recognition. Then he confessed that he had been so absorbed in thought about some other matters that he had not been aware of you, until your intentional collision with him. You were there, yet he did not see you. Though actually in your presence, he was nevertheless as unconscious of you as if you did not exist.

That is a persistent failure of the unemancipated consciousness. It can be so preoccupied by lesser realities that it does not sense the presence of the divine Reality surrounding and sustaining it. Something has to happen to end that absorption in other affairs, so that it can turn its attention to God.

Sometimes events will do it. One encounters God in a crisis that, as we say, "brings one to one's senses." Death, disaster, sickness, the collapse of friendship, are like the collision on the street. They shatter the tyranny of an idea or a dream, and release consciousness for the awareness of something greater than the idea or the dream—God himself.

It would be a very poor sort of life that was aware of people only when it collided with them, or was brought up standing by some decisive act of theirs. And it is a tragic life that becomes conscious of God only in those events that shatter its habitual thoughts and dreams and compel it to recognize his presence and activity.

What makes life splendid is the constant awareness of God. What transforms the spirit into his likeness is intimate fellowship with him. We are saved—from our pettiness and earthiness and selfishness and sin—by conscious communion with his greatness and love and holiness.

—From *Discipline and Discovery* by Albert Edward Day

❧ The fire of God, which is his essential being, his love, his creative power, is a fire unlike its earthly symbol in this, that it is only at a distance it burns—that the farther from him it burns the worse, and that when we turn and begin to approach him, the burning begins to change to comfort, which comfort will grow to such bliss that the heart at length cries out with a gladness no other gladness can reach, "Whom have I in heaven but thee? and there is nothing upon earth that I desire besides thee!"

—From *Creation in Christ* by George MacDonald

Hymn: O Little Town of Bethlehem

O little town of Bethlehem,
How still we see thee lie!
Above thy deep and dreamless sleep
The silent stars go by;
Yet in the dark streets shineth
The everlasting light;
The hopes and fears of all the years
Are met in thee tonight.

For Christ is born of Mary,
And gathered all above,
While mortals sleep, the angels keep
Their watch of wondering love.
O morning stars, together

Proclaim the holy birth,
And praises sing to God the King,
And peace to all on earth!

How silently, how silently
The wondrous gift is given!
So God imparts to human hearts
The blessings of his heaven.
No ear may hear his coming,
But in this world of sin,
Where meek souls will receive him, still
The dear Christ enters in.

O holy Child of Bethlehem,
Descend on us, we pray;
Cast out our sin, and enter in,
Be born in us today.
We hear the Christmas angels
The great glad tidings tell;
O come to us, abide in us,
Our Lord Emmanuel! Amen.
—Phillips Brooks

5: *All Things New*

I. Invocation
    O Lord, the house of my soul is narrow; enlarge it that thou mayest enter in. It is ruinous, O repair it! It displeases thy sight; I confess it, I know. But who shall cleanse it, or to whom shall I cry but unto thee? Cleanse me from my secret faults, O Lord, and spare thy servant from strange sins.
    —Saint Augustine

II. Psalm 65

III. Daily Scripture Readings
Monday	Isaiah 43:1-13
Tuesday	Galatians 3:23–4:7
Wednesday	2 Corinthians 5:16-21
Thursday	Ephesians 4:17-32
Friday	John 3:1-8
Saturday	Revelation 21:1-7
Sunday	A. Isaiah 63:7-9; Psalm 111; Hebrews 2:10-18; Matthew 2:13-15, 19-23
	B. Isaiah 61:10–62:3; Psalm 111; Galatians 4:4-7; Luke 2:22-40
	C. 1 Samuel 2:18-20, 26; Psalm 111; Colossians 3:12-17; Luke 2:41-52

IV. Readings for Reflection

V. Prayers: for the church, for others, for myself

VI. Reflection: silent and written

VII. Hymn: "Let All Together Praise Our God"

VIII. Benediction
    And now may the spirit which was in Jesus Christ be in me, enabling me to know God's will and empowering me to do God's will. Amen.

Readings for Reflection

❧ Years ago I came across this sentence in an old book: "Never indulge, at the close of an action, in any self-reflective acts of any kind, whether of self-congratulation or of self-despair. Forget the things that are behind, the moment they are past, leaving them with God." This has been of unspeakable value to me. When the temptation comes, as it mostly does to every worker after the performance of any service, to indulge in these reflections, either of one sort or the other, I turn from them at once and positively refuse to think about my work at all, leaving it with the Lord to overrule the mistakes, and to bless it as he chooses. I believe there would be far fewer "blue Mondays" for ministers of the Gospel than there are now if they would adopt this plan; and I am sure all workers would find their work far less wearing.

—From *The Christian's Secret of a Happy Life* by Hannah
   Whitall Smith

❧ The love of our neighbor is the love which comes down from God to man. It precedes that which rises from men to God. God is longing to come down to those in affliction. As soon as a soul is disposed to consent, though it were the last, the most miserable, the most deformed of souls, God will precipitate himself into it in order, through it, to look at and listen to the afflicted. Only as time passes does the soul become aware that he is there. But, though it finds no name for him, wherever the afflicted are loved for themselves alone, it is God who is present.

God is not present, even if we invoke him, where the afflicted are merely regarded as an occasion for doing good. They may even be loved on this account, but then they are in their natural role, the role of matter and of things. We have to bring to them in their inert, anonymous condition a personal love.

—From *Waiting for God* by Simone Weil

❧ In terms of time the eternal Lord of all order appears to be the Lord of misrule. No wonder the pharisees, who seem to have been always wholly serious, had to have Jesus put down. He couldn't be allowed to go on indefinitely standing everything on its head and making their piety look ridiculous. Why, in the end, they might even laugh themselves, and that would be the ultimate catastrophe. Who in reality had ever witnessed a pious man blowing a trumpet before he put a pound note in the church box? The notion was irresponsibly misleading. And then there were camels going through the eyes of needles, not to mention camels being swallowed easily by those who choked when they swallowed a gnat. And if people did sometimes get a speck in their eye who ever heard of a man, and an improving teacher at that, who had a log in his? And worse: idlers who were given full pay, stewards who were successful cheats, spendthrift and debauched sons being feted on their return home—what had all this pernicious nonsense to do with religion? It could only undermine the morals of society, and, being socially dangerous had to be stopped; stopped before the contagion of eternal love showed up the whole solemn system of moralism and religiosity as a complete knockabout farce. So the Jester had to be crucified.

But Eternity had the last laugh after all. For that is the final joke—the resurrection. Here are Caiaphas and all his crowd, Pilate and Herod and all theirs, sitting complacently in a state of grave and dignified self-congratulation. They have done their duty and justified the authority vested in them by efficiently disposing once and for all of a dangerous fool. He is safely dead. And with solemn calm again restored they can concentrate once more on the really serious matters to which their lives are dedicated. But behind their backs, without them having the slightest inkling of what is going on, the fool has popped up again like a Jack-in-the-box and is dancing about even more vigorously than before and even more compellingly. People here, there and everywhere are falling under his spell. But the brass hats and mitred heads and stuffed shirts are facing the other way and can't see what is going on. So they continue with their dignified mutual congratulation and their serious business.

If that isn't funny, nothing is. It is the supreme, the final, the ultimate joke—that than which nothing could be funnier. And since laughter, although not irresistible is none the less highly contagious, perhaps the brass hats themselves will in time catch the disease, turn around, see

the joke, and laugh with the rest of creation because the kingdom of God has drawn near.
—From *Tensions* by H. A. Williams

ॐ The biblical Christian can only pray empty-handed, as the thirteenth-century Dominican preacher William Peraldus expressed it. Or, as Augustine observed, "The best disposition for praying is that of being desolate, forsaken, stripped of everything." Unlike the ritualist, we know that any sacrifice we bring before God is stained by sin and therefore unworthy of acceptance apart from the mediation and intercession of Jesus Christ. Our hope depends not on the right technique or the proper phrase or gesture, which borders on magic, but on the promises of God to look with favor on those who throw themselves on his mercy and who acknowledge the efficacy of the atoning sacrifice of his Son, Jesus Christ, for their redemption.

As I see it, true prayer is neither mystical rapture nor ritual observance nor philosophical reflection: it is the outpouring of the soul before a living God, the crying to God "out of the depths." Such prayer can only be uttered by one convicted of sin by the grace of God and moved to confession by the Spirit of God. True prayer is an encounter with the Holy in which we realize not only our creatureliness and guilt but also the joy of knowing that our sins are forgiven through the atoning death of the divine savior, Jesus Christ. In such an encounter, we are impelled not only to bow before God and seek his mercy but also to offer thanksgiving for grace that goes out to undeserving sinners.
—From *The Struggle of Prayer* by Donald G. Bloesch

ॐ Men can never escape from obedience to God. A creature cannot but obey. The only choice given to men, as intelligent and free creatures, is to desire obedience or not to desire it. If a man does not desire it, he obeys nevertheless, perpetually, inasmuch as he is a thing subject to mechanical necessity. If he desires it, he is still subject to mechanical necessity, but a new necessity is added to it, a necessity constituted by laws belonging to supernatural things. Certain actions become impossible for him; others are done by his agency, sometimes almost in spite of himself.

When we have the feeling that on some occasion we have disobeyed God, it simply means that for a time we have ceased to desire obedience.
—From *Waiting for God* by Simone Weil

❧ I did this day receive as much honor and work as ever I shall be able to know what to do with. Lord Jesus, proportion supplies accordingly.
—Philip Henry

❧ Bishop Walpole, the father of Hugh Walpole, the novelist, once said to a friend who was weighing a call:
"If you are uncertain of which of two paths to take, choose the one on which the shadow of the cross falls."
—From *Hugh Walpole, A Biography* by Rupert Hart-Davis

❧ I beg you, do not look upon Dortmund as a stepping-stone, but rather say: Here I shall stay as long as it pleases God; if it be his will, until I die. Look upon every child, your confirmands, every member of the congregation as if you will have to give account for every soul on the day of the Lord Jesus. Every day commit all these human souls from the worst and weakest of hands, namely, your own, into the best and strongest of hands. Then you will be able to carry on your ministry not only without care but also with joy overflowing and joyful hope.
—Friedrich von Bodelschwingh

❧ Then one begins wondering about the most essential, common things: the supernatural versus politics—verticalism versus horizontalism—immanence versus transcendence—human revolution versus eschatological revolution.
And if one does not take care, one can set out unwittingly on quite a wrong road—live with the renouncing angelists in a hypothetical, spiritualist heaven; or turn to the error of reincarnating Jesus' message in a new culture or ideology which is destined, like all the others, to perish, incapable of expressing God's thought and fit only to be a vehicle of suffering for Christians yet to come.
No, it is not easy, even for the Church, to read in the message of Jesus that even though we are his intimate spouse, we can become distracted by the things of earth, and

we constantly run the risk of either saying old things which serve no purpose or being silent when we should speak.

In the gospel of Jesus, God remains a mystery. The face on the Father, which Jesus came to trace out for us here on earth, remains the face of the unknowable One. Let us not forget it.

But there is a way to unveil the unknowable, to read his intimate thoughts, to gain knowledge of him—the way of love.

That way is to enter the enclosure of love, guided by love, so that we can reach knowledge of the Father: "He who loves, has eternal life." And eternal life is knowledge of God.

—From *The God Who Comes* by Carlo Carretto

&. But how is one to find his [or her] true place in life? Is there any means whereby you may discover what it really is that God wishes you to do? You may feel inclined to say: "Even if it be true that God has some splendid thing that he wishes me to do, and to be, how can I possibly find out what it is?" Perhaps you may even be tempted to add: "I am a very plain, everyday sort of person; my circumstances are extremely restricted; the conditions of my life are just drab commonplace. How then can there be something wonderful, beautiful, splendid awaiting me? Or, even if there were, how could I possibly get to know about it?" And the answer is Divinely simple—Already in your past life from time to time, God himself has whispered into your heart just that very wonderful thing, whatever it is, that he is wishing you to be, and to do, and to have. And that wonderful thing is nothing less than what is called *Your Heart's Desire*. Nothing less than that. The most secret, sacred wish that lies deep down at the bottom of your heart, the wonderful thing that you hardly dare to look at, or to think about—the thing that you would rather die than have anyone else know of, because it seems so far beyond anything that you are, or have at the present time, that you fear that you would be cruelly ridiculed if the mere thought of it were known—that is just the very thing that God is wishing you to do or to be for him. And the birth of that marvelous wish in your soul—the dawning of that secret dream—was the Voice of God himself telling you to arise and come up higher because he had need of you.

—From *Your Heart's Desire* by Emmet Fox

Hymn: Let All Together Praise Our God

Let all together praise our God
Upon his lofty throne;
For he uncloses heaven today
And gives to us his Son,
And gives to us his Son.

He lays aside his majesty
And seems as nothing worth,
And takes on him a servant's form,
Who made the heaven and earth,
Who made the heaven and earth.

Behold the wonderful exchange
Our Lord with us doth make!
Lo, he assumes our flesh and blood,
And we of heaven partake,
And we of heaven partake.

The glorious gates of paradise
The angel guards no more;
This day again those gates unfold.
With praise our God adore,
With praise our God adore! Amen.

—Nicolaus Hermann

6: Chosen to Be God's Children

I.   Invocation
     Almighty God, look upon my life and cause all
     darkness and doubt to vanish beneath your gaze.
     Look upon my ministry and banish all barriers to
     effectiveness and faithfulness. Fill my life and min-
     istry with your Holy Spirit to the end that I may this
     day be led into paths of fruitful service. Through
     Jesus Christ. Amen.

II. Psalm 146

III. Daily Scripture Readings
     | Monday | John 15:12-17 |
     | Tuesday | 2 Peter 1:3-11 |
     | Wednesday | Isaiah 55:1-5 |
     | Thursday | Ezekiel 34:25-31 |
     | Friday | Romans 8 |
     | Saturday | 1 Peter 2:1-10 |

     Sunday   A. Isaiah 60:1-6; Psalm 72:1-14;
                 Ephesians 3:1-12; Matthew 2:1-12
              B. Isaiah 60:1-6; Psalm 72:1-14;
                 Ephesians 3:1-12; Matthew 2:1-12
              C. Isaiah 60:1-6; Psalm 72:1-14;
                 Ephesians 3:1-12; Matthew 2:1-12

IV. Readings for Reflection

V.   Prayers: for the church, for others, for myself

VI. Reflection: silent and written

VII. Hymn: "Children of the Heavenly King"

VIII. Benediction
      The grace of the Lord Jesus Christ be with you.
      Amen.

*If this is First Sunday after Epiphany, use Week 7.

Readings for Reflection

❦ As soon as even service is done for the honor and not for the service sake, the doer is that moment outside the kingdom. But when we receive the child in the name of Christ, the very childhood that we receive to our arms is humanity. We love its humanity in its childhood, for childhood is the deepest heart of humanity—its divine heart; and so in the name of the child we receive all humanity.
—From *Creation in Christ* by George MacDonald

❦ How terribly, then, have the theologians misrepresented God! Nearly all of them represent him as a great King on a grand throne, thinking how grand he is, and making it the business of his being and the end of his universe to keep up his glory, wielding the bolts of a Jupiter against them that take his name in vain. They would not allow this, but follow out what they say, and it comes much to this.

Brothers, have you found our king? There he is, kissing little children and saying they are like God. There he is at table with the head of a fisherman lying on his bosom, and somewhat heavy at heart that even he, the beloved disciple, cannot yet understand him well. The simplest peasant who loves his children and his sheep were—no, not a truer, for the other is false, but—a true type of our God beside that monstrosity of a monarch.
—From *Creation in Christ* by George MacDonald

❦ Therefore, with angels and with archangels, with the spirits of the just made perfect, with the little children of the kingdom, yea, with the Lord himself, and for all them that know him not, we praise and magnify and laud his name in itself, saying *Our Father*. We do not draw back for that we are unworthy, nor even for that we are hard-hearted and care not for the good. For it is his childlikeness that makes him our God and Father. The perfection of his relation to us swallows up all our imperfections, all our defects, all our evils; for our childhood is born of his fatherhood. That man is perfect in faith who can come to God in the utter dearth of his feelings and his desires, without a glow or an aspiration, with the weight of low thoughts, failures, neglects, and wandering forgetfulness, and say to him, "You are my refuge, because you are my home."

—From *Creation in Christ* by George MacDonald

❧ There is something new for women, too. Read carefully.

Today, a woman must hear the words of Jesus as a man hears them; and if Jesus says, "Go and make disciples of all nations," it must no longer be that a man hears this in one way and a woman in another.

How you must re-think everything!

And how I would like to say to women of today, "Go!" with all the force of which my spirit is capable, and all my anxiety for the immense needs of a world athirst for the Gospel. This is an urgent invitation.

Transform your home into a convent—an ideal, spiritual one, as Saint Catherine did. Let prayer reign there, good counsel, and peace. Let your toil, wherever it is, be illumined by the power of your calling—for you were made to love, to comfort, to serve.

Do not copy men. Be authentic. Seek, in your femaleness, the root that distinguishes you from them. It is unmistakable, for it has been willed and created by God himself. Repeat to yourselves every day: A man is not a woman.

Waste no time in approaching men in order somehow to resemble them. Rather seek to remove yourselves as far as possible from their model. It is not yours, and it is rather marred and muddled even so.

I think there is a model for you women in the world. Mary of Nazareth.

It is scarcely possible that Jesus would not have thought of this during the thirty years of his earthly existence, or that he would not have sought to mold and shape a model for women.

Mary was so close to him!

And she was so attentive to him!

And she was altogether the Daughter of the Father, the Mother of the Word, the Spouse of the Spirit.

We have not yet sufficiently considered this exceptional woman.

We have not plumbed the depths of her reality as "woman of this earth," as our sister. We have not sufficiently considered her freedom, her autonomy, her self-fulfillment, day by day in her everyday life.

You women are going to have to be the ones to dig out something of the mystery of Mary, in prayer.

There has been too much sentimentality, and too much useless triumphalism! Especially coming from men. Especially if they are not married.

And one more thing.

Do not let yourselves be guided by men any longer just because they are men. If you let them lead you do so because they are saints, and do not disdain the help of persons like Clare—who, though she is a woman, can tell you things of utility and power.

—From *I, Francis* by Carlo Carretto

ॐ The failure of perception, the inability to apprehend him directly is the sad paradox of our religious existence. It was an extraordinary moment when man was ready to exclaim:

This is my God, I will glorify him;
The God of my father, I will exalt him. —Exodus 15:2

The normal situation is expressed in the words of Job:
Lo, he goes by me, and I see him not;
He passes on also, but I perceive him not. —Job 9:11

However, God is not indifferent to man's quest of him. He is in need of man, in need of man's share in redemption. God who created the world is not at home in the world, in its dark alleys of misery, callousness and defiance. . . .

The words, "I am a stranger on earth" (Psalm 119:19), were interpreted to refer to God. God is a stranger in the world. The *Shechinah*, the presence of God, is in exile. Our task is to bring God back into the world, into our lives. To worship is to expand the presence of God in the world. To have faith in God is to reveal what is concealed.

—From *God in Search of Man* by Abraham Joshua Heschel

ॐ The position of intelligence is the key to this harmony, because the intelligence is a specifically and rigorously individual thing. This harmony exists wherever the intelligence, remaining in its place, can be exercised without hindrance and can reach the complete fulfillment of its function. That is what Saint Thomas says admirably of all the parts of the soul of Christ, with reference to his sensitiveness to pain during the crucifixion.

The special function of the intelligence requires total liberty, implying the right to deny everything, and allowing of no domination. Wherever it usurps control there is an excess of individualism. Wherever it is hampered or uneasy there is an oppressive collectivism, or several of them.

—From *Waiting for God* by Simone Weil

❧ My God, I desire to love thee perfectly,
    With all my heart which thou madest for thyself
With all my mind, which only thou canst satisfy
    With all my soul, which feign would soar to thee.
With all my strength, my feeble strength, which shrinks
    before
So great a task and yet can choose naught else but
    spend itself
In loving thee.
    Claim thou my heart,
    Fill thou my mind,
    Uplift my soul and
    Reinforce my strength,
    That when I fail thou mayest succeed in me
    And make me love thee perfectly.

—From *Love Is My Meaning* by Elizabeth Basset

❧ Ministers are like trumpets, which make no sound if breath be not breathed into them. Or like Ezekiel's wheels, which move not unless the Spirit move them. Or like Elisha's servants whose presence does no good unless Elisha's spirit be there also.

—John Flavel

❧ Loving Jesu, gentle Lamb,
    In thy gracious hands I am;
    Make me, Saviour, what thou art!
    Live thyself within my heart.

I shall then show forth thy praise;
Serve thee all my happy days;
Then the world shall always see
Christ, the Holy Child, in me.
—Charles Wesley

Hymn: Children of the Heavenly King

Children of the heavenly King,
As we journey let us sing;
Sing our Savior's worthy praise,
Glorious in his works and ways.

We are traveling home to God,
In the way our fathers trod;
They are happy now, and we
Soon their happiness shall see.

Fear not, brethren; joyful stand
On the borders of our land;
Jesus Christ, our Father's Son,
Bids us undismayed go on.

Lord, obediently we'll go,
Gladly leaving all below;
Only thou our leader be,
And we still will follow thee.

Lift your eyes, ye sons of light,
Zion's city is in sight;
There our endless home shall be,
There our Lord we soon shall see. Amen.
—John Cennick

First Sunday after Epiphany
(between January 7 and 13)

7: The Son of God

I. Invocation
    O God of grace, who at this time didst give Jesus
    Christ to be our Savior: We beseech thee to over-
    come our darkness with his light, our selfishness
    with his love, our indolence and cowardice with
    his steadfast devotion, that we may live ever as in
    thy presence, and perform faithfully our appointed
    tasks, and finally come to everlasting life; through
    the same Jesus Christ our Lord. Amen.
    —From *The Book of Worship*

II. Psalm 93

III. Daily Scripture Readings
Monday	Mark 1:21-28
Tuesday	John 1:35-42
Wednesday	John 5:19-24
Thursday	Luke 10:1, 3, 17-24
Friday	Hebrews 1:1-12
Saturday	1 John 4

    Sunday A. Isaiah 42:1-9; Psalm 29;
                Acts 10:34-43; Matthew 3:13-17
            B. Genesis 1:1-5; Psalm 29; Acts 19:1-7;
                Mark 1:4-11
            C. Isaiah 61:1-4; Psalm 29; Acts 8:14-17;
                Luke 3:15-17, 21-22

IV. Readings for Reflection

V. Prayers: for the church, for others, for myself

VI. Reflection: silent and written

VII. Hymn: "Be Thou My Vision"

VIII. Benediction
    May the peace of God fill my heart, mind, and activ-
    ity all this day long. Amen.

Readings for Reflection

❧ The Master prayed as naturally as a child breathes. Sometimes he prayed in triumph as on the Mount of Transfiguration when as he prayed, "the fashion of his countenance was altered" (Luke 9:29); sometimes he prayed in grief, as in the Garden of Gethsemane, of which it is written that "Being in an agony he prayed more earnestly; and his sweat became as it were great drops of blood" (Luke 22:44). He spent whole nights in prayer, arose long before day to pray, or at the sunset hour withdrew alone to commune with God (Luke 6:12; Mark 1:35; Mark 6:46, 47). He preceded the crises of his life and followed his hard and perplexing labors with prayer, and if the solitude of place was lacking, he could withdraw into the solitude of his own soul. "It came to pass, as he was praying apart," says Luke, "the disciples were with him" (Luke 9:18). He was a soul so great in spiritual apprehension that our best adjectives pass rather for impertinence than praise, and yet his prayers are as simple as a child's. "Father, into thy hands I commend my spirit," is the trustful self-commitment which he makes even in the crucifixion's agony. Yet so impressive was it to hear him pray that one of his biographers, referring in parenthesis to a geographical locality, describes it by saying, "The place where they ate the bread, after the Lord had given thanks" (John 6:23). Just one thing the disciples are reported to have asked the Master to teach them; they wanted him to teach them to pray.

Out of such a life no deed could come, no virtue could emerge that was not distinguished by the quality of its source. All the elements in the Master's goodness which we have studied, his joy, his fearlessness, his fortitude, his magnanimity, are separate as incandescent arcs are, but they all burn with the same fire. This explains why it is often possible to find bravery or sacrificial devotion in other lives than his, that seem to equal the same virtues in him; but it is never possible to find the same quality which suffuses his courage and makes his sacrificial devotion a symbol of the love of God. *No virtue in him was the whole of itself; his spirit was the rest of it.* The Master's preeminence comes not chiefly from his describable virtues, but from those deep sources of his life with God, out of which his virtues flowed, begotten not made, and fragrant, every one of them, with the quality of his perfect fellowship with the Father.

This could be illustrated in many ways, but we may note especially the quality of humility in the Master as manifestly the consequence of his life with God. It is only in the light of such an attitude on Jesus' part as John records, "I can of myself do nothing" (John 5:30), that we can understand the seeming contradiction between Jesus' amazing claims for himself on the one side and on the other his teaching of humility, and the impression which he makes of being "meek and lowly in heart." Many of the Master's words do not at all have a humble note in them: "Heaven and earth shall pass away; but my words shall not pass away" (Mark 13:31); "The Son of man shall come in his glory, and all the angels with him, then shall he sit on the throne of his glory: and before him shall be gathered all nations" (Matt. 25:31); "He that loveth father or mother more than me is not worthy of me" (Matt. 10:37); "He that denieth me in the presence of men shall be denied before the angels of God" (Luke 12:9).

—From *The Manhood of the Master* by Harry Emerson Fosdick

&. *Nothing will help us more to make of these disciplines what they ought to be than a continuing remembrance of Jesus.*

He was the most wisely disciplined person in history. Name the disciplines one by one. Then recall his perfect illustration of their meaning and purpose:

Obedience: "Not my will be done"—"my meat and drink is to do the will of him who sent me and to finish his work." As Paul Tillich said, Jesus lived in unbroken unity with God and yet sought nothing for himself by that unity.

Simplicity: He lived simply—"foxes have holes and birds of the air have nests, but the Son of man hath not where to lay his head"; there was no effort to make an impression—he refused the spectacular, he spoke the language of the people; there was no pose of any kind; he kept silent when he did not know the answers—"of that day and hour no one knows, not even the angels of heaven nor the Son."

Humility: "Why do you call me good? No one is good but God"; "take my yoke upon you and learn of me, for I am gentle and lowly in heart."

Frugality: "How hard it will be for those who have riches to enter the kingdom of God"; "for our sakes he became poor that we through his poverty might be rich"; "man shall not live by bread alone but by every word that proceeds from the mouth of God"; "those who wear soft raiment are in kings' houses." Frugal in food, he fasted long days in the wilderness. Frugal in sleep, he spent whole nights in prayer alone with God. Frugal in personal relationships, he loved people but could get along without them if his truth offended them; "will ye also go away?"

Generosity: He gave everything to God, everything! His days and nights, his dreams and deeds, his labors and his life itself, were God's. He gave himself without stint to people, sharing with them his truth, ministering to their souls, healing their sickness, listening to their questions, "for many were coming and going and there was no leisure even to eat"; "he had compassion on them, because they were like sheep without a shepherd."

Truthfulness: Even his enemies had to say, "we know that you are true . . . you do not regard the position of men but teach the way of God." Deceit, evasion, double-talk, ambiguity, exaggeration, flattery, guile never appeared in his life even when, by common strategy, they promised advantage to his selfless cause.

Purity: Not even a look in the direction of evil, no mixed motives, no service adulterated by sly self-interest, nothing that did not fit the concept of God-likeness: He not only said, "Blessed are the pure in heart," he was that!

Charity: Paul's deathless portrayal of charity had Jesus as its model. Every quality of life that good usage names charity was Christ's in abundance—gentleness, graciousness, quick forgiveness, bountifulness, courtesy, self-sacrifice, universal good will, channeling God's love toward all people—of all this Jesus was the perfect incarnation.

Nor were all these superlative qualities of life sheer native endowment. They were his because God was in him, true! But God was in him because he did what the rest of us must do—by dedication and discipline keep one's life open to God.

—From *Discipline and Discovery* by Albert Edward Day

❧ There is within me a me which is both greater than me and at the same time authentically myself. One way of approaching this mysterious fact would be by what is called the paradox of grace. The more God gives me his grace (i. e. himself), the more I am myself. The more I discover within me the greater than me the more I discover that that greater than me is authentically me.

—From *Tensions* by H. A. Williams

❧ I keep thinking it is an awesome thing to look into the face of the living God. I feel God is turning the screws so I will get into an ultimate position of transition, but I also feel that the centre of the circle is buoying me up, holding me in suspension as though I were in God's hands. And God, terrible and loving, is with me now in his presence.

—From *And a Time to Die* by Mark Pelgrin

❧ Lord, I know not what I ought to ask of thee; thou only knowest what I need. . . . I simply present myself before thee, I open my heart to thee. Behold my needs which I know not myself. Smite, or heal; depress me, or raise me up; I adore all thy purposes without knowing them; I am silent; I offer myself in sacrifice; I yield myself to thee; I would have no other desire than to accomplish thy Will. Teach me to pray. Pray thyself in me. Amen.

—François Fénelon

❧ The Lord's Supper is then essentially *a fellowship, koinonia, communio,* and in a double sense. First and foremost the Lord's Supper is *a fellowship in Christ:* Christians are called to fellowship with the Son, the Lord (1 Cor. 1:9).

—From *The Church* by Hans Küng

❧ The Lord's Supper is fellowship with Christ, and so *fellowship with other Christians;* their common union with Christ naturally leads to a union of those who share the Lord's Supper, a communion of Christians among themselves. The one is not possible without the other, because they all partake of the same bread, Christ.

—From *The Church* by Hans Küng

৯ So much is clear: the Lord's Supper is the centre of the Church and of its various acts of worship. Here the Church is truly itself, because it is wholly with its Lord; here the Church of Christ is gathered for its most intimate fellowship, as sharers in a meal. In this fellowship they draw strength for their service in the world. Because this meal is a meal of recollection and thanksgiving, the Church is essentially a community which remembers and thanks. And because this meal is a meal of covenant and fellowship, the Church is essentially a community, which loves without ceasing. And because finally this meal is an anticipation of the eschatological meal, the Church is essentially a community which looks to the future with confidence. Essentially, therefore, the Church must be a meal-fellowship, a koinonia or communio, must be a fellowship with Christ and with Christians, or it is not the Church of Christ. In the Lord's Supper it is stated with incomparable clarity that the Church is the ecclesia, the congregation, the community of God. In the Lord's Supper in fact the Church is constantly constituted anew. If the Church owes to baptism the fact that it *is* a Church, and does not have to become a Church through its own pious works, the Church owes to the Lord's Supper the fact that it *remains* a Church, despite any falling away and failure. From God's viewpoint this means that while baptism is the sign of electing and justifying grace, the Lord's Supper is the sign of sustaining and perfecting grace. From the human viewpoint it means that while baptism is above all the sign of the response of faith and obedience, the Lord's Supper is the sign of the response of love and hope.
—From *The Church* by Hans Küng

৯ O Lord, my heart is not proud
   nor haughty my eyes.
   I have not gone after things too great
   nor marvels beyond me.
   Truly I have set my soul
   in silence and peace.

   A weaned child on its mother's breast,
   even so is my soul. (Ps. 130)

This is the psalm of contemplative prayer. Men and women on the way to the roots of their being, towards their end, their creator, after having passed the first degrees of prayer, after having been purified by the suffering dryness of human pleasure and selfishness, find themselves at the doorway of eternity. Their own strength can do nothing, meditation itself becomes impossible, and words, once so effortless, can only repeat some monosyllable of love and lament.

No image sums all this up so exactly as that of a child that has been weaned in its mother's arms. And it is still Jesus who tells us, "Unless you turn and become like little children, you will not enter into the Kingdom of Heaven."
—From *Letters from the Desert* by Carlo Carretto

Hymn: Be Thou My Vision

Be thou my Vision, O Lord of my heart;
Naught be all else to me, save that thou art;
Thou my best thought, by day or by night,
Waking or sleeping, thy presence my light.

Be thou my Wisdom, and thou my true Word;
I ever with thee and thou with me, Lord;
Thou my great Parent, and I thy true child,
Thou in me dwelling and I with thee one.

Riches I heed not, nor all empty praise;
Thou mine inheritance, now and always;
Thou and thou only, first in my heart,
High King of heaven, my treasure thou art.

High King of heaven, my victory won,
May I reach heaven's joys, O bright heaven's Sun!
Heart of my own heart, whatever befall,
Still be my Vision, O Ruler of all. Amen.
—From *The Poem Book of the Gael* edited by Eleanor Hull

8: *Come Follow Me*

I.   Invocation
Almighty God, you who continually call your people to yourself, draw us by the power of your Holy Spirit into such a warm and binding relationship that we may faithfully follow you all the days of our lives. We pray in the name of Jesus Christ. Amen.

II. Psalm 128

III. Daily Scripture Readings

Monday		John 1:35-51
Tuesday		Matthew 4:17-22
Wednesday		Luke 9:23-27, 57-62
Thursday		Matthew 10:34-42
Friday		Matthew 11:25-30
Saturday		Matthew 19:16-30
Sunday	A.	Isaiah 49:1-7; Psalm 40:1-11; 1 Corinthians 1:1-9; John 1:29-34
	B.	1 Samuel 3:1-10, (11-20); Psalm 63:1-8; 1 Corinthians 6:12-20; John 1:35-42
	C.	Isaiah 62:1-5; Psalm 36:5-10; 1 Corinthians 12:1-11; John 2:1-11

IV. Readings for Reflection

V.   Prayers: for the church, for others, for myself

VI. Reflection: silent and written

VII. Hymn: "Guide Me, O Thou Great Jehovah"

VIII. Benediction
Today walk in the power and presence of God, Father, Son, and Holy Spirit. Amen.

Readings for Reflection

❧ "But I do not know how to awake and arise!"

I will tell you. Get up, and do something the Master tells you; so make yourself his disciple at once. Instead of asking yourself whether you believe or not, ask yourself whether you have this day done one thing because he said, Do it, or once abstained because he said, Do not do it. It is simply absurd to say you believe, or even want to believe in him, if you do not anything he tells you. If you can think of nothing he ever said as having had an atom of influence on your doing or not doing, you have too good ground to consider yourself no disciple of his.

But you can begin at once to *be* a disciple of the Living One—by obeying him in the first thing you can think of in which you are not obeying him. We must learn to obey him in everything, and so must begin somewhere. Let it be at once, and in the very next thing that lies at the door of our conscience! Oh fools and slow of heart, if you think of nothing but Christ, and do not set yourselves to do his words! You but build your houses on the sand.
—From *Creation in Christ* by George MacDonald

❧ Our Lord asks great faith from us, and he is right. We owe him great faith. After Our Lord said 'Come' to him, Peter had no more fear and walked upon the waters. So that when Jesus has quite certainly called us to certain circumstances in life, given us a certain vocation, we need fear nothing, but should attack the most insurmountable obstacles without hesitation. If Jesus has said 'Come,' we have the grace to walk upon the waters. It may seem to us impossible, but Jesus overmasters the impossible. So we need three things: first, to call out to Our Lord very clearly, and then, when we have distinctly heard his 'Come' (without this summons we have not the right to throw ourselves into the waters—it would be presumptuous, imprudent and rash, and a risk to the life of the soul; it would be sinful, even to mortal sin, for to risk the life of the soul is even graver than to risk the life of the body), once his 'Come' is heard by the soul (till that moment our duty is simply to pray and wait), we must hesitate no more but throw ourselves into the waters like S. Peter and, confident in the call that God has given, walk over the waves, without hesitation, without the least doubt or fear, sure that if we go forward in faith and confidence the path that Jesus calls to us to follow will become easy to us by the virtue of his call 'Come.' So let us walk with perfect faith in the way along which he calls us, for heaven and earth shall pass away but his words shall not pass.

—From *Meditations of a Hermit* by Charles de Foucauld

ᏧᎠ The movement from illusion to prayer is hard to make since it leads us from false certainties to true uncertainties, from an easy support system to a risky surrender, and from the many 'safe' gods to the God whose love has no limits.

—From *Reaching Out* by Henri J. M. Nouwen

ᏧᎠ Everyone, at some time and in some areas, is a follower, and it is just as important to be discriminating in choosing whom to follow as it is to prepare to lead.

—From *Servant Leadership* by Robert K. Greenleaf

ᏧᎠ O God, you are the fountain of all truth; we ask you to protect your church from all false teaching.

> Protect the Church
>> From all teaching and preaching which would
>>> destroy men's faith;
>> From all that removes the old foundations
>>> without putting anything in their place;
>> From all that confuses the simple,
>>> that perplexes the seeker,
>>> that bewilders the way-faring man.

> And yet at the same time protect the Church
>> From the failure to face new truth;
>> From devotion to words and ideas
>>> which the passing of the years has rendered
>>> unintelligible;
>> From all intellectual cowardice
>>> and from all mental lethargy and sloth.
> O God, send to your Church teachers,
>> Whose minds are wise with wisdom;
>> Whose hearts are warm with love;

Whose lips are eloquent with truth.
Send to your Church teachers
Whose desire is to build and not to destroy;
Who are adventurous with the wise,
and yet gentle with the simple;
Who strenuously exercise the intellect,
and who yet remember that the heart has reasons
of its own.

Give to your Church preachers and teachers who can make known the Lord Christ to others because they know him themselves; and give to your Church hearers, who, being freed from prejudice, will follow truth as blind men long for light. This we ask through Jesus Christ our Lord. Amen.
—From *Prayers for the Christian Year* by William Barclay

❧ We are sorely in need of strong ethical leaders to go out ahead to show the way so that the moral standards and the perceptions of the many will be raised, and so that they will serve better with what they have and what they know.
—From *Servant Leadership* by Robert K. Greenleaf

❧ Hospitality is the virtue which allows us to break through the narrowness of our own fears and to open our houses to the stranger, with the intuition that salvation comes to us in the form of a tired traveler. Hospitality makes anxious disciples into powerful witnesses, makes suspicious owners into generous givers, and makes closed-minded sectarians into interested recipients of new ideas and insights.

But it has become very difficult for us today to fully understand the implications of hospitality. Like the Semitic nomads, we live in a desert with many lonely travelers who are looking for a moment of peace, for a fresh drink and for a sign of encouragement so that they can continue their mysterious search for freedom.

What does hospitality as a healing power require? It requires first of all that the host feel at home in his own house, and secondly that he create a free and fearless place for the unexpected visitor. Therefore, hospitality embraces two concepts: concentration and community.
—From *The Wounded Healer* by Henri J. M. Nouwen

꽃 The fathers of the early church who went out into the desert are popularly thought to have been fleeing the evils of civilization. But this is a simplification. They thought of themselves more properly as going out to fight evil. The demons, as well as the angels, were believed to live in the wilderness and there could be confronted and bested in all their horrible destructiveness.

The besetting sin of the desert fathers was acedia or *accidie*, tellingly described as "the devil of the noon-day sun." Acedia is spiritual boredom, an indifference to matters of religion, or simple laziness. Symeon the New Theologian wrote to his monks, "Do not forget your special tasks and your handicraft to walk about aimlessly and in dissipation and so expose yourselves to the demon of accidie." His remark is almost a commentary on the axiom, "Idle hands are the devil's workshop."

The ancient sin of acedia lies at the root of the pastor's or priest's refusal to heed the calling to be the instrument of spiritual growth. In 1977 Carlyle Marney, a distinguished Baptist "pastor to pastors," spoke at the seminary where I serve. I remember him asking our students if they thought after ten years they would still love the Lord Jesus or if instead would have become "hand tamed by the gentry." Of course, he would have been exceedingly surprised if any had confessed that probably the latter would be the case, but the fact is that many ordained persons quickly lose a sense of the excitement of the spiritual quest. They succumb to acedia in those forms that are to a degree peculiar to our times, and yet share much with previous centuries of clergy.

Many of us when we think of the sins of the clergy recall the "fallen priest" in literature, such as the Reverend T. Lawrence Shannon in Tennessee Williams' play, *The Night of the Iguana*. He was a boozer, a wencher, and had lost his faith. Yet, such a person is less a sinner than he is a casualty. American religion is obsessed with the "warm sins" such as illicit sex and gluttony. Because many of us are Donatists—believing that the validity of the sacrament depends upon the moral character of its minister, which was condemned as a heresy long ago—we become inordinately concerned when the warm sins are committed by the ordained. What we fail to realize is that pastor or priest who succumbs to the sins of passion is fallen in the same manner as a fallen soldier.

These are the demons that threaten anyone who sets out upon the path through chaos. Some will lose.

The sins that should concern us far more deeply are those that prevent the ordained from ever exercising their spiritual vocation. These "cold sins" truly violate the mission of the pastor to be a symbol, symbol-bearer, and hermeneut. They arise not from an excess of passion, but from a fear of passion. They are the product of a calculated apathy, sustained only by the embers of a dying soul.

Acedia is the root sin of the clergy as spiritual guides. Like a cancer it eats away at our abandonment to the love for God and his creation. It takes a number of forms, which have much in common with those of other centuries but also have their own peculiar twist in our times.
—From *Spirituality for Ministry* by Urban T. Holmes III

Hymn: Guide Me, O Thou Great Jehovah

Guide me, O thou great Jehovah,
Pilgrim through this barren land;
I am weak, but thou art mighty;
Hold me with thy powerful hand;
Bread of heaven, bread of heaven,
Feed me till I want no more,
Feed me till I want no more.

Open now the crystal fountain,
Whence the healing stream doth flow;
Let the fire and cloudy pillar
Lead me all my journey through;
Strong deliverer, strong deliverer,
Be thou still my strength and shield,
Be thou still my strength and shield.

When I tread the verge of Jordan,
Bid my anxious fears subside;
Death of death and hell's destruction,
Land me safe on Canaan's side;
Songs of praises, songs of praises
I will ever give to thee,
I will ever give to thee. Amen.
—William Williams

9: The Call to Ministry

I. Invocation
    Almighty God, in every age you have called out men and women to be your faithful servants. We believe you have now called us to join that great company who seek to follow you. Grant unto us today and always a clear vision of your call and strength to fulfill the ministry assigned to us. We pray in the name of Christ. Amen.

II. Psalm 62

III. Daily Scripture Readings
Monday	Isaiah 6:1-8
Tuesday	Luke 5:1-11
Wednesday	Acts 9:1-22
Thursday	1 Corinthians 1:26-31
Friday	2 Corinthians 4
Saturday	John 21:15-19

    Sunday A Isaiah 9:1-4; Psalm 27:1-6; 1 Corinthians 1:10-17; Matthew 4:12-23

    B. Jonah 3:1-5, 10; Psalm 62:5-12; 1 Corinthians 7:29-31, (32-35); Mark 1:14-20

    C. Nehemiah 8:1-4a, 5-6, 8-10; Psalm 19:7-14; 1 Corinthians 12:12-30; Luke 4:14-21

IV. Readings for Reflection

V. Prayers: for the church, for others, for myself

VI. Reflection: silent and written

VII. Hymn: "Take My Life, and Let It Be Consecrated"

VIII. Benediction
    Go forth now as God's servant. Remember God's presence often and draw strength from the knowledge that the One who calls and sends also sustains. Amen.

Readings For Reflection

❧ Is there then anything you will not leave for Christ? You cannot know him—and yet he is the Truth, the one thing alone that can be known! Do you not care to be imperfect? Would you rather keep this or that, with imperfection, than part with it to be perfect? You cannot know Christ, for the very principle of his life was the simple absolute relation of realities; his one idea was to be a perfect child to his Father. He who will not part with all for Christ, is not worthy of him, and cannot know him; and the Lord is true, and cannot acknowledge him. . . .

To let their light shine, not to force on them their interpretations of God's designs, is the duty of Christians toward their fellows. If you who set yourselves to explain the theory of Christianity, had set yourselves instead to do the will of the Master, the one object for which the Gospel was preached to you, how different would now be the condition of that portion of the world with which you come into contact! Had you given yourselves to the understanding of his word that you might do it, and not to the quarrying from it of material wherewith to buttress your systems, in many a heart by this time would the name of the Lord be loved where now it remains unknown. The word of life would then by you have been held out indeed.

Men, undeterred by your explanations of Christianity —for you would not be forcing them on their acceptance— and attracted by your behavior, would be saying to each other, as Moses said to himself when he saw the bush that burned with fire and was not consumed, "I will turn aside and see this great sight!" They would be drawing nigh to behold how these Christians loved one another, and how just and fair they were to every one that had to do with them! to note that their goods were the best, their weight surest, their prices most reasonable, their word most certain! that in their families was neither jealousy nor emulation! that their children were as diligently taught to share, as some are to save, or to lay out only upon self—their mothers more anxious lest a child should hoard than lest he should squander; that in no house of theirs was religion one thing, and the daily life another.

—From *Creation in Christ* by George MacDonald

❧ Obedience is indispensable. *Not to a static code*, however helpful it may be at times. *But obedience to God*, who is present with us in every situation and is speaking to us all the time. Every obedience, however small (if any obedience is ever small) quickens our sensitivity to him and our capacity to understand him and so makes more real our sense of his presence.

—From *The Captivating Presence* by Albert Edward Day

❧ It was not God's forgetfulness of us, but his true, raw way of digging out of the depths of us free love and naked faith.

It was not chaos, clutching at men and women's throats to make them cry out and curse the day they were born, but the motherly lap that would give them birth, bear them to the Kingdom.

From that moment I had no more doubts: Poverty was the dwelling place of the divine, the highest school of true love, the mighty pull of mercy, the encounter with God made easy, the surest way to cross this earth.

I espoused my Lady Poverty in desire, and from that moment all fear died within me.

Or rather, true freedom began.

—From *I, Francis* by Carlo Carretto

❧ Faith in the value and meaning of life, even in the face of despair and death, is the second principle of Christian leadership. This seems so obvious that it is often taken for granted and overlooked.

But for a man with a deep-rooted faith in the value and meaning of life, every experience holds a new promise, every encounter carries a new insight, and every event brings a new message. But these promises, insights, and messages have to be discovered and made visible. A Christian leader is not a leader because he announced a new idea and tries to convince others of its worth; he is a leader because he faces the world with eyes full of expectation, with the expertise to take away the veil that covers its hidden potential. Christian leadership is called ministry precisely to express that in the service of others new life can be brought about. It is this service which gives eyes to see the flower breaking through the cracks in the street, ears to hear a word of forgiveness muted by hatred and hostility, and hands to feel new life under the cover of death and destruction.

—From *The Wounded Healer* by Henri J. M. Nouwen

  While personal concern is sustained by a continuously growing faith in the value and meaning of life, the deepest motivation for leading our fellow man to the future is hope. For hope makes it possible to look beyond the fulfillment of urgent wishes and pressing desires and offers a vision beyond human suffering and even death. A Christian leader is a man of hope whose strength in the final analysis is based neither on self-confidence derived from his personality, nor on specific expectations for the future, but on a promise given to him.

This promise not only made Abraham travel to unknown territory; it not only inspired Moses to lead his people out of slavery; it is also the guiding motive for any Christian who keeps pointing to new life even in the face of corruption and death.

Without this hope, we will never be able to see value and meaning in the encounter with a decaying human being and become personally concerned. This hope stretches far beyond the limitations of one's own psychological strength, for it is anchored not just in the soul of the individual but in God's self-disclosure in history. Leadership therefore is not called Christian because it is permeated with optimism against all the odds of life, but because it is grounded in the historic Christ-event which is understood as a definitive breach in the deterministic chain of human trial and error, and as a dramatic affirmation that there is light on the other side of darkness.

Every attempt to attach this hope of visible symptoms in our surroundings becomes a temptation when it prevents us from the realization that promises, not concrete successes, are the basis of Christian leadership. Many ministers, priests and Christian laymen have become disillusioned, bitter and even hostile when years of hard work bear no fruit, when little change is accomplished. Building a vocation on the expectations of concrete results, however conceived, is like building a house on sand instead of on solid rock, and even takes away the ability to accept successes as free gifts.

Hope prevents us from clinging to what we have and frees us to move away from the safe place and enter unknown and fearful territory. This might sound romantic, but when a man enters with his fellow man into his fear of death and is able to wait for him right there, "leaving the safe place" might turn out to be a very difficult act of leadership. It is an act of discipleship in which we follow the hard road of Christ, who entered death with nothing but bare hope.

—From *The Wounded Healer* by Henri J. M. Nouwen

&. So those who imagine that they are called to contemplation because they are attracted by contemplation, when the common duties of existence steadily block this path, do well to realise that our own feelings and preferences are very poor guides when it comes to the robust realities and stern demands of the Spirit.

St. Paul did not want to be an apostle to the Gentiles. He wanted to be a clever and appreciated young Jewish scholar, and kicked against the pricks. St. Ambrose and St. Augustine did not want to be overworked and worried bishops. Nothing was farther from their intention. St. Cuthbert wanted the solitude and freedom of his hermitage on the Farne; but he did not often get there. St. Francis Xavier's preference was for an ordered life close to his beloved master, St. Ignatius. At a few hours' notice he was sent out to be the Apostle of the Indies and never returned to Europe again. Henry Martyn, the fragile and exquisite scholar, was compelled to sacrifice the intellectual life to which he was so perfectly fitted for the missionary life to which he felt he was decisively called. In all these, a power beyond themselves decided the direction of life. Yet in all we recognise not frustration, but the highest of all types of achievement. Things like this—and they are constantly happening—gradually convince us that the over-ruling reality of life is the Will and Choice of a Spirit acting not in a mechanical but in a living and personal way; and that the spiritual life does not consist in mere individual betterment, or assiduous attention to one's own soul, but in a free and unconditional response to that Spirit's pressure and call, whatever the cost may be.

—From *The Spiritual Life* by Evelyn Underhill

Hymn: Take My Life, and Let It Be Consecrated

Take my life, and let it be
Consecrated, Lord, to thee.
Take my moments and my days;
Let them flow in ceaseless praise.
Take my hands, and let them move
At the impulse of thy love.
Take my feet, and let them be
Swift and beautiful for thee.

Take my voice, and let me sing
Always, only, for my King.
Take my lips, and let them be
Filled with messages from thee.
Take my silver and my gold;
Not a mite would I withhold.
Take my intellect, and use
Every power as thou shalt choose.

Take my will, and make it thine;
It shall be no longer mine.
Take my heart, it is thine own;
It shall be thy royal throne.
Take my love; my Lord, I pour
At thy feet its treasure store.
Take myself, and I will be
Ever, only, all for thee. Amen.
—Frances R. Havergal

10: The Authority of God's Word

I. Invocation
Almighty God, whose word is authority and power and whose way is love, grant unto us today clear minds, understanding hearts, and willing spirits so that we may wisely appropriate your word of truth. In the name of Christ. Amen.

II. Psalm 9

III. Daily Scripture Readings
Monday   Genesis 1
Tuesday   John 15:1-11
Wednesday   Acts 27:21-26
Thursday   Acts 10:1-43
Friday   Luke 6:17-45
Saturday   Luke 8:40-56
Sunday   A. Micah 6:1-8; Psalm 37:1-11;
               1 Corinthians 1:18-31; Matthew 5:1-12
            B. Deuteronomy 18:15-20; Psalm 111;
               1 Corinthians 8:1-13; Mark 1:21-28
            C. Jeremiah 1:4-10; Psalm 71:1-6;
               1 Corinthians 13:1-13; Luke 4:21-30

IV. Readings for Reflection

V. Prayers: for the church, for others, for myself

VI. Reflection: silent and written

VII. Hymn: "Holy Spirit, Truth Divine"

VIII. Benediction
The grace of the Lord Jesus Christ, and the love of God, and the fellowship of the Holy Spirit be with you all. Amen. —2 Corinthians 13:14

*If this is the Last Sunday after Epiphany, use Week 15.

Readings for Reflection

ﻬ Merton once told me to quit trying so hard in prayer. He said: "How does an apple ripen? It just sits in the sun." A small green apple cannot ripen in one night by tightening all its muscles, squinting its eyes and tightening its jaw in order to find itself the next morning miraculously large, red, ripe, and juicy beside its small green counterparts. Like the birth of a baby or the opening of a rose, the birth of the true self takes place in God's time. We must wait for God, we must be awake; we must trust in his hidden action within us.
—From *Merton's Palace of Nowhere* by James Finley

ﻬ We seldom get rid of an evil merely by understanding its causes . . . and for all our insight, obstinate habits do not disappear until replaced by other habits. But habits are won only by exercise, and appropriate education is the sole means to this end. The patient must be *drawn out* of himself into other paths, which is the true meaning of "education," and this can only be achieved by an educative will. . . .

. . . no amount of confession and no amount of explaining can make the crooked plant grow straight; it must be trained upon the trellis of the norm by the gardener's art.
—From *The Practice of Psychotherapy* by Carl G. Jung

ﻬ The creature has nothing else in its power but the free use of its will, and its free will hath no other power but that of concurring with, or resisting, the working of God in nature.
—From *A Serious Call to a Devout and Holy Life* by William Law

ﻬ The distresses of choice are our chance to be blessed.
—From *For the Time Being* by W. H. Auden

ﻬ Represent to your imagination that your bed is your grave; that all things are ready for your interment; that you are to have no more to do with this world; and that it will be owing to God's great mercy if you ever see the light of the sun again or have another day to add to your works of piety. Then commit yourself to sleep as one that is to have no more opportunities of doing good, but is to awake among spirits that are separate from the body and waiting for the judgment of the last great day.

Such a solemn resignation of yourself into the hands of God every evening, and parting with all the world as if you were never to see it any more—and all this in the silence and darkness of the night—is a practice that will soon have excellent effects upon your spirit. For this time of the night is exceeding proper for such prayers and meditations. The likeness which sleep and darkness have to death will contribute very much to make your thoughts about it the more deep and affecting. So that I hope you will not let a time so proper for such prayers be ever passed over without them.
—From *A Serious Call to a Devout and Holy Life* by William Law

ᐓ We live in a world of unreality and dreams. To give up our imaginary position as the center, to renounce it, not only intellectually but in the imaginative part of our soul, that means to awaken to what is real and eternal, to see the true light and hear the true silence. A transformation then takes place at the very roots of our sensibility, in our immediate reception of sense impressions and psychological impressions. It is a transformation analogous to that which takes place in the dusk of evening on a road, where we suddenly discern as a tree what we had at first seen as a stooping man; or where we suddenly recognize as a rustling of leaves what we thought at first was whispering voices. We see the same colors; we hear the same sounds, but not in the same way.

To empty ourselves of our false divinity, to deny ourselves, to give up being the center of the world in imagination, to discern that all points in the world are equally centers and that the true center is outside the world, this is to consent to the rule of mechanical necessity in matter and of free choice at the center of each soul. Such consent is love. The face of this love, which is turned toward thinking persons, is the love of our neighbor; the face turned toward matter is love of the order of the world, or love of the beauty of the world which is the same thing.
—From *Waiting for God* by Simone Weil

ᐓ Just as physical pain is a warning that all is not well with us and something needs to be done, so neurosis is a similar warning. It is a call to repentance—not to repentance in its all too familiar garb of moralism and religiosity, but to real repentance: a fundamental change in our whole outlook and attitude, a radical reorientation of our lives, a new beginning which is like being born again.

—From *Tensions* by H. A. Williams

❧ We need loving communication, we need the presence of the Spirit.

That is why I do not believe in theologians who do not pray, who are not in humble communication of love with God.

Neither do I believe in the existence of any human power to pass on authentic knowledge of God.

Only God can speak about himself, and only the Holy Spirit, who is love, can communicate this knowledge to us.

When there is a crisis in the Church, it is always here: a crisis of contemplation.

The Church wants to feel able to explain about her spouse even when she has lost sight of him; even when, although she has not been divorced, she no longer knows his embrace, because curiosity has gotten the better of her and she has gone searching for other people and other things.

The revelation of a triune God in the unity of a single nature, the revelation of a divine Holy Spirit present in us, is not on the human level; it does not belong to the realm of reason. It is a personal communication which God alone can give, and the task of giving it belongs to the Holy Spirit, who is the same love which unites the Father and the Son.

The Holy Spirit is the fullness and the joy of God.

It is so difficult to speak of these things. We have to babble like children, but at least, like children, we can say over and over again, tirelessly, "Spirit of God, reveal yourself to me, your child."

And we can avoid pretending that knowledge of God could be the fruit of our gray matter.

Then, and only then, shall we be capable of prayer; borne to the frontier of our radical incapacity, which love has made the beatitude of poverty, we shall be able to invoke God's coming to us, "Come, creator Spirit!"

—From *The God Who Comes* by Carlo Carretto

ᴥ O God, we thank you for all those in whose words and in whose writings your truth has come to us.

For the historians, the psalmists and the prophets,
 who wrote the Old Testament;
For those who wrote the Gospels and the Letters
 of the New Testament;
For all who in every generation
 have taught and explained and expounded and
 preached
  the word of Scripture:
We thank you, O God.
Grant, O God, that no false teaching may ever have
any power to deceive us
or to seduce us from the truth.
 Grant, O God, that we may never listen to any
 teaching which would encourage us to think
 sin less serious, vice more attractive,
 or virtue less important;
Grant, O God, that we may never listen to any
 teaching which would dethrone
Jesus Christ from the topmost place;
Grant, O God, that we may never listen to any
 teaching
which for its own purposes perverts the truth.
O God, our Father, establish us immovably in the truth.
Give us minds which can see at once the difference
 between the true and the false;
Make us able to test everything, and to hold fast to that
 which is good;
Give us such a love of truth,
that no false thing may ever be able to lure us from it.
So grant that all our lives we may know, and love,
 and live the truth; through Jesus Christ our Lord.
 Amen.

—From *Prayers for the Christian Year* by William Barclay

Hymn: Holy Spirit, Truth Divine

Holy Spirit, Truth Divine,
Dawn upon this soul of mine;
Word of God and inward light,
Wake my spirit, clear my sight.

Holy Spirit, Love divine,
Glow within this heart of mine;
Kindle every high desire;
Perish self in thy pure fire.

Holy Spirit, Power divine,
Fill and nerve this will of mine;
By thee may I strongly live,
Bravely bear and nobly strive.

Holy Spirit, Right divine,
King within my conscience reign;
Be my Lord, and I shall be
Firmly bound, forever free. Amen.
—Samuel Longfellow

11: The Cost of Ministry

I. Invocation

Almighty God, who sent Jesus to suffer and die for our sake, help us to count the cost of ministry and by your grace to follow through suffering to joy and through death to resurrection. Through Christ our Lord, we pray. Amen.

II. Psalm 28

III. Daily Scripture Readings

Monday	Luke 9:57-62
Tuesday	1 Kings 19
Wednesday	Philippians 1:19-30
Thursday	1 Peter 5:1-11
Friday	Luke 22:24-27
Saturday	John 13:1-17
Sunday	A. Isaiah 58:3-9a; Psalm 112:4-9; 1 Corinthians 2:1-11; Matthew 5:13-16
	B. Job 7:1-7; Psalm 147:1-11; 1 Corinthians 9:16-23; Mark 1:29-39
	C. Isaiah 6:1-8 (9-13); Psalm 138; 1 Corinthians 15:1-11; Luke 5:1-11

IV. Readings for Reflection

V. Prayers: for the church, for others, for myself

VI. Reflection: silent and written

VII. Hymn: "Breathe on Me, Breath of God"

VIII. Benediction

You have been in communion with your Lord. Go forth now in the strength and assurance that the Lord Jesus Christ goes with you. Amen.

If this is the Last Sunday after Epiphany, use Week 15.

Readings for Reflection

ᴥ A man can keep his sanity and stay alive as long as there is at least one person who is waiting for him. The mind of man can indeed rule his body even when there is little health left. A dying mother can stay alive to see her son before she gives up the struggle, a soldier can prevent his mental and physical disintegration when he knows that his wife and children are waiting for him. But when "nothing and nobody" is waiting, there is no chance to survive in the struggle for life.

—From *The Wounded Healer* by Henri J. M. Nouwen

ᴥ On the one hand, no minister can keep his own experience of life hidden from those he wants to help. Nor should he want to keep it hidden. While a doctor can still be a good doctor even when his private life is severely disrupted, no minister can offer service without a constant and vital acknowledgment of his own experiences. On the other hand, it would be very easy to misuse the concept of the wounded healer by defending a form of spiritual exhibitionism. A minister who talks in the pulpit about his own personal problems is of no help to his congregation, for no suffering human being is helped by someone who tells him that he has the same problems. Remarks such as, "Don't worry because I suffer from the same depression, confusion and anxiety as you do," help no one. This spiritual exhibitionism adds little faith to little faith and creates narrow-mindedness instead of new perspectives. Open wounds stink and do not heal.

Making one's own wounds a source of healing, therefore, does not call for a sharing of superficial personal pains but for a constant willingness to see one's own pain and suffering as rising from the depth of the human condition which all men share.

—From *The Wounded Healer* by Henri J. M. Nouwen

ᴥ How baffling you are, oh Church, and yet how I love you!

How you have made me suffer, and yet how much I owe you!

I should like to see you destroyed, and yet I need your presence.

You have given me so much scandal and yet you have made me understand sanctity.

I have seen nothing in the world more devoted to obscurity, more compromised, more false, and I have touched nothing more pure, more generous, more beautiful. How often I have wanted to shut the doors of my soul in your face, and how often I have prayed to die in the safety of your arms.

No, I cannot free myself from you, because I am you, although not completely.

And where should I go?
—From *The God Who Comes* by Carlo Carretto

❧ Real training for service asks for a hard and often painful process of self-emptying. The main problem of service is to be the way without being 'in the way.' And if there are any tools, techniques and skills to be learned they are primarily to plow the field, to cut the weeds and to clip the branches, that is, to take away the obstacles for real growth and development. Training for service is not a training to become rich but to become voluntarily poor; not to fulfill ourselves but to empty ourselves; not to conquer God but to surrender to his saving power. All this is very hard to accept in our contemporary world, which tells us about the importance of power and influence. But it is important that in this world there remain a few voices crying out that if there is anything to boast of, we should boast of our weakness. Our fulfillment is in offering emptiness, our usefulness in becoming useless, our power in becoming powerless.
—From *Reaching Out* by Henri J. M. Nouwen

❧ Twelve ministers and theologians of all faiths and twelve psychiatrists of all faiths had convened for a two-day off-the-record seminar on the one-word theme of *healing*. The chairman, a psychiatrist, opened the seminar with this question: 'We are all healers, whether we are ministers or doctors. Why are we in this business? What is our motivation?' There followed only ten minutes of intense discussion and they were all agreed, doctors and ministers, Catholics, Jews, and Protestants. 'For our own healing,' they said.

This is an interesting word, healing, with its meaning, 'to make whole.' The example above suggests that one really never makes it. It is always something sought. Perhaps, as with the minister and the doctor, the servant-leader might also acknowledge that his own healing is his motivation. There is something subtle communicated to one who is being served and led if, implicit in the compact between servant-leader and led, is the understanding that the search for wholeness is something they share.

—From *Servant Leadership* by Robert K. Greenleaf

   In my interviews of clergy there was a general awareness of the issue of the church and the poor and oppressed, often joined by a sincere feeling of ambivalence about what this meant for their style of life. The following statement is an honest, characteristic reflection:

> I struggle with [the issue of poverty] a lot. I had some friends in my last church—we thought in terms of communal living. We thought of cutting way back in our lifestyle as far as the physical things. I don't know. Right now my feeling is a little more like—I wouldn't mind having a little more money to spend. I don't know whether that was just an age factor thing or what, but I'm not as strongly connected in my spirituality with my poverty. I think it gets very, very bad when things begin to provide the meaning for your life. At the same time I don't mind enjoying things. I'm probably a little less ascetic than I was five or six years ago.

The contrast between his nostalgia for a youthful enthusiasm and his present position tempered by inflation, family responsibilities, and a forgivable *joie de vivre* is rather poignant. The principle is clear: things must not provide the meaning for life. This man lived in a modest manse with a wife who worked and one child. With him I had no sense of someone who indulged himself, yet he struggled.

The struggle can be more intentional, that is, more purposeful and directed, if we understand poverty in the daily life of the ordained person as a symbol. We need to remind ourselves repeatedly that to classify something as a symbol does not make it less real, as our culture often thinks; rather we are designating it as a central image in our reality.

Poverty as symbol becomes poverty as a way of seeing and living in the world.

Poverty does not mean penury. One does not have to become indigent, suffering from hunger and cold, to embrace poverty. Analogously, one does not have to become chemically dependent (i.e., an alcoholic, a drug addict) to know the horror of loneliness. The preponderance of evidence from the New Testament would suggest that our Lord and his disciples did not suffer from penury. It was noted that Judas Iscariot was the one who kept the common purse (John 13:29), so we can assume they had some means of support.

Penury is a problem to be overcome as poverty is a symbol to be embraced. Whether or not penury will ever be solved is another matter. The Fourth Evangelist is less sanguine—"For you have the poor among you always" (John 12:8)—than many modern social engineers. But we must be careful not to romanticize the poor, as Pusey appeared to do. There is no reason for thinking that poor folk are more holy than everyone else. Whatever Jesus may have meant in saying it is easier for a camel to pass through the eye of a needle than for a rich man to enter the Kingdom of Heaven, he was not recommending starvation as a means of acquiring the Kingdom of God. He was talking about poverty as a way of seeing and acting in the world (Matt. 19:24).

Poverty as a symbol has to do with receiving and giving. The priest or pastor is an instrumental image of the spiritual life, which life is an openness to God and a consequent openness to one another. The life in the spirit flows from a new transcendent awareness to an action grounded in the vision one shares with God. It is a continuous movement of receiving from God the gift of his presence and giving that gift to others. Poverty allows the freedom of that flow of God's presence through the life of the person, particularly the one who is ordained.

"Human fulfillment," says H. A. Williams, "cannot be reached along the road of gratified greed." The investment of the self in things chokes the spirit, so that it is not capable of allowing the Spirit to slip into one's life. It is like going to an art gallery to view a painting. If one stands before a masterpiece with a mind filled with the countless interpretations from the past, there is little possibility that the painting may touch that person in a new and revealing manner. One must come empty to the painting; not empty in the sense of barren, but empty in the sense of being in an imaginal space full of possibilities.

—From *Spirituality for Ministry* by Urban T. Holmes III

❧ At the root of acedia and clerical sins of un-passion lies the fear of failure.

It has become the practice in some dioceses within the Episcopal Church to interview a selected group of priests who are willing to be nominated for bishop in that diocese. In one such selection process a question was asked of the candidates: "How do you handle failure?" One man, a demonstrably successful cardinal rector, probably lost the election on the basis of his answer to that question alone which was, "I don't recall ever having failed."

How can we serve a Lord, the symbol of whose failure is above our altars, on top of our churches, on our stationery, and around our necks, and claim to be a stranger to failure? The power of Christ's Passion is that every human being can identify with it, if he or she just gives it some thought. Despite our best intentions and our fervent hopes, each of us is nailed to his or her cross daily. Certainly this is true of the ordained person, who is called to be "another Christ" and to risk living by values that the world not only rejects but perceives as subversive of its goals and objectives.

—From *Spirituality for Ministry* by Urban T. Holmes III

❧ The vocation of ordination is a call to power. But it is not the pastor's or priest's power, it is Christ's power. In at least some of the denominations surveyed in this study ordination bestows upon the recipient the power to forgive sins. It is, of course, not his or her authority, but that authority which Christ claims for the Son of Man in the Gospels: "Is it easier to say, 'Your sins are forgiven you,' or to say, 'Stand up and walk'? But to convince you that the Son of Man has the right [*exousian*, power or authority] on earth to forgive sins . . . 'I say to you, stand up, take your bed, and go home'" (Luke 5:23-24). In what way Christ identified himself with the Son of Man is widely debated, but certainly the church understood this reference to be to Christ himself.

The word the Evangelist uses for right, power, or authority to forgive sins is important. *Exousia* means literally in Greek "out of being." It is an authority or power which flows from the inside out and is grounded not in our status or role, but in our center of being, who we are. It is a power rooted in the authenticity of the person; he or she is who he or she appears to be. But such authenticity comes at a high price, as I shall insist again and again throughout this book. At the very least, it will not make us popular.
—From *Spirituality for Ministry* by Urban T. Holmes III

Hymn: Breathe on Me, Breath of God

Breathe on me, Breath of God,
Fill me with life anew,
That I may love what thou dost love,
And do what thou wouldst do.

Breathe on me, Breath of God,
Until my heart is pure,
Until with thee I will one will,
To do and to endure.

Breathe on me, Breath of God,
Till I am wholly thine,
Till all this earthly part of me
Glows with thy fire divine.

Breathe on me, Breath of God,
So shall I never die,
But live with thee the perfect life
Of thine eternity. Amen.
—Edwin Hatch

12: *The Rewards of Ministry*

I.   Invocation
Lord Jesus Christ, you have promised never to forsake or leave us. Teach us day by day the deep rewards of faithful ministry and most of all help us to know always the reward of being near to you. In the name of Christ. Amen.

II.   Psalm 27

III.   Daily Scripture Readings

Monday	1 Thessalonians 4:9-18
Tuesday	1 Timothy 6:6-20
Wednesday	Philippians 3
Thursday	Ezekiel 33:30-33
Friday	2 Timothy 1:8-14
Saturday	Romans 6:1-11

Sunday   A. Deuteronomy 30:15-20;
Psalm 119:1-8; 1 Corinthians 3:1-9;
Matthew 5:17-26

            B. 2 Kings 5:1-14; Psalm 32;
1 Corinthians 9:24-27; Mark 1:40-45

            C. Jeremiah 17:5-10; Psalm 1;
1 Corinthians 15:12-20; Luke 6:17-26

IV.   Readings for Reflection

V.   Prayers: for the church, for others, for myself

VI.   Reflection: silent and written

VII.   Hymn: "Close to Thee"

VIII.   Benediction
Be filled with hope, joy, and peace by the power of the Holy Spirit. Amen.

*If this is the Last Sunday after Epiphany, use Week 15.

Readings for Reflection

❧ If you asked twenty good men to-day what they thought the highest of the virtues, nineteen of them would reply, Unselfishness. But if you asked almost any of the great Christians of old he would have replied, Love. You see what has happened? A negative term has been substituted for a positive, and this is of more than philosophical importance. The negative ideal of Unselfishness carries with it the suggestion not primarily of securing good things for others, but of going without them ourselves, as if our abstinence and not their happiness was the important point. I do not think this is the Christian virtue of Love. The New Testament has lots to say about self-denial, but not about self-denial as an end in itself. We are told to deny ourselves and to take up our crosses in order that we may follow Christ; and nearly every description of what we shall ultimately find if we do so contains an appeal to desire. If there lurks in most modern minds the notion that to desire our own good and earnestly to hope for the enjoyment of it is a bad thing, I submit that this notion has crept in from Kant and the Stoics and is no part of the Christian faith. Indeed, if we consider the unblushing promises of reward and the staggering nature of the rewards promised in the Gospels, it would seem that Our Lord finds our desires, not too strong, but too weak. We are half-hearted creatures, fooling about with drink and sex and ambition when infinite joy is offered us, like an ignorant child who wants to go on making mud pies in a slum because he cannot imagine what is meant by the offer of a holiday at the sea. We are far too easily pleased.

—From *The Weight of Glory* by C. S. Lewis

❧ Our place is not the auditorium but the stage—or, as the case may be, the field, workshop, study, laboratory—because we ourselves form part of the creative apparatus of God, or at least are meant to form part of the creative apparatus of God. He made us in order to use us, and use us in the most profitable way; for his purpose, not ours. To live a spiritual life means subordinating all other interests to that single fact. Sometimes our position seems to be that of tools; taken up when wanted, used in ways which we had not expected for an object on which our opinion is not asked, and then laid down. Sometimes we are the currency used in some great operation, of which the purpose is not revealed to us. Sometimes we are servants, left year in, year out to the same monotonous job. Sometimes we are conscious fellow-workers with the Perfect, striving to bring the Kingdom in. But whatever our particular place or job may be, it means the austere conditions of the workshop, not the free-lance activities of the messy but well-meaning amateur; clocking in at the right time and tending the machine in the right way. Sometimes, perhaps, carrying on for years with a machine we do not very well understand and do not enjoy; because it needs doing, and no one else is available. Or accepting the situation quite quietly, when a job we felt that we were managing excellently is taken away. Taking responsibility if we are called to it, or just bringing the workers their dinner, cleaning and sharpening the tools. All self-willed choices and obstinacy drained out of what we thought to be our work; so that it becomes more and more God's work in us.

—From *The Spiritual Life* by Evelyn Underhill

&. We are the agents of the Creative Spirit in this world. Real advance in the spiritual life, then, means accepting this vocation with all it involves. Not merely turning over the pages of an engineering magazine and enjoying the pictures, but putting on overalls and getting on with the job. The real spiritual life must be horizontal as well as vertical; spread more and more as well as aspire more and more.

—From *The Spiritual Life* by Evelyn Underhill

&. This River has been a Terror to many, yea, the thoughts of it also have often frightened me. But now methinks I stand easy, my Foot is fixed upon that upon which the Feet of the Priests that bare the Ark of the Covenant stood while Israel went over this Jordan. The Waters indeed are to the Palate bitter and to the Stomach cold, yet the thoughts of what I am going to, and of the Conduct that waits for me on the other side, doth lie as a glowing Coal at my Heart.

I see myself now at the end of my Journey, my toilsome days are ended. I am going now to see that Head that was crowned with Thorns, and that Face that was spit upon for me.

I have formerly lived by Hearsay and Faith, but now I go where I shall live by sight, and shall be with him in whose Company I delight myself.

—From *The Pilgrim's Progress* by John Bunyan

ॐ Osuna says that God plays a game with the soul called "the loser wins"; a game in which the one who holds the poorest cards does best. The Pharisee's consciousness that he had such an excellent hand really prevented him from taking a single trick.

—From *The Spiritual Life* by Evelyn Underhill

ॐ One obvious reason for this sense of God's unreality, which often makes helpful prayer impossible, lies of course in *character*. Isaiah was dealing with a universal truth when he said: "Your iniquities have separated between you and your God, and your sins have hid his face from you" (Isaiah 59:2). One has only to consider that frivolous American who in the Rembrandt room of the Amsterdam Gallery looked lackadaisically around and asked: "I wonder if there is anything here worth seeing"; one has only to recall the women who climbed an Alpine height on an autumn day, when the riot of color in the valley sobered into the green of the pines upon the heights, and over all stood the crests of eternal snow, and who inquired in the full sight of all this, "We heard there was a view up here; where is it?" to see that there is a spiritual qualification for every experience, and that without it nothing fine and beautiful can ever be real to any one. "Mr. Turner," a man once said to the artist, "I never see any sunsets like yours." And the artist answered grimly, "No, sir. Don't you wish you could?" How clearly then must the sense of God's reality be a progressive and often laborious achievement of the spirit! It is not a matter to be taken for granted, as though any one could saunter into God's presence at any time, in any mood, with any sort of life behind him, and at once perceive God there.

—From *The Meaning of Prayer* by Harry Emerson Fosdick

ë&. If the Church really sees itself as the people of God, it is obvious that it can never be a static and supra-historical phenomenon, which exists undisturbed by earthly space and historical time. The Church is always and everywhere a living people, gathered together from the peoples of this world and journeying through the midst of time. The Church is essentially *en route*, on a journey, a pilgrimage. A Church which pitches its tents without looking out constantly for new horizons, which does not continually strike camp, is being untrue to its calling. The historical nature of the Church is revealed by the fact that it remains the pilgrim people of God. It renews and continues the history of the ancient people of the covenant and fulfills it in the new covenant. At the same time it journeys through history, through a time of complex imperfection, towards the final perfection, the eschatological kingdom of God, led by God himself. It is essentially an interim Church, a Church in transition, and therefore not a Church of fear but of expectation and hope: a Church which is directed towards the consummation of the world by God.

—From *The Church* by Hans Küng

ë&. O God, you are our refuge.
When we are exhausted by life's efforts;
    When we are bewildered by life's problems;
    When we are wounded by life's sorrows:
        We come for refuge to you.
O God, you are our strength.
    When our tasks are beyond our powers;
    When our temptations are too strong for us;
    When duty calls for more than we have to give to it:
        We come for strength to you.
O God, it is from you that all goodness comes.
    It is from you that our ideals come;
    It is from you that there comes to us the spur
        of high desire and the restraint of conscience.
    It is from you that there has come the strength
        to resist any temptation,
        and to do any good thing.
And now as we pray to you,
    Help us to believe in your love,
    so that we may be certain

that you will hear our prayer;
Help us to believe in your power,
so that we may be certain
that you are able to do for us
above all that we ask or think;
Help us to believe in your wisdom,
so that we may be certain
that you will answer,
not as our ignorance asks,
but as your perfect wisdom knows best.
All this we ask through Jesus Christ our Lord. Amen.
—From *Prayers for the Christian Year* by William Barclay

Hymn: Close to Thee

Thou my everlasting portion,
More than friend or life to me,
All along my pilgrim journey,
Savior, let me walk with thee.

Close to thee, close to thee,
Close to thee, close to thee;
All along my pilgrim journey,
Savior, let me walk with thee.

Not for ease or worldly pleasure,
Nor for fame my prayer shall be;
Gladly will I toil and suffer,
Only let me walk with thee.

Close to thee, close to thee,
Close to thee, close to thee;
All along my pilgrim journey,
Savior, let me walk with thee.

Lead me through the vale of shadows,
Bear me o'er life's fitful sea;
Then the gate of life eternal
May I enter, Lord, with thee.

Close to thee, close to thee,
Close to thee, close to thee;
All along my pilgrim journey,
Savior, let me walk with thee. Amen.
—Fanny J. Crosby

Seventh Sunday after Epiphany*
(between February 18 and 24)

13: *Unchanging Truths*

I. Invocation
    God of power unconquerable and light unquench-
    able look with favor upon your servant. By the
    power of your Spirit at work within, transform and
    make fruitful my life and ministry. In the name and
    Spirit of Christ. Amen.

II. Psalm 40

III. Daily Scripture Readings
Monday	Ephesians 6:10-17
Tuesday	Hebrews 12:1-17
Wednesday	1 Peter 2:7-12
Thursday	Philippians 3:12-21
Friday	Matthew 23:1-12
Saturday	Matthew 7:13-23
Sunday	A. Isaiah 49:8-13; Psalm 62:5-12; 1 Corinthians 3:10-11, 16-23; Matthew 5:27-37
	B. Isaiah 43:18-25; Psalm 41; 2 Corinthians 1:18-22; Mark 2:1-12
	C. Genesis 45:3-11, 15; Psalm 37:1-11; 1 Corinthians 15:35-38, 42-50; Luke 6:27-38

IV. Readings for Reflection

V. Prayers: for the church, for others, for myself

VI. Reflection: silent and written

VII. Hymn: "I Want a Principle Within"

VIII. Benediction
       Embrace the will of God. Obey the call of God.
       Receive the power of God. Reflect the peace of God.
       Amen.

*If this is the Last Sunday after Epiphany, use Week 15.

Readings for Reflection

⁋ True holiness is a witness that cannot be ignored. Real sainthood is a phenomenon to which even the worldling pays tribute. The power of a life, where Christ is exalted, would arrest and subdue those who are bored to tears by our thin version of Christianity and wholly uninterested in mere churchmanship.

We have talked much of salvation by faith, but there has been little realization that all real faith involves discipline. Faith is not a blithe "turning it all over to Jesus." Faith is such confidence in Jesus that it takes seriously his summons, "If any man will come after me, let him deny himself, and take up his cross, and follow me."

We have loudly proclaimed our dependence upon the grace of God, never guessing that *the grace of God is given only to those who practice the grace of self-mastery*. "Work out your own salvation with fear and trembling for God is at work in you both to will and to work his good pleasure." People working out, God working in—that is the New Testament synthesis.

Humans, working out their salvation alone, are a pathetic spectacle—hopelessly defeated moralists trying to elevate themselves by their own bootstraps.

God, seeking to work in a person who offers no disciplined cooperation, is a heartbreaking spectacle—a defeated Savior trying to free, from sins and earthiness, a person who will not lift his or her face out of the dust, or shake off the shackles of the egocentric self.

Real discipline is not vain effort to save one's self. It is an intelligent application to the self of those psychological principles which enable the self to enter into life-giving fellowship with God who is our salvation.

In all Christian literature there is no writer who had a clearer conviction concerning the salvation provided only in Christ than has Paul. His self-despair ended in that marvelous, ageless insight, "I thank God, through Jesus Christ my Lord." "I know whom I have believed," he cried in an ecstasy of confident gladness, "and am persuaded that he is able." Paul was a salvationist, in the noblest sense.

But Paul was also a disciplinarian. "I beat my body to keep it in subjection." "They that are Christ's have crucified the flesh with its affections and lusts." "So fight I, not as one who beateth the air." "Mortify therefore your members which are upon earth." "Laying aside every weight and the sin which doth so easily beset us." "No man that warreth, entangleth himself with the affairs of this life." These are not the words of a man who scorned discipline!

One might multiply such statements as these from Paul—all of them the almost spontaneous evidence of the disciplines which he, trusting in Christ, imposed upon himself in his eager effort to give Christ that co-operation without which not even Christ can save a soul and make a saint.

We must recover for ourselves the significance and the necessity of the spiritual disciplines. Without them we shall continue to be impotent witnesses for Christ. Without them Christ will be impotent in his efforts to use us to save our society from disintegration and death.

—From *Discipline and Discovery* by Albert Edward Day

❧ And I drew, too, the way my father once looked at a bird lying on its side against the curb near our house. It was Shabbos and we were on our way back from the synagogue.

"Is it dead, Papa?" I was six and could not bring myself to look at it.

"Yes," I heard him say in a sad and distant way.

"Why did it die?"

"Everything that lives must die."

"Everything?"

"Yes."

"You, too, Papa? And Mama?"

"Yes."

"And me?"

"Yes," he said. Then he added in Yiddish, "But may it be only after you live a long and good life, my Asher."

I couldn't grasp it. I forced myself to look at the bird. Everything alive would one day be as still as that bird?

"Why?" I asked.

"That's the way the Ribbono Shel Olom made his world, Asher."

"Why?"

"So life would be precious, Asher. Something that is yours forever is never precious."

—From *My Name Is Asher Lev* by Chaim Potok

  ❧ Supposing there is some old root—greed, lust, jealousy, or hate—that seems so ingrained in your very bones, in your very nervous system, in your very blood, that there is no way of getting it out. Then, lean back and let the Christ work the miracle.

When you recover from an illness is it because *you* do anything? No. All you do is to lie on the bed and rest, and the cleansing blood, continuously flowing through your veins, brings the healing. . . .

Open your heart in absolute trust while this "purest and most precious blood in all history" brings you complete cleansing and healing. Open your soul while the love of Christ—"the acme of all spiritual love"—the love which has the power to save, and redeem the most hopeless of sinners—takes complete dominion over every area of your life. "Greater love hath no man than this, that a man lay down his life for his friends."

—From *I Will Lift Up Mine Eyes* by Glenn Clark

  ❧ Mother Teresa of Calcutta said, "Pray for me that I not loosen my grip on the hands of Jesus even under the guise of ministering to the poor." That is our first task: to grip the hands of Jesus with such tenacity that we are obliged to follow his lead, to seek first his Kingdom.

The [next] step is so simple I am almost embarrassed to mention it, and yet it is so important that I must. Begin now to obey him in every way you can.

—From *Freedom of Simplicity* by Richard J. Foster

Hymn: I Want a Principle Within

I want a principle within,
Of watchful, godly fear,
A sensibility of sin,
A pain to feel it near.
Help me the first approach to feel
Of pride or wrong desire,

To catch the wandering of my will,
And quench the kindling fire.

If to the right or left I stray,
That moment, Lord, reprove,
And let me weep my life away
For having grieved thy love.
Give me to feel an idle thought
As actual wickedness,
And mourn for the minutest fault
In exquisite distress.

From thee that I no more may stray,
No more thy goodness grieve,
Grant me the filial awe, I pray,
The tender conscience give;
Quick as the apple of an eye,
O God, my conscience make!
Awake my soul when sin is nigh,
And keep it still awake.

Almighty God of truth and love,
To me thy power impart;
The burden from my soul remove,
The hardness from my heart.
O may the least omission pain
My reawakened soul,
And drive me to that grace again,
Which makes the wounded whole. Amen.
—Charles Wesley

Eighth Sunday after Epiphany*
(between February 25 and 29)

14: Protected by God

I.   Invocation
Almighty God, may your strong hand defend, guide, and empower my life and ministry today. In the name of Christ. Amen.

II. Psalm 94

III. Daily Scripture Readings
Monday		John 10:1-18
Tuesday		Luke 15:1-10
Wednesday		Luke 12:22-34
Thursday		Psalm 121
Friday		Revelation 22:1-5, 17
Saturday		Jeremiah 31:27-34
Sunday	A.	Leviticus 19:1-2, 9-18; Psalm 119:33-40; 1 Corinthians 4:1-5; Matthew 5:38-48
	B.	Hosea 2:14-20; Psalm 103:1-13; 2 Corinthians 3:1-6; Mark 2:18-22
	C.	Isaiah 55:10-13; Psalm 92:1-4, 12-15; 1 Corinthians 15:51-58; Luke 6:39-49

IV. Readings for Reflection

V.   Prayers: for the church, for others, for myself

VI. Reflection: silent and written

VII. Hymn: "Jesus, Thou Joy of Loving Hearts"

VIII. Benediction
May the Almighty and ever-present God guide, direct, and enable your life and ministry. Amen.

*If this is the Last Sunday after Epiphany, use Week 15.

Readings for Reflection

ð Through his illustrious missionary and literary career, Frank Laubach bore repeated witness to this reality. His diaries and books on prayer are peppered with his many experiments to remain in constant communion with God. On the first day of 1937 he wrote in his diary, "God, I want to give you every minute of this year. I shall try to keep You in mind every moment of my waking hours. . . . I shall try to let You be the speaker and direct every word. I shall try to let You direct my acts. I shall try to learn Your language." What a marvelous resolve for the new year! Three months later, he noted his progress in learning to practice God's presence: "Thank Thee . . . that the habit of constant conversation grows easier each day. I really do believe *all* thought can be conversations with Thee."

Think of the number of people who have been encouraged in this way by the simple writings and profound life of Brother Lawrence. How vastly enriched we are that he was finally persuaded, almost against his will, to write down how he had learned *The Practice of the Presence of God*. His famous words still throb with life and joy. "The time of business does not with me differ from the time of prayer; and in the noise and clatter of my kitchen, while several persons are at the same time calling for different things, I possess God in as great tranquillity as if I were upon my knees at the blessed sacrament." Every thought, every decision, every action stemmed from the divine Root. A simple kitchen monk, who meekly referred to himself as the "lord of all pots and pans," found it to be possible. We can too!

But we fool ourselves if we think that such a sacramental way of living is automatic. This kind of living communion does not just fall on our heads. We must desire it and seek it out. Like the deer that pants for the flowing stream, so we thirst for the living Spring. We must order our lives in particular ways. We must take up a consciously chosen course of action that will draw us more deeply into perpetual communion with the Father.

I have discovered one delightful means to this end to be prayer experiments that open us to God's presence every

waking moment. The idea is extraordinarily simple. Seek to discover as many ways as possible to keep God constantly in mind. "There is nothing new in that," you may say. "That practice is very ancient and very orthodox." Exactly! This desire to practice the presence of God is the secret of all the saints.
—From *Freedom of Simplicity* by Richard J. Foster

    ᐣ There's not a plant or flower below,
        But makes thy glories known;
        And clouds arise, and tempests blow,
        By order from thy throne,
        While all that borrows life from thee
        Is ever in thy care,
        And everywhere that man can be,
        Thou, God, art present there.
        —Isaac Watts

    ᐣ The vision for wholeness and peace, which shines like a beacon of light through the Old Covenant, gives us important insights into Christian simplicity. This theme is wonderfully gathered up in the Hebrew word *shalom*, a full-bodied concept that resonates with wholeness, unity, balance. Gathering in (but much broader than) peace, it means a harmonious, caring community with God at its center as the prime sustainer and most glorious inhabitant. This great vision of *shalom* begins and ends our Bible. In the creation narrative, God brought order and harmony out of chaos; in the Apocalypse of John, we have the glorious wholeness of a new heaven and a new earth. The messianic child to be born is to be the Prince of Peace (Isa. 9:6). Justice and righteousness and peace are to characterize his unending kingdom (Isa. 9:7). Central to the dream of *shalom* is the wonderful vision of all nations streaming to the mountain of the temple of God to be taught his ways and to walk in his paths; to beat their swords into plowshares and their spears into pruning hooks (Isa. 2:2-5; Mic. 4:1-4). *Shalom* even carries the idea of a harmonious unity in the natural order: the cow and the bear become friends, the lion and the lamb lie down together, and a little child leads them (Isa. 1:1-9). We are in harmony with God—faithfulness and loyalty prevail. We are in harmony with our neighbor—justice and mercy abound. We are in harmony with nature—peace and unity reign.

Economically and socially, the vision of *shalom* is captured in what Bishop John Taylor calls "The Theology of Enough." The greed of the rich is tempered by the need of the poor. Justice, harmony, equilibrium prevail. "It meant a dancing kind of inter-relationship, seeking something more free than equality, more generous than equity, the evershifting equipoise of a life-system." Excessive extravagance, vaunting ambition, ravaging greed—all are foreign to the complete contented brotherhood of *shalom*. Under the reign of God's *shalom* the poor are no longer oppressed, because covetousness no longer rules.

In a particularly tender scene, Jeremiah lamented the fraud and greed of prophet and priest, saying, "They have healed the wound of my people lightly, saying, 'Peace, peace,' when there is no peace" (Jer. 6:14). In essence, Jeremiah had filed a malpractice suit against the self-styled religious quacks. They had put a Band-Aid over a gaping social wound and said, "*Shalom, shalom*—all will be well." But Jeremiah thundered, in effect, "*En shalom*—all is not well. Justice is spurned, the poor oppressed, the orphan ignored. There is no wholeness or healing here!"

But the healing peace of God will not be spurned forever. Isaiah saw a day when the reconciliation between people will be a reality, a day when justice and righteousness will reign, a time when the wholeness of God's peace will rule and people will "walk in the light of the Lord" (Isa. 2:4-5).

In an especially poignant passage, Scripture brings together the three Hebrew concepts we have studied: justice, compassion, and peace. The Psalmist points to the day when "Steadfast love and faithfulness will meet; righteousness and peace will kiss each other" (Ps. 85:10).

—From *Freedom of Simplicity* by Richard J. Foster

❧ Write thy blessed name, O Lord, upon my heart, there to remain so indelibly engraven, that no prosperity, no adversity shall ever move me from thy love. Be thou to me a strong tower of defence, a comforter in tribulation, a deliverer in distress, a very present help in trouble, and a guide

to heaven through the many temptations and dangers of this life. Amen.
—Thomas à Kempis

Hymn: Jesus, Thou Joy of Loving Hearts

Jesus, thou joy of loving hearts!
Thou fount of life! Thou light of all!
From the best bliss that earth imparts,
We turn unfilled to thee again.

Thy truth unchanged hath ever stood;
Thou savest those that on thee call;
To them that seek thee, thou art good;
To them that find thee, all-in-all.

We taste thee, O thou living bread,
And long to feast upon thee still;
We drink of thee, the fountainhead,
And thirst our souls from thee to fill!

Our restless spirits yearn for thee
Where'er our changeful lot is cast,
Glad, when thy gracious smile we see,
Blest, when our faith can hold thee fast.

O Jesus, ever with us stay;
Make all our moments calm and bright;
Chase the dark night of sin away;
Shed o'er the world thy holy light! Amen.
—Bernard of Clairvaux

15: Listen to Jesus Christ

I.   Invocation
Almighty God, you have chosen to speak to us through prophets and wise leaders and most clearly through your son, Jesus Christ. Grant unto us now the ability to hear, understand, and obey him whom you have sent. Amen.

II.   Psalm 78

III.   Daily Scripture Readings

Monday	Matthew 18:1-9
Tuesday	Matthew 15:1-20
Wednesday	Mark 10:35-45
Thursday	Matthew 5:1-12
Friday	Matthew 5:13-16
Saturday	Matthew 6:25-34

Sunday   A. Exodus 24:12-18; Psalm 2:6-11; 2 Peter 1:16-21; Matthew 17:1-9

             B. 2 Kings 2:1-12a; Psalm 50:1-6; 2 Corinthians 4:3-6; Mark 9:2-9

             C. Exodus 34:29-35; Psalm 99; 2 Corinthians 3:12–4:2; Luke 9:28-36

IV.   Readings for Reflection

V.   Prayers: for the church, for others, for myself

VI.   Reflection: silent and written

VII.   Hymn: "Christ, Whose Glory Fills the Skies"

VIII.   Benediction
Bless with your presence my life and ministry all this day long and when night comes grant your servant rest and peace. Amen.

Readings for Reflection

🙠 Boehme advises us once an hour "to fling ourselves beyond every creature." But in order to find God it is perhaps not always necessary to leave the creatures behind. We may ignore, but we can nowhere evade, the presence of God. The world is crowded with him. He walks everywhere *incognito*. And the *incognito* is not always hard to penetrate. The real labour is to remember, to attend. In fact, to come awake. Still more, to remain awake.

Oddly enough, what corroborates me in this faith is the fact, otherwise so infinitely deplorable, that the awareness of this presence has so often been unwelcome. I call upon him in prayer. Often he might reply—I think he does reply—"But you have been evading me for hours." For he comes not only to raise up but to cast down; to deny, to rebuke, to interrupt. The prayer "prevent us in all our doings" is often answered as if the word *prevent* had its modern meaning. The presence which we voluntarily evade is often, and we know it, his presence in wrath.

—From *Letters to Malcolm: Chiefly on Prayer* by C. S. Lewis

🙠 Love bade me welcome: yet my soul drew back,
    Guilty of dust and sin.
But quick-eyed Love, observing me grow slack
    From my first entrance in,
Drew nearer to me, sweetly questioning
    If I lacked anything.
"A guest," I answered, "worthy to be here."
    Love said, "You shall be he."
"I the unkind, the ungrateful? Ah, my dear,
    I cannot look on thee."
Love took my hand, and smiling did reply,
    "Who made the eyes but I?"
"Truth, Lord, but I have marred them: let my shame
    Go where it doth deserve."
"And know you not," says Love, "who bore the blame?"
    "My dear, then I will serve."
"You must sit down," says Love, "and taste my meat,"
    So I did sit and eat.

—"Love Bade Me Welcome" by George Herbert

Everyone has warned me not to tell you what I am going to tell you. . . . They all say "the ordinary reader does not want Theology; give him plain practical religion." I have rejected their advice. I do not think the ordinary reader is such a fool. Theology means "the science of God," and I think any man who wants to think about God at all would like to have the clearest and most accurate ideas about him which are available. You are not children: why should you be treated like children?

In a way I quite understand why some people are put off by Theology. I remember once when I had been giving a talk to the R.A.F., an old, hard-bitten officer got up and said, "I've no use for all that stuff. But, mind you, I'm a religious man too. I *know* there's a God. I've *felt* him: out alone in the desert at night: the tremendous mystery. And that's just why I don't believe all your neat little dogmas and formulas about him. To anyone who's met the real thing they all seem so petty and pedantic and unreal!"

Now in a sense I quite agreed with that man. I think he had probably a real experience of God in the desert. And when he turned from that experience to the Christian creeds, I think he really was turning from something real, to something less real. In the same way, if a man has once looked at the Atlantic from the beach, and then goes and looks at a map of the Atlantic, he also will be turning from real waves to a bit of colored paper. But here comes the point. The map is admittedly only colored paper, but there are two things you have to remember about it. In the first place, it is based on what hundreds and thousands of people have found out by sailing the real Atlantic. In that way it has behind it masses of experience just as real as the one you could have from the beach; only, while yours would be a single isolated glimpse, the map fits all those different experiences together. In the second place, if you want to go anywhere, the map is absolutely necessary. As long as you are content with walks on the beach, your own glimpses are far more fun than looking at a map. But the map is going to be more use than walks on the beach if you want to get to America.

Now Theology is like the map. Merely learning and thinking about the Christian doctrines, if you stop there, is less real and less exciting than the sort of thing my friend got in the desert. Doctrines are not God: they are only a kind of map. But the map is based on the experience of hundreds of people who really were in touch with God—experiences compared with which any thrills or pious feelings you or I are likely to get on our own way are very elementary and very confused. And secondly, if you want to get any further, you must use the map. You see, what happened to that man in the desert may have been real, and was certainly exciting, but nothing comes of it. It leads nowhere. There is nothing to do about it. In fact, that is just why a vague religion—all about feeling God in nature, and so on—is so attractive. It is all thrills and no work; like watching the waves from the beach. But you will not get to Newfoundland by studying the Atlantic that way, and you will not get eternal life by simply feeling the presence of God in flowers or music. Neither will you get anywhere by looking at maps without going to sea. Nor will you be very safe if you go to sea without a map.

—From *The Joyful Christian* by C. S. Lewis

❧ Most of the discussion of prayer I had ever heard centered on whether God answers prayer and how we can know that he does. But during the past decade I have come to believe that prayer is not a matter of my calling in an attempt to get God's attention, but of my finally *listening to the call of God*, which has been constant, patient, and insistent in my inner being. In relationship to God, I am not the seeker, the initiator, the one who loves more greatly. In prayer, as in the whole salvation story unfolded by Scripture, God is reaching out to me, speaking to me, and it is up to me to learn to be polite enough to pay attention. When I do have something to say to God, I am rendering a response to the divine initiative. So the questions of whether or not and how God answers prayer now seem to me bogus questions. God speaks, all right. The big question is do I answer, do I respond, to an invitation that is always open.

I do not mean to imply that I have no use for liturgical or communal prayer, which serves as a concrete enactment of my oneness with the other members of the family of God. But I know, and I think every honest person knows, that communal prayers are sometimes real to my inner experience, and sometimes not, and that the difference lies in the kind of internal focus I am able to give to them. I think that those who attack traditional liturgy, ritual, and communal prayer as meaningless to modern humanity are bogging themselves down in a great muddle. Religious communal celebrations enact, reinforce, and incarnate the human sense of mortal interrelationship, divine interrelationship, and divine-human interrelationship.

—From *Speech, Silence, Action!* by Virginia Ramey Mollenkott

ঌ Awe is a way of being in rapport with the mystery of all reality. The awe that we sense or ought to sense when standing in the presence of a human being is a moment of intuition for the likeness of God which is concealed in his essence. Not only man; even inanimate things stand in a relation to the Creator. The secret of every being is the divine care and concern that are invested in it. Something sacred is at stake in every event.

Awe is an intuition for the creaturely dignity of all things and their preciousness to God; a realization that things not only are what they are but also stand, however remotely, for something absolute. Awe is a sense for the transcendence, for the reference everywhere to him who is beyond all things. It is an insight better conveyed in attitudes than in words. The more eager we are to express it, the less remains of it.

—From *God in Search of Man* by Abraham Joshua Heschel

ঌ O God, Our Father, we know our own weakness.
>Our minds are darkened,
>>and by ourselves we cannot find and know the truth.
>Our wills are weak,
>>and by ourselves we cannot resist temptation, or bring to its completion that which we resolve to do.
>Our hearts are fickle,
>>and by ourselves we cannot give to you the loyalty which is your due.
>Our steps are faltering,
>>and by ourselves we cannot walk in your straight way.
>So this day we ask you,
>To enlighten us;
>To strengthen us;

To guide us,
>> that we may know you, and love you, and follow you all the days of our life.

Give to your Church your blessing and your protection.
> Guide her in her thinking,
>> that she may be saved from the heresies, which destroy the faith.

> Strengthen her in her witness,
>> that she may bring no discredit on the name she bears.

> Inspire her in her fellowship,
>> that those who enter her may find within her your friendship and the friendship of their fellow men.

—From *Prayers for the Christian Year* by William Barclay

Hymn: Christ, Whose Glory Fills the Skies

Christ, whose glory fills the skies,
Christ, the true, the only light,
Sun of Righteousness, arise,
Triumph o'er the shades of night;
Day-spring from on high, be near;
Day-star, in my heart appear.

Dark and cheerless is the morn
Unaccompanied by thee;
Joyless is the day's return
Till thy mercy's beams I see;
Till they inward light impart,
Cheer my eyes and warm my heart.

Visit, then, this soul of mine;
Pierce the gloom of sin and grief;
Fill me, Radiancy divine;
Scatter all my unbelief;
More and more thyself display,
Shining to the perfect day. Amen.
—Charles Wesley

16: Preparation for Ministry

I. Invocation

Almighty God, you who call me to prayer and who offer yourself to all who seek your face, pour out your Holy Spirit upon me today and deliver me from coldness of heart, a wandering mind, and wrongful desire. By the power of your spirit place within me steadfast love and devotion, so that today I may worship and serve you with all of my life; through Jesus Christ my Lord. Amen.

II. Psalm 15

III. Daily Scripture Readings

Monday	Isaiah 6
Tuesday	Luke 9:57-62
Wednesday	Acts 9:1-30
Thursday	Colossians 1:24-29
Friday	Galatians 1:11-24
Saturday	2 Peter 1:1-11
Sunday	A. Genesis 2:4b-9, 15-17, 25–3:7; Psalm 130; Romans 5:12-19; Matthew 4:1-11
	B. Genesis 9:8-17; Psalm 25:1-10; 1 Peter 3:18-22; Mark 1:9-15
	C. Deuteronomy 26:1-11; Psalm 91:9-16; Romans 10:8b-13; Luke 4:1-13

IV. Readings for Reflection

V. Prayers: for the church, for others, for myself

VI. Reflection: silent and written

VII. Hymn: "Dear Master, in Whose Life I See"

VIII. Benediction

Almighty God, cause your good gifts to flow in and through my life and ministry this day and always. Amen.

Readings for Reflection

❧ Ministry is service in the name of the Lord. It is bringing the good news to the poor, proclaiming liberty to captives and new sight to the blind, setting the downtrodden free and announcing the Lord's year of favor (Luke 4:18). Spirituality is attention to the life of the spirit in us; it is going out to the desert or up to the mountain to pray; it is standing before the Lord with open heart and open mind; it is crying out, "Abba, Father"; it is contemplating the unspeakable beauty of our loving God.

We have fallen into the temptation of separating ministry from spirituality, service from prayer. Our demon says: "We are too busy to pray; we have too many needs to attend to, too many people to respond to, too many wounds to heal. Prayer is a luxury, something to do during a free hour, a day away from work or on a retreat. The few who are exclusively concerned with prayer—such as Trappists, Poor Clares, and some isolated hermits—are really not involved in ministry. They are set free for single-minded contemplation and leave Christian service to others." But to think this way is harmful; harmful for ministers as well as for contemplatives. Service and prayer can never be separated; they are related to each other as the Yin and Yang of the Japanese Circle.

—From *The Living Reminder* by Henri J. M. Nouwen

❧ We often hear the criticism that the Church is afflicted with piety, but the real trouble is that its piety is not deep enough! Since the materials are available, all that is needed is the recognition of where they are, and the will to employ them. An important contribution would be the liberation of the term "piety" from its present damaging connotations, reinstating it as a term of respect. We, indeed, still have a little piety; we say a few hasty prayers; we sing meaningfully a few hymns; we read snatches from the Bible. But all of this is far removed from the massive dose that we sorely need if we are to be the men and women who can perform a healing service in our generation. The seat of our disease, says Helmut Thielicke, "is not in the branches of our nerves at all but rather in our roots which are stunted and starved." The eloquent German points out that Martin Luther prayed four hours each day, "not despite his busy life but because only so could he accomplish his gigantic labors." Luther worked so hard that a little desultory praying would not suffice. "To work without praying and without listening," continues Thielicke, "means only to grow and spread oneself upward, without striking roots and without an equivalent in the earth." Trees can grow well in rocky soil, as I can attest by looking out the window of my mountain writing cabin, but they do this only by finding crevices in the rocks where the roots are able to penetrate deeply.

—From *The New Man for Our Time* by Elton Trueblood

ن The Bible does not prescribe the time or length of prayer, but it does offer guidelines. In Psalm 88 prayer is offered in the early morning (v. 13), and in Psalm 55 prayers are said evening, morning and noon (v. 17). The author of Psalm 119 advocates prayer seven times a day (v. 164). Daniel knelt for devotions three times a day (Daniel 6:10). Jesus prayed before sunrise (Mark 1:35) and in the evening when the day's work was over (Mark 6:46). Peter prayed at the third, sixth, and ninth hours.

Despite their aversion to prescribed formulas in the life of prayer that function as a new law, the Reformers did make general recommendations. On the basis of the Scriptural testimony Luther suggested that prayer should be "the first business of the morning and the last at night." He advised: "Cultivate the habit of falling asleep with the Lord's Prayer on your lips every evening when you go to bed and again every morning when you get up. And if occasion, place, and time permit, pray before you do anything else." Calvin urged that we offer prayer "when we arise in the morning, before we begin daily work, when we sit down to a meal, when by God's blessing we have eaten, when we are getting ready to retire."

Just as the Christian is not bound to ritual laws that regulate the preparation for prayer, so he is not absolutely bound to set times for prayer. Yet there are times that are more appropriate for prayer than others: the gathering together for worship, the hours before work and bedtime, the time right before meals, when we need to remind ourselves of the goodness of God. But a Christian should feel

free to pray anywhere, anytime, in the midst of daily work and play as well as in the solitude of his room in the early morning or late in the evening.
—From *The Struggle of Prayer* by Donald G. Bloesch

❧ It is the crucifixion of Jesus that is the decisive criticism of the royal consciousness. The crucifixion of Jesus is not to be understood simply in good liberal fashion as the sacrifice of a noble man, nor should we too quickly assign a cultic, priestly theory of atonement to the event. Rather, we might see in the crucifixion of Jesus the ultimate act of prophetic criticism in which Jesus announces the end of a world of death (the same announcement as that of Jeremiah) and takes that death into his own person. Therefore we say that the ultimate criticism is that God himself embraces the death that his people must die. The criticism consists not in standing over against but in standing with; the ultimate criticism is not one of triumphant indignation but one of the passion and compassion that completely and irresistibly undermine the world of competence and competition. The contrast is stark and total: this *passionate* man set in the midst of *numbed* Jerusalem. And only the *passion* can finally penetrate the *numbness*.
—From *The Prophetic Imagination* by Walter Brueggemann

❧ The cross is the ultimate metaphor of prophetic criticism because it means the end of the old consciousness that brings death on everyone. The crucifixion articulates God's odd freedom, his strange justice, and his peculiar power. It is this *freedom* (read religion of God's freedom), *justice* (read economics of sharing), and *power* (read politics of justice) which break the power of the old age and bring it to death. Without the cross, prophetic imagination will likely be as strident and as destructive as that which it criticizes. The cross is the assurance that effective prophetic criticism is done not by an outsider but always by one who must embrace the grief, enter into the death, and know the pain of the criticized one.
—From *The Prophetic Imagination* by Walter Brueggemann

❧ If anyone could show that we need not *always* act as in the divine presence, that we need not consider and use *everything* as the gift of God, and that we need not *always* live by reason—the same arguments would show that we need *never* act as in the presence of God nor need we make religion and reason the measure of *any* of our actions. If, therefore, we are to live unto God at any time or in any place, we are to live unto him at all times and in all places. If we are to use anything as the gift of God, we are to use everything as his gift. If we are to do anything by strict rules of reason, we are to do everything in the same manner.

They, therefore, who confine religion to times and places, and who think that it is being too strict and rigid to make religion give laws to all their actions and ways of living—they who think thus mistake the whole nature of religion. They may well be said to mistake the whole nature of wisdom who do not think it desirable to be always wise. He has not learned the nature of piety who thinks it too much to be pious in all his actions.

—From *A Serious Call to a Devout and Holy Life* by William Law

❧ I have come to learn certain things about private prayer. You cannot pray to order. You can get on your knees to order; but how to pray? I have found nothing more important than to learn how to get oneself into that frame and condition in which one can pray. You have to learn how to start yourself off, and it is just here that this knowledge of yourself is so important. What I have generally found is that to read something which can be characterized in general as devotional is of great value. By devotional I do not mean something sentimental, I mean something with a true element of worship in it. Notice that I do not say that you should start yourself in prayer by always reading the Scriptures; because you can have precisely the same difficulty there. Start by reading something that will warm your spirit. Get rid of a coldness that may have developed in your spirit. You have to learn how to kindle a flame in your spirit, to warm yourself up, to give yourself a start. It is comparable, if you like, to starting a car when it is cold. You have to learn how to use a spiritual choke. I have found it most rewarding to do that, and not to struggle vainly. When one finds oneself in this condition, and that it is difficult to pray, do not struggle in prayer for the time being, but read something that will warm and stimulate you, and you will

find that it will put you into a condition in which you will be able to pray more freely.
—From *Preaching and Preachers* by D. Martyn Lloyd-Jones

&. I ran away and stayed away; Mother Teresa moved in and stayed. That was the difference. She, a nun, rather slightly built, with a few rupees in her pocket; not particularly clever, or particularly gifted in the arts of persuasion. Just with this Christian love shining about her; in her heart and on her lips. Just prepared to follow her Lord, and in accordance with his instructions regard every derelict left to die in the streets as him; to hear in the cry of every abandoned child, even in the tiny squeak of the discarded fetus, the cry of the Bethlehem child; to recognize in every leper's stumps the hands which once touched sightless eyes and made them see, rested on distracted heads and made them calm, brought back health to sick flesh and twisted limbs. As for my expatiations on Bengal's wretched social conditions —I regret to say that I doubt whether, in any divine accounting, they will equal one single quizzical half smile bestowed by Mother Teresa on a street urchin who happened to catch her eye.
—From *Something Beautiful for God* by Malcolm Muggeridge

Hymn: Dear Master, in Whose Life I See

Dear Master, in whose life I see
All that I would, but fail to be,
Let thy clear light forever shine,
To shame and guide this life of mine.

Though what I dream and what I do
In my weak days are always two,
Help me, oppressed by things undone,
O thou, whose deeds and dreams were one! Amen.
—John Hunter

17: *The Cost of Discipleship*

I. Invocation
    Almighty God, by the power of your Holy Spirit open our eyes, ears, hearts, and very lives to your presence so that today we may worship and serve you in faithfulness, be blessing and healing reminders of your love to all whose lives we touch. We offer our prayers in the name of Christ. Amen.

II. Psalm 25

III. Daily Scripture Readings
Monday	John 13:1-20
Tuesday	Matthew 10:16-42
Wednesday	John 15:12-27
Thursday	Acts 6:8-15
Friday	James 1:2-18
Saturday	1 Peter 4:12-19
Sunday	A. Genesis 12:1-4a, (4b-8); Psalm 33:18-22; Romans 4:1-5, (6-12), 13-17; John 3:1-17
	B. Genesis 17:1-10, 15-19; Psalm 105:1-11; Romans 4:16-25; Mark 8:31-38
	C. Genesis 15:1-12, 17-18; Psalm 127; Philippians 3:17–4:1; Luke 13:31-35

IV. Readings for Reflection

V. Prayers: for the church, for others, for myself

VI. Reflection: silent and written

VII. Hymn: "O God, Our Help in Ages Past"

VIII. Benediction
    May the God of steadfastness and encouragement grant you to live in such harmony with one another, in accord with Christ Jesus, that together you may with one voice glorify the God and Father of our Lord Jesus Christ. Amen. —Romans 15:5-6

Readings for Reflection

❧ Though it might be argued, theoretically, that a Christianity in which men know how to picket, but not how to pray, is bound to wither, theorizing is not required, because we can already observe the logic of events. The fact is that emphasis upon the life of outer service, without a corresponding emphasis upon the life of devotion, has already led to obviously damaging results, one of which is calculated arrogance. How different it might be if the angry activists were to heed the words found in *The Imitation of Christ*, "Be not angry that you cannot make others as you wish them to be, since you cannot make yourself as you wish to be."

The essence of pietism, by contrast, is the limitation of primary interest to personal salvation. Even today, by the highways, we can see signs paid for by somebody, which urge us to "get right with God." The evil of this well-intentioned effort lies not in what it says, but in what it so evidently omits. The assumption is that salvation is nothing more than a private transaction between the individual and God and that it can become an accomplished, dated event.
—From *The New Man for Our Time* by Elton Trueblood

❧ It must be realized that the true sign of spiritual endeavour and the price of success in it is suffering. One who proceeds without suffering will bear no fruit. Pain of the heart and physical striving bring to light the gift of the Holy Spirit, bestowed in holy baptism upon every believer, buried in passions through our negligence in fulfilling the commandments, and brought once more to life by repentance, through the ineffable mercy of God. Do not, because of the suffering that accompanies them, cease to make painstaking efforts, lest you be condemned for fruitlessness and hear the words, 'Take the talent from him' (Matt. xxv. 28).

Every struggle in the soul's training, whether physical or mental, that is not accompanied by suffering, that does not require the utmost effort, will bear no fruit. 'The kingdom of heaven suffereth violence, and the violent take it by force' (Matt. xi. 12). Many people have worked and continue to work without pain, but because of its absence they are strangers to purity and out of communion with the

Holy Spirit, because they have turned aside from the severity of suffering. Those who work feebly and carelessly may go through the movements of making great efforts, but they harvest no fruit, because they undergo no suffering. According to the prophet, unless our loins are broken, weakened by the labour of fasting, unless we undergo an agony of contrition, unless we suffer like a woman in travail, we shall not succeed in bringing to birth the spirit of salvation in the ground of our heart.

—Theophan the Recluse

᷍ Perhaps the peculiar mark of the modern saint is that he or she faces this crisis [the crisis that forms our existence] in his or her own life, and is therefore driven at least by the desire to experience Christianity in a pristine form beyond the decaying cultural forms that no longer serve to bring us to conversation. There is about such a life a minimum of self-betrayal.

—From "The Incarnation of Thomas Merton" by Charles E. Kinzie in *Contemplative Review* (Fall 1981)

᷍ What I call the haven, as you know, is the Cross. If it cannot be given me to deserve one day to share the Cross of Christ, at least may I share that of the good thief. Of all the beings other than Christ of whom the Gospel tells us, the good thief is by far the one I most envy. To have been at the side of Christ and in the same state during the crucifixion seems to me a far more enviable privilege than to be at the right hand of his glory.

—From *Waiting for God* by Simone Weil

᷍ Such a way of discerning the sovereign power of his gracious compassion leads directly to the *resurrection of Jesus*. The resurrection of Jesus is the ultimate energizing for the new future. The wrenching of Friday had left only the despair of Saturday (Luke 24:21) and there was no reason to expect Sunday after that Friday. There is not any way to explain the resurrection out of the previously existing reality. The resurrection can only be received and affirmed and celebrated as the new action of God whose province it is to create new futures for people and to let them be amazed in the midst of despair. . . . The resurrection of Jesus is not to be understood in good liberal fashion as a spiritual development in the church. Nor should it be too quickly handled as an oddity in the history of God or as an isolated act of God's power. Rather, it is the ultimate act of prophetic energizing in which a new history is initiated. It is a new history open to all but peculiarly received by the marginal victims of the old order.

—From *The Prophetic Imagination* by Walter Brueggemann

   I put my body through its paces like a war horse; I keep it clean, sturdy, prepared. I harden it and I pity it. I have no other steed.

I keep my brain wide awake, lucid, unmerciful. I unleash it to battle relentlessly so that, all light, it may devour the darkness of the flesh. I have no other workshop where I may transform darkness into light.

I keep my heart flaming, courageous, restless. I feel in my heart all commotions and all contradictions, the joys and sorrows of life. But I struggle to subdue them to a rhythm superior to that of the mind, harsher than that of my heart—to the ascending rhythm of the Universe.

The Cry within me is a call to arms. It shouts: "I, the Cry, am the Lord your God! I am not an asylum. I am not hope and a home. I am not the Father nor the Son nor the Holy Ghost. I am your General!

"You are not my slave, nor a plaything in my hands. You are not my friend, you are not my child. You are my comrade-in-arms!

"Hold courageously the passes which I entrusted to you; do not betray them. You are in duty bound, and you may act heroically by remaining at your own battle station.

"Love danger. What is most difficult? That is what I want! Which road should you take? The most craggy ascent! It is the one I also take: follow me!

"Learn to obey. Only he who obeys a rhythm superior to his own is free.

"Learn to command. Only he who can give commands may represent me here on earth.

"Love responsibility. Say: 'It is my duty, and mine alone, to save the earth. If it is not saved, then I alone am to blame.'"

—From *The Saviors of God: Spiritual Exercises* by Nikos Kazantzakis

❨ My prayer is not the whimpering of a beggar nor a confession of love. Nor is it the trivial reckoning of a small tradesman: Give me and I shall give you.

My prayer is the report of a soldier to his general: This is what I did today, this is how I fought to save the entire battle in my own sector, these are the obstacles I found, this is how I plan to fight tomorrow.

My God and I are horsemen galloping in the burning sun or under drizzling rain. Pale, starving, but unsubdued, we ride and converse.

"Leader!" I cry. He turns his face towards me, and I shudder to confront his anguish.

Our love for each other is rough and ready, we sit at the same table, we drink the same wine in this low tavern of life.

—From *The Saviors of God: Spiritual Exercises* by Nikos Kazantzakis

❨ Recognizing that the earth and the fulness thereof is a gift from our gracious God, and that we are called to cherish, nurture, and provide loving stewardship for the earth's resources.

And recognizing that life itself is a gift, and a call to responsibility, joy, and celebration, I make the following declarations:

1. I declare myself to be a world citizen.
2. I commit myself to lead an ecologically sound life.
3. I commit myself to lead a life of creative simplicity and to share my personal wealth with the world's poor.
4. I commit myself to join with others in reshaping institutions in order to bring about a more just global society in which each person has full access to the needed resources for their physical, emotional, intellectual, and spiritual growth.
5. I commit myself to occupational accountability, and in so doing I will seek to avoid the creation of products which cause harm to others.
6. I affirm the gift of my body, and commit myself to its proper nourishment and physical well-being.
7. I commit myself to examine continually my relations with others, and to attempt to relate honestly, morally, and lovingly to those around me.

8. I commit myself to personal renewal through prayer, meditation and study.
9. I commit myself to responsible participation in a community of faith.

—"Shakertown Pledge" in *Visions of a World Hungry* by Thomas G. Pettepiece

Hymn: O God, Our Help in Ages Past

O God, our help in ages past,
Our hope for years to come,
Our shelter from the stormy blast,
And our eternal home!

Under the shadow of thy throne
Still may we dwell secure;
Sufficient is thine arm alone,
And our defense is sure.

Before the hills in order stood,
Or earth received her frame,
From everlasting thou art God,
To endless years the same.

A thousand ages, in thy sight,
Are like an evening gone;
Short as the watch that ends the night
Before the rising sun.

Time, like an ever rolling stream,
Bears all who breathe away;
They fly forgotten, as a dream
Dies at the opening day.

O God, our help in ages past,
Our hope for years to come;
Be thou our guide while life shall last,
And our eternal home. Amen.
—Isaac Watts

Third Sunday in Lent
18: Thirsting for God

I. Invocation
    Lord of life and love, help us to worship thee in the
    holiness of beauty, that some beauty of holiness
    may appear in us. Quiet our souls in thy presence
    with the stillness of a wise trust. Lift us above dark
    moods, and the shadow of sin, that we may find
    thy will for our lives; through Jesus Christ our Lord.
    Amen. —From *The Book of Worship*

II. Psalm 42

III. Daily Scripture Readings
     Monday   Psalm 63:1-8
     Tuesday   Isaiah 55
     Wednesday   John 7:37-44
     Thursday   John 6:22-40
     Friday   Romans 8:18-25
     Saturday   Psalm 84
     Sunday   A. Exodus 17:3-7; Psalm 95;
                     Romans 5:1-11; John 4:5-26, (27-42)
                 B. Exodus 20:1-17; Psalm 19:7-14;
                     1 Corinthians 1:22-25; John 2:13-22
                 C. Exodus 3:1-15; Psalm 103:1-13;
                     1 Corinthians 10:1-13; Luke 13:1-9

IV. Readings for Reflection

V.   Prayers: for the church, for others, for myself

VI. Reflection: silent and written

VII. Hymn: "As Pants the Hart for Cooling Streams"

VIII. Benediction
      May God be your source of peace and power all day
      long. Amen.

Readings for Reflection

&. Listen, O Lord, to my prayers. Listen to my desire to be with you, to dwell in your house, and to let my whole being be filled with your presence. But none of this is possible without you. When you are not the one who fills me, I am soon filled with endless thoughts and concerns that divide me and tear me away from you. Even thoughts about you, good spiritual thoughts, can be little more than distractions when you are not their author.

O Lord, thinking about you, being fascinated with theological ideas and discussions, being excited about histories of Christian spirituality and stimulated by thoughts and ideas about prayer and meditation, all of this can be as much an expression of greed as the unruly desire for food, possessions, or power.

Every day I see again that only you can teach me to pray, only you can set my heart at rest, only you can let me dwell in your presence. No book, no idea, no concept or theory will ever bring me close to you unless you yourself are the one who lets these instruments become the way to you.

But Lord, let me at least remain open to your initiative; let me wait patiently and attentively for that hour when you will come and break through all the walls I have erected. Teach me, O Lord, to pray. Amen.

—From *A Cry for Mercy* by Henri J. M. Nouwen

&. I cannot resist quoting, to finish up with, from an unknown medieval English writer who translated the famous *Scala Claustralium* of Guigo II into English, interpolating merrily as he went little gems of his own devising. This is one of his interpolations: "So doth God almighty to his lovers in contemplation as a taverner that hath good wine to sell doth to good drinkers that will drink well of his wine and largely spend. Well he knoweth what they be when he seeth them in the street. Privily he goeth and whispereth them in the ear and saith to them that he hath a claret and that all fine for their own mouth. He taketh them to house and giveth them a taste. Soon when they have tasted thereof, and they think the drink good and greatly to their pleasure, then they drink day and night and the more they drink, the more they want. Such liking they have of that drink that of none other wine they think, but only for to drink their fill and to have of this drink all their will. And so they spend what they have, and then they spend or pledge their coat or hood and all that they may, to drink with liking as long as they desire. Thus it fareth sometime by God's lovers, that from the time that they had tasted of the sweetness of God, such liking they found therein that as drunken men they did spend what they had and gave themselves to fasting and to keeping vigil and to doing other penance. And when they had no more to spend, they laid off their weeds, as apostles, martyrs and maidens, young of years, did in their time." Scarcely a puritanical conception of the Christian life! Yet how firmly and dramatically it leads to the true austerities involved. In the Canticle (5:1), the bridegroom invites us, his friends, to "drink deep and get drunk." That is the context for all our discipline, our ascetic efforts, our self-sacrifice. God himself, like a shrewd taverner, has come to us first, to seduce us from the narrow path of worldly duty, to know the sweetness of his love. Are we ready to be the prodigal come home, welcomed with a party? Or are we going to insist on being the good boy, the elder brother, prepared only to do his duty, but not to celebrate the feast of love?

Well, for the moment we do not have to decide in any very definitive way; as long as life lasts in this world we can be both brothers in turn. But eventually the question will be put. And which way we answer it, will depend to a very considerable extent on the picture we encourage ourselves to have of ourselves, of human life, of our place in the world.

—From *Prayer* by Simon Tugwell

&. Our doctrines are not photographs of Reality. They are the attempted description of heavenly things by means of the hints and guesses which earthly things provide.
—From *Tensions* by H. A. Williams

&. You will find it a great help to put your reckoning into words, and say over and over to yourself and to your God, "Lord, I am thine; I do yield myself up entirely to thee, and I believe that thou dost take me. I leave myself with thee.

Work in me all the good pleasure of thy will, and I will only lie still in thy hands and trust thee."

Make this a daily, definite act of your will, and many times a day recur to it, as being your continual attitude before the Lord. Confess it to yourself. Confess it to your God. Confess it to your friends. Avouch the Lord to be your God, continually and unwaveringly, and declare your purpose of walking in his ways and keeping his statutes; and sooner or later, you will find in practical experience that he has avouched you to be one of his peculiar people, and will enable you to keep all his commandments, and that you are being made into "an holy people unto the Lord, as he hath spoken."

> For thou art making me, I think thee Sire.
> What thou hast done and doest, thou knowest well;
> And I will help thee: gently in thy fire
> I will lie burning; on thy potter's wheel
> I will whirl patient, though my brain should reel;
> Thy grace shall be enough my grief to quell,
> And growing strength perfect through weakness dire.

—From *The Christian's Secret of a Happy Life* by Hannah Whitall Smith

❧ I have often reminded you, my dear sister, about the remembrance of God, and now I tell you again: unless you work and sweat to impress on your heart and mind this awe-inspiring Name, you keep silence in vain, you sing in vain, you fast in vain, you watch in vain. In short, all a nun's work will be useless without this activity, without recollection of God. This is the beginning of silence for the Lord's sake, and it is also the end. This most desirable Name is the soul of stillness and silence. By calling it to mind we gain joy and gladness, forgiveness of sins and a wealth of virtues. Few have been able to find this most glorious Name, save only in stillness and silence. We can attain it in no other way, even with great effort. Therefore, knowing the power of this advice, I entreat you for the love of Christ always to be still and silent, since these virtues enrich remembrance of God within us.
—Theophan the Recluse

❧ From all I have said about the minister as a sustaining reminder, it becomes clear that a certain unavailability is essential for the spiritual life of the minister. I am not trying to build a religious argument for a game of golf, a trip to a conference, a cruise to the Caribbean, or a sabbatical. These arguments have been made and they all strike me as quite unconvincing in the midst of our suffering world. No, I would like to make a plea for prayer as the creative way of being unavailable.

How would it sound when the question, "Can I speak to the minister?" is not answered by "I am sorry, he has someone in his office" but by "I am sorry, he is praying." When someone says, "The minister is unavailable because this is his day of solitude, this is his day in the hermitage, this is his desert day," could that not be a consoling ministry? What it says is that the minister is unavailable to me, not because he is more available to others, but because he is with God, and God alone—the God who is our God.
—From *The Living Reminder* by Henri J. M. Nouwen

Hymn: As Pants the Hart for Cooling Streams

As pants the hart for cooling streams,
When heated in the chase,
So longs my soul, O God for thee
And thy refreshing grace.

For thee, my God, the living God,
My thirsty soul doth pine;
O when shall I behold thy face,
Thou Majesty divine!

I sigh to think of happier days,
When thou, O Lord, wast nigh;
When every heart was tuned to praise,
And none more blest than I.

Why restless, why cast down, my soul?
Hope still, and thou shalt sing
The praise of him who is thy God,
Thy Savior, and thy King. Amen.
—Nahum Tate and Nicholas Brady

Fourth Sunday in Lent
19: Crucial Choices

I. Invocation
    Lord God, you who are the source of all truth, wisdom, justice, and love, lead me through this time of worship and throughout this day of service to you. Help me constantly to rest my life upon the eternal foundations of your love and presence. Save me from haste and confusion, from wrongful desire, and the net of evil. Through the inspiration of your Holy Spirit, enlighten, instruct, and guide me all the day long. In the name of Jesus. Amen.

II. Psalm 143

III. Daily Scripture Readings
Monday	Deuteronomy 30:15-20
Tuesday	Joshua 24:14-28
Wednesday	Hebrews 2:1-18
Thursday	Philemon 8-21
Friday	Colossians 3:1-17
Saturday	Romans 12

Sunday
   A. 1 Samuel 16:1-13; Psalm 23; Ephesians 5:8-14; John 9:1-41
   B. 2 Chronicles 36:14-23; Psalm 137:1-6; Ephesians 2:4-10; John 3:14-21
   C. Joshua 5:9-12; Psalm 34:1-8; 2 Corinthians 5:16-21; Luke 15:1-3,11-32

IV. Readings for Reflection

V. Prayers: for the church, for others, for myself

VI. Reflection: silent and written

VII. Hymn: "Arise, My Soul, Arise"

VIII. Benediction
    May the Lord make you strong to do the work of ministry. Amen.

Readings for Reflection

❧ Often we're not as pressed for time as much as we *feel* we're pressed for time. I remember several years ago becoming so pressed by the demands of teaching at Yale that I took a prayer sabbatical to the Trappist monastery at Geneseo, New York. No teaching, lecturing, or counseling— just solitude and prayer.

The second day there, a group of students from Geneseo College walked in and asked, "Henri, can you give us a retreat?"

Of course at the monastery that was not my decision, but I said to the abbot, "I came here from the university to get away from that type of thing. These students have asked for five meditations, an enormous amount of work and preparation. I don't want to do it."

The abbot said, "You're going to do it."

"What do you mean? Why should I spend my sabbatical time preparing all those things?"

"Prepare?" he replied. "You've been a Christian for forty years and a priest for twenty, and a few high school students want to have a retreat. Why do you have to prepare? What those boys and girls want is to be a part of your life in God for a few days. If you pray half an hour in the morning, sing in our choir for an hour, and do your spiritual reading, you will have so much to say you could give ten retreats."

The question, you see, is not to prepare but to live in a state of ongoing preparedness so that, when someone who is drowning in the world comes into your world, you are ready to reach out and help. It may be at four o'clock, six o'clock, or nine o'clock. One time you call it preaching, the next time teaching, then counseling, or later administration. But let them be part of your life in God—that's ministering.

—From "Time Enough to Minister" by Henri J. M. Nouwen
   in *Leadership* (Spring 1982)

❧ Because we are come out of the divine nature, which chooses to be divine, we must *choose* to be divine, to be *of God, to be one with God,* loving and living as he loves and lives, and so be partakers of the divine nature, or we perish.

Man cannot originate this life; it must be shown him, and he must choose it. God is the father of Jesus and of us—of every possibility of our being; but while God is the father of his children, Jesus is the father of their sonship. For in him is made the life which is sonship to the Father—the recognition, namely, in fact and life, that the Father has his claim upon his sons and daughters.

We are not and cannot become true sons without our will willing his will, our doing following His making. It was the will of Jesus to be the thing God willed and meant him, that made him the true son of God. He was not the son of God because he could not help it, but because he willed to be in himself the son that he was in the divine idea.

So with us: we must *be* the sons we are. We are not made to be what we cannot help being; sons and daughters are not after such fashion! We are sons and daughters in God's claim; we must be sons and daughters in our will. And we can be sons and daughters, saved into the original necessity and bliss of our being, only by choosing God for the father he is, and doing his will—yielding ourselves true sons to the absolute Father. Therein lies human bliss—only and essential. The working out of this our salvation must be pain, and the handing of it down to them that are below must ever be in pain; but the eternal form of the will of God in and for us, is intensity of bliss.

—From *Creation in Christ* by George MacDonald

&. People often think of Christian morality as a kind of bargain in which God says, "If you keep a lot of rules, I'll reward you, and if you don't I'll do the other thing." I do not think that is the best way of looking at it. I would much rather say that every time you make a choice you are turning the central part of you, the part of you that chooses, into something a little different from what it was before. And taking your life as a whole, with all your innumerable choices, all your life long you are slowly turning this central thing either into a Heaven creature or into a hellish creature: either into a creature that is in harmony with God, and with other creatures, and with itself, or else into one that is in a state of war and hatred with God, and with its fellow creatures, and with itself. To be the one kind of creature is Heaven: that is, it is joy, and peace, and knowledge, and power. To be the other means madness, horror, idiocy, rage, impotence, and eternal loneliness. Each of us at each moment is progressing to the one state or the other.

—From *The Joyful Christian* by C. S. Lewis

❧ According to Christian teachers, the essential vice, the utmost evil, is Pride. Unchastity, anger, greed, drunkenness, and all that, are mere fleabites in comparison: it was through Pride that the devil became the devil: Pride leads to every other vice: it is the complete anti-God state of mind.

Does this seem exaggerated? If so, think it over. I pointed out a moment ago that the more pride one had, the more one disliked pride in others. In fact, if you want to find out how proud you are, the easiest way is to ask yourself, "How much do I dislike it when other people snub me, or refuse to take any notice of me, or shove their oar in, or patronize me, or show off?" The point is that each person's pride is in competition with everyone else's pride. It is because I wanted to be the big noise at the party that I am so annoyed at someone else being the big noise. Two of a trade never agree. Now what you want to get clear is that Pride is *essentially* competitive—is competitive by its very nature— while the other vices are competitive only, so to speak, by accident. Pride gets no pleasure out of having something, only out of having more of it than the next man. We say that people are proud of being rich, or clever, or good-looking, but they are not. They are proud of being richer, or cleverer, or better-looking than others. If everyone else became equally rich, or clever, or good-looking, there would be nothing to be proud about. It is the comparison that makes you proud: the pleasure of being above the rest. Once the element of competition has gone, pride has gone. That is why I say that Pride is essentially competitive in a way the other vices are not. The sexual impulse may drive two men into competition if they both want the same girl. But that is only by accident; they might just as likely have wanted two different girls. But a proud man will take your girl from you, not because he wants her, but just to prove to himself that he is a better man than you. Greed may drive men into competition if there is not enough to go round; but the proud man, even when he has got more than he can possibly want, will try to get still more just to assert his power. Nearly all those evils in the world which people put down to greed or self-ishness are really far more the result of Pride.

—From *The Joyful Christian* by C. S. Lewis

৯. O God, our Father, we know that the issues of life and death are in your hands, and we know what you are loving us with an everlasting love. If it is your will, grant to us to live in happiness and in peace.

> In all our undertakings,
> > Grant us prosperity and good success.
> In all our friendships,
> > Grant us to find our friends faithful and true.
> In all bodily things,
> > Make us fit and healthy,
> > > Able for the work of the day.
> In all the things of the mind,
> > Make us calm and serene,
> > > Free from anxiety and worry.
> In material things,
> > Save us from poverty and from want.
> In spiritual things,
> > Save us from doubt and from distrust.
> Grant us
> > In our work satisfaction;
> > In our study true wisdom;
> > In our pleasure gladness;
> > In our love loyalty.

And if misfortune does come to us, grant that any trial may only bring us closer to one another and closer to you; and grant that nothing may shake our certainty that you work all things together for good, and that a Father's hand will never cause his child a needless tear. Hear this our prayer; through Jesus Christ our Lord. Amen.

—From *Prayers for the Christian Year* by William Barclay

Hymn: Arise, My Soul, Arise

Arise, my soul, arise;
Shake off thy guilty fears;
The bleeding sacrifice
In my behalf appears:
Before the throne my surety stands,
Before the throne my surety stands,
My name is written on his hands.

He ever lives above,
For me to intercede;
His all redeeming love,
His precious blood, to plead:
His blood atoned for all our race,
His blood atoned for all our race,
And sprinkles now the throne of grace.

Five bleeding wounds he bears,
Received on Calvary;
They pour effectual prayers;
They strongly plead for me:
"Forgive him, O forgive," they cry,
"Forgive him, O forgive," they cry,
"Nor let that ransomed sinner die!"

The Father hears him pray,
His dear anointed One;
He cannot turn away
The presence of his Son:
His spirit answers to the blood,
His spirit answers to the blood,
And tells me I am born of God.

My God is reconciled;
His pardoning voice I hear;
He owns me for his child;
I can no longer fear:
With confidence I now draw nigh,
With confidence I now draw nigh,
And, "Father, Abba, Father," cry. Amen.
—Charles Wesley

20: *From Death to Life*

I. Invocation
    O God our Father, renew our spirits and draw our hearts to thyself, that our work may not be to us a burden but a delight; and give us such love to thee as may sweeten all our obedience. Help us that we may serve thee with the cheerfulness and gladness of children, delighting ourselves in thee and rejoicing in all that is to the honor of thy name; through Jesus Christ our Lord. Amen.
    —From *The Book of Worship*

II. Psalm 32

III. Daily Scripture Readings
Monday	Matthew 11:2-19
Tuesday	1 Corinthians 15:1-28
Wednesday	Romans 1:1-7, 16-17
Thursday	Isaiah 25:1-9
Friday	Colossians 3:1-17
Saturday	Romans 8:31-39

    Sunday
    A. Ezekiel 37:1-14; Psalm 116:1-9; Romans 8:6-11; John 11:(1-16), 17-45
    B. Jeremiah 31:31-34; Psalm 51:10-17; Hebrews 5:7-10; John 12:20-33
    C. Isaiah 43:16-21; Psalm 126; Philippians 3:8-14; John 12:1-8

IV. Readings for Reflection

V. Prayers: for the church, for others, for myself

VI. Reflection: silent and written

VII. Hymn: "O Love Divine, What Hast Thou Done"

VIII. Benediction
    Be bound to Christ for this day and always. Amen.

Readings for Reflection

❧ We are not happy because we are unforgiving, and we are unforgiving because we feel superior to others.

Mercy is the fruit of the highest degree of love, because love creates equals, and a greater love makes us inferior.

First let us establish three premises:

Those who do not love feel superior to everyone else.

Those who love feel equal to everyone else.

Those who love much gladly take the lower place.

Each one of us can identify his position somewhere along this spectrum, which comprises the three degrees of the spiritual life here on earth:

Death for those who do not love.

Life for those who love.

Holiness for those who love much.

The beatitude of the merciful relates, like all the beatitudes, to the realm of holiness and we have to admit that Jesus set his sights high when he had the courage and confidence to place this lofty ideal before us. It is the beatitude that he himself lived to the full, stooping, out of love, to the lowest place, even to the extent of being rejected as a common criminal, fit only to be hung on a gibbet.

—From *In Search of the Beyond* by Carlo Carretto

❧ The Skin Horse had lived longer in the nursery than any of the others. He was so old that his brown coat was bald in patches and showed the seams underneath, and most of the hairs in his tail had been pulled out to string bead necklaces. He was wise, for he had seen a long succession of mechanical toys arrive to boast and swagger, and by-and-by break their mainsprings and pass away, and he knew that they were only toys, and would never turn into anything else. For nursery magic is very strange and wonderful, and only those playthings that are old and wise and experienced like the Skin Horse understand all about it.

"What is REAL?" asked the [Velveteen] Rabbit one day, when they were lying side by side near the nursery fender, before Nana came to tidy the room. "Does it mean having things that buzz inside you and a stick-out handle?"

"Real isn't how you are made," said the Skin Horse. "It's a thing that happens to you. When a child loves you for a long, long time, not just to play with, but REALLY loves you, then you become Real."

"Does it hurt?" asked the Rabbit.

"Sometimes," said the Skin Horse, for he was always truthful. "When you are Real you don't mind being hurt."

"Does it happen all at once, like being wound up," he asked, "or bit by bit?"

"It doesn't happen all at once," said the Skin Horse. "You become. It takes a long time. That's why it doesn't often happen to people who break easily, or have sharp edges, or who have to be carefully kept. Generally, by the time you are Real, most of your hair has been loved off, and your eyes drop out and you get loose in the joints and very shabby. But these things don't matter at all, because once you are Real you can't be ugly, except to people who don't understand."

—From *The Velveteen Rabbit* by Margery Williams

ð Only very late do we learn the price of the risk of believing, because only very late do we face up to the idea of death.

This is what is difficult: believing truly means dying. Dying to everything: to our reasoning, to our plans, to our past, to our childhood dreams, to our attachment to earth, and sometimes even to the sunlight, as at the moment of our physical death.

That is why faith is so difficult. It is so difficult to hear from Jesus a cry of anguish for us and our difficulties in believing, "Oh, if only you could believe!"

Because not even he can take our place in the leap of Faith; it is up to us. It *is* like dying! It is up to us, and no one is able to take our place.

This mature act of faith is terribly, uniquely personal. Its risk involves us down to the core; the truest and greatest prototype of this act of faith that we, as the People of God, possess is the biblical account of the trial of Abraham. "God said, 'Take your son Isaac, your only one whom you love, and go to the land of Moriah. There you shall offer him up as a holocaust on a height that I will point out to you'" (Gen. 22:2).

That is a leap of pure faith proposed to Abraham!

It is a personal act, and it is an act of death.

Without love it is impossible to understand such a proposal; on the contrary, it is scandalous.

But for anyone who loves?

Seeing God wrapt round the colossal figure of this patriarch, alone in the desert beside his tent . . . no, that is no scandal, but quite the contrary.

God wants to communicate with the depths of Abraham's being and tear him from himself and his involvement with his own problems, which are like self-centered possessions; he wants to make this creature of his "more his," this man who is destined not for the tents of earth, but for those of Heaven. So God asks of him an absurd trial, as love is absurd for anyone who does not live it, but as true and relentless as love for anyone who possesses it. " 'Take your son . . .' " (Gen. 22:2).

I believe that at dawn that morning the angels from every corner of Heaven were busy preparing the mountain on which a man was about to carry out such a tragic and radical rite of love!

I believe that at sunrise on that eastern morning the space around Abraham was quilted by the invisible eyes of all who had died before him, wanting to see what the ending would be!

What a drama was in the poor heart of that man! God had asked the supreme sacrifice. If Abraham had had to turn the knife on himself it would have been easier!

An act of pure faith is the death of what we love most so it may be offered to the loved one because only love is stronger than death. . . .

At the ultimate moment of trial, when we try to pierce the invisible, with the sharpened spear of every possibility we can find, we realize that the three theological virtues—faith, hope, and charity—are really only one, and they have such a power of penetration that they could disrupt the entire universe.

On Mount Moriah, in the trial of Abraham, humankind embraced God as never before. The experience of this embrace reverberates through the religious history of the world as an epic of a love greater than our endless frailty.

—From *The God Who Comes* by Carlo Carretto

ờ That we may have to strive after goodness with an effort of our will is one of the lies invented by the mediocre part of ourselves in its fear of being destroyed. Such an effort does not threaten it in any way, it does not even disturb its comfort—not even when it entails a great deal of fatigue and suffering. For the mediocre part of ourselves is not afraid of fatigue and suffering; it is afraid of being killed.

There are people who try to raise their souls like a man continually taking standing jumps in the hopes that, if he jumps higher every day, a time may come when he will no longer fall back but will go right up to the sky. Thus occupied he cannot look at the sky. We cannot take a single step toward heaven. It is not in our power to travel in a vertical direction. If however we look heavenward for a long time, God comes and takes us up. He raises us easily.

—From *Waiting for God* by Simone Weil

ờ The world needs more than the secret holiness of individual inwardness. It needs more than sacred sentiments and good intentions. God asks for the heart because He needs the lives. It is by lives that the world will be redeemed, by lives that beat in concordance with God, by deeds that outbeat the finite charity of the human heart.

Man's power of action is less vague than his power of intention. And an action has intrinsic meaning; its value to the world is independent of what it means to the person performing it. The act of giving food to a helpless child is meaningful regardless of whether or not the moral intention is present. God asks for the heart, and we must spell our answer in terms of deeds.

It would be a device of conceit, if not presumption, to insist that purity of the heart is the exclusive test of piety. Perfect purity is something we rarely know how to obtain or how to retain. No one can claim to have purged all the dross even from his finest desire. The self is finite, but selfishness is infinite.

God asks for the heart, but the heart is oppressed with uncertainty in its own twilight. God asks for faith, and the heart is not sure of its own faith. It is good that there is a dawn of decision for the sight of the heart; deeds to objectify faith, definite forms to verify belief.

The heart is often a lonely voice in the marketplace of living. Man may entertain lofty ideals and behave like the ass that, as the saying goes, "carries gold and eats thistles." The problem of the soul is how to live nobly in an animal environment; how to persuade and train the tongue and the senses to behave in agreement with the insights of the soul.

The integrity of life is not exclusively a thing of the heart; it implies more than consciousness of the moral law. The innermost chamber must be guarded at the uttermost outposts. Religion is not the same as spiritualism; what man does in his concrete, physical existence is directly relevant to the divine. Spirituality is the goal, not the way of man. In this world music is played on physical instruments, and to the Jew the mitsvot are the instruments on which the holy is carried out. If man were only mind, worship in thought would be the form in which to commune with God. But man is body and soul, and his goal is so to live that both *his heart and his flesh should sing to the living God.*

—From *God in Search of Man* by Abraham Joshua Heschel

ᔌ After this it was noised abroad that Mr. Valiant-for-truth was taken with a Summons by the same Post as the other, and had this for a Token that the Summons was true, That his Pitcher was broken at the Fountain. When he understood it, he called for his Friends, and told them of it. Then said he, I am going to my Father's, and though with great difficulty I am got hither, yet now I do not repent me of all the Trouble I have been at to arrive where I am. My Sword I give to him that shall succeed me in my Pilgrimage, and my Courage and Skill to him that can get it. My Marks and Scars I carry with me, to be a witness for me that I have fought his Battles who now will be my Rewarder. When the day that he must go hence was come, many accompanied him to the Riverside, into which as he went he said, Death, where is thy Sting? And as he went down deeper he said, Grave, where is thy Victory? So he passed over, and all the Trumpets sounded for him on the other side.

—From *The Pilgrim's Progress* by John Bunyan

ᔌ Indeed, the Church has a future; it has *the* future. This is the eighth day which passes description and cannot be foreseen, the day on which God will complete his work of

creation, the Church will reach the goal of its pilgrimage and the world will recognize its Lord. "And that seventh age will be our sabbath, a day that knows no evening, but is followed by the day of the Lord, an everlasting eighth day, hallowed by the resurrection of Christ, prefiguring the eternal rest not only of the spirit, but of the body as well. Then we shall have holiday and we shall see, we shall see and we shall love, we shall love and we shall praise. Behold, this is how it shall be at the end without end. For what else is our end, but to come to that kingdom which has no end?"
—From *The Church* by Hans Küng

Hymn: O Love Divine, What Hast Thou Done

O love divine, what hast thou done!
Th'incarnate God hath died for me!
The Father's coeternal Son
Bore all my sins upon the tree!
The Son of God for me hath died:
My Lord, my Love, is crucified:

Is crucified for me and you,
To bring us rebels near to God;
Believe, believe the record true,
Ye all are bought with Jesus' blood;
Pardon for all flows from his side:
My Lord, my Love, is crucified.

Behold him, all ye that pass by,
The bleeding Prince of life and peace!
Come, sinners, see your Savior die,
And say, was ever grief like his?
Come, feel with me his blood applied:
My Lord, my Love, is crucified. Amen.
—Charles Wesley

21: The Wounds and Sorrows of Ministry

I. Invocation
    Almighty God, you are the light and life of every
    soul and my only source of hope. Grant that in this
    time of worship I may experience your transforming
    power preparing me for the ministry of this day. In
    the name of Jesus Christ. Amen.

II. Psalm 56

III. Daily Scripture Readings
     Monday   Acts 14:19-28
     Tuesday   1 Peter 2:21-25
     Wednesday   2 Corinthians 1:3-11
     Thursday   Isaiah 53:1-6
     Friday   Isaiah 53:7-9
     Saturday   Isaiah 53:10-12
     Sunday   A. Isaiah 50:4-9a; Psalm 118:19-29;
                     Philippians 2:5-11; Matthew 21:1-11
                 B. Isaiah 50:4-9a; Psalm 118:19-29;
                     Philippians 2:5-11; Mark 11:1-11
                 C. Isaiah 50:4-9a; Psalm 118:19-29;
                     Philippians 2:5-11; Luke 19:28-40

IV.   Readings for Reflection

V.   Prayers: for the church, for others, for myself

VI.   Reflection: silent and written

VII. Hymn: "O Sacred Head, Now Wounded"

VIII. Benediction
      Go forth into this day with the strong name of Jesus
      Christ to sustain you. Amen.

Readings for Reflection

❧ In the evening I went very unwillingly to a society in Aldersgate Street, where one was reading Luther's preface to the Epistle to the Romans. About a quarter before nine, while he was describing the change which God works in the heart through faith in Christ, I felt my heart strangely warmed. I felt I did trust in Christ, Christ alone for salvation: And an assurance was given me, that he had taken away *my* sins, even *mine*, and saved *me* from the law of sin and death.

—John Wesley

❧ Many persons, ordained or not, live in a fairly constant state of noise, with their unresolved past and the uncertain present breaking in on them. They lack a still center and it is only for such a quiet point that we can listen attentively. When I was in my first parish, which was located in the middle of the city, a constant stream of indigents came through. One came into my office and wanted to tell me his story. I sat as if to listen but was deeply troubled inside over some issue now long forgotten. I remember I was fiddling with a pencil. The man stopped his story, looked at me and said, "Young Father, the least you can do is listen." He was right. There was no still center in me.

Thomas Merton (1915–1968), the fascinating Cistercian monk whose writings continue to increase in popularity, found the busy life of a Trappist very disconcerting. Despite the fact that speaking is severely curtailed in a Cistercian monastery, he found the place incredibly noisy. For many years he sought permission to live as a hermit on the property of the monastery. He needed the quiet that he might listen. Too frequently we do not understand the hermit's discipline, a discipline that needs to be ours in spirit, if not in fact.

—From *Spirituality for Ministry* by Urban T. Holmes III

❧ I believe that the possibility of passion is a primary prophetic agenda and that it is precisely what the royal consciousness means to eradicate. . . . Passion as the capacity and readiness to care, to suffer, to die, and to feel is the enemy of imperial reality. Imperial economics is designed to keep people satiated so that they do not notice. Its politics is intended to block out the cries of the denied ones. Its religion is to be an opiate so that no one discerns misery alive in the heart of God.

—From *The Prophetic Imagination* by Walter Brueggemann

৯ Marital love is an image, however, pale, of the reality which develops little by little between the Absolute and the creature, between God and humankind, between Yahweh and Israel.

In marital love it is not enough to study the beloved, write poems, or receive cards from far away. Couples must marry, say "yes" to one another, go behind the veil of intimacy, delight in one another—exultantly, become close, cultivate friendship, stay together as much as possible, coalesce their wills, make two things one, as scripture says.

But pretending to know the other just by studying him in books or photographs means remaining outside real knowledge, real mystery.

Today, many persons who seek or study God do just that. They study him in books, make him an object of speculation, approach him from intellectual curiosity.

With what result? The more we study, the more our ideas become confused; the more we get caught up in discussions, the farther we go from him.

I think this is the nature of the crisis in the Church today; it is a crisis of prayer, it is a crisis of contemplation.

Study is no longer the light of spirituality, and curiosity has taken the place of humility.

Self-assurance and derision of the past are the false light which guides man's pride in the labyrinth of God's "unknowing," pretending to seize the truth with the strength of intelligence only.

But God's truth is the same, truth is the secret of things "up there," and no one can know it without revelation from God.

Has Christ not already said so?

In the upper room, replying to the worried question put to him by Judas (not Judas Iscariot) about why he was not manifesting himself to the world, but only to his intimate friends, he replied with extreme clarity: "'Anyone who loves me will be true to my word, and my Father will

love him; we will come to him and make our dwelling place
with him' " (John 14:23).

Only love brings God's coming to us, his living presence within us, and his consequent revelation.

He who obeys the commandments he has from me
is the man who loves me;
and he who loves me will be loved by my Father.
I too will love him
and reveal myself to him.
(John 14:21)

—From *The God Who Comes* by Carlo Carretto

ک۔ Thy will be done. I yield up everything.
"The life is more than meat"—then more than health;
The body more than raiment"—then than wealth;
The hairs I made not, thou art numbering.
Thou art my life—I the brook, thou the spring.
Because thine eyes are open, I can see;
Because thou art thyself, 'tis therefore I am me.
—From *Diary of an Old Soul* by George MacDonald

ک۔ Care thou for mine whom I must leave behind;
Care that they know who 'tis for them takes care;
Thy present patience help them still to bear;
Lord, keep them clearing, growing, heart and mind;
In one thy oneness us together bind;
Last earthly prayer with which to thee I cling—
Grant that, save love, we owe not anything.
—From *Diary of an Old Soul* by George MacDonald

ک۔ The minister, as a living memory of God's great deeds
in history, is called to heal by reminding people of their
wounded past and by connecting their wounds with the
wounds of all humanity, redeemed by the suffering of God
in Christ. But what are the implications of such a viewpoint
for the personal life of the minister? The temptation is
strong to ask the "how" question: "How do I become a living memory of God; how do I accept and connect; how do I
lift up the individual story into the divine history?" These
questions are temptations insofar as they avoid the more
basic question: "Who am I as a living memory of God?"

The main question indeed is not a question of doing, but a question of being. When we speak about the minister as a living reminder of God, we are not speaking about a technical specialty which can be mastered through the acquisition of specific tools, techniques, and skills, but about a way of being which embraces the totality of life: working and resting, eating and drinking, praying and playing, acting and waiting. Before any professional skill, we need a spirituality, a way of living in the spirit by which all we are and all we do becomes a form of reminding.

One way to express this is to say that in order to be a living reminder of the Lord, we must walk in his presence as Abraham did. To walk in the presence of the Lord means to move forward in life in such a way that all our desires, thoughts, and actions are constantly guided by him. When we walk in the Lord's presence, everything we see, hear, touch, or taste reminds us of him. This is what is meant by a prayerful life. It is not a life in which we say many prayers, but a life in which nothing, absolutely nothing, is done, said, or understood independently of him who is the origin and purpose of our existence.

—From *The Living Reminder* by Henri J. M. Nouwen

❧ It is in affliction itself that the splendor of God's mercy shines, from its very depths, in the heart of its inconsolable bitterness. If still persevering in our love, we fall to the point where the soul cannot keep back the cry "My God, why hast thou forsaken me?" if we remain at this point without ceasing to love, we end by touching something that is not affliction, not joy, something that is the central essence, necessary and pure, something not of the senses, common to joy and sorrow: the very love of God.

We know then that joy is the sweetness of contact with the love of God, that affliction is the wound of this same contact when it is painful, and that only the contact matters, not the manner of it.

It is the same as when we see someone very dear to us after a long absence; the words we exchange with him do not matter, but only the sound of his voice, which assures us of his presence.

The knowledge of this presence of God does not afford consolation; it takes nothing from the fearful bitterness of

affliction; nor does it heal the mutilation of the soul. But we know quite certainly that God's love for us is the very substance of this bitterness and this mutilation.
—From *Waiting for God* by Simone Weil

&. I try to give to the poor people for love what the rich could get for money. No, I wouldn't touch a leper for a thousand pounds; yet I willingly cure him for the love of God.
—From *A Gift for God* by Mother Teresa

Hymn: O Sacred Head, Now Wounded

O sacred Head, now wounded,
With grief and shame weighed down,
Now scornfully surrounded
With thorns, thine only crown:
How pale thou art with anguish,
With sore abuse and scorn!
How does this visage languish
Which once was bright as morn!

What thou, my Lord, hast suffered
Was all for sinners' gain;
Mine, mine was the transgression,
But thine the deadly pain.
Lo, here I fall, my Savior!
'Tis I deserve thy place;
Look on me with thy favor,
Vouchsafe to me thy grace.

What language shall I borrow
To thank thee, dearest friend,
For this thy dying sorrow,
Thy pity without end?
O make me thine forever;
And should I fainting be,
Lord, let me never, never
Outlive my love to thee. Amen.
—Anonymous

22: *Christ Lives*

I.   Invocation
Almighty God, you who have sent Jesus into the world to suffer, die, and rise again for our sake, help us to experience your transforming resurrection power within our lives and ministry. We offer our prayers in the name and spirit of Jesus Christ, our Lord. Amen.

II. Psalm 23

III. Daily Scripture Readings
Monday	John 12:1-11	
Tuesday	Ezekiel 37:1-14	
Wednesday	John 13:21-38	
Thursday	Mark 14:12-26	
Friday	John 18–19	
Saturday	John 21:1-14	
Sunday	A.	Acts 10:34-43; Psalm 118:14-24; Colossians 3:1-4; John 20:1-18
	B.	Isaiah 25:6-9; Psalm 118:14-24; Acts 10:34-43; Mark 16:1-8
	C.	Acts 10:34-43; Psalm 118:14-24; 1 Corinthians 15:19-26; John 20:1-18

IV. Readings for Reflection

V.   Prayers: for the church, for others, for myself

VI. Reflection: silent and written

VII. Hymn: "The Lord's My Shepherd, I'll Not Want"

VIII. Benediction
The Lord bless you and keep you: the Lord make his face to shine upon you, and be gracious to you: the Lord lift up his countenance upon you, and give you peace. Amen. —Numbers 6:24-26

Readings for Reflection

🍃 Today is Resurrection Sunday. My first Easter in prison. Surely the regime can't continue to keep almost 10,000 political prisoners in its gaols! In here, it is much easier to understand how the men in the Bible felt, stripping themselves of everything that was superfluous. Many of the prisoners have already heard that they have lost their homes, their furniture, and everything they owned. Our families are broken up. Many of our children are wandering the streets, their father in one prison, their mother in another.

There is not a single cup. But a score of Christian prisoners experienced the joy of celebrating communion—without bread or wine. The communion of empty hands. The non-Christians said: "We will help you; we will talk quietly so that you can meet." Too dense a silence would have drawn the guards' attention as surely as the lone voice of the preacher. "We have no bread, nor water to use instead of wine," I told them, "but we will act as though we had."

"This meal in which we take part," I said, "reminds us of the prison, the torture, the death and final victory of the resurrection of Jesus Christ. The bread is the body which he gave for humanity. The fact that we have none represents very well the lack of bread in the hunger of so many millions of human beings. The wine, which we don't have today, is his blood and represents our dream of a united humanity, of a just society, without difference of race or class."

I held out my empty hand to the first person on my right, and placed it over his open hand, and the same with the others: "Take, eat, this is my body which is given for you; do this in remembrance of me." Afterward, all of us raised our hands to our mouths, receiving the body of Christ in silence. "Take, drink, this is the blood of Christ which was shed to seal the new covenant of God with men. Let us give thanks, sure that Christ is here with us, strengthening us."

We gave thanks to God, and finally stood up and embraced each other. A while later, another non-Christian prisoner said to me: "You people have something special, which I would like to have." The father of the dead girl came up to me and said: "Pastor, this was a real experience! I

believe that today I discovered what faith is. Now, I believe
that I am on the road."
—From *Visions of a World Hungry* by Thomas G. Pettepiece

    Long, long, long ago;
    Way before this winter's snow
    First fell upon these weathered fields;
    I used to sit and watch and feel
    And dream of how the spring would be,
    When through the winter's stormy sea
    She'd raise her green and growing head,
    Her warmth would resurrect the dead.

    Long before this winter's snow
    I dreamt of this day's sunny glow
    And thought somehow my pain would pass
    With winter's pain, and peace like grass
    Would simply grow. The pain's not gone.
    It's still as cold and hard and long
    As lonely pain has ever been,
    It cuts so deep and far within.

    Long before this winter's snow
    I ran from pain, looked high and low
    For some fast way to get around
    Its hurt and cold. I'd have found,
    If I had looked at what was there,
    That things don't follow fast or fair.
    That life goes on, and times do change,
    And grass does grow despite life's pains.

    Long before this winter's snow
    I thought that this day's sunny glow,
    The smiling children and growing things
    And flowers bright were brought by spring.
    Now, I know the sun does shine,
    That children smile, and from the dark, cold, grime
    A flower comes. It groans, yet sings,
    And through its pain, its peace begins.
    —"Resurrection" by Mary Ann Bernard

&. God created through love and for love. God did not create anything except love itself, and the means to love. He created love in all its forms. He created beings capable of love from all possible distances. Because no other could do it, he himself went to the greatest possible distance, the infinite distance. This infinite distance between God and God, this supreme tearing apart, this agony beyond all others, this marvel of love, is the crucifixion. Nothing can be further from God than that which has been made accursed.

This tearing apart, over which supreme love places the bond of supreme union, echoes perpetually across the universe in the midst of the silence, like two notes, separate yet melting into one, like pure and heart-rending harmony. This is the Word of God. The whole creation is nothing but its vibration. When human music in its greatest purity pierces our soul, this is what we hear through it. When we have learned to hear the silence, this is what we grasp more distinctly through it.

Those who persevere in love hear this note from the very lowest depths into which affliction has thrust them. From that moment they can no longer have any doubt.

Men struck down by affliction are at the foot of the Cross, almost at the greatest possible distance from God. It must not be thought that sin is a greater distance. Sin is not a distance, it is a turning of our gaze in the wrong direction.
—From *Waiting for God* by Simone Weil

&. The purpose of God in the history of man was accomplished when Jesus breathed his last upon the cross. The cry "It is finished" was not the mere gasp of a wornout life; it was not the cry of satisfaction with which a career of pain and sorrow is terminated; it was the deliberate utterance of a clear consciousness on the part of God's appointed Revealer that now all had been done that could be done to make God known to men and to identify him with men. God's purpose had ever been one and indivisible—declared to men in various ways, a hint here, a broad light there, now by a gleam of insight in the mind of a prophet, now by a deed of heroism in king or leader, through rude symbolic contrivances and through the tenderest of human affections and the highest human thoughts. God had been making men ever more and more sensible that his one purpose was to come closer and closer into fellowship with them, and to draw them into a perfect harmony with him. Forgiveness and deliverance from sin were provided for them, knowledge of God's law and will, thus they might learn to know and to serve him—all these were secured when Jesus cried, "It is finished."

—From *Footsteps in the Path of Life* by Marcus Dods

ἐ▲. Astonishing! The Son of God—who, more than anyone else, was free to choose what he would—chose not only a mother and a people, but also a social position. And he wanted to be a wage earner.

That Jesus had *voluntarily* lost himself in an obscure Middle Eastern village; annihilated himself in the daily monotony of thirty years' rough, miserable work; separated himself from the society that "counts"; and died in total anonymity.

—From *Letters from the Desert* by Carlo Carretto

ἐ▲. O God, our Father, at Easter time we remember the great hope of eternal life which you have set before us, and we feel within our hearts the longings for goodness and for you. Grant that nothing may hinder the hope of eternal life from coming true, and the desire for goodness and for you from being realized.

—From *Prayers for the Christian Year* by William Barclay

ἐ▲. The Day of Resurrection has dawned upon us, the day of true light and life, wherein Christ, the life of believers, arose from the dead. Let us give abundant thanks and praise to God, that while we solemnly celebrate the day of our Lord's resurrection, he may be pleased to bestow on us quiet peace and special gladness; so that being protected from morning to night by his favoring mercy, we may rejoice in the gift of our Redeemer. Amen.

—Mozarabic Sacramentary

Hymn: The Lord's My Shepherd, I'll Not Want

The Lord's my Shepherd, I'll not want;
He makes me down to lie
In pastures green;
He leadeth me
The quiet waters by.

My soul he doth restore again;
And me to walk doth make
Within the paths of righteousness,
E'en for his own name's sake.

Yea, though I walk in death's dark vale,
Yet will I fear no ill;
For thou art with me, and thy rod
And staff me comfort still.

My table thou hast furnished
In presence of my foes;
My head thou dost with oil anoint,
And my cup overflows.

Goodness and mercy all my life
Shall surely follow me;
And in God's house for evermore
My dwelling place shall be. Amen.
—Scottish Psalter

23: *Partakers of Eternal Life*

I. Invocation
    O God, who through the grace of thy Holy Spirit
    dost pour the gift of love into the hearts of thy faith-
    ful people: Grant us health, both of mind and body,
    that we may love thee with our whole strength, and
    with glad hearts may perform those things which
    are pleasing unto thee; through Jesus Christ our
    Lord. Amen. —From *The Book of Worship*

II. Psalm 46

III. Daily Scripture Readings
Monday	Acts 11:19-26
Tuesday	John 10:1-18
Wednesday	2 Corinthians 5:1-10
Thursday	2 Corinthians 4
Friday	1 John 3:11-24
Saturday	John 15:1-11
Sunday	A. Acts 2:14a, 22-32; Psalm 16:5-11; 1 Peter 1:3-9; John 20:19-31
	B. Acts 4:32-35; Psalm 133; 1 John 1:1–2:2; John 20:19-31
	C. Acts 5:27-32; Psalm 2; Revelation 1:4-8; John 20:19-31

IV. Readings for Reflection

V. Prayers: for the church, for others, for myself

VI. Reflection: silent and written

VII. Hymn: "Some Day"

VIII. Benediction
    Lord, allow me your servant to go in peace. I have
    experienced your salvation which you have pre-
    pared for everyone. Uphold me as I seek to serve in
    your name. Amen.

Readings for Reflection

❧ O Lord, who else or what else can I desire but you? You are my Lord, Lord of my heart, mind, and soul. You know me through and through. In and through you everything that is finds its origin and goal. You embrace all that exists and care for it with divine love and compassion. Why, then, do I keep expecting happiness and satisfaction outside of you? Why do I keep relating to you as one of my many relationships, instead of my only relationship, in which all other ones are grounded? Why do I keep looking for popularity, respect from others, success, acclaim, and sensual pleasures? Why, Lord, is it so hard for me to make you the only one? Why do I keep hesitating to surrender myself totally to you?

Help me, O Lord, to let my old self die, to let die the thousand big and small ways in which I am still building up my false self and trying to cling to my false desires. Let me be reborn in you and see through you the world in the right way, so that all my actions, words, and thought can become a hymn of praise to you.

I need your loving grace to travel on this hard road that leads to the death of my old self and to a new life in and for you. I know and trust that this is the road to freedom.

Lord, dispel my mistrust and help me become a trusting friend. Amen.

—From *A Cry for Mercy* by Henri J. M. Nouwen

❧ Still the pain of loss, while the emergence is coming about, can drive one to desperation, trying to fulfill heart's desire in spite of circumstances, or to despair, giving up heart's desire because of circumstances. In the desperation and the despair there is an element of ignorance, not understanding one's heart's desire, and an element of guilt, not waiting to understand it. "Because of impatience we were driven out," Kafka says, speaking of the sin that caused mankind to be driven out of paradise, "because of impatience we cannot return."

Waiting to understand the heart's desire, one is waiting to become heart-free and heart-whole. One is waiting to be purified of desperation and despair. The waiting itself is already the beginning. If one continues to wait, one finds oneself going against a current of fear, the fear that leads back towards desperation and despair. It is fear that leads one to act in desperation, one realizes. It is fear that leads one to give up in despair. Fear of what? Of nothingness, Kierkegaard says. Of death, we could say. The desperation and the despair arise when one's life opens up before one all the way to death. There is a loneliness one experiences in the face of death, the loneliness of having to die one's own death just as one has to live one's own life, the loneliness of having to live and die alone. It is the same deep loneliness, it seems, that we found at the core of human relationships. As the heart kindles, on the other hand, one enters into a love that "casts out fear." It is a love that casts out the fear leading to desperation and despair, the fear of death and nothingness. "There is no fear in love," it is said in the First Epistle of John, "but perfect love casts out fear."

"Now is my soul troubled" even Jesus can say, even in the Gospel of John, when he is facing death. "Now shall the ruler of this world be cast out," he says, though, when he goes through fear to courage. One goes through fear to courage, it seems, through desperation and despair to hope, through sorrow to joy, through conflict to peace, through circumstances to heart's desire. The way to necessity is the way of circumstance and conflict and suffering and guilt and death. The way of possibility is the way of "going through." "God is how things stand" for one who sees only the way of necessity. "God is that all things are possible" for one who sees the way of possibility. What is God we can ask, for one who actually does "go through"?
—From *The Reasons of the Heart* by John S. Dunne

🙢   Yestereve, Death came, and knocked at my thin door.
    I from my window looked: the thing I saw,
    The shape uncouth, I had not seen before.
    I was disturbed—with fear, in sooth, not awe;
    Whereof ashamed, I instantly did rouse
    My will to seek thee—only to fear the more:
    Alas! I could not find thee in the house.
    I was like Peter when he began to sink.
    To thee a new prayer therefore I have got—
    That, when Death comes in earnest to my door,
    Thou wouldst thyself go, when the latch doth clink,

And lead him to my room, up to my cot;
Then hold thy child's hand, hold and leave him not,
Till Death has done with him for evermore.

Till Death has done with him? Ah, leave me then!
And Death has done with me, oh, nevermore!
He comes—and goes—to leave me in thy arms,
Nearer thy heart, oh, nearer than before!
To lay thy child, naked, new-born again
Of mother earth, crept free through many harms,
Upon thy bosom—still to the very core.
—From *Diary of an Old Soul* by George MacDonald

&. Scripture and tradition habitually put the joys of Heaven into the scale against the sufferings of earth, and no solution of the problem of pain which does not do so can be called a Christian one. We are very shy nowadays of even mentioning Heaven. We are afraid of the jeer about "pie in the sky," and of being told that we are trying to "escape" from the duty of making a happy world here and now into dreams of a happy world elsewhere. But either there is "pie in the sky" or there is not. If there is not, then Christianity is false, for this doctrine is woven into its whole fabric. If there is, then this truth, like any other, must be faced, whether it is useful at political meetings or no. Again, we are afraid that Heaven is a bribe, and that if we make it our goal we shall no longer be disinterested. It is not so. Heaven offers nothing that a mercenary soul can desire. It is safe to tell the pure in heart that they shall see God, for only the pure in heart want to. There are rewards that do not sully motives. A man's love for a woman is not mercenary because he wants to marry her, nor his love for poetry mercenary because he wants to read it, nor his love of exercise less disinterested because he wants to run and leap and walk. Love, by definition, seeks to enjoy its object.
—From *The Problem of Pain* by C. S. Lewis

&. O God, our Father, in the life and death and resurrection of Jesus you have given us the remedy for sin. In him you have opened to us the way to forgiveness for all our past sins, and you have given us the strength and the power to live in purity and in truth.

Help us to put away all evil things.
　　Silence the evil word;
　　Forbid the evil deed;
　　Break the evil habit;
　　Banish the evil thought;
　　Take away the evil desire and the evil ambition;
　　　　and make our lives to shine like lights
　　　　in this dark world.

Help us to live in purity.
　　Make all our words so pure
　　　　that you may hear them;
　　Make all our deeds so pure
　　　　that you may see them;
　　Make all our thoughts and desires so pure
　　　　that they may bear your scrutiny.
　　And so grant that we being pure in heart
　　　　may see you.

Help us to live in truth.
　　Grant
　　　　That we may never speak or act a lie;
　　　　That we may never be misled by false or
　　　　　　mistaken beliefs;
　　　　That we may never evade the truth,
　　　　　　even when we do not want to see it.

Grant to us at all times
　　　　To seek and to find;
　　　　To know and to love;
　　　　To obey and to live
　　　　　　the truth.

This we ask for the sake of him who is the Way, the Truth
and the Life, even for the sake of Jesus Christ our Lord.
Amen.
—From *Prayers for the Christian Year* by William Barclay

Hymn: Some Day

Beams of heaven, as I go,
Through this wilderness below,
Guide my feet in peaceful ways,
Turn my midnights into days;
When in the darkness I would grope,
Faith always sees a star of hope,
And soon from all life's grief and danger,
I shall be free some day.

Often-times my sky is clear,
Joy abounds without a tear.
Though a day so bright begun,
Clouds may hide tomorrow's sun.
There'll be a day that's always bright,
A day that never yields to night,
And in its light the streets of glory
I shall behold some day.

Harder yet may be the fight,
Right may often yield to might,
Wickedness awhile may reign,
Satan's cause may seem to gain;
There is a God that rules above,
With hand of pow'r and heart of love,
If I am right, he'll fight my battle,
I shall have peace some day.

Burdens now may crush me down,
Disappointments all around,
Troubles speak in mournful sigh,
Sorrow through a tear-stained eye;
There is a world where pleasure reigns,
No mourning soul shall roam its plains,
And to that land of peace and glory
I want to go some day.

Refrain:
I do not know how long 'twill be,
Nor what the future holds for me,
But this I know if Jesus leads me
I shall get home some day.
—Charles A. Tindley

24: *The Lord Is with Us*

I.   Invocation
Lord, you have promised to meet those who seek your face. Come now and reveal your presence to me as I make myself present to you. In the name of Jesus Christ my Lord. Amen.

II.   Psalm 121

III.   Daily Scripture Readings

Monday	Acts 13:44-52
Tuesday	Acts 18:5-11
Wednesday	Romans 8:1-11
Thursday	Galatians 2:11-20
Friday	Leviticus 26:1-13
Saturday	Acts 4:23-37
Sunday	A. Acts 2:14a, 36-41; Psalm 116:12-19; 1 Peter 1:17-23; Luke 24:13-35
	B. Acts 3:12-19; Psalm 4; 1 John 3:1-7; Luke 24:35-48
	C. Acts 9:1-20; Psalm 30:4-12; Revelation 5:11-14; John 21:1-19

IV.   Readings for Reflection

V.   Prayers: for the church, for others, for myself

VI.   Reflection: silent and written

VII.   Hymn: "O Love That Wilt Not Let Me Go"

VIII.   Benediction
Go forth into the activity of this day as companion of Jesus Christ the Lord. Amen.

Readings for Reflection

❧   After my return home, I was much buffeted with temptations; but cried out, and they fled away. They returned again and again. I as often lifted up my eyes, and he "sent me help from his holy place." And herein I found the difference between this and my former state chiefly consisted. I was striving, yea, fighting with all my might under the law, as well as under grace. But then I was sometimes, if not often, conquered; now, I was always conqueror.
—John Wesley

❧   As for me, I began to know Jesus as soon as I accepted Jesus as the truth; I found true peace when I actively sought his friendship; and above all I experienced joy, true joy, that stands above the vicissitudes of life, as soon as I tasted and experienced for myself the gift he came to bestow on us: eternal life.

But Jesus is not only the Image of the Father, the Revealer of the dark knowledge of God. That would be of little avail to me in my weakness and my sinfulness: he is also my *Saviour*.

On my journey towards him, I was completely worn out, unable to take another step forward. By my errors, my sinful rebellions, my desperate efforts to find joy far from his joy, I had reduced myself to a mass of virulent sores which repelled both heaven and earth.

What sin was there that I had not committed? Or what sin had I as yet not committed simply because the opportunity had not come my way?

Yet it was he, and he alone, who got down off his horse, like the good Samaritan on the way to Jericho; he alone had the courage to approach me in order to staunch with bandages the few drops of blood that still remained in my veins, blood that would certainly have flowed away, had he not intervened.

Jesus became a *sacrament* for me, the cause of my salvation, he brought my time in hell to an end, and put a stop to my inner disintegration. He washed me patiently in the waters of baptism, he filled me with the exhilarating joy of the Holy Spirit in confirmation, he nourished me with the bread of his word. Above all, he forgave me, he forgot everything, he did not even wish me to remember my past myself.

When, through my tears, I began to tell him something of the years during which I betrayed him, he lovingly placed his hand over my mouth in order to silence me. His one concern was that I should muster courage enough to pick myself up again, to try and carry on walking in spite of my weakness, and to believe in his love in spite of my fears. But there was one thing he did, the value of which cannot be measured, something truly unbelievable, something only God could do.

While I continued to have doubts about my own salvation, to tell him that my sins could not be forgiven, and that justice, too, had its rights, he appeared on the Cross before me one Friday towards midday.

I was at its foot, and found myself bathed with the blood which flowed from the gaping holes made in his flesh by the nails. He remained there for three hours until he expired.

I realized that he had died in order that I might stop turning to him with questions about justice, and believe instead, deep within myself, that the scales had come down overflowing on the side of love, and that even though all, through unbelief or madness, had offended him, he had conquered for ever, and drawn all things everlastingly to himself.

Then later, so that I should never forget that Friday and abandon the Cross, as one forgets a postcard on the table or a picture in the worn-out book that had been feeding one's devotion, he led me on to discover that in order to be with me continually, not simply as an affectionate remembrance but as a living presence, he had devised the Eucharist.

What a discovery that was!

Under the sacramental sign of bread, Jesus was there each morning to renew the sacrifice of the Cross and make of it the living sacrifice of his bride, the Church, a pure offering to the Divine Majesty.

And still that was not all.

He led me on to understand that the sign of bread testified to his hidden presence, not only during the Great

Sacrifice, but at all times, since the Eucharist was not an isolated moment in my day, but a line which stretched over twenty-four hours: he is God-with-us, the realization of what had been foretold by the *cloud* that went before the people of God during their journey through the desert, and the *darkness* which filled the tabernacle in the temple at Jerusalem.

I must emphasize that this vital realization that the sign of bread concealed and pointed out for me the uninterrupted presence of Jesus beside me was a unique grace in my life. From that moment he led me along the path to intimacy, and friendship with himself.

I understood that he longed to be present like this beside each one of us.

Jesus was not only bread, he was a friend.

A home without bread is not a home, but a home without friendship is nothing.

That is why Jesus became a friend, concealed under the sign of bread. I learned to stay with him for hours on end, listening to the mysterious voices that welled up from the abysses of Being and to receive the rays of that light whose source was in the uncreated light of God.

I have experienced such sweetness in the eucharistic presence of Christ.

I have learned to appreciate why the saints remained in contemplation before this bread to beseech, to adore and to love.

How I wish that everyone might take the Eucharist home, and having made a little oratory in some quiet comer, might find joy in sitting quietly before it, in order to make his dialogue with God easier and more immediate, in intimate union with Christ.

But still that was not enough.

Jesus did not overcome the insuperable obstacle presented by the divinity and enter the human sphere simply to be our saviour. Had that been all, his work would have remained unfinished, his mission of love unfulfilled.

He broke through the wall surrounding the invisible, and came down into the visible world to bear witness to 'the things that are above,' to reveal to us 'the secrets of his Father's house,' to give us in concrete form what he called eternal life.

What exactly is it, this famous 'eternal life'?

He himself defined it in the Gospel: 'And eternal life is this: to know you, the only true God, and Jesus Christ whom you have sent' (Jn 17:3). So eternal life is, first and foremost, knowledge. It is a matter of knowing the Father, knowing Jesus. But it is not a question of any external, historical, analogical knowledge which we could more or less imagine, possess perhaps, even now; it is rather a question of real, supernatural knowledge which, although it is still surrounded here by the darkness of faith, is already the same as the knowledge we will have when the veil is torn aside and we see God face to face. It is a question of knowing God *as he is*, not as he may appear to us or as we may imagine him. This is the heart of the mystery I have tried to describe as *the beyond*, and which is the key to the secret of intimacy with God and the substance of contemplative prayer.

In giving us 'eternal life' Jesus gives us that knowledge of the Father which is already our first experience of living, here on earth, the divine life; which is a vital participation, here and now, in the family of God; and which means that while we remain sons of man, we are at the same time sons of God. . . .

Jesus is the Image of the Father, the centre of the universe and of history.

Jesus is our salvation, the radiance of the God we cannot see, the unquenchable fire of love, the one for whom the angels sigh, the Holy one of God, the true adorer, the eternal High Priest, the Lord of the Ages, the glory of God.

Jesus is also our brother, and as such he takes his place beside us, to teach us the path we must follow to reach the invisible. And to make sure that we understand, he translates into visible terms the invisible things he has seen—as man he acts as God would act; he introduces the ways of the family of God on to the earth and into the family of man.

—From *In Search of the Beyond* by Carlo Carretto

Three men shared death upon a hill,
But only one man dies;
The other two—
A thief and God himself—
Made rendezvous.

Three crosses still
Are borne up Calvary's Hill,
Where Sin still lifts them high:
Upon the one, sag broken men
Who, cursing, die;
Another holds the praying thief,
Or those who penitent as he,
Still find the Christ
Beside them on the tree.
—"Upon a Hill" by Miriam LeFevre Crouse

Hymn: O Love That Wilt Not Let Me Go

O Love that wilt not let me go,
I rest my weary soul in thee;
I give thee back the life I owe,
That in thine ocean depths its flow
May richer, fuller be.

O Light that followest all my way,
I yield my flickering torch to thee;
My heart restores its borrowed ray,
That in thy sunshine's blaze its day
May brighter, fairer be.

O Joy that seekest me through pain,
I cannot close my heart to thee;
I trace the rainbow through the rain,
And feel the promise is not vain
That morn shall tearless be.

O Cross that liftest up my head,
I dare not ask to fly from thee;
I lay in dust life's glory dead,
And from the ground there blossoms red
Life that shall endless be. Amen.
—George Matheson

Fourth Sunday of Easter
25: *The Good Shepherd*

I.   Invocation
     Lord God, in whom I find life, health, and strength,
     through whose gifts I am clothed and fed, through
     whose mercy I have been forgiven and cleansed, be
     for me guide, strength, Savior, and Lord all the days
     of my life. I offer my prayers through Christ. Amen.

II. Psalm 131

III. Daily Scripture Readings
     Monday   Jeremiah 23
     Tuesday   1 Peter 5:1-11
     Wednesday   Ezekiel 34:11-16
     Thursday   Isaiah 40:9-11
     Friday   1 Timothy 3:1-13
     Saturday   2 Corinthians 4
     Sunday   A. Acts 2:42-47; Psalm 23;
                     1 Peter 2:19-25; John 10:1-10
                  B. Acts 4:8-12; Psalm 23;
                     1 John 3:18-24; John 10:11-18
                  C. Acts 13:15-16, 26-33; Psalm 23;
                     Revelation 7:9-17; John 10:22-30

IV. Readings for Reflection

V.   Prayers: for the church, for others, for myself

VI. Reflection: silent and written

VII. Hymn: "Savior, Like a Shepherd Lead Us"

VIII. Benediction
     And now may the spirit which was in Jesus Christ
     be in me, enabling me to know God's will and
     empowering me to do God's will. Amen.

Readings for Reflection

❧ Joy or sadness, war or peace, love or hate, purity or impurity, charity or greed, all are tremendous realities which are the hinges of our interior life. Everyday things, relationships with other people, daily work, love of our family—all these may breed saints.

Jesus at Nazareth taught us to live every hour of the day as saints. Every hour of the day is useful and may lead to divine inspiration, the will of the Father, the prayer of contemplation—holiness. Every hour of the day is holy. What matters is to live it as Jesus taught us.

And for this one does not have to shut oneself in a monastery or fix strange and inhumane regimes for one's life. It is enough to accept the realities of life. Work is one of these realities; motherhood, the rearing of children, family life with all its obligations are others.

—From *Letters from the Desert* by Carlo Carretto

❧ Another picture that our Lord loves to use is that of the shepherd who goes out to look for the sheep that is lost (*Mt 18:12ff*). So long as we imagine that it is we who have to look for God, then we must often lose heart. But it is the other way about: he is looking for us. And so we can afford to recognise that very often we are not looking for God; far from it, we are in full flight from him, in high rebellion against him. And he knows that and has taken it into account. He has followed us into our own darkness; there where we thought finally to escape him, we run straight into his arms.

So we do not have to erect a false piety for ourselves, to give us hope of salvation. Our hope is in his determination to save us. And he will not give in!

This should free us from that crippling anxiety which prevents any real growth, giving us room to do whatever we can do, to accept the small but genuine responsibilities that we do have. Our part is not to shoulder the whole burden of our salvation, the initiative and the programme are not in our hands: our part is to consent, to learn how to love him in return whose love came to us so freely while we were quite uninterested in him.

Also we can let ourselves off that desperate question, "Am I in the right place?" "Have I done the right thing?" Of course, we must sometimes acknowledge sins and mistakes and we must try to learn from them; but we should not foster the kind of worry that leads to despair. God's providence means that *wherever* we have got to, *whatever* we have done, that is precisely where the road to heaven begins. However many cues we have missed, however many wrong turnings we have taken, however unnecessarily we may have complicated our journey, the road still beckons, and the Lord still "waits to be gracious" to us *(Isaiah 30:18)*.

If we let these things really speak to us, then we can surely accept our Lord's invitation, indeed his command, to cast all our cares upon him *(I Pet. 5:7)* and let him care for them. We can give space in our hearts for Christ to dwell there, and it is faith that gives him space *(cf. Eph 3:17)*. We can let him dethrone us from being God in our own hearts, and establish there his own rule. We can then let him give us to ourselves, just as at the beginning he gave Adam to Adam. Then we can receive from him all that is ours, all our faculties, all our freedom, our capacity to take initiatives, to make our own decisions, so that our own true independence no longer challenges God's sovereignty but is precisely a most wonderful expression of it, as we receive our freedom day by day, minute by minute, from the creative love of God.

—From *Prayer* by Simon Tugwell

ఴ In any case, when I think of the act by which I should enter the Church as something concrete, which might happen quite soon, nothing gives me more pain than the idea of separating myself from the immense and unfortunate multitude of unbelievers. I have the essential need, and I think I can say the vocation, to move among men of every class and complexion, mixing with them and sharing their life and outlook, so far that is to say as conscience allows, merging into the crowd and disappearing among them, so that they show themselves as they are, putting off all disguises with me. It is because I long to know them so as to love them just as they are. For if I do not love them as they are, it will not be they whom I love, and my love will be unreal.

I do not speak of helping them, because as far as that goes I am unfortunately quite incapable of doing anything as yet.
—From *Waiting for God* by Simone Weil

ʘ Jesus in his solidarity with the marginal ones is *moved to compassion*. Compassion constitutes a radical form of criticism, for it announces that the hurt is to be taken seriously, that the hurt is not to be accepted as normal and natural but is an abnormal and unacceptable condition for humanness. In the arrangement of "lawfulness" in Jesus' time, as in the ancient empire of Pharaoh, the one unpermitted quality of relation was compassion. Empires are never built or maintained on the basis of compassion. The norms of law (social control) are never accommodated to persons, but persons are accommodated to the norms. Otherwise the norms will collapse and with them the whole power arrangement. Thus the compassion of Jesus is to be understood not simply as a personal emotional reaction but as a public criticism in which he dares to act upon his concern against the entire numbness of his social context.
—From *The Prophetic Imagination* by Walter Brueggemann

ʘ O Lord,
 you know me.
You know when I sit
 and when I stand.
You have me always present
 in your mind.
For this, Lord, I thank you.
You know the path for my life
 and what is best for me.
Lord, reveal to me the path
 I am to walk.
Bless me and guide me
 and be Lord to me
so that whichever road I take
 I may do all for your glory.
 In Jesus' name. Amen.
—"Vocation Prayer" from the Beech Grove Benedictine Community

ⲥ Prayer is really an attitude of our hearts toward God. As such it finds expression, at times in words and at times without words, precisely as when two people love each other. As conscious personalities we must and should give expression to our attitudes in words one to another. It is this faculty which lifts the fellowship of human beings to such a high plane and makes it so rich.

But at the same time let us remind ourselves that life, in the last analysis, is inexpressible. There is something in our lives, also in our fellowships, which can never be formulated in words, but which can be the common experience, nevertheless, of two who share with each other everything that can be expressed in words.

In the soul's fellowship with God in prayer, too, there are things which can and should be formulated in words. We have spoken of that in the preceding. But there are also things for which we can find no words. Likely it is this to which the apostle makes reference when he speaks in Romans 8:26 of the "groanings which cannot be uttered."

My little boy came in one day and stuck his little head into the doorway of my study. Now he knew that he was not supposed to disturb me during working hours. And his conscience troubled him a little on account of this. But he looked at me nevertheless with his kind, round baby eyes and said, "Papa, dear, I will sit still all the time if you will only let me be here with you!"

That he received permission when he approached my father-heart in that way, every father knows.

That little experience gave me a great deal to think about.

Is not that just the way we often feel with regard to our heavenly Father? We do so love to be with him, just to be in his presence! Moreover, we never disturb him, no matter when we come nor how often we come!

We pray to God. We speak to him about everything we have on our minds both concerning others and ourselves. There come times, not so seldom with me at least, when I have nothing more to tell God. If I were to continue to pray in words, I would have to repeat what I have already said. At such times it is wonderful to say to God, "May I be in thy presence, Lord? I have nothing more to say to thee, but I do love to be in thy presence."

We can spend time in silence together with people whom we know real well. That we cannot do with others. We must converse with them, entertain them either with interesting or profound things as the case may be. But with our own dear ones we can speak freely about common and insignificant things. In their presence, too, we can be silent. Similarly, it is not necessary to maintain a conversation when we are in the presence of God. We can come into his presence and rest our weary souls in quiet contemplation of him. Our groanings, which cannot be uttered, rise to him and tell him better than words how dependent we are on him.

As evening drew nigh, and our little fellow had played until he was tired, I noticed that he drew closer and closer to his mother. At last he found the place he was longing for, mother's lap. He did not have a great deal to say either. He simply lay there, and let his mother caress him to sleep.

We, too, become tired, deadly tired, of ourselves, of others, of the world, of life, of everything! Then it is blessed to know of a place where we can lay our tired head and heart, our heavenly Father's arms, and say to him, 'I can do no more. And I have nothing to tell you. May I lie here a while and rest? Everything will soon be well again if I can only rest in your arms a while.'

—From *Prayer* by O. Hallesby

❧ Say that I am musical and attend a concert. From one point of view I am totally passive. Indeed, unless I am passive, unless I cease from activity in the usual sense, the music is wasted on me. But after the concert is over I find that I am quite tired, happily tired no doubt, but tired none the less. My tiredness shows that my passivity in the concert hall was also a deep form of activity. To receive and take in the music was spending of energy. So also in the prayer of contemplation, when the mind and the feelings are quietened and we become passively receptive in the presence of God, our passivity is a deep and costly form of activity. It is action of the highest human order which always consists of letting go and letting God take on. And when at prayer we are thus receptively passively active so that we let go and let God take on, then it inevitably colours and gives wings to all we are and do. That is why, at regular times, we should cease from action in the more superficial sense in order at prayer to find that receptive passivity which is action at its human highest because it is the point where our letting go is God taking on. And this in turn gives the depth of God's own love to what we do in the ordinary sense in the workaday world.

—From *Tensions* by H. A. Williams

Hymn: Savior, Like a Shepherd Lead Us

Savior, like a shepherd lead us,
Much we need thy tender care;
In thy pleasant pastures feed us,
For our use thy folds prepare:
Blessed Jesus, blessed Jesus!
Thou hast bought us, thine we are.

We are thine, do thou befriend us,
Be the guardian of our way;
Keep thy flock, from sin defend us,
Seek us when we go astray:
Blessed Jesus, blessed Jesus!
Hear, O hear us, when we pray.

Thou hast promised to receive us,
Poor and sinful though we be;
Thou hast mercy to relieve us,
Grace to cleanse and power to free:
Blessed Jesus, blessed Jesus!
We will early turn to thee.

Early let us seek thy favor,
Early let us do thy will;
Blessed Lord and only Savior,
With thy love our bosoms fill:
Blessed Jesus, Blessed Jesus!
Thou hast loved us, love us still. Amen.

—Attributed to Dorothy A. Thrupp

26: *Love Is the Sign*

I. Invocation
O Thou who has ordered this wondrous world, and who knowest all things in earth and heaven: So fill our hearts with trust in thee that by night and day, at all times and in all seasons, we may without fear commit all that we have and hope to be to thy never-failing love, for this life and the life to come; through Jesus Christ our Lord. Amen.
—From *The Book of Worship*

II. Psalm 136

III. Daily Scripture Readings
Monday	Galatians 5:13-24
Tuesday	Romans 5:1-11
Wednesday	Ephesians 5:1-20
Thursday	Hebrews 13:1-6
Friday	Deuteronomy 7:6-16
Saturday	1 Corinthians 13:1-13
Sunday	A. Acts 7:55-60; Psalm 31:1-8; 1 Peter 2:2-10; John 14:1-14
	B. Acts 8:26-40; Psalm 22:25-31; 1 John 4:7-12; John 15:1-8
	C. Acts 14:8-18; Psalm 145:13b-21; Revelation 21:1-6; John 13:31-35

IV. Readings for Reflection

V. Prayers: for the church, for others, for myself

VI. Reflection: silent and written

VII. Hymn: "Love Divine, All Loves Excelling"

VIII. Benediction
The grace of the Lord Jesus Christ be with you. Amen.

Readings for Reflection

 ❧ Now what is the deepest in God? His power? No, for power could not make him what we mean when we say *God*. Evil could, of course, never create one atom; but let us understand very plainly, that a being whose essence was only power would be such a negation of the divine that no righteous worship could be offered him: his service must be fear, and fear only. Such a being, even were he righteous in judgment, yet could not be God.

The God himself whom we love could not be righteous were he not something deeper and better still than we generally mean by the word—but, alas, how little can language say without seeming to say something wrong! In one word, God is Love. Love is the deepest depth, the essence of his nature, at the root of all his being. It is not merely that he could not be God, if he had made no creatures to whom to be God; but love is the heart and hand of his creation; it is his right to create, and his power to create as well. The love that foresees creation is itself the power to create.

—From *Creation in Christ* by George MacDonald

 ❧ James considers it natural that a person with faith also has works. It is not a heavy and moralistic Christian duty; it is the Christian possibility and life-style—response comes with true faith.

On this theme, the Bible is clear and direct in both Testaments—God loves and cares for the poor. Jesus said to be perfect. In other words, to be imitators of the perfect God, to do as God does. If we are to love God, we are to love and care for the poor and hungry, too. "You will know them by their fruits" (Matt. 7:16*a* RSV) he said, and he meant that we are known by our ethical behavior as illustrated by life experience.

—From *Visions of a World Hungry* by Thomas G. Pettepiece

 ❧ Oh, my sisters, what nothingness is all that we have given up, and all that we are doing, or can ever do, for a God who is pleased to communicate himself in this way to a worm! If we have the hope of enjoying this blessing while we are still in this life, what are we doing about it and why are we waiting? What sufficient reason is there for delaying even a short time instead of seeking this Lord, as the Bride did, through streets and squares? Oh, what a mockery is everything in the world if it does not lead us and help us on the way towards this end,—and would be even though all the worldly delights and riches and joys that we can imagine were to last for ever! For everything is cloying and degrading by comparison with these treasures, which we shall enjoy eternally. And even these are nothing by comparison with having for our own the Lord of all treasures and of Heaven and earth.

Oh, human blindness! How long, how long shall it be before this dust is removed from our eyes? For although, as far as we ourselves are concerned, it seems not to be bad enough to blind us altogether, I can see some motes and particles which, if we allow them to become more numerous, will be sufficient to do us great harm. For the love of God, then, sisters, let us profit by these faults and learn from them what wretched creatures we are, and may they give us clearer sight, as did the clay to the blind man who was healed by our Spouse; and thus, realizing our own imperfections, we shall beseech him more and more earnestly to bring good out of our wretchedness, so that we may please his Majesty in everything.

Without realizing it, I have strayed far from my theme. Forgive me, sisters; and believe me, now that I have come to these great things of God (come to write about them, I mean), I cannot help feeling the pity of it when I see how much we are losing, and all through our own fault. For, true though it is that these are things which the Lord gives to whom he will, he would give them to us all if we loved him as he loves us. For he desires nothing else but to have those to whom he may give them, and his riches are not diminished by his readiness to give.

—From *Interior Castle* by Saint Teresa of Avila

❧ If you wish to know whether you have made progress, my daughters, here is the measure for each of you: that you consider yourself the most imperfect of all and that you show this belief by actions conducing to the advancement and good of others. Consolations in prayer and ecstasies, visions, or any such favors which the Lord may give are not the signs to look for; we must wait until the next world to understand their value. The knowledge of yourself is current money, an unfailing revenue, an estate in perpetuity; it is no annuity subject to cancellation. Extraordinary favors, however, may come and go. Our true treasure consists in humility, mortification, and such perfect obedience that we would not make the slightest move contrary to the Superior's orders, knowing that it is God who commands us since she stands in his place.

—From *Way of Perfection* by Saint Teresa of Avila

 ❧ I have said this before and I would say it many, many times, for fear seriously constrains people who do not wholly understand God's goodness by personal experience, although they know it by faith. It is truly a wonderful thing to know by experience the friendship and the tenderness with which he treats those who go by this road and to see how he defrays, as it were, all the expenses of the journey.

 I do not find it strange that those who have not known this attention should wish for assurance of some interest. Yet you know that it is one hundred to one, even in this life, and that Our Lord has said: "Ask, and you shall receive." If you do not believe his Majesty when he says this several times in his Gospel, it is certainly of little use for me to wear myself out, sisters, telling you the same thing. However, if any of you still doubt it, I assure her she has little to lose in putting it to the proof. That is the wonderful thing about this journey: one is given more than one ever asks or even dreams of desiring. This is absolutely certain; I know it to be true. If you should find it untrue, never believe anything else I tell you.

—From *Way of Perfection* by Saint Teresa of Avila

 ❧ I give you only one bit of advice: do not think that you will ever attain the prayer of quiet by dint of your own efforts. They would be unavailing, and after having had devotion, you would become cold. But simply and humbly, for humility obtained everything, say: THY WILL BE DONE.

—From *Way of Perfection* by Saint Teresa of Avila

❧ What a different life it must be not to desire death! How different then is the inclination of our will from the will of God! His will would have us love the truth; we love the life. It would have us desire eternal things; we incline to what is passing. It would have us desire lofty and sublime things; we want vile and earthly things. It would have us desire only what is certain; we love dubious things. It is mockery, my daughters, to ask anything of God but that he deliver us from all these dangers and from all evil, for eternity. Even though we do not make the petition perfectly, let us force ourselves to make it. Does it cost us anything to ask for a great deal, since we are asking One who is powerful? It would be shameful to ask a great emperor for a penny. But, that we may better succeed, let us leave the giving to his will, since we have already given him ours. May his name ever be glorified in heaven and on earth and may his will be always done in me. Amen.

—From *Way of Perfection* by Saint Teresa of Avila

❧ Let us not be satisfied with just giving money. Money is not enough, money can be got, but they need your hearts to love them. So, spread love everywhere you go: first of all in your own home. Give love to your children, to your wife or husband, to a next-door neighbor.

—From *A Gift for God* by Mother Teresa

❧ Some people came to Calcutta, and before leaving, they begged me: 'Tell us something that will help us to live our lives better.' And I said: 'Smile at each other; smile at your wife, smile at your husband, smile at your children, smile at each other—it doesn't matter who it is—and that will help you to grow up in greater love for each other.' And then one of them asked me: 'Are you married?' and I said: 'Yes, and I find it difficult sometimes to smile at Jesus.' And it is true, Jesus can be very demanding also, and it is at those times when he is so demanding that to give him a big smile is very beautiful.

—From *A Gift for God* by Mother Teresa

Hymn: Love Divine, All Loves Excelling

Love divine, all loves excelling
Joy of heaven, to earth come down;
Fix in us thy humble dwelling;
All thy faithful mercies crown!
Jesus thou art all compassion,
Pure, unbounded love thou art;
Visit us with thy salvation;
Enter every trembling heart.

Breathe, O breathe thy loving spirit
Into every troubled breast!
Let us all in thee inherit;
Let us find that second rest.
Take away our bent to sinning;
Alpha and Omega be;
End of faith, as its beginning,
Set our hearts at liberty.

Come, Almighty to deliver,
Let us all thy life receive;
Suddenly return and never,
Nevermore thy temples leave,
Thee we would be always blessing,
Serve thee as thy hosts above,
Pray and praise thee without ceasing,
Glory in thy perfect love.

Finish, then, thy new creation;
Pure and spotless let us be.
Let us see thy great salvation
Perfectly restored in thee:
Changed from glory into glory,
Till in heaven we take our place,
Till we cast our crowns before thee,
Lost in wonder, love, and praise. Amen.
—Charles Wesley

Sixth Sunday of Easter
27: *Chosen by God*

I. Invocation
    Almighty God, you have created us, called us, chosen us to be your people. We wait now to receive your word of guidance and blessing. Grant unto us ears to hear, eyes to see, and faith to respond to your love and leadership. In the name of Christ. Amen.

II. Psalm 126

III. Daily Scripture Readings
    Monday   Isaiah 63:7-9
    Tuesday   Isaiah 45:1-8
    Wednesday   Genesis 9:8-17
    Thursday   Romans 5:1-11
    Friday   Joel 2:18-27
    Saturday   1 Peter 2:1-10
    Sunday   A. Acts 17:22-31; Psalm 66:8-20;
                   1 Peter 3:13-22; John 14:15-21
                B. Acts 10:44-48; Psalm 98;
                   1 John 5:1-6; John 15:9-17
                C. Acts 15:1-2, 22-29; Psalm 67;
                   Revelation 21:10, 22-27;
                   John 14:23-29

IV. Readings for Reflection

V. Prayers: for the church, for others, for myself

VI. Reflection: silent and written

VII. Hymn: "God, Who Touchest Earth with Beauty"

VIII. Benediction
    May the peace of God fill my heart, mind, and activity all this day long. Amen.

Readings for Reflection

❧ The God-who-is has always been searching for me. By his choice, his relationship with me is presence, as a call, as a guide; he is not satisfied with speaking to me, or showing things to me, or asking things of me. He does much more.

He is Life, and he knows his creature can do nothing without him; he knows his child would die of hunger without bread.

But our bread is God himself, and God gives himself to us as food.

Only eternal life can feed one who is destined for eternal life.

The bread of earth can nourish us only for this finite earth; it can sustain us only as far as the frontier of the Invisible. If we want to penetrate this frontier, the bread from our fields is not sufficient; if we want to march along the roads of the Invisible, we must feed on bread from heaven.

This bread from heaven is God himself. He becomes food to us walking in the Invisible.

—From *The God Who Comes* by Carlo Carretto

❧ Let us, then, take care not to quench the Spirit. All evil actions extinguish this light: slander, offences and the like. The nature of fire is such that everything foreign to it destroys it, and everything akin to it gives it further strength. This light of the Spirit reacts in the same manner.

This is the way in which the spirit of grace manifests itself in Christians. Through repentance and faith it descends into the soul of each man in the sacrament of baptism, or else is restored to him in the sacrament of repentance. The fire of zeal is its essence. But it can take different directions according to the individual. The spirit of grace leads one man to concentrate entirely on his own sanctification by severe ascetic feats, another it guides preeminently to works of charity, another it inspires to devote his life to the good organization of Christian society, and again another it directs to spread the Gospel by preaching:

as for example Apollos, who, burning in spirit, spoke and taught about our Lord (Acts xviii, 25).
—From *The Art of Prayer*

  Ah, Lord God, thou holy Lover of my soul, when thou comest into my soul, all that is within me shall rejoice. Thou art my Glory and the exultation of my heart; thou art my Hope and Refuge in the day of my trouble. Set me free from all evil passions, and heal my heart of all inordinate affections; that, being inwardly cured and thoroughly cleansed, I may be made fit to love, courageous to suffer, steady to persevere. Nothing is sweeter than Love, nothing more courageous, nothing fuller nor better in heaven and earth; because Love is born of God, and cannot rest but in God, above all created things. Let me love thee more than myself, nor love myself but for thee. Amen.
—Thomas à Kempis

  We should try to be so closely united to Our Lord that we reproduce his life in our own, that our thoughts and words and actions should proclaim his teaching, so that he reigns in us, lives in us. He so often enters within us in Holy Communion. May his Kingdom reign in us.

If he sends us happiness let us accept it gratefully. Like the Good Shepherd he sets us in a rich pasture to strengthen us to follow him later into barren lands. If he sends us crosses let us embrace them and say '*Bona Crux*,' for this is the greatest grace of all. It means walking through life hand in hand with our Lord, helping him to carry his Cross like Simon of Cyrene. It is our Beloved asking us to prove how much we love him. Whether in mental suffering or bodily pain 'let us rejoice and tremble with joy.' Our Lord calls us and asks us to tell him of our love and repeat it over and over again all through our sufferings.

Every cross, great or small, even small annoyances, are the voice of the Beloved. He is asking for a declaration of love from us to last whilst the suffering lasts.

Oh, when one thinks of this one would like the suffering to last forever. It will last as long as Our Lord wishes. However sweet the suffering may become to us, we only desire it at such times as Our Lord sends it. Your will be done, my Brother Jesus, and not mine. We long to forget ourselves, we ask nothing, only your glory.

—From *Meditations of a Hermit* by Charles de Foucauld

&. God presents himself to us little by little. The whole story of salvation is the story of the God who comes.

It is always he who comes, even if he has not yet come in his fullness. But there is indeed one unique moment in his coming; the others were only preparations and announcement.

The hour of his coming is the Incarnation.

The Incarnation brings the world his presence. It is a presence so complete that it overshadows every presence before it.

God is made human in Christ. God makes himself present to us with such a special presence, such an obvious presence, as to overthrow all the complicated calculations made about him in the past.

"The invisible, intangible God has made himself visible and tangible in Christ."

If Jesus is truly God, everything is clear; if I cannot believe this, everything darkens again.

—From *The God Who Comes* by Carlo Carretto

&. "There is a dream dreaming us," a Bushman once told Laurens Van der Post. We are part of a dream, according to this, part of a vision. What is more, we can become aware of it. Although we are far removed from the Bushmen and their vision, it seems we can indeed come to a sense of being dreamed, being seen, being known. Our minds' desire is to know, to understand; but our heart's desire is intimacy, to be known, to be understood. To see God with our mind would be to know God, to understand God; but to see God with our heart would be to have a sense of being known by God, of being understood by God.

If there is a dream dreaming us, it will be God's vision of us, and if we have a sense of being part of that dream, it will be our heart's vision of God. Nicholas of Cusa in his *Vision of God*, while speaking of our vision of God, speaks even more of God's vision of us. He has it that our seeing God consists of our having a sense of God seeing us: to see

God is to see one who sees; it is to have an experience of being seen. It is like looking at one of those portraits, he says, where the eyes are so contrived as to follow the beholder wherever he moves. No matter where the beholder stands, the eyes of the portrait seem to be looking at him. Or better, we could say, it is like feeling the gaze of another person, feeling the gaze without seeing the other's eyes. Or it can be like meeting the gaze of another. Or it can even be like looking into the eyes of another and seeing there the pupil, the *pupilla*, the "little doll," the tiny image of oneself reflected in the other's eyes.

—From *The Reasons of the Heart* by John S. Dunne

Hymn: God, Who Touchest Earth with Beauty

God, who touchest earth with beauty,
Make my heart anew;
With thy spirit recreate me,
Pure and strong and true.

Like thy springs and running waters
Make me crystal pure;
Like thy rocks of towering grandeur
Make me strong and sure.

Like thy dancing waves in sunlight
Make me glad and free;
Like the straightness of the pine trees
Let me upright be.

Like the arching of the heavens
Lift my thoughts above;
Turn my dreams to noble action,
Ministries of love.

God, who touchest earth with beauty,
Make my heart anew;
Keep me ever, by thy spirit,
Pure and strong and true. Amen.
—Mary S. Edgar

28: *Life Together*

I.   Invocation
Almighty God, you have called the church into being and have gathered us into one family. By the power of your Holy Spirit help us to live in unity and peace with all of your children. May our actions this day be fruit of our faith in your kingdom. In the name of Christ. Amen.

II. Psalm 133

III. Daily Scripture Readings

Monday	Ephesians 4:1-16
Tuesday	Philemon
Wednesday	1 Corinthians 6:1-10
Thursday	1 Corinthians 3:5-23
Friday	Romans 12:1-21
Saturday	Colossians 3:5-17
Sunday	A. Acts 1:6-14; Psalm 68:1-10; 1 Peter 4:12-14; 5:6-11; John 17:1-11
	B. Acts 1:15-17, 21-26; Psalm 1; 1 John 5:9-13; John 17:11b-19
	C. Acts 16:16-34; Psalm 97; Revelation 22:12-14, 16-17, 20; John 17:20-26

IV. Readings for Reflection

V.   Prayers: for the church, for others, for myself

VI. Reflection: silent and written

VII. Hymn: "O Spirit of the Living God"

VIII. Benediction
Be held in the center of God's will today and know the joy, freedom, and power of walking by faith and in faithfulness. Amen.

Readings for Reflection

&. By way of encouragement, God tells us in scripture: "I will remove the stony heart from their bodies, and replace it with a natural heart . . . " (Ezek. 11:19). But I'm still waiting, asking myself when and how this will happen.

In our community the other day there wasn't much coffee. Coffee does me good down here in the desert . . . it helps me. . . . I am old.

I was worried about not having any, about spending a few hours feeling dull and weak, and so—without perceiving the evil I was doing—I went into the kitchen before the others and drank up all that was left.

Afterwards, having suffered all day and made my confession, I thought in shame of my selfishness, of the ease with which I had excluded my two brothers from those black, bitter remains.

It seems a tiny thing, yet in that cup of coffee, taken and not shared with my brothers, is the root of all the evil which disturbs us, the poison of all the arrogance which selfishness, riches, and power create.

The difference between me and Jesus is right here, in an affair that seems simple but isn't at all; after a whole life time it is still there to make you think. Jesus would have left the coffee for his brothers; I excluded my brothers.

No, it isn't easy to live with hearts like ours: let us confess it.

—From *The God Who Comes* by Carlo Carretto

&. Let him who cannot be alone beware of community. He will only do harm to himself and to the community. Alone you stood before God when he called you; alone you had to answer that call; alone you had to struggle and pray; and alone you will die and give an account to God. You cannot escape from yourself; for God has singled you out. If you refuse to be alone you are rejecting Christ's call to you, and you can have no part in the community of those who are called. "The challenge of death comes to us all, and no one can die for another. Everyone must fight his own battle with death by himself, alone . . . I will not be with you then, nor you with me" (Luther).

But the reverse is also true: Let him who is not in community beware of being alone. Into the community you were called, the call was not meant for you alone; in the community of the called you bear your cross, you struggle, you pray. You are not alone, even in death, and on the Last Day you will be only one member of the great congregation of Jesus Christ. If you scorn the fellowship of the brethren, you reject the call of Jesus Christ, and thus your solitude can only be hurtful to you. "If I die, then I am not alone in death; if I suffer they [the fellowship] suffer with me" (Luther).
—From *Life Together* by Dietrich Bonhoeffer

&. An ancient saying suggested that there are two wings by which we rise, one being personal piety and the other community charity. No one can fly by flapping only one wing. It is impossible to be sincere in our worship of God without expecting to do the will of God. It is equally impossible to do the full will of God without the guidance and empowerment of a vital personal relationship with God. As Allan Hunter has said, "Those who picket should also pray, and those who pray should also picket." The same combination of devotional vitality and social action is also emphasized in the two great commandments of Jesus—to love God with all one's being and to love other persons as ourselves (Matt. 22:36-40).
—From *Liberation of Life* by Harvey and Lois Seifert

&. To make way for a new birth of authentic being, we are not only willing, but even eager to give up present habits and imperfections and prejudices. No matter how far we have moved in the Christian life, we can still know that every opinion we hold and every act we perform is something less than the best. We never have the Holy Spirit in our pockets, completely domesticated and supporting everything we are doing. Any such sanctifying of present imperfections is an obstacle to further growth. Instead of clutching fiercely to my foibles and fallacies, I had better cultivate the ability to change my mind, my political opinions, and my lifestyle when it becomes clear that this is the will of God.
—From *Liberation of Life* by Harvey and Lois Seifert

❧ An old rabbi was once asked why so few people were finding God. He wisely replied that people are not willing to look that low. Jesus was born in a stable, and God is especially concerned for the poorest, the lowliest, the lost, and the neglected.
—From *Liberation of Life* by Harvey and Lois Seifert

❧ Here is the miracle of love: to discover that all creation is one, flung out into space by a God who is a Father, and that if you present yourself to it as he does—unarmed, and full of peace—creation will recognize you and meet you with a smile.

This is a principle of nonviolence, and I should like to recommend it to you with all the enthusiasm of which I am capable.

I have you not to speak over much of poverty today. Your environment is too ambiguous in its regard, and it is too difficult to explain your position in your bourgeois and socialist milieu. Instead, I tell you this, and I tell you most emphatically: Speak of nonviolence, be apostles of nonviolence, become nonviolent.

Now is the hour to do so, in fact it may be the last hour, in as much as you are all sitting on top of a stockpile of bombs, and you can blow up at any moment now.
—From *I, Francis* by Carlo Carretto

❧ There are certain personal attitudes and feelings that contribute to creative relationships with others. They include, for one thing, warm acceptance and understanding instead of rejection or hostility. Even when we disagree with or regret the action of another, we can emphasize "I still love you," instead of "You really were a fool." When disagreement is called for, we can be honest and open instead of masked and hidden. Instead of remaining silent, we can speak out when a different position needs to be expressed. But such a reaction can be held within a framework of basic support for the other. We can help others feel that we are still on their side when it comes to appreciating and encouraging them as persons.
—From *Liberation of Life* by Harvey and Lois Seifert

᪥ In an atmosphere of security and trust, persons are likely to be more ready to change. The child who trusts the mother lets go and takes the first unaided step. A social prophet is better received when listeners have learned to appreciate his or her integrity and friendship. Healthy growth more easily takes place when all participants interact in a mutually supportive environment rather than when some manipulate others to secure the ends of the manipulators.

—From *Liberation of Life* by Harvey and Lois Seifert

᪥ This internalizing of openness to God and concern for neighbors is what it means to *be* a Christian, rather than simply to *act like* a Christian. That the church can produce this kind of person is a persuasive recommendation for the church.

Within the fellowship of the church, we help one another become such Christians. Here we can become comrades of our better selves. We support one another in our highest resolves. An entire searching congregation turns our attention to the liberation of unrealized possibilities as we respond to the upward call of God. Even one other person or a small subgroup within the church can sustain our determination to spend more time at devotions and to act differently in society.

In such a combination, we are to love both God and neighbor. We cannot fully do either without the other. We reach the ecstatic heights of a devotional life only as we also act creatively in society. Full creativity as consumer, worker, citizen, and friend is possible only with the vision and power that comes from vital devotion. To "turn on" is to "turn up" toward God and to "turn out" toward neighbor. The two wings of soaring, liberated life are indeed devotion and action.

—From *Liberation of Life* by Harvey and Lois Seifert

᪥ Without the solitude of heart, the intimacy of friendship, marriage and community life cannot be creative. Without the solitude of heart, our relationships with others easily become needy and greedy, sticky and clinging, dependent and sentimental, exploitative and parasitic, because without the solitude of heart we cannot experience the others as different from ourselves but only as people

who can be used for the fulfillment of our own, often hidden, needs.
—From *Reaching Out* by Henri J. M. Nouwen

Hymn: O Spirit of the Living God

O Spirit of the Living God,
Thou light and fire divine,
Descend upon thy Church once more,
And make it truly thine!
Fill it with love and joy and power,
With righteousness and peace,
Till Christ shall dwell in human hearts,
And sin and sorrow cease.

Blow, wind of God! With wisdom blow
Until our minds are free
From mists of error, clouds of doubt,
Which blind our eyes to thee!
Burn, winged fire! Inspire our lips
With flaming love and zeal,
To preach to all thy great good news,
God's glorious commonweal!

Teach us to utter living words
Of truth which all may hear,
The language we all understand
When love speaks loud and clear;
Till every age and race and clime
Shall blend their creeds in one,
And earth shall form one brotherhood
By whom thy will is done.

So shall we know the power of him
Who came us all to save.
So shall we rise with him to life
Which soars beyond the grave;
And earth shall win true holiness,
Which makes thy children whole,
Till, perfected by thee, we reach
Creation's glorious goal! Amen.
—Henry H. Tweedy

Pentecost Sunday
29: *The Church of the Spirit*

I. Invocation
    Almighty God, send your Holy Spirit upon us so
    that we may perfectly love you and faithfully fol-
    low you today and always. In the name and spirit of
    Christ. Amen.

II. Psalm 107

III. Daily Scripture Readings
Monday	Acts 2:43-47
Tuesday	Acts 3:1-10
Wednesday	Acts 4:32-37
Thursday	Zechariah 4:1 -10
Friday	Ephesians 4:17–5:2
Saturday	Romans 8:1-17

    Sunday A. Acts 2:1-21; Psalm 104:24-34;
    1 Corinthians 12:3b-13; John 20:19-23
    B. Ezekiel 37:1-14; Psalm 104:24-34;
    Romans 8:22-27; John 16:4b-15
    C. Acts 2:1-21; Psalm 104:24-34;
    Romans 8:14-17; John 14:8-17, 25-27

IV. Readings for Reflection

V. Prayers: for the church, for others, for myself

VI. Reflection: silent and written

VII. Hymn: "Spirit of God, Descend upon My Heart"

VIII. Benediction
    Be filled with hope, joy, and peace by the power of
    the Holy Spirit. Amen.

Readings for Reflection

   That structural position in the Church which the humblest Christian occupies is eternal and even cosmic. The Church will outlive the universe; in it the individual person will outlive the universe. Everything that is joined to the immortal Head will share his immortality. We hear little of this from the Christian pulpit to-day. What has come of our silence may be judged from the fact that recently addressing the Forces on this subject, I found that one of my audience regarded this doctrine as "theosophical." If we do not believe it let us be honest and relegate the Christian faith to museums. If we do, let us give up the pretence that it makes no difference. For this is the real answer to every excessive claim made by the collective. It is mortal; we shall live for ever. There will come a time when every culture, every institution, every nation, the human race, all biological life, is extinct, and every one of us is still alive. Immortality is promised to us, not to these generalities. It was not for societies or states that Christ died, but for men. In that sense Christianity must seem to secular collectivists to involve an almost frantic assertion of individuality. But then it is not the individual as such who will share Christ's victory over death. We shall share the victory by being the Victor. A rejection, or in Scripture's strong language, a crucifixion of the natural self is the passport to everlasting life. Nothing that has not died will be resurrected.

—From *The Weight of Glory* by C. S. Lewis

   So the Church is not to be understood primarily as a means to the end of transforming society. This would be to trample over the uniqueness and infinite worth to God of the Christian community. Besides, the amazing and profound fact is that the Church most transforms society when it is itself growing and being perfected in the love of Christ. In fact when the Church is taken merely as a means to transform society, very little is accomplished. For in that case the uniqueness of the Church is denied and we enter the battle on the same terms as secular and godless forces. We assume the battle for right and justice can be won by force, by technique, by doing. It can't. These very clearly are not the weapons of Christian warfare (Eph. 6:10-20). Truly Christian transformation of culture comes through Christlike (and hence sacrificial) love, community and being.

But this fact by no means cancels out the responsibility to do, to act, to walk in the words of God. Rather, the being and the doing go together. The being is fundamental, but the doing is the natural result.

—From *The Community of the King* by Howard A. Snyder

ৰ্ই If Jesus Christ actually gave more time to preparing a community of disciples than to proclaiming the good news (which he did), then the contemporary church must also recognize the importance of community for proclamation. I would emphasize the priority of community in two directions: in relation to the individual believer and in relation to witness.

In the first place community is important for the individual believer. Mainline Protestantism, from its structures to its hymns and gospel songs, has emphasized the individual over the community. It has had a keen sense of the individual person's responsibility before God but little corresponding sense of the communal life of the Christian. Too often the Church has been seen more as a mere collection of saved souls than as a community of interacting personalities. Christian growth has been a matter of individual soul culture rather than the building of the community of the Spirit. Saints who lived isolated, solitary lives were often placed on a pedestal above those whose lives were spent in true community. These tendencies, of course, were part of Protestantism's pre-Reformation heritage.

But four biblical truths should call us back to the priority of community: (1) the concept of the people of God, (2) the model of Christ with his disciples, (3) the example of the early church, and (4) the explicit teachings of Jesus and the apostles.

—From *The Community of the King* by Howard A. Snyder

ৰ্ই The Spirit is thus the earthly presence of the glorified Lord. In the Spirit Christ becomes Lord of his Church, and in the Spirit the resurrected Lord acts both in the community and in the individual. The power of his resurrection is more than a power of ecstasy and miracle; it produces a

new creation. The Spirit opens up for the believer the way to the saving action of God in Christ. He does this not as a magic power which man cannot resist; he creates the possibility of man's replying with a responsible and conscious affirmative. He gives him, through the knowledge of the crucified Christ, the realization that in Jesus Christ God acted for him. The Spirit gives faith in the cross and resurrection of Christ and gives the power to live a life of faith. He is the "spirit of faith" (II Cor. 4:13; cf. II Cor. 5:5, 7). The Spirit is not man's own potential, but entirely the gift, the power and strength of God. The Holy Spirit, as *God's* Spirit, must be distinguished from *man's* own spirit, since he is the *Holy* Spirit, free from all sin. The Holy Spirit is always entirely God's Spirit and is not absorbed into the individual spirit of man (cf. Rom 8:16; I Cor. 2:10 f.). At the same time, God's Spirit can win power and dominion over man, so that he becomes man's inner self, so that a man no longer lives by his own strength, but by God's (cf. Rom. 8:9-15, 26 f.). In this way God's Spirit does not work, as in the gnostic view, as an automatically divinizing substance. The Spirit is the power which creates faith, and the norm according to which the believer is constantly summoned to live: "If we live by the Spirit, let us also walk by the Spirit" (Gal. 5:25; cf. 6:8).
—From *The Church* by Hans Küng

&. The Church on its pilgrimage is not deserted or forgotten by God; it is not wandering totally in the dark. Even though it is not the kingdom of God which is to come, it is already under the reign of God which has begun; though looking forward to the final victory of the reign of God, it can look back to the decisive victory: in Jesus the Christ; while still wandering in the shadow of death, it has the resurrection not only ahead of it, but in its decisive form behind it: in Jesus the risen Kyrios. This living Kyrios is with it, remains with it, all days until the consummation of the world, until the coming of the kingdom of God in glory. Until that time it is under the reign of this Kyrios, the reign of Christ, which will also continue until the coming of the reign of God. The reign of Christ, the hidden ruler of the whole world, is already effective in the Church: in the preaching of the word, which already has power to forgive sins, to renew men and so to proclaim the consummation of all things; in the giving of baptism, a visible sign and action which makes men members of the eschatological community, in which the old man is buried in penance and the new man arises in faith to become part of the new creation; in the celebration of the Lord's Supper which proclaims and represents the eschatological meal of salvation in the glory of the Father and is shared by the heirs of God's kingdom until the Lord comes again. The Church has already been granted the Holy Spirit, if only as a guarantee. So at work in the Church, though constantly in jeopardy, is the love which will remain with it and in it always.

—From *The Church* by Hans Küng

❧ It is possible either to sustain and strengthen this burning of the spirit, or to quench it. It is warmed above all by acts of love towards God and our neighbour—this, indeed, is the essence of the spiritual life—by a general fidelity to all God's commandments, with a quiet conscience, by deeds that are pitiless to our own soul and body, and by prayer and thoughts of God. The spirit is quenched by distraction of the attention from God and God's works, by excessive anxiety about worldly matters, by indulgence in sensual pleasure, by pandering to carnal desires, and by infatuation with material things. If this spirit is quenched, then the Christian life will be quenched too.

—From *The Art of Prayer*

❧ Cast aside everything that might extinguish this small flame which is beginning to burn within you, and surround yourself with everything which can feed and fan it into a strong fire. Isolate yourself, pray, think over for yourself what you should do. The order of life, of occupation and work, which you forced yourself to adopt when you were seeking for grace, is also the most helpful in prolonging within you the action of grace which has now begun. What you need most in your present position is solitude, prayer, and meditation. Your solitude must become more collected, your prayer deeper, and your meditation more forceful.

How did our ascetics, fathers, and teachers warm the spirit of prayer inwardly, and establish themselves firmly in prayer? Their great object was to make the heart burn unceasingly towards the Lord alone. God claims the heart because within it lies the source of life. Where the heart is, there is consciousness, attention, mind; there is the whole soul.

—From *The Art of Prayer*

Hymn: Spirit of God, Descend upon My Heart

Spirit of God, descend upon my heart;
Wean it from earth;
Through all its pulses move;
Stoop to my weakness,
Mighty as thou art,
And make me love thee as I ought to love.

I ask no dream, no prophet ecstasies,
No sudden rending of the veil of clay,
No angel visitant, no opening skies;
But take the dimness of my soul away.

Hast thou not bid me love thee, God and King?
All, all thine own, soul, heart and strength and mind.
I see thy cross;
There teach my heart to cling:
O let me seek thee, and O let me find!

Teach me to feel that thou art always nigh;
Teach me the struggles of the soul to bear,
To check the rising doubt, the rebel sigh;
Teach me the patience of unanswered prayer.

Teach me to love thee as thine angels love,
One holy passion filling all my frame
The kindling of the heaven-descended Dove,
My heart an altar, and thy love the flame. Amen.
—George Croly

30: The Triune God

I. Invocation
Almighty God, you have made yourself known to us as Father, Son, and Holy Spirit. Make yourself known to us in such a way that we may understand your will and purpose for our lives today. We offer our prayers in the name and spirit of Christ. Amen.

II. Psalm 150

III. Daily Scripture Readings

Monday		Deuteronomy 6:4-25
Tuesday		John 5:19-47
Wednesday		1 Corinthians 12:1-11
Thursday		Ephesians 1:3-14
Friday		Ephesians 3:14-20
Saturday		Colossians 2:1-15
Sunday	A.	Deuteronomy 4:32-40; Psalm 33:1-12; 2 Corinthians 13:5-14; Matthew 28:16-20
	B.	Isaiah 6:1-8; Psalm 29; Romans 8:12-17; John 3:1-17
	C.	Proverbs 8:22-31; Psalm 8; Romans 5:1-5; John 16:12-15

IV. Readings for Reflection

V. Prayers: for the church, for others, for myself

VI. Reflection: silent and written

VII. Hymn: "Joyful, Joyful, We Adore Thee"

VIII. Benediction
May Christ be made known to you and through you today. Amen.

Readings for Reflection

❧ *The Spirit as an eschatological gift.* In the messianic time of salvation, according to the prophetic expectation of salvation, not only individual prophets and wise men, warriors, singers and kings, were to be fulfilled by the spirit of God, by God's creating power and strength of life; it was to be given to the whole people.

"For I will pour water on thirsty land, and streams on the dry ground; I will pour my Spirit upon your descendants and my blessing on your offspring" (Is. 44:3; cf. 63:14). "And I will put my spirit within you, and cause you to walk in my statutes and be careful to observe my ordinances" (Ez. 36:27; cf. Zech. 4:6).

The early Christian communities, the Pauline communities as well as that in Jerusalem, saw the expectation of the prophets as having been fulfilled in reality. The pouring out of the Spirit is the signal for the beginning of the eschatological event—the pouring out of the Spirit upon *all* mankind: on sons and on daughters, on old men and young men, on menservants and maidservants, as well as on their masters (Joel 2:28 f.). Spirit in this context, in the Old and New Testament alike, is not used, as the word often was, in the sense of breath, or angel or demon (or ghost or spirit of the departed), nor in the sense of soul or source of life, nor in the sense of the seat of knowledge and volition, the living ego of a man. No, in this context the Spirit of *God* is referred to, the *Holy* Spirit; its holiness separates it distinctly from the spirit of man and of the world. This Spirit is not some magical, mysteriously supernatural aura of a dynamistic kind, nor a magical being of an animistic kind, but God himself in his especially personal and self-giving aspect: as a power which creates life. The Spirit is God himself, a merciful power establishing his reign over man's heart, over the whole of man, inwardly present to man and apparent in his workings to man's human spirit.

—From *The Church* by Hans Küng

❧ The Spirit works *where* he wills. The Spirit of God cannot be restricted in his operation by the Church; he is at work not only in the offices of the Church, but where he wills: in the whole people of God. He is at work not only in the "holy city," but where he wills: in all the churches of the one Church. He is at work not only in the Catholic Church, but where he wills: in Christianity as a whole. And finally he is at work not only in Christianity, but where he wills: in the whole world.

The power of the Spirit of God can pass through *all* walls, even church walls. It is true that the Holy Spirit has his dwelling and his temple in the Church, which he fills and which he governs. Here his power is especially revealed, since in the Church and through the Church the word of God is preached and his sacraments are administered. But the Spirit of God, if domiciled in the Church, is not domesticated in it. He is and remains the free Spirit of the free Lord not only of the "holy city", not only of Church offices, not only of the Catholic Church, not only of Christians, but of the whole world. . . .

The Spirit is at work *when* he wills. The Spirit of God is not, of course, a Spirit of arbitrariness or apparent freedom, but of real freedom; he is a Spirit of order, not chaos; peace, not contradictions, in the Church as well as in the world. This is what Paul had to remind the Corinthians, who, proud of their spiritual gifts, had neglected order in the Church: "God is not a God of confusion but of peace" (I Cor. 14:33). Arbitrariness, disorder and chaos in the Church cannot be the work of the Holy Spirit.

At the same time, God's Spirit does not blow when he *must*, but only when he *wills*. No decrees of the Church, in doctrine or practice, can force him to act or not to act at a given time. True, God is absolutely free, and is thus free even with regard to his freedom.

—From *The Church* by Hans Küng

❧ God himself must free the man who is unfree and incapable of winning his own freedom, must free him for freedom. He can turn "slaves of sin" into "slaves of God," who have been "set free from sin" (Rom. 6:20, 22). God does this for the man who believes, whether Jew or Gentile, through his eschatological act of salvation in Jesus Christ. In Christ, the new free man, God promised and revealed and created the way to a new and true freedom. Sinful man thinks he can find freedom by self-confidently controlling himself and his own life. But he is warned that he can only win freedom by abdicating this control to another—not to men, who would reduce him to the rank of a slave, but to God, who will accept him as his child. To be able to do what one wants is only the appearance of freedom; true freedom is to will what God does.

—From *The Church* by Hans Küng

  {} God, Creator and Author of Life, warned anew of the threats to human survival, we confess that the way we live and order society sets us against one another and alienates us from your creation, exploiting as though dead, things to which you have given life. Separated from you we live in emptiness. We long in our own lives for a new spirituality of intention, thought, and action. Help us to struggle to conserve the earth for future generations, and free us to share together, that all may be free.

God of love, who through Jesus Christ shares our suffering, forgives our sins, and delivers from the bondage of oppression, help us to desire and nourish in ourselves sustaining community with our brothers and sisters everywhere. Give us courage to share suffering when it comes. Restore to us the joy of Resurrection, that in the midst of situations we can hardly bear we may sing out:

Hallelujah

God of hope, whose spirit gives light and power to your people, empower us to witness to your name in all the nations, to struggle for your own justice against all principalities and powers and to persevere with faith and humor in the tasks that you have given to us. Without you we are powerless. Therefore we cry together:

Maranatha

—From *Visions of a World Hungry* by Thomas G. Pettepiece

  {} The catechism is not enough, theology is not enough, formulas are not enough to explain the Unity and Trinity of God.

We need loving communication, we need the presence of the Spirit.

That is why I do not believe in theologians who do not pray, who are not in humble communication of love with God.

Neither do I believe in the existence of any human power to pass on authentic knowledge of God.

Only God can speak about himself, and only the Holy Spirit, who is love, can communicate this knowledge to us.

When there is a crisis in the Church, it is always here: a crisis of contemplation.

The Church wants to feel able to explain about her spouse even when she has lost sight of him; even when, although she has not been divorced, she no longer knows his embrace, because curiosity has gotten the better of her and she has gone searching for other people and other things.

The revelation of a triune God in the unity of a single nature, the revelation of a divine Holy Spirit present in us, is not on the human level; it does not belong to the realm of reason. It is a personal communication which God alone can give, and the task of giving it belongs to the Holy Spirit, who is the same love which unites the Father and the Son.

The Holy Spirit is the fullness and the joy of God.

It is so difficult to speak of these things. We have to babble like children, but at least, like children, we can say over and over again, tirelessly, "Spirit of God, reveal yourself to me, your child."

—From *The God Who Comes* by Carlo Carretto

ᏋᏗ Christian prayer rests upon the irreversible fact of the self-revelation of God in Jesus Christ and its confirmation in our hearts by the Holy Spirit. The Holy Trinity is the basis of true prayer as well as its goal. Prayer, as biblical faith understands it, is made possible by the triune God and is directed to this God.

To gain a true awareness of the depth and breadth of Christian prayer, it is necessary to understand something of the nature of the God who originates such prayer. This God is first of all a Personal Spirit who is self-sustaining and who is the ground of everything that is. He not only exists but he also coexists as a Trinity. He is capable of having fellowship with humanity because he has fellowship within himself. He is capable of caring because he embodies love within himself.

The God of the Bible is a living God, not a philosophical first principle or a moral ideal. As the psalmist expresses it, "He who planted the ear, does he not hear? He who formed the eye, does he not see?" (Ps. 94:9). He is not divinity in the abstract, but a divine person. He is supremely personal, yet he infinitely transcends human personhood. He is a personal-infinite God (Francis Schaeffer), who is at the same time all-powerful and all-loving. He is a gregarious God, seeking to include man in fellowship with himself. Such a God can be approached in prayer because he not only can hear but also has the power to act on the requests of his children.

The biblical picture of God as "heavenly Father" reinforces the idea that he is loving and caring. We do not ask as beggars but as sons and daughters, since he is the Father of all by creation and the Father of Christians in particular by adoption. God is also likened in the Bible to a divine Mother who seeks to gather her children together as a hen would gather her brood under her wings (Matt. 23:37).

In the Christian tradition, some mystics have sought to transcend the Trinity by positing a "God above God," an infinite abyss that lies beyond personality and diversity. The God that is thus depicted is incontestably other than the God of Abraham, Isaac, and Jacob: he resembles more the Prime Mover or Infinite One of Hellenistic philosophy. Such a God transcends pity as well as anger. He is infinitely removed from temporality as well as materiality. This is the God described by the seventeenth-century mystical poet, Angelus Silesius: "How often have I prayed 'Lord do your will'. . . . But see: He does no willing—motionless he is and still." Far from being a static absolute beyond history, the God of the Bible is living and dynamic will who enters into history in order to have fellowship with his people.

—From *The Struggle of Prayer* by Donald G. Bloesch

Hymn: Joyful, Joyful, We Adore Thee

Joyful, joyful, we adore thee,
God of glory, Lord of love;
Hearts unfold like flowers before thee,
Opening to the sun above.
Melt the clouds of sin and sadness;
Drive the dark of doubt away;
Giver of immortal gladness,
Fill us with the light of day!

All thy works with joy surround thee,
Earth and heav'n reflect thy rays,
Stars and angels sing around thee,
Center of unbroken praise;
Field and forest, vale and mountain,
Flowery meadow, flashing sea,
Chanting bird and flowing fountain,
Call us to rejoice in thee.

Thou art giving and forgiving,
Ever blessing, ever blest,
Well-spring of the joy of living,
Ocean-depth of happy rest!
Thou our Father, Christ our brother,
All who live in love are thine;
Teach us how to love each other,
Lift us to the joy divine.
—Henry Van Dyke

Sunday between May 29 and June 4*
  (if after Trinity Sunday—otherwise turn to next Sunday)

31: Mercy, Justice, and Love

I. Invocation
    Lord God, creator and redeemer, claim my life and
    ministry for your high and holy purpose. Help me
    to remain faithful and steadfast all day long, and
    when evening comes grant a peaceful rest in your
    presence. In the name of Jesus. Amen.

II. Psalm 103

III. Daily Scripture Readings
Monday	1 Peter 2:21-25
Tuesday	James 5:13-20
Wednesday	Acts 28:7-10
Thursday	Acts 3:1-10
Friday	Acts 9:32-42
Saturday	Acts 16:11-18

Sunday
A. Genesis 12:1-9; Psalm 33:12-22;
    Romans 3:21-28; Matthew 7:21-29
B. 1 Samuel 16:1-13; Psalm 20;
    2 Corinthians 4:5-12; Mark 2:23–3:6
C. 1 Kings 8:22-23, 41-43; Psalm 100;
    Galatians 1:1-10; Luke 7:1-10

IV. Readings for Reflection

V. Prayers: for the church, for others, for myself

VI. Reflection: silent and written

VII. Hymn: "Oh Thou, in Whose Presence"

VIII. Benediction
    Almighty and merciful God, surround your servants
    with peace and power all day long and bring us at
    last to life abundant and eternal. Amen.

**If the Sunday between May 24 and 28 follows Trinity Sunday, use Week
14.*

Readings for Reflection

&. Then we come to understand the dimensions of heaven; then we see things as they really are, and we see God as really God!

But then, too, we realize that this cannot last, that in order to keep its gratuitous quality, the fragrance of that hour must be paid for in a harsh and severe way.

Perhaps because it would all be too beautiful?

Perhaps because contemplation would destroy the roots of action?

Perhaps because you would never again get anything done, as though you were on too perfect a honeymoon?

Perhaps because heaven would start here and now, whereas the way is still long, and possession of the Beloved is feeble?

Yes, all this and many other things are true.

But there is one other thing which seems to me still more true, and I understood it only very late:

You would not be free any longer.

And God is terribly concerned about your freedom in loving him.

He knows that you can be suffocated by the greatness and the quantity of his gifts.

It is difficult to make a marriage between two persons who are in such different circumstances.

He brings you his all, while you can only bring him your nothing.

How can one set about reconciling such differences?

How can he be certain that you are not seeking him out of self-interest?

That you are not going to him only because you have found no one else?

That you are not going to him for the pleasure you get out of it?

That would be too easy and too shallow a love.

When the Bible says that God is a jealous God, it is speaking truly.

But God's jealousy is not like ours. He is jealous because he is afraid that, instead of loving him in his naked being, we love his creation, his riches, his gifts, the joy he bestows, the peace he brings, and the truth he makes us a present of.

God is not only jealous in his love. He is tragic. Before making you his, before letting himself be possessed, he tears you to shreds—rather, he makes history tear you to shreds. . . .

For much of my life, I asked myself why God acted in such a strange way.

Why is he silent so long? Why is faith so bitter?

He can do everything, so why does he not reveal himself to us in a more sensational way?

What would it cost him to come out into the streets, among those who cry "God does not exist," give a hard slap to the noisiest, and say—better still, shout—"Don't believe these fools! I am here indeed! To convince you, let's make an appointment to meet tomorrow evening in Leningrad's museum of atheism. You'll see what I'll do! I'll crush you and reduce you to souvenir envelopes!"

But it seems that God does his best to remain silent, as if to demonstrate that he does not exist, that it is useless for us to follow him, that we would do better if we went all out to possess the earth.

And are there not those who, when faced with his silence, convince themselves that he does not exist? And are there not others who are scandalized merely by the way the world goes?

If God exists, why evil? If God is love, why sorrow?

If God is a Father, why death?

If I have knocked, why has he not opened to me?

I used to think all this and more, when I was new to this school.

But then, walking patiently, not allowing myself to become frightened off by the first difficulties, hounding his door with the determination of a man on a hunger strike, and, above all, believing his gospel true and unrelenting, I began to see the way things are, I began to discover how God goes about what he is doing, I began to distinguish his stealthy footsteps. . . .

It was for him to open it, not me, always in a hurry.

Sin lies in Adam's haste, and my lust for possession is stronger than my true love for him. Wait! Oh, the anguish of that "wait," the emptiness of that absence!

But then, little by little, I began to understand, as never before, that he was present in the emptiness, in the waiting.
—From *The God Who Comes* by Carlo Carretto

❧ The great illusion of leadership is to think that man can be led out of the desert by someone who has never been there. Our lives are filled with examples which tell us that leadership asks for understanding and that understanding requires sharing. So long as we define leadership in terms of preventing or establishing precedents, or in terms of being responsible for some kind of abstract "general good," we have forgotten that no God can save us except a suffering God, and that no man can lead his people except the man who is crushed by its sins. Personal concern means making Mr. Harrison the only one who counts, the one for whom I am willing to forget my many other obligations, my scheduled appointments and long-prepared meetings, not because they are not important but because they lose their urgency in the face of Mr. Harrison's agony. Personal concern makes it possible to experience that going after the "lost sheep" is really a service to those who were left alone.

Many will put their trust in him who went all the way, out of concern for just one of them. The remark "He really cares for us" is often illustrated by stories which show that forgetting the many for the one is a sign of true leadership.

It is not just curiosity which makes people listen to a preacher when he speaks directly to a man and a woman whose marriage he blesses or to the children of the man whom he buries in the ground. They listen in the deep-seated hope that a personal concern might give the preacher words that carry beyond the ears of those whose joy or suffering he shares. Few listen to a sermon which is intended to be applicable to everyone, but most pay careful attention to words born out of concern for only a few.

All this suggests that when one has the courage to enter where life is experienced as most unique and most private, one touches the soul of the community. The man who has spent many hours trying to understand, feel, and clarify the alienation and confusion of one of his fellow men might well be the best equipped to speak to the needs of the many, because all men are one at the well-spring of pain and joy.

This is what Carl Rogers pointed out when he wrote: ". . . I have—found that the very feeling which has seemed to me most private, most personal and hence most incomprehensible by others, has turned out to be an expression for which there is a resonance in many other people. It has led me to believe that what is most personal and unique in each one of us is probably the very element which would, if it were shared or expressed, speak most deeply to others. This has helped me to understand artists and poets who have dared to express the unique in themselves." It indeed seems that the Christian leader is first of all the artist who can bind together many people by his courage in giving expression to his most personal concern.
—From *The Wounded Healer* by Henri J. M. Nouwen

Hymn: O Thou, in Whose Presence

O Thou, in whose presence my soul takes delight,
On whom in affliction I call,
My comfort by day and my song in the night,
My hope, my salvation, my all!

Where dost thou, dear Shepherd, resort with thy sheep,
To feed them in pastures of love?
Say, why in the valley of death should I weep,
Or alone in this wilderness rove?

O why should I wander, an alien from thee,
Or cry in the desert for bread?
Thy foes will rejoice when my sorrows they see,
And smile at the tears I have shed.

Restore, my dear Savior, the light of thy face;
Thy soul-cheering comfort impart;
And let the sweet tokens of pardoning grace
Bring joy to my desolate heart.

He looks! and ten thousands of angels rejoice,
And myriads wait for his word;
He speaks! and eternity, filled with his voice,
Reechoes the praise of the Lord. Amen.
—Joseph Swain

32: God's Gracious Love

I. Invocation
Loving God, clothe me in yourself and enable me to live and serve after the pattern of Jesus. Amen.

II. Psalm 51

III. Daily Scripture Readings
Monday		Luke 15:1-10
Tuesday		Acts 3:17-26
Wednesday		Ephesians 2:1-10
Thursday		Romans 6:1-14
Friday		Luke 7:36-50
Saturday		John 4:7-42
Sunday	A.	Genesis 22:1-18; Psalm 13; Romans 4:13-18; Matthew 9:9-13
	B.	1 Samuel 16:14-23; Psalm 57; 2 Corinthians 4:13–5:1; Mark 3:20-35
	C.	1 Kings 17:17-24; Psalm 113; Galatians 1:11-24; Luke 7:11-17

IV. Readings for Reflection

V. Prayers: for the church, for others, for myself

VI. Reflection: silent and written

VII. Hymn: "Come Down, O Love Divine"

VIII. Benediction
Go forth with the calm assurance that the unparalleled love of God surrounds, upholds, and preserves your life and ministry. Amen.

Readings for Reflection

   ᢀ Pastors also need to take courage and share boldly and tenderly. People need the truth. It does them no good to remain ignorant. They need the freedom that comes through the grace of simplicity. And if we are to bring the whole counsel of God, we must give attention to these issues that enslave people so savagely. Martin Luther is reported to have said, "If you preach the Gospel in all aspects with the exception of the issues which deal specifically with your time you are not preaching the Gospel at all." Given the contemporary milieu, several dimensions of simplicity seem to me to need careful attention in the teaching ministry of the Church.

We must boldly teach the essential connection between the inner and outer aspects of simplicity. We can no longer allow people to engage in pious exercises that are divorced from the hard social realities of life. Nor can we tolerate a radical social witness that is devoid of inward spiritual vitality. Our preaching and teaching needs to hold these elements in unity. If our teaching is centered in the biblical text, we will find literally hundreds of examples—from Abraham to St. John, from the wisdom literature to the apocalyptic writings.

—From *Freedom of Simplicity* by Richard J. Foster

   ᢀ Any good gardener knows that beautiful roses require careful pruning. Pieces of living plant have to die. It cannot just grow wild. We cannot simply "celebrate growth." It is more than to be regretted, it is tragic that we seem to have lost the insight that growth in Christ requires careful pruning. Pieces of us by our intentional action need to die if we are to become the person that is in God's vision. We are not cutting away a cancerous growth, but making room for intended growth. Mortification refers to that intentional action of pruning of life that better life might grow by God's grace—just as better roses grow by God's grace.

Undoubtedly there have been people who have thought that by mortifying themselves they earned merit with God. . . . There is always this temptation. For Becket it was to die that he might be remembered as a great martyr. In Eliot's play

Becket found the *right* reason for being martyred. Similarly, finding the wrong reasons for mortification does not mean there are no right reasons. One right reason for mortification is to remind us of our humanity—what is and what might be—as the court jesters did for the kings of old.

Mortification is the intentional denial of legitimate pleasures in the spirit of Christian poverty that one might become more human. In my tradition Lent has long been considered a time for mortification, although one would not use such a "medieval" word. We gave up eating desserts, going to movies, or telling dirty jokes, all of which in the face of world problems seemed rather trivial. Once rendered silly, we dismissed the idea of "giving up" and talked of "taking on." What we failed to understand was that a life incapable of significant sacrifice is also incapable of courageous action.
—From *Spirituality for Ministry* by Urban T. Holmes III

❧ You have more wealth than before, and you talk more of poverty. You are middle class and you play "poor Church." You talk more of community, and you live more isolated, more divorced, from one another.

"Many a slip 'twixt the cup and the lip," they say—and there is a whole ocean of slips between what you say and what you do.

It is the ocean of your chatter, and you are drowning in it in every regard.

Now would you care to know why I am not inclined to give you a "tough talking-to?" Because you are the tough ones, not I.

All one has to do is to listen to you when you gather together.

It is a terrible thing, how hard, unyielding, and radical you are.

What a pity that this hardness, this radicalism, is always directed against others and never against yourselves.

One would say that your great passion is to convert others!

And I, Francis, tell you, aim at your own conversions. You will see that you will understand things better.

Above all, understand this: it is of no use to think you can change the Franciscans, the Capuchins, and Conventuals, and to continue, the Jesuits, the Salesians, the Little Brothers.

It is simply not possible!

What is possible is the conversion of a person—especially if that person happens to be you who are listening to me at this moment.

History has its own laws, and no institution escapes the ravages of time, however holy and great its founder.

Only naked human beings, as naked as possible, can escape the ravages of time, and are able to place themselves before the nakedness of the Gospel and make it their own.

My children—this is what I shall call you, since you call me Father Francis—do not believe in the reform of your Order. Believe in your personal reform.

My brothers and sisters—for you call me Friar Francis—be holy, and the world will appear to you as holy.
—From *I, Francis* by Carlo Carretto

&. For the Desert Fathers, the flight to the desert was a way of escaping conformity to the world. The world, including the Church, had become so dominated by secular materialism that, for them, the only way to witness against it was to withdraw from it. Thomas Merton writes in the introduction to his *Wisdom of the Desert*, "Society . . . was regarded by the Desert Fathers as a shipwreck from which each single individual man had to swim for his life."

They were seeking to revive true Christian devotion and simplicity of life by intense renunciation. Their experience has particular relevance, because modern society is uncomfortably like the world that they attacked so vigorously. Their world asked, "How can I get more?" The Desert Fathers asked, "What can I do without?" Their world asked, "How can I find myself?" The Desert Fathers asked, "How can I lose myself?" Their world asked, "How can I win friends and influence people?" The Desert Fathers asked, "How can I love God?"

Anthony, the "father of monks" (A.D. 251–356), was about eighteen years old when he heard the Gospel words, "Go, sell what you possess and give to the poor . . . and come, follow me" (Matt. 19:21). Going out from the church, he immediately gave away his inherited land, sold all of his possessions, and distributed the proceeds among the poor, saving only enough to care for his sister. After living at the edge of his village for a time, he retreated into the desert, where for twenty years he lived in complete solitude. In the solitude he was forced to face his false, empty self. He learned to die to the opinions of others. He came out of a bondage to human beings. Violent and many were the temptations he faced.

When he emerged from the solitude of the desert, he was marked with graciousness, love, kindness, endurance, meekness, freedom from anger, and the practice of prayer. People recognized in him a unique compassion and power. Many sought him out for spiritual counsel and healing power. Even the Emperor Constantine sought his advice. . . . In the final years of his life he retreated again to the solitude of the desert, where he died in his 105th year.
—From *Freedom of Simplicity* by Richard J. Foster

Hymn: Come Down, O Love Divine

Come down, O Love divine,
Seek thou this soul of mine,
And visit it with thine own ardor glowing;
O Comforter, draw near,
Within my heart appear,
And kindle it, thy holy flame bestowing.

O let it freely burn,
Till earthly passions turn
To dust and ashes in its heat consuming;
And let thy glorious light
Shine ever on my sight,
And clothe me round the while my path illuming.

And so the yearning strong,
With which the soul will long,
Shall far outpass the power of human telling;
For none can guess its grade,
Till he become the place
Wherein the Holy Spirit makes his dwelling. Amen.
—Bianco da Siena

33: Christian Maturity

I. Invocation
    O God our Father, renew our spirits and draw our hearts to thyself, that our work may not be to us a burden but a delight; and give us such love to thee as may sweeten all our obedience. Help us that we may serve thee with the cheerfulness and gladness of children, delighting ourselves in thee and rejoicing in all that is to the honor of thy name; through Jesus Christ our Lord. Amen.
    —From *The Book of Worship*

II. Psalm 84

III. Daily Scripture Readings
Monday	Luke 18:18-30
Tuesday	Galatians 5:16-24
Wednesday	Philippians 2:12-18
Thursday	1 Timothy 4:6-16
Friday	2 Timothy 2:1-13
Saturday	1 John 4
Sunday	A. Genesis 25:19-34; Psalm 46; Romans 5:6-11; Matthew 9:35–10:8
	B. 2 Samuel 1:1, 17-27; Psalm 46; 2 Corinthians 5:6-10, 14-17; Mark 4:26-34
	C. 1 Kings 19:1-8; Psalm 42; Galatians 2:15-21; Luke 7:36–8:3

IV. Readings for Reflection

V. Prayers: for the church, for others, for myself

VI. Reflection: silent and written

VII. Hymn: "Dear Lord and Father of Us All"

VIII. Benediction
    You have been in communion with your Lord. Go forth now in the strength and assurance that the Lord Jesus Christ goes with you. Amen.

Readings for Reflection

❧ God will know how to draw glory even from our faults. Not to be downcast after committing a fault is one of the marks of true sanctity.
—Dom Augustin Guillerand

❧ So often we are too full of what we think should be happening to us in our spiritual formation to notice what God is actually teaching us. We must be still enough, simple enough, humble enough, to let him plan the course, and use whatever opportunities there may be for our instruction.

We must not think that as we progress in prayer everything will necessarily become much more overtly holy. What it will become is more simple, more humble, more actual.

St. Ambrose gave his congregation some very good advice. Using the old Christian symbol, he compared them in this stormy world to fish swimming in the sea. And to them too he said: "Be a fish." We must learn how not to be swamped by the situations that we find ourselves in. We must learn how to get through them with a minimum of damage, and a maximum of profit.

One aspect of this is simply learning to get through situations, and not always to want to take them with us. There is a story told of two monks in Japan, "travelling together down a muddy road. A heavy rain was still falling. Coming around a bend, they met a lovely girl in a silk kimono and sash, unable to cross the intersection. 'Come on, girl,' said Tanzan at once. Lifting her in his arms, he carried her over the mud. Ekido did not speak again until that night when they reached a lodging temple. Then he no longer could restrain himself. 'We monks don't go near females,' he told Tanzan, 'especially not young and lovely ones. It is dangerous. Why did you do that?' 'I left the girl there,' said Tanzan. 'Are you still carrying her?'"

We must learn to pass through situations like a fish, rather than carrying them all with us like a snail. We should certainly emerge with a little bit more experience of life, but there is no need to carry more with us than we have to—each situation carries quite enough trouble with it by itself!
—From *Prayer* by Simon Tugwell

❧ Lord, make me an
instrument of your peace!
Where there is hatred,
let me sow love;
where there is injury, pardon;
where there is doubt, faith;
where there is despair, hope;
where there is darkness, light;
and where there is sadness, joy.

O Divine Master,
grant that I may not
so much seek to be consoled
as to console;
to be understood
as to understand;
to be loved
as to love;
for it is in giving
that we receive;
it is in pardoning
that we are pardoned;
and it is in dying
that we are born to Eternal Life.
—Saint Francis of Assisi

❧ If, then, we desire a simple test of the quality of our spiritual life, a consideration of the tranquillity, gentleness and strength with which we deal with the circumstances of our outward life will serve us better than anything that is based on the loftiness of our religious notions, or fervour of our religious feelings. It is a test that can be applied anywhere and at any time. Tranquillity, gentleness and strength, carrying us through the changes of weather, the ups and downs of the route, the varied surface of the road; the inequalities of family life, emotional and professional disappointments, the sudden intervention of bad fortune or bad health, the rising and falling of our religious temperature. This is the threefold imprint of the Spirit on the souls surrendered to his great action.
—From *The Spiritual Life* by Evelyn Underhill

❧ A doll of salt, after a long pilgrimage on dry land, came to the sea and discovered something she had never seen and could not possibly understand. She stood on the firm ground, a solid little doll of salt, and saw there was another ground that was mobile, insecure, noisy, strange and unknown. She asked the sea, 'But what are you?' and it said, 'I am the sea.' And the doll said, 'What is the sea?' to which the answer was, 'It is me.' Then the doll said, 'I cannot understand, but I want to; how can I?' The sea answered, 'Touch me.' So the doll shyly put forward a foot and touched the water and she got a strange impression that it was something that began to be knowable. She withdrew her leg, looked and saw that her toes had gone, and she was afraid and said, 'Oh, but where is my toe, what have you done to me?' And the sea said, 'You have given something in order to understand.' Gradually the water took away small bits of the doll's salt and the doll went farther and farther into the sea and at every moment she had a sense of understanding more and more, and yet of not being able to say what the sea was. As she went deeper, she melted more and more, repeating: 'But what is the sea?' At last a wave dissolved the rest of her and the doll said: 'It is I!' She had discovered what the sea was, but not yet what the water was.

Without drawing an absolute parallel between the buddhist doll and christian knowledge of God, one can see much truth in this little story. St. Maxim uses the example of a sword that becomes red hot: the sword does not know where the fire ends and the fire does not know where the sword begins, so that one can, as he says, cut with fire and burn with iron. The doll knew what the sea was when she had become, minute as she was, the vastness of the sea. So also when we enter into the knowledge of God, we do not contain God, but are contained in him, and we become ourselves in this encounter with God, secure in his vastness. . . .

We grow into the knowledge of God gradually from year to year until the end of our life and we will continue to do so through all eternity, without coming to a point when we shall be able to say that now we know all that is knowable of God. This process of the gradual discovery of God leads us at every moment to stand with our past experience behind us and the mystery of God knowable and still unknown before us. The little we know of God makes it difficult for us to learn more, because the more cannot simply be added to the little, since every meeting brings such a change of perspective that what was known before becomes almost untrue in the light of what is known later.

—From *Living Prayer* by Anthony Bloom

ᔰ Father in Heaven! What is a human being without thee! What is all that one knows, vast accumulation though it be, but a chipped fragment if one does not know thee! What is all striving, could it ever encompass a world, but a half-finished work if one does not know thee: thee the One, who art one thing and who art all! So may thou give to the intellect, wisdom to comprehend that one thing; to the heart, sincerity to receive this understanding; to the will, purity that wills only one thing. In prosperity may thou grant perseverance to will one thing; amid distractions, collectedness to will one thing; in suffering, patience to will one thing. Oh, thou that givest both the beginning and the completion, may thou early, at the dawn of day, give to the young person the resolution to will one thing. As the day wanes, may thou give the older person a renewed remembrance of the first resolution, that the first may be like the last, the last like the first, in possession of a life that has willed only one thing. Alas, but this has indeed not come to pass. Something has come in between. The separation of sin lies in between. Each day, and day after day something is being placed in between: delay, blockage, interruption, delusion, corruption. So in this time of repentance may thou give the courage once again to will one thing. True, it is an interruption of our ordinary tasks; we do lay down our work as though it were a day of rest, when the penitent (and it is only in a time of repentance that the heavy-laden worker may be quiet in the confession of sin) is alone before thee in self-accusation.

This is indeed an interruption. But it is an interruption that searches back into its very beginnings that it might bind up anew that which sin has separated, that in its grief it may atone for lost time, that in its anxiety it might bring to completion that which lies before it. Oh, thou that givest both the beginning and the completion, give thou victory in the day of need so that what neither a burning wish nor

determined resolution may attain to, may be granted in the sorrowing of repentance: to will only one thing.
—From *The Prayers of Kierkegaard* by Søren Kierkegaard

Hymn: Dear Lord and Father of Us All

Dear Lord and Father of us all,
Forgive our foolish ways;
Reclothe us in our rightful mind,
In purer lives thy service find,
In deeper reverence praise.

In simple trust like theirs who heard,
Beside the Syrian sea,
The gracious calling of the Lord,
Let us, like them, without a word
Rise up and follow thee.

O sabbath rest by Galilee!
O calm of hills above,
Where Jesus knelt to share with thee
The silence of eternity,
Interpreted by love!

Drop thy still dews of quietness,
Till all our strivings cease;
Take from our souls the strain and stress,
And let our ordered lives confess
The beauty of thy peace.

Breathe through the pulses of desire
Thy coolness and thy balm;
Let sense be dumb, let flesh retire;
Speak through the earthquake, wind, and fire,
O still, small voice of calm. Amen.
—John Greenleaf Whittier

34: Our Weakness and God's Strength

I. Invocation
Almighty God, through the power of your Holy
Spirit you enable us to do and be more than we can
think or imagine. Come now, dwell within us, and
make us strong to do your work and will. Through
Christ our Lord. Amen.

II. Psalm 46

III. Daily Scripture Readings

Monday		1 Corinthians 2:1-13
Tuesday		Psalm 28
Wednesday		Isaiah 40:12-31
Thursday		Philippians 4:10-20
Friday		2 Corinthians 9:6-15
Saturday		Ephesians 3:14-21
Sunday	A.	Genesis 28:10-17; Psalm 91:1-10; Romans 5:12-19; Matthew 10:24-33
	B.	2 Samuel 5:1-12; Psalm 48; 2 Corinthians 5:18–6:2; Mark 4:35-41
	C.	1 Kings 19:9-14; Psalm 43; Galatians 3:23-29; Luke 9:18-24

IV. Readings for Reflection

V. Prayers: for the church, for others, for myself

VI. Reflection: silent and written

VII. Hymn: "Just as I Am, Without One Plea"

VIII. Benediction
May the power, peace, and presence of Jesus Christ
uphold, sustain, direct, and keep you always. Amen.

Readings for Reflection

❧ It is assumed that if God is omnipotent he can do anything; but this is not strictly true. What God's omnipotence does mean is that nothing can obstruct him, nothing can prevent his being fully and eternally himself.

But this means that it is actually a part of his omnipotence that God does not contradict himself. He is free to determine the manner of his own working; and in fact, as we know from revelation, he has chosen to work in such a way that we can interfere, and interfere very drastically, with his creation. God made man such that man could rebel against him, and set up his own "world" in opposition to God. Of course, God is not without allies even in "our" world; he knows that we can never really be satisfied with any world of our own devising, so that it will always be vulnerable to his influence in one way or another; and God exploits this to the full. But he always respects the freedom and independence that he has given us.

—From *Prayer* by Simon Tugwell

❧ When Hercules wrestled with Antaeus he found that every time he threw him down upon the ground the enemy arose stronger than before. But when he discovered that Gaea—the Earth—was the mother of the giant, and that every time her son fell back upon her bosom he rose with renewed strength, then Hercules changed his tactics. Lifting Antaeus high in the air, away from the source of strength, he held him there till he brought him into subjection.

We, who are not children of Earth but children of God, could learn much from the lesson of Antaeus. We too, whenever troubles cast us back upon the bosom of our Father, rise with renewed strength. But just as Antaeus let Hercules, who was smaller in stature than he, lift him away from the source of his power, so circumstances, infinitely small and trivial, may drag us away from God. Troubles, misfortunes, disappointments, and handicaps, if they but throw us back upon God, if they merely give us opportunity of bringing into play our God-directed imagination and our heaven-blessed sense of humor, may become converted into marvelous good fortune. For trouble, if it merely turns us to God and hence renews our strength, ceases to be evil, and becomes good; it becomes the best thing that could possibly come to us, next to God himself. For our growth in power and happiness depends upon the number of seconds out of each twenty-four hours that we are resting in God.

—From *The Soul's Sincere Desire* by Glenn Clark

ès You give your help, not in proportion to our merit, but to our needs. You came for the sick and not for the healthy. How true I feel this is. I feel your love as you hold me to your Sacred Heart, my Beloved Jesus, my God, my Master, but I feel, too, the need I have of your tenderness, and of your caress because of my infinite weakness.

—From *Meditations of a Hermit* by Charles de Foucauld

ès Lord Jesus, I believe that thou art able and willing to deliver me from all the care and unrest and bondage of my Christian life. I believe thou didst die to set me free, not only in the future, but now and here. I believe thou art stronger than sin, and that thou canst keep me, even me, in my extreme of weakness, from falling in its snares or yielding obedience to its commands. And Lord, I am going to trust thee to keep me. I have tried keeping myself, and have failed, and failed, most grievously. I am absolutely helpless. So now I will trust thee. I give myself to thee. I keep back no reserves. Body, soul and spirit, I present myself to thee as a piece of clay, to be fashioned into anything thy love and thy wisdom shall choose. And now I *am* thine. I believe thou dost accept that which I present to thee; I believe that this poor, weak, foolish heart has been taken possession of by thee, and that thou hast even at this very moment begun to work in me to will and to do of thy good pleasure. I trust thee *utterly*, and I trust thee now.

—From *The Christian's Secret of a Happy Life* by Hannah
  Whitall Smith

ès Consider the battlefield of Gethsemane. Was there ever a more eventful engagement than that? It was a struggle for clear vision to see and strength to do the will of God.

Peter Annet, an old Deist, used to say that praying men are like sailors who have cast anchor on a rock, and who imagine they are pulling the rock to themselves, when they are really pulling themselves to the rock. But that is a caricature of what praying men at their best think. The Master here was deliberately trying to pull himself to the rock. That was the objective of the struggle in the garden. The will of God was settled; he wanted clearly to see it and strongly to be apprehended by it, and he called God in to fight the narrower self will that opposed the larger devotion. What a deep experience such praying brings into any life that knows it! As Phillips Brooks exclaimed: "God's mercy seat is no mere stall set by the vulgar road side, where every careless passer-by may put an easy hand out to snatch any glittering blessing that catches his eye. It stands in the holiest of holies. We can come to it only through veils and by altars of purification. To enter into it, we must enter into God."

—From *The Meaning of Prayer* by Harry Emerson Fosdick

ৰ During a dry season in the New Hebrides, John G. Paton the missionary awakened the derision of the natives by digging for water. They said water always came down from heaven, not up through the earth. But Paton revealed a larger truth than they had seen before by discovering to them that heaven could give them water through their own land. So men insist on waiting for God to send them blessing in some supernormal way, when all the while he is giving them abundant supply if they would only learn to retreat into the fertile places of their own spirits where, as Jesus said, the wells of living waters seek to rise. We need to learn Eckhart's lesson, "God is nearer to me than I am to myself; he is just as near to wood and stone, but they do not know it."

—From *The Meaning of Prayer* by Harry Emerson Fosdick

ৰ Our progress in holiness depends on God and ourselves—on God's grace and on our will to be holy. We must have a real living determination to reach holiness.

—From *A Gift for God* by Mother Teresa

ৰ I Need Thy Sense of Time
> Always I have an underlying anxiety about things.
> Sometimes I am in a hurry to achieve my ends
> And am completely without patience. It is hard for
> me to realize

That some growth is slow,
That all processes are not swift. I cannot always
    discriminate
Between what takes time to develop and what can
    be rushed,
Because my sense of time is dulled.
I measure things in terms of happenings.
O to understand the meaning of perspective
That I may do all things with a profound sense of
    leisure
    —of time.

I Need Thy Sense of Order
    The confusion of the details of living
    Is sometimes overwhelming. The little things
    Keep getting in my way providing ready-made
    Excuses for failure to do and be
    What I know I ought to do and be.
    Much time is spent on things that are not very
        important
    While significant things are put into an insignificant
        place
    In my scheme of order. I must unscramble my
        affairs
    So that my life will become order. O God, I need
        thy sense of order.

I Need Thy Sense of the Future
    Teach me to know that life is ever
    On the side of the future.
    Keep alive in me the forward look, the high hope,
    The onward surge. Let me not be frozen
    Either by the past or the present.
    Grant me, O patient Father, thy sense of the future
    Without which all life would sicken and die.
—From *Deep Is the Hunger* by Howard Thurman

   You write that at times, during prayer, a solution to some problem that perplexes you in your spiritual life comes of itself from an unknown source. This is good. It is the true Christian way of being taught God's truth. Here the promise is fulfilled, 'And they shall be taught of God' (John vi. 45).

So indeed it is. Truths are inscribed in the heart by the finger of God, and remain there firm and indelible. Do not neglect these truths which God inscribes, but write them down.
—From *The Art of Prayer*

Hymn: Just as I Am, Without One Plea

Just as I am, without one plea,
But that thy blood was shed for me,
And that thou bidst me come to thee,
O Lamb of God,
I come, I come!

Just as I am, and waiting not
To rid my soul of one dark blot,
To thee whose blood can cleanse each spot,
O Lamb of God,
I come, I come!

Just as I am, though tossed about
With many a conflict, many a doubt,
Fightings and fears within, without,
O Lamb of God,
I come, I come!

Just as I am, thou wilt receive,
Wilt welcome, pardon, cleanse, relieve;
Because thy promise I believe,
O Lamb of God,
I come, I come!

Just as I am, thy love unknown,
Hath broken every barrier down;
Now to be thine, yea, thine alone,
O Lamb of God,
I come, I come! Amen.
—Charlotte Elliott

35: The Cost of Servanthood

I. Invocation

Lord Jesus Christ, you have shown us what it means to be a servant. We ask now for your grace and strength to faithfully follow in the footsteps of servanthood. We pray in the name and spirit of Jesus. Amen.

II. Psalm 31

III. Daily Scripture Readings

Monday		Luke 14:25-33
Tuesday		Matthew 12:46-50
Wednesday		Acts 7:54-60
Thursday		2 Corinthians 4:7-18
Friday		2 Corinthians 13:5-10
Saturday		John 21:15-23
Sunday	A.	Genesis 32:22-32; Psalm 17:1-7, 15; Romans 6:3-11; Matthew 10:34-42
	B.	2 Samuel 6:1-15; Psalm 24; 2 Corinthians 8:7-15; Mark 5:21-43
	C.	1 Kings 19:15-21; Psalm 44:1-8; Galatians 5:1, 13-25; Luke 9:51-62

IV. Readings for Reflection

V. Prayers: for the church, for others, for myself

VI. Reflection: silent and written

VII. Hymn: "I'll Go Where You Want Me to Go"

VIII. Benediction

Go forth now as God's servant. Remember God's presence often and draw strength from the knowledge that the One who calls and sends also sustains. Amen.

Readings for Reflection

❧ The first lesson God gives us in training our will is in making us go halfway with him. He first puts us through a series of disciplines to see if we are worthy to make his team. After this lesson is learned we discover that there are many, many times that God goes *all* the way with *us*. Over and over again he gives us far more than we have any right to ask. We call this "his Grace," which goes so much farther than "his law" requires that he should go. God's mercy goes so much farther than mere human justice goes.

And then there are many times when God gives us the opportunity to go *all* the way with him. He did that with Job. He did it with Abraham. He used it as a school for many of his greatest saints and leaders. One of the great privileges he may give to you—if he is preparing for you great leadership—is the opportunity sometime of going *all* the way with him. One of those who did this was Thomas à Kempis. Hear his profession of faith:

> O Lord, thou knowest what is the better way; let this or that be done as thou shalt please. Give what thou wilt, and how much thou wilt, and when thou wilt. Deal with me as thou knowest, and best pleaseth thee, and is most for thy honor. Set me where thou wilt, and deal with me in all things as thou wilt. I am in thy hand; turn me round and turn me back again, even as a wheel. Behold I am thy servant, prepared for all things; for I desire not to live unto myself, but unto thee; and Oh that I could do it worthy and perfectly!

—From *I Will Lift Up Mine Eyes* by Glenn Clark

❧ When you undertake some special endeavour, do not concentrate your attention and heart on it, but look upon it as something secondary; and by entire surrender to God open yourself up to God's grace, like a vessel laid out ready to receive it. Whoever finds grace finds it by means of faith and zeal, says St. Gregory of Sinai, and not by zeal alone. However painstaking our work, so long as we omit to surrender ourselves to God while performing it, we fail to attract God's grace, and our efforts build up within us not so much a true spirit of grace but the spirit of a Pharisee. Grace is the soul of the struggle. Our efforts will be rightly directed so long as we preserve self-abasement, contrition, fear of God, devotion to him, and the realisation of our dependence on divine help. If we are self-satisfied and contented with our efforts, it is a sign that they are not performed in the right way, or that we lack wisdom.

—From *The Art of Prayer*

For too long we have thought of the Christian life as essentially either involvement in political, economic, social concerns that wear us out and result in depression or activity which keeps the church intact and doctrinally pure. Our primary orientation cannot be an institution or some great cause or even other people, but first and forever to God. Unless our identity is hid in God we will never know who we are or what we are to do. Our first act must be prayer, *Oratio*. To be human is to pray, to meditate both day and night on the love and activity of God. We are called to be continuously formed and transformed by the thought of God within us. Prayer is a disciplined dedication to paying attention. Without the singleminded attentiveness of prayer we will rarely hear anything worth repeating or catch a vision worth asking anyone else to gaze upon.

—From *The Spiritual Life* by John H. Westerhoff III and John D. Eusden

That God of Israel, who makes a divine promise to live by: "Fear not, I shall be with you. I will lead you. You will conquer!"

The infallibility of Christ did not rest on the weakness of human beings, but on the divine omnipotence.

It was not the result of human virtue, but of the love of God, which, in spite of human beings' little virtue and their infantile mistakes, will succeed, with his invincible will, in leading his people to their goal.

In establishing Moses, Saint Peter, and Innocent III as heads of his people, God did not remove from them their hardness of mind or the dross of their heart—but in spite of the hardness and the dross he guaranteed his people that they would reach the Kingdom.

It was not a matter of switching leaders, then, and founding another Church. It was a matter of believing that the Church had already been founded, and that we should trust in the Spirit that guided it as he had guided Moses, as he had guided David, as he had guided Peter, and as he now guided Innocent III, whom he had seen in all his weakness but a few days before.

Yes, what was needed was to believe that the Church had already been founded before we appeared on the scene, and that we would not have been better than the others.

Perish the thought that we would have been more skillful because we were ill clad and lived in huts!

Perish the temptation that once we had come on the scene things would have taken a sharp turn for the better!

No.

We, as church, would have continued to be saints and sinners, capable of high ideals and base enormities, the dwelling place of peace and a jungle of violence.

All would have depended upon personal sanctity—on the commitment and the prayer of saints, on the sacrifice of the humble, on the true love of Christ's followers.

But one thing was sure: even if we had failed, overwhelmed by our sins and our faithlessness, the Church would not have failed—as neither did God's people fail in the desert, or in the terrible loneliness of Babylon.

—From *I, Francis* by Carlo Carretto

❧ "Why is the Church so sad?

"Why is the priesthood so boring that it even has to ask itself the nature of its identity and reasons for its existence?

"There is only one reply. In practice—not in theory—'They have forsaken Me, the source of living waters;/they have dug themselves cisterns,/broken cisterns, that hold no water' (Jer. 2:13).

"Oh, return to Me—the prophet would say—and put Me to the test: 'Shall I not open for you the floodgates of heaven to pour down blessing upon you without measure' (Mal. 3:10)? For 'Is My hand too short to ransom' (Isa. 50:2)? Have I become incapable of helping you?"

"You will live in my love if you keep my commandments, even as I have kept my Father's commandments, and live in His love" (John 15:10).

"Leave your idols, which cannot help you.

"Do not believe in the strength of money, do not rely on the powerful. Rely on Me, who am God.

"Live on in my love," and rest in peace. "'I have overcome the world' (John 16:33).

"Do not place yourselves with that world that I have overcome, which is power, money, sensuality, a world that I shall crush because it is a damned thing 'under the evil one' (1 John 5:19), a world for which I do not pray (cf. John 17:9).

"Do not begin the day by reading the newspaper; that will make you slaves of public opinion, even though involuntarily. Rather, begin your daily labors waiting for the dawn in prayer, as the Psalm suggests to you: 'Awake, O my soul; awake, lyre and harp; I will wake the dawn' (Ps. 108:3). All those who have signed the story of my presence in the world have done so.

"Come to me, all you who are weary and find life burdensome, and I will refresh you. Take my yoke upon your shoulders and learn from Me, for I am gentle and humble of heart. Your souls will find rest . . ." (Matt. 11: 28-29).

—From *The God Who Comes* by Carlo Carretto

❧ It is not what you are nor what you have been that God sees with his all-merciful eyes, but what you desire to be. St. Gregory declares that "all holy desires heighten in intensity with the delay of fulfillment, and desire which fades with delay was never holy desire at all." For if you experience less and less joy when you discover anew the sudden presence of great desires you had formerly pursued, your first desire was not holy desire. Possibly you felt a natural tendency toward the good but this should not be confused with holy desire. St. Augustine explains what I mean by holy desire when he says that "the entire life of a good Christian is nothing less than holy desire."

—From *The Cloud of Unknowing*

Hymn: I'll Go Where You Want Me to Go

It may not be on the mountain's height,
Or over the stormy sea;
It may not be at the battle's front
My Lord will have need of me;
But if by a still, small voice he calls
To paths I do not know,
I'll answer dear Lord with my hand in thine,
I'll go where you want me to go.

I'll go where you want me to go, dear Lord,
O'er mountain, or plain or sea;
I'll say what you want me to say, dear Lord.
I'll be what you want me to be.

Perhaps today there are loving words
Which Jesus would have me speak;
There may be now, in the paths of sin,
Some wanderer whom I should seek.
O Savior, if thou wilt be my Guide,
Tho' dark and rugged the way,
My voice shall echo the message sweet,
I'll say what you want me to say.

There's surely somewhere a lowly place
In earth's harvest fields so wide,
Where I may labor thro life's short day
For Jesus the Crucified.
So, trusting my all unto thy care,
I know thou lovest me!
I'll do thy will with a heart sincere,
I'll be what you want me to be.
—Mary Brown

36: The Power of the Gospel

I.   Invocation
     Almighty God, may the transforming power of your gospel be at work in my life today and always. Amen.

II. Psalm 4

III. Daily Scripture Readings
Monday	Romans 1:1-17
Tuesday	Colossians 1:9-23
Wednesday	Ephesians 1:1-14
Thursday	2 Corinthians 12:1-10
Friday	1 Peter 1: 1-9
Saturday	1 Corinthians 1: 18-31

     Sunday   A . Exodus 1:6-14, 22–2:10; Psalm 124; Romans 7:14-25a; Matthew 11:25-30
              B. 2 Samuel 7:1-17; Psalm 89:20-37; 2 Corinthians 12:1-10; Mark 6:1-6
              C. 1 Kings 21:1-3, 17-21; Psalm 5:1-8; Galatians 6:7-18; Luke 10:1-12, 17-20

IV. Readings for Reflection

V.   Prayers: for the church, for others, for myself

VI. Reflection: silent and written

VII. Hymn: "O Holy Savior, Friend Unseen"

VIII. Benediction
      Go forth to serve in the strength, love, and presence of the Lord Jesus Christ. Amen.

Readings for Reflection

ৈ And so when we had a decision to make, we would open the Gospel at random, after having said a little prayer, and then we did whatever was written, without adding anything.

This manner of action gave us a boundless liberty, and nurtured simplicity of heart with some solid food.

Another important element taking shape in the community we were forming was the primacy of faith instead of structures.

We felt ourselves to be a community in search of God, not a seminary for the priesthood.

What made us one was Christ, and the imitation of him gave meaning to the manner of living of each one of us.

There was the whole expression around us of the life of a simple Christian.

—From *I, Francis* by Carlo Carretto

ৈ When we begin to ask what the conditions of inner renewal are, we receive essentially the same answers from nearly all of those whom we have most reason to respect. One major answer is the emphasis upon discipline. In the conduct of one's own life it is soon obvious, as many have learned the hard way, that empty freedom is a snare and a delusion. In following what comes naturally or easily, life simply ends in confusion, and in consequent disaster. Without the discipline of time, we spoil the next day the night before, and without the discipline of prayer, we are likely to end by having practically no experience of the divine-human encounter. However compassionate we may be with others, we dare not be soft or indulgent with ourselves. Excellence comes at a price, and one of the major prices is that of inner control.

We have not advanced very far in our spiritual lives if we have not encountered the basic paradox of freedom, to the effect that we are most free when we are bound. But not just any way of being bound will suffice; what matters is the character of our binding. The one who would like to be an athlete, but who is unwilling to discipline his body by regular exercise and by abstinence, is not free to excel on the field or the track. His failure to train rigorously and to live abstemiously denies him the freedom to go over the bar at the desired height, or to run with the desired speed and endurance. With one concerted voice the giants of the devotional life apply the same principle to the whole of life with the dictum: *Discipline is the price of freedom.*

—From *The New Man for Our Time* by Elton Trueblood

&. We sat down to table and the officer began his story: "I have served in the army ever since I was quite young. I knew my duties and was a favorite of my superiors as a conscientious officer. But I was young, as were also my friends, and unhappily I started drinking. It went from bad to worse until drinking became an illness. When I did not drink, I was a good officer, but when I would start drinking, then I would have to go to bed for six weeks. My superiors were patient with me for a long time, but finally, for rudeness to the commanding officer while I was drunk, they reduced my rank to private and transferred me to a garrison for three years. They threatened me with more severe punishment if I would not improve and give up drinking. In this unfortunate condition all my efforts at self-control were of no avail and I could not stay sober for any length of time. Then I heard that I was to be sent to the guardhouse and I was beside myself with anguish.

"One day I was sitting in the barracks deep in thought. A monk came in to beg alms for the church. Those who had money gave what they could. When he approached me he asked, 'Why are you so downcast?' We started talking and I told him the cause of my grief. The monk sympathized with my situation and said, 'My brother was once in a similar position, and I will tell you how he was cured. His spiritual father gave him a copy of the Gospels and strongly urged him to read a chapter whenever he wanted to take a drink. If the desire for a drink did not leave him after he read one chapter he was encouraged to read another and if necessary still another. My brother followed this advice, and after some time he lost all desire for alcoholic beverages. It is now fifteen years since he has touched a drop of alcohol. Why don't you do the same, and you will discover how beneficial the reading of the Gospels can be. I have a copy at home and will gladly bring it to you.'

"I wasn't very open to this idea so I objected, 'How can your Gospels help when neither my efforts at self-control nor medical aid could keep me sober?' I spoke in this way because I never read the Gospels.

"'Give it a chance,' continued the monk reassuringly, 'and you will find it very helpful.'

"The next day he brought me this copy of the Gospels. I opened it, browsed through it, and said, 'I will not take it, for I cannot understand it; I am not accustomed to reading Church Slavonic.'

"The monk did not give up but continued to encourage me and explained that God's special power is present in the Gospel through his words. He went on, 'At the beginning be concerned only with reading it diligently; understanding will come later. One holy man says that "even when you don't understand the word of God, the demons do, and they tremble"; and the passion for drink is without a doubt their work. And St. John Chrysostom in speaking about the power of the word of God says that the very room where the Gospel is kept has the power to ward off the spirits of darkness and thwart their intrigues.'

"I do not recall what I gave the monk when I took the copy of the Gospels from him, but I placed the book in my trunk with my other belongings and forgot about it. Some time later a strong desire to have a drink took hold of me and I opened the trunk to get some money and run to the tavern. But I saw the copy of the Gospels before I got to the money and I remembered clearly what the monk had told me. I opened the book and read the first chapter of Matthew without understanding anything. Again I remembered the monk's words, 'At the beginning be concerned only with reading it diligently; understanding will come later.' So I read another chapter and found it a bit more comprehensible. Shortly after I began reading the third chapter, the curfew bell rang and it was no longer possible for me to leave the barracks.

"In the morning my first thought was to get a drink, but then I decided to read another chapter to see what would happen. I read it and did not go. Again I wanted a drink, but I started reading and I felt better. This gave me courage, and with every temptation for a drink I began reading a chapter from the Gospels. The more I read, the easier it became, and when I finally finished reading all four Gospels the compulsion for drink had disappeared completely; I was repelled by the very thought of it. It is now twenty years since I stopped drinking alcoholic beverages.

"Everyone was surprised at the change that took place in me, and after three years I was reinstated as an officer and then climbed up the ranks until I was made a commanding officer. Later I married a fine woman; we have saved some money, which we now share with the poor. Now I have a grown son who is a fine lad and he also is an officer in the army."

—From *The Way of a Pilgrim*

ॐ Miracles are unpopular today—to the scientifically minded because they seem to conflict with so-called scientific miracles, like bumping television programmes across the world by satellite, or going to the moon; to the ostensibly religiously minded because they remind them of miraculous claims made in the past and now discredited, which they wish to forget.

—From *Something Beautiful for God* by Malcolm Muggeridge

ॐ The Sacred Scriptures contain
the Word of God
and, since they are inspired,
really are the Word of God. . . .

This sacred Synod urges all the Christian faithful
to learn by frequent reading of the divine Scriptures
the "excelling knowledge of Jesus Christ."
"For ignorance of the Scriptures
is ignorance of Christ."

Therefore, they should gladly put themselves
in touch with the sacred text itself. . . .

And let them remember that prayer should accompany
the reading of Sacred Scripture,
so that God and man may talk together;

for "we speak to him when we pray;
we hear him when we read the divine saying."
—From *Dogmatic Constitution on Divine Revelation* by
Second Vatican Council

  Our Father, we have listened to thy word, and loved it;
we have found comfort and inspiration in song and psalter;
we have enjoyed the companionship of those who, with
kindred minds and hearts, have praised and worshiped
thee. Now help us understand that, as we leave this sacred
House of God, we shall become thy Church in the street.
—Anonymous

Hymn: O Holy Savior, Friend Unseen

O Holy Savior, friend unseen,
Since on thine arm thou bidst me lean,
Help me, throughout life's changing scene,
By faith to cling to thee.

What though the world deceitful prove,
And earthly friends and hopes remove;
With patient, uncomplaining love,
Still would I cling to thee.

Though oft I seem to tread alone
Life's dreary waste, with thorns o'ergrown,
Thy voice of love, in gentlest tone,
Still whispers, "Cling to me!"

Though faith and hope may long be tried,
I ask not, need not, aught beside;
How safe, how calm, how satisfied,
The soul that clings to thee! Amen.
—Charlotte Elliott

Sunday between July 10 and 16
37: The Church for Others

I. Invocation
    Lord Jesus Christ, pour out your spirit upon your church so that she may faithfully and constantly serve you and your children. In the name of Christ. Amen.

II. Psalm 24

III. Daily Scripture Readings
Monday	Isaiah 1:10-17
Tuesday	Matthew 10:1-10
Wednesday	Romans 15:1-13
Thursday	1 Corinthians 9:15-23
Friday	John 17:20-26
Saturday	Romans 14

    Sunday
    A. Exodus 2:11-22; Psalm 69:6-15; Romans 8:9-17; Matthew 13:1-9, 18-23
    B. 2 Samuel 7:18-29; Psalm 132:11-18; Ephesians 1:1-10; Mark 6:7-13
    C. 2 Kings 2:1, 6-14; Psalm 139:1-12; Colossians 1:1-14; Luke 10:25-37

IV. Readings for Reflection

V. Prayers: for the church, for others, for myself

VI. Reflection: silent and written

VII. Hymn: "When the Storms of Life Are Raging"

VIII. Benediction
    May grace, mercy, love, and peace flow through your life and ministry all the day long. Amen.

Readings for Reflection

&c. When the child of God speaks, when the Church—the society of faith and grace speaks—there is no need for aesthetics, for technology, for culture. Prophecy, being divine by nature, has the power of casting light on our march towards freedom; charity, having its origin in the theological love of God, has an exact vision of things and knows what is really good for us.

And let us remember: what is good for us always comes to the light of history screened by three unequivocal words: life, light, love. These are the same words which indicate the Person of the Father, the Person of the Son, and the Person of the Holy Spirit.

Defending life, witnessing light, living out love; these remain forever and for every occasion the divine background of prophecy; they are the specific duty of anyone who calls upon God, following Christ's unmistakable example.

An assembly where people do not love each other, where they accuse each other, where there is rancor or hatred, cannot call itself prophetic.

A person who keeps silent about the truth, who hides the light, is not a prophet.

A people which kills, which deteriorates the quality of life, which suffocates the poor, which is not free, is not a prophetic people.

That is why it is not enough for just any assembly to call itself Church, just as it is not enough to be a bishop or a pope in order to possess prophecy.

A group of young people which meets for sports or outings with the "do everything" blessing of the up-to-date parish, another group which meets to camouflage some political position cannot be called Church, even if the sports are refereed by a famous devout layman and the social ideas are worked out by a priest.

To call itself Church, an assembly must mirror the first assembly that met in the Upper Room with Christ: an assembly of faith and grace, an assembly of love and Eucharist, an assembly of prayer and prophecy.

But it is not easy to prophesy; it is terribly costly. It has to be drawn from the silence of God, and there is need to

swim against the stream, need to pray at length, need to be without fear.
—From *The God Who Comes* by Carlo Carretto

&. Accompanying Mother Teresa, as we did, to these different activities for the purpose of filming them—to the Home for the Dying, to the lepers and unwanted children, I found I went through three phases. The first was horror mixed with pity, the second compassion pure and simple, and the third, reaching far beyond compassion, something I had never experienced before—an awareness that these dying and derelict men and women, these lepers with stumps instead of hands, these unwanted children, were not pitiable, repulsive or forlorn, but rather dear and delightful; as it might be, friends of long standing, brothers and sisters. How is it to be explained—the very heart and mystery of the Christian faith? To soothe those battered old heads, to grasp those poor stumps, to take in one's arms those children consigned to dustbins, because it is his head, as they are his stumps and his children, of whom he said that whosoever received one such child in his name received him.
—From *Something Beautiful for God* by Malcolm Muggeridge

&. The essential part of the Christian message is the idea of salvation for the whole community of people, of which the individual is a member. Closely linked to the idea of the Christian's message is the outward sign which is at once a sign of grace and vocation for the individual and of his reception into the community of the people of God: baptism (cf. Eph. 4:1-5). Since God's call precedes any action and any faith on the part of the individual, and since this call is addressed to the whole people of God, the individual never stands alone, but within the community, just as the individual communities are part of the one community, the Church. The Church begins, not with a pious individual, but with God.
—From *The Church* by Hans Küng

&. Love to pray. Feel often during the day the need for prayer, and take trouble to pray. Prayer enlarges the heart until it is capable of containing God's gift of himself. Ask and seek, and your heart will grow big enough to receive him and keep him as your own.

—From *A Gift for God* by Mother Teresa

❧ It is impressive to see how prayer opens one's eyes to nature. Prayer makes men contemplative and attentive. In place of manipulating, the man who prays stands receptive before the world. He no longer grabs but caresses, he no longer bites, but kisses, he no longer examines but admires. To this man, as for Merton, nature can show itself completely renewed. Instead of an obstacle, it becomes a way; instead of an invulnerable shield, it becomes a veil which gives a preview of unknown horizons.

—From *Thomas Merton: Contemplative Critic* by Henri J. M. Nouwen

❧ Few men have summed up the sanctity of common things so well as did Gandhi in his writings:

> If when we plunge our hand
>   into a bowl of water,
> Or stir up the fire with the bellows
> Or tabulate interminable columns of figures
>   on our book-keeping table,
> Or, burnt by the sun, we are plunged in
>   the mud of the rice-field,
> Or standing by the smelter's furnace
> We do not fulfill the same religious life
>   as if in prayer in a monastery,
>   the world will never be saved.

Jesus was himself the carrier of the message; he was at the same time the Supreme Intelligence, capable of devising the best way of making himself understood, and of carrying out the divine plans.

Well, what did he do? He did not open hospitals or found orphanages. He became flesh, lived among people and he embodied the Gospel message in its entirety, *Coepit facere*. He began to act.

He *lived* his message before he *spoke* of it. He preached it by his life before explaining it in words. This was Jesus' method and we too easily forget it.

In many cases catechesis is reduced to words rather than to 'life,' to discussions rather than to the pursuit of Christian living.

And here, perhaps, is the reason for the poor results, and still more, the reason for so much of the apathy and indifference among Christians today. Teaching is ineffective because it is not life-centered; there is no life because there is no example; there is no example because empty words have taken the place of faith and charity.

"I want to preach the Gospel with my life," Charles de Foucauld often said. He was convinced that the most effective method of preaching the Gospel was to live it. Especially today, people no longer want to listen to sermons. They want to see the Gospel in action.

—From *Letters from the Desert* by Carlo Carretto

&. Lord, I already know the best way to alter my life-style to the best advantage for all—live like Jesus. The Christian existence ideally is to imitate what you do. You send the sun and rain on everyone, you want me to get back to the basic facts of life, to love without reservation, to distinguish between life's needs and life itself, and seek first your kingdom knowing you will meet all my other needs.

Still it is easy to trust in the "things" of today and feel like it is up to me to see that humanity survives. Keep me from undue worry and pride. Remind me that life is a gift—not a right, and that my attitude toward the ultimate resources and values in life will determine how the earth's resources will be handled and provided for those who need them. I have already formed many habits of consuming and acting. Guide me in aligning my personal priorities to conform to my awareness of a world hungry. May my life-style become more compatible with our biosphere and supportive of peoples around the world.

Lord, help me choose a simpler life-style that promotes solidarity with the world's poor, helps me appreciate nature more, affords greater opportunity to work together with my neighbors, reduces use of limited resources, creates greater inner harmony, saves money, allows time for meditation and prayer, incites me to take political and social action.

May all my decisions about my style of life celebrate the joy of life that comes from loving you. *Amen*.
—From *Visions of a World Hungry* by Thomas G. Pettepiece

Hymn: When the Storms of Life Are Raging

When the storms of life are raging,
Stand by me;
When the storms of life are raging,
Stand by me.
When the world is tossing me
Like a ship upon the sea,
Thou who rulest wind and water,
Stand by me.

In the midst of tribulation,
Stand by me;
In the midst of tribulation,
Stand by me.
When the hosts of sin assail,
And my strength begins to fail,
Thou who never lost a battle,
Stand by me.

In the midst of faults and failures,
Stand by me;
In the midst of faults and failures,
Stand by me.
When I've done the best I can,
And my friends misunderstand,
Thou who knowest all about me,
Stand by me.

When I'm growing old and feeble,
Stand by me;
When I'm growing old and feeble,
Stand by me.
When my life becomes a burden,
And I'm nearing chilly Jordan,
O thou Lily of the Valley,
Stand by me. Amen.
—Charles A. Tindley

38: *Patience*

I. Invocation
O God, prepare us, through the active presence of thy Spirit, to come before thee worthily and to ask of thee rightly; enlighten our understanding; purify our every desire; quicken our wills into instant obedience to thy Word; strengthen every right purpose; direct this hour of worship to the magnifying of thy name, and to the enduring good of us thy children and servants; through Jesus Christ our Lord. Amen.
—From *The Book of Worship*

II. Psalm 37

III. Daily Scripture Readings
Monday		Psalm 25:1-21
Tuesday		Luke 12:35-40
Wednesday		Micah 7
Thursday		Colossians 3:12-17
Friday		Luke 8:11-15
Saturday		James 5:7-11
Sunday	A.	Exodus 3:1-12; Psalm 103:1-13; Romans 8:18-25; Matthew 13:24-30, 36-43
	B.	2 Samuel 11:1-15; Psalm 53; Ephesians 2:11-22; Mark 6:30-34
	C.	2 Kings 4:8-17; Psalm 139:13-18; Colossians 1:21-29; Luke 10:38-42

IV. Readings for Reflection

V. Prayers: for the church, for others, for myself

VI. Reflection: silent and written

VII. Hymn: "Jesus, I My Cross Have Taken"

VIII. Benediction
Live today in Christ's presence, remembering he is near and will sustain you as you serve in his name. Amen.

Readings for Reflection

❧ I call to you, O Lord, from my quiet darkness. Show me your mercy and love. Let me see your face, hear your voice, touch the hem of your cloak. I want to love you, be with you, speak to you and simply stand in your presence. But I cannot make it happen. Pressing my eyes against my hands is not praying, and reading about your presence is not living in it.

But there is that moment in which you will come to me, as you did to your fearful disciples, and say, "Do not be afraid; it is I." Let that moment come soon, O Lord. And if you want to delay it, then make me patient. Amen.

—From *A Cry for Mercy* by Henri J. M. Nouwen

❧ O never star
Was lost; here
We all aspire to heaven and there is heaven
Above us.
If I stoop
Into a dark tremendous sea of cloud,
It is but for a time; I press God's lamp
Close to my breast; its splendor soon or late
Will pierce the gloom. I shall emerge some day.
—"Faith" by Robert Browning

❧ God comes like the sun in the morning—when it is time.

We must assume an attitude of waiting, accepting the fact that we are creatures and not creator.

We must do this because it is not our right to do anything else; the initiative is God's, not ours. We are able to initiate nothing; we are able only to accept.

If God does not call, no calling takes place. If God does not come, there is no history! History is the coming of God to us, and the way in which we reply.

Only God created the heavens and the earth; only God can create history. We carry it out through our response, but the inspiration, the design, and the strength to carry it out come from him.

In short, he is what creates, and we creatures are in an act of becoming.

—From *The God Who Comes* by Carlo Carretto

◢ And Friends, though you may have tasted of the power and been convinced and have felt the light, yet afterwards you may feel winter storms, tempests, and hail, and be frozen, in frost and cold and a wilderness and temptations. Be patient and still in the power and still in the light that doth convince you, to keep your minds to God; in that be quiet, that you may come to the summer, that your flight be not in the winter. For if you sit still in the patience which overcomes in the power of God, there will be no flying. For the husbandman, after he hath sown his seed, he is patient. For by the power and by the light you will come to see through and feel over winter storms, tempests, and all the coldness, barrenness, emptyness. And the same light and power will go over the tempter's head, which power and light were before he was. And so in the light standing still you will see your salvation, you will see the Lord's strength, you will feel the small rain, you will feel the fresh springs in the power and light, your minds being kept low; for that which is out of the power and light lifts up. But in the power and light you will see God revealing his secrets, inspiring, and his gifts coming unto you, through which your hearts will be filled with God's love; praise to him that lives for ever more, in which light and power his blessings are received. And so the eternal power of the Lord Jesus Christ preserve and keep you in that. And so live everyone in the power of God that you may all come to be heirs of that and know that to be your portion, and the kingdom that hath no end, and an endless life, which the seed is heir of. And so feel that over all set, which hath the promise and blessing of God.

—From *The Journal of George Fox*

◢ God, we believe, accepts us, accepts all men, unconditionally, warts and all. Laughter is the purest form of our response to God's acceptance of us. For when I laugh at myself I accept myself and when I laugh at other people in genuine mirth I accept them. Self-acceptance in laughter is the very opposite of self-satisfaction or pride. For in laughter I accept myself not because I'm some sort of super-person, but precisely because I'm not. There is nothing funny about a super-person. There is everything funny about a man who thinks he is. In laughing at my own claims to importance or regard I receive myself in a sort of loving

forgiveness which is an echo of God's forgiveness of me. In much conventional contrition there is a selfishness and pride which are scarcely hidden. In our desperate self-concern we blame ourselves for not being the super-persons we think we really are. But in laughter we sit light to ourselves. That is why laughter is the purest form of our response to God.
—From *Tensions* by H. A. Williams

❧ Our requests spurt up like intermittent geysers; we cry out and fall back again. We are not in earnest. "Easiness of desire," said Jeremy Taylor, "is a great enemy to the success of a good man's prayer. It must be an intent, zealous, busy, operative prayer. For consider what a huge indecency it is that a man should speak to God for a thing that he values not. Our prayers upbraid our spirits when we beg tamely for those things for which we ought to die." This, then, is the rationale of importunity in prayer, not that it is needed to coax God, but that it is needed alike to express and by expressing to deepen our eager readiness for the good we seek. *Some things God cannot give to a man until the man has prepared and proved his spirit by persistent prayer.* Such praying cleans the house, cleanses the windows, hangs the curtains, sets the table, opens the door, until God says, "Lo! The house is ready. Now may the guest come in."
—From *The Meaning of Prayer* by Harry Emerson Fosdick

❧ Complete serenity of mind is a gift of God; but this serenity is not given without our own intense effort. You will achieve nothing by your own efforts alone; yet God will not give you anything, unless you work with all your strength. This is an unbreakable law.
—From *The Art of Prayer*

❧ Grant, O God,
    That we may never lose the way through our self-will,
        and so end up in the far countries of the soul;
    That we may never abandon the struggle,
        but that we may endure to the end,
        and so be saved;
    That we may never drop out of the race,
        but that we may ever press forward
        to the goal of our high calling;

That we may never choose the cheap and passing
    things, and let go the precious things
    that last for ever;
That we may never take the easy way,
    and so leave the right way;
That we may never forget
    that sweat is the price of all things,
    and that without the cross, there cannot
    be the crown.

So keep us and strengthen us by your grace that no disobedience and no weakness and no failure may stop us from
entering into the blessedness which awaits those who are
faithful in all the changes and the chances of life down even
to the gates of death; through Jesus Christ our Lord. Amen.
—From *Prayers for the Christian Year* by William Barclay

૏ God withholds an answer to our prayers not only when
they are unworthy but when he finds in us such greatness,
such depth—depth and power of faith—that he can rely
upon us to remain faithful even in the face of his silence.

I remember a young woman with an incurable disease
and after years of the awareness of God's presence, she suddenly sensed God's absence—some sort of real absence—
and she wrote to me saying, 'Pray to God, please, that I
should never yield to the temptation of building up an
illusion of his presence, rather than accept his absence.' Her
faith was great. She was able to stand this temptation and
God gave her this experience of his silent absence.

Remember these examples, think them over because
one day you will surely have to face the same situation.

I cannot give you any exercise, but I only want you to
remember that we should always keep our faith intact, both
in the love of God and in our honest, truthful faith, and
when this temptation comes upon us, let us say this prayer,
which is made of two sentences pronounced by Jesus Christ
himself:

'Into Thy hands I commend my spirit,
Thy Will, not mine, be done.'

—From *Living Prayer* by Anthony Bloom

Hymn: Jesus, I My Cross Have Taken

Jesus, I my cross have taken,
All to leave and follow thee;
Destitute, despised, forsaken,
Thou, from hence, my all shalt be.
Perish every fond ambition,
All I've sought or hoped or known;
Yet how rich is my condition:
God and heaven are still my own!

Let the world despise and leave me;
They have left my Savior, too.
Human hearts and looks deceive me;
Thou art not, like those, untrue.
And, while thou shalt smile upon me,
God of wisdom, love, and might,
Foes may hate, and friends may shun me;
Show thy face, and all is bright.

Haste thee on from grace to glory,
Armed by faith and winged by prayer;
Heaven's eternal days before thee,
God's own hand shall guide thee there.
Soon shall close thy earthly mansion;
Swift shall pass thy pilgrim days;
Hope shall change to glad fruition,
Faith to sight, and prayer to praise. Amen.
—Henry F. Lyte

39: *God, Our Source of Hope*

I. Invocation
O God, from whom all holy desires, all good coun-
sels, and all just works do proceed: Give unto thy
servants that peace which the world cannot give; that
our hearts may be set to obey thy commandments,
and also that by thee we, being defended from the
fear of our enemies, may pass our time in rest and
quietness; through the merits of Jesus Christ our
Savior. Amen. —From *The Book of Worship*

II. Psalm 16

III. Daily Scripture Readings
Monday	Psalm 44:1-8
Tuesday	Isaiah 41:1-10
Wednesday	Hebrews 10:19-25
Thursday	Revelation 21:1-8
Friday	1 Corinthians 1:9
Saturday	Hebrews 6:13-20
Sunday	A. Exodus 3:13-20; Psalm 105:1-11; Romans 8:26-30; Matthew 13:44-52
	B. 2 Samuel 12:1-14; Psalm 32; Ephesians 3:14-21; John 6:1-15
	C. 2 Kings 5:1-15ab; Psalm 21:1-7; Colossians 2:6-15; Luke 11:1-13

IV. Readings for Reflection

V. Prayers: for the church, for others, for myself

VI. Reflection: silent and written

VII. Hymn: "A Mighty Fortress Is Our God"

VIII. Benediction
The grace of the Lord Jesus Christ and the love of
God and the fellowship of the Holy Spirit be with
you all. Amen. —2 Corinthians 13:14

Readings for Reflection

❧ But in the epiphany of that night of darkness and pain and near despair, *the holiness of God became an ecstasy, a captivity of adoration, a heart-smiting and heart-cleansing and heart-possessing reality.* I was caught up and then bowed in enthralled worship. I wanted to be wholly so engaged forever. I wanted everything I said or did to be an act of worship. What I had become aware of thrillingly and exclusively, was *a holiness that is wholeness!* It includes everything the human heart at its best craves, everything the human mind in its greatest moments reaches after, everything the authentic self needs for its fulfillment. It was goodness of infinite dimensions, truth transcending all limitations; beauty endlessly satisfying; mercy without limit; forgiveness equal to every desperate sin; restoration transcending every prodigality; wisdom surpassing all human knowledge; everything of value in time and eternity; and always there, without variation, for everybody, in every situation!

In the Presence thus manifested there was nothing that at any time diminishes his perfections, dilutes his redemptive powers, modifies his living eagerness to help his creatures fulfill their destiny. I was ravishingly made aware that *the Presence is always the Presence-in-the-fullness-of-his-being, in his concern for all of us, in the inexhaustibleness of his saving energies, in the responsibility he assumes for every one of his children.*

—From *The Captivating Presence* by Albert Edward Day

❧ When we say that God is holy, we are not naming an attribute among many others such as love and mercy and wisdom and power. We are attempting to designate something that *applies to all his attributes,* something that gives them an awesome dimension. We are saying that he is the changeless One. His love never fluctuates; his mercy is inexhaustible; his wisdom cherishes all that is truly good; his power can always be trusted to act redemptively. *The supreme wonder and unrivalled glory is that he is all that he is, unchangeably.*

"In him is no variableness", is the New Testament assurance.

So we need not speculate what will be his response whenever we turn to him, whether it be from an hour of victory or from a night of defeat; from an act of which we are proud, or from one of which we are heartily ashamed. Our heads may be held high or bent very low. We may come jubilantly to thank him for what he has done or to barely utter a faint cry for help. It matters not who we are or where we are, a holy God is a God in whom there is nothing to adulterate or diminish or alter the transcendent qualities which our weakness or our sinfulness need. *He is always God.* Nothing is ever missing from him if he is to be what all mankind must have to make and keep it truly human on the way to its fulfillment in him. Sometimes the best of us have days when our dearest friend must say, "you are not yourself today." That fact gives them a hard time and sends them away deprived of what they should have from us. BUT GOD IS ALWAYS GOD.

—From *The Captivating Presence* by Albert Edward Day

ॐ Lord, there are people who have curled up and died in a corner for no reason other than they lost hope. When there is no hope, there is no life. Without hope we give up—we lose our will to fight, to trust, to live.

There are too many people in this world today who have begun to lose hope—those who hunger for life's basic needs but see no relief; those who see too many problems and cannot find a solution.

When I begin to lose hope, too often I have forgotten that hope is inseparably connected to love and faith . . . your love which powerfully confirms that you are not only the bringer of life, but you *are* Life . . . faith that receives love humbly and enables me to respond with hope to even the most complicated problems.

Lord, the hunger problem seems hopeless to many, the victims and the bystanders. But hope needs opportunity, and just as Paul adapted to his situation in life, you have given me now an unparalleled chance to be a part of conquering this condition, conscious of your presence which supplies me with strength and with hope.

Together we as believers can never repay you for supplying our needs, but we can trust in the hope that you will continue to supply them through us and through all the means available today. Empowered by hope in you, we can do even greater works than you did on earth—if only we keep hope.

Lord, we do not hope in ourselves, our technology, our governments, our laws, our tenacity, our courage, or our will, though these things are all necessary to conquer hunger and provide justice. We hope in you. Amen.

—From *Visions of a World Hungry* by Thomas G. Pettepiece

    ❧ This urging to bring hope to public expression is based on a conviction about believing folks. It is premised on the capacity to evoke and bring to expression the hope that is within us (see 1 Pet. 3:15). It is there within and among us, for we are ordained of God to be people of hope. It is there by virtue of our being in the image of the promissory God. It is sealed there in the sacrament of baptism. It is dramatized in the Eucharist—"until he comes." It is the structure of every creed that ends by trusting in God's promises. Hope is the decision to which God invites Israel, a decision against despair, against permanent consignment to chaos (Isa. 45:18), oppression, barrenness, and exile.

Hope is the primary prophetic idiom not because of the general dynamic of history or because of the signs of the times but because the prophet speaks to a people who, willy-nilly, are God's people. Hope is what this community must do because it is God's community invited to be in God's pilgrimage. And as Israel is invited to grieve God's grief over the ending, so Israel is now invited to hope in God's promises. That very act of hope is the confession that we are not children of the royal consciousness.

Of course prophetic hope easily lends itself to distortion. It can be made so grandiose that it does not touch reality; it can be trivialized so that it does not impact reality; it can be "bread and circuses" so that it only supports and abets the general despair. But a prophet has another purpose in bringing hope to public expression, and that is to return the community to its single referent, the sovereign faithfulness of God.

—From *The Prophetic Imagination* by Walter Brueggemann

&. Bad religion has always favored escape, passivity, irresponsibility. By dint of fixing one's eyes on heaven above, one does not see what takes place on earth here below.

The upward-looking must come to an understanding with the forward-looking.

We believe that our God (up above) calls us to go forward. Our faith in an absolute does not immobilize us in contemplation, but invites us to discover him according to our means of creating a world inspired by his love: a world where justice dwells and where people love one another.

—From *In the Christian Spirit* by Louis Evely

&. We guide by calling to mind men and women in whom the great vision becomes visible, people with whom we can identify, yet people who have broken out of the constraints of their time and place and moved into unknown fields with great courage and confidence. The rabbis guide their people with stories; ministers usually guide with ideas and theories. We need to become story-tellers again, and so multiply our ministry by calling around us the great witnesses who in different ways offer guidance to doubting hearts.

One of the remarkable qualities of the story is that it creates space. We can dwell in a story, walk around, find our own place. The story confronts but does not oppress; the story inspires but does not manipulate. The story invites us to an encounter, a dialog, a mutual sharing.

A story that guides is a story that opens a door and offers us space in which to search and boundaries to help us find what we seek, but it does not tell us what to do or how to do it. The story brings us into touch with the vision and so guides us. Wiesel writes, "God made man because he loves stories." As long as we have stories to tell to each other there is hope. As long as we can remind each other of the lives of men and women in whom the love of God becomes manifest, there is reason to move forward to new land in which new stories are hidden.

—From *The Living Reminder* by Henri J. M. Nouwen

Hymn: A Mighty Fortress Is Our God

A mighty fortress is our God,
A bulwark never failing;
Our helper he amid the flood
Of mortal ills prevailing:
For still our ancient foe
Doth seek to work us woe;
His craft and power are great,
And, armed with cruel hate,
On earth is not his equal.

Did we in our own strength confide,
Our striving would be losing,
Were not the right man on our side,
The man of God's own choosing:
Dost ask who that may be?
Christ Jesus, it is he;
Lord Sabaoth, his name,
From age to age the same,
And he must win the battle.

And though this world, with devils filled,
Should threaten to undo us,
We will not fear, for God hath willed
His truth to triumph through us:
The Prince of Darkness grim,
We tremble not for him;
His rage we can endure,
For lo, his doom is sure;
One little word shall fell him.

That word above all earthly powers,
No thanks to them, abideth;
The Spirit and the gifts are ours
Through him who with us sideth:
Let goods and kindred go,
This mortal life also;
The body they may kill:
God's truth abideth still;
His kingdom is forever. Amen.
—Martin Luther

40: God's Abundant Provision

I.   Invocation
Almighty God, in wisdom you have created us and all things. Provide our daily needs and grant us grace and strength to fulfill the ministry to which we have been called. We offer our prayers in the name and spirit of Christ. Amen.

II.   Psalm 105

III.   Daily Scripture Readings

Monday		Deuteronomy 7:6-14
Tuesday		Exodus 16:1-21
Wednesday		Romans 8:31-39
Thursday		2 Corinthians 5:16-21
Friday		Colossians 1:1-14
Saturday		Revelation 19:1-10
Sunday	A.	Exodus 12:1-14; Psalm 143:1-10; Romans 8:31-39; Matthew 14:13-21
	B.	2 Samuel 12:15b-24; Psalm 34:11-22; Ephesians 4:1-6; John 6:24-35
	C.	2 Kings 13:14-20a; Psalm 28; Colossians 3:1-11; Luke 12:13-21

IV.   Readings for Reflection

V.   Prayers: for the church, for others, for myself

VI.   Reflection: silent and written

VII.   Hymn: "One Holy Church of God Appears"

VIII.   Benediction
Today walk in the power and presence of God, Father, Son, and Holy Spirit. Amen.

Readings for Reflection

ᘐ Before we get too carried away with thoughts of God's power, we should listen attentively to what St. Paul says about the "weakness of God" (1 Cor. 1:25), which is a vital part of God's self-revelation. If we look at the way in which he discloses himself in Jesus Christ we have to acknowledge that he does not come into our world with a great display of superior power; in fact, this was one of the temptations which our Lord had to resist as being contrary to his mission, contrary to his true nature. (*Mt.* 4:5ff). He does not come in strength but in weakness, and he chooses the foolish and weak and unimportant things of the world, things that are nothing at all, to overthrow the strength and impressiveness of the world. As we saw earlier, he is like the judo expert who uses the strength of his opponent to bring him to the ground; it is the art of self-defence proper to the weak.

This is why, if we keep clamouring for things we want from God, we may often find ourselves disappointed, because we have forgotten the weakness of God and what we may call the poverty of God. We had thought of God as the dispenser of all the good things we would possibly desire; but in a very real sense, God has nothing to give at all except himself.

—From *Prayer* by Simon Tugwell

ᘐ We are the agents of the Creative Spirit in this world. Real advance in the spiritual life, then, means accepting this vocation with all it involves. Not merely turning over the pages of an engineering magazine and enjoying the pictures, but putting on overalls and getting on with the job. The real spiritual life must be horizontal as well as vertical; spread more and more as well as aspire more and more.

—From *The Spiritual Life* by Evelyn Underhill

ᘐ So those who imagine that they are called to contemplation because they are attracted by contemplation, when the common duties of existence steadily block this path, do well to realise that our own feelings and preferences are very poor guides when it comes to the robust realities and stern demands of the Spirit.

St. Paul did not want to be an apostle to the Gentiles. He wanted to be a clever and appreciated young Jewish scholar, and kicked against the pricks. St. Ambrose and St. Augustine did not want to be overworked and worried bishops. Nothing was farther from their intention. St. Cuthbert wanted the solitude and freedom of his hermitage on the Farne; but he did not often get there. St. Francis Xavier's preference was for an ordered life close to his beloved master, St. Ignatius. At a few hours' notice he was sent out to be the apostle of the Indies and never returned to Europe again. Henry Martyn, the fragile and exquisite scholar, was compelled to sacrifice the intellectual life to which he was so perfectly fitted for the missionary life to which he felt he was decisively called. In all these, a power beyond themselves decided the direction of life. Yet in all we recognise not frustration, but the highest of all types of achievement. Things like this—and they are constantly happening—gradually convince us that the overruling reality of life is the Will and Choice of a Spirit acting not in a mechanical but in a living and personal way; and that the spiritual life does not consist in mere individual betterment, or assiduous attention to one's own soul, but in a free and unconditional response to that Spirit's pressure and call, whatever the cost may be.

—From *The Spiritual Life* by Evelyn Underhill

❧ How are we to know, or find out, what the Will of God is? I do not think that any general answer can be given to this. In clear moral or political issues, we must surely judge and act by the great truths and demands of Christianity; and if we have the pluck to do this, then, as we act, more and more we shall perceive the direction of the Will. That choice, cause, or action, which is least tainted by self-interest, which makes for the increase of happiness— health—beauty—peace—cleanses and harmonises life, must always be in accordance with the Will of the Spirit which is drawing life towards perfection. The difficulty comes when there is a conflict of loyalties, or a choice between two apparent gods. At such points many people feel unaware of any guidance, unable to discern or understand the signals of

God; not because the signals are not given, but because the mind is too troubled, clouded and hurried to receive them. "He who is in a hurry," said St. Vincent de Paul, "delays the things of God." But when those who are at least attempting to live the life of the Spirit, and have consequently become more or less sensitive to its movements to have no clear light, they will often become aware, if they will wait in quietness, of a subtle yet insistent pressure in favour of the path which they should take. The early Friends were accustomed to trust implicitly in indications of this kind, and were usually justified. When there is no such pressure, then our conduct should be decided by charity and common sense; qualities which are given to us by God in order that they may be used.

—From *The Spiritual Life* by Evelyn Underhill

❧ Suffering is increasing in the world today. People are hungry for something more beautiful, for something greater than people round about can give. There is a great hunger for God in the world today. Everywhere there is much suffering, but there is also great hunger for God and love for each other.

—From *A Gift for God* by Mother Teresa

❧ Christian ministry is more than doing good. Ministry is an act of service performed either consciously or unconsciously in the name of Christ. Ministry is Jesus Christ expressing his life through us. It is born, therefore, not in activity, but in solitude, where through the spirit we experience the power of life from within. No one becomes a "minister." Rather in trust we so open ourselves to the Spirit that Jesus Christ can express his ministry through us. Prayer and ministry, therefore, are indissoluable. In the stillness of meditative prayer we are confronted by God's loving claim upon us—the most intense intimacy a human being can experience. To know this intimacy we have only to let go. Instead of relying on our own initiative, where we are in control, we discover that we are participating in what God has already initiated within us.

—From *Ministry and Solitude* by James C. Fenhagen

A Christian lady who had this feeling was once expressing to a friend how impossible she found it to say, "Thy will be done," and how afraid she should be to do it. She was the mother of an only little boy, who was the heir to a great fortune, and the idol of her heart. After she had stated her difficulties fully, her friend said, "Suppose your little Charley should come running to you to-morrow and say, 'Mother, I have made up my mind to let you have your own way with me from this time forward. I am always going to obey you, and I want you to do just whatever you think best with me. I will trust your love.' How would you feel towards him? Would you say to yourself, 'Ah, now I shall have a chance to make Charley miserable. I will take away all his pleasures, and fill his life with every hard and disagreeable thing that I can find. I will compel him to do just the things that are the most difficult for him to do, and will give him all sorts of impossible commands.'" "Oh, no, no, no!" exclaimed the indignant mother. "You know I would not. You know I would hug him to my heart and cover him with kisses, and would hasten to fill his life with all that was sweetest and best." "And are you more tender and more loving than God?" asked her friend. "Ah, no!" was the reply; "I see my mistake. Of course I must not be any more afraid of saying, 'Thy will be done,' to my Heavenly Father than I would want my Charley to be of saying it to me."

Better and sweeter than health, or friends, or money, or fame, or ease, or prosperity, is the adorable will of our God. It gilds the darkest hours with a divine halo, and sheds brightest sunshine on the gloomiest paths. He always reigns who has made it his kingdom, and nothing can go amiss to him. Surely, then, it is only a glorious privilege that is opening before you when I tell you that the first step you must take in order to enter into the life hid with Christ in God is that of entire consecration. I beg of you not to look at it as a hard and stern demand.

—From *The Christian's Secret of a Happy Life* by Hannah Whitall Smith

Hymn: One Holy Church of God Appears

One holy Church of God appears
Through every age and race,
Unwasted by the lapse of years,
Unchanged by changing place.

From oldest time, or farthest shores,
Beneath the pine or palm,
One unseen Presence she adores,
With silence, or with psalm.

The truth is her prophetic gift,
The soul, her sacred page;
And feet on mercy's errand swift
Do make her pilgrimage.

O living Church, thine errand speed;
Fulfill thy task sublime;
With bread of life earth's hunger feed;
Redeem the evil time! Amen.
—Samuel Longfellow

41: Prayers and Promises

I.   Invocation
Lord Jesus Christ, you have promised never to forsake or leave me. Accept my life and ministry as a living sacrifice to you and grant me strength to keep my promises to you. In the name of Christ. Amen.

II.   Psalm 127

III.   Daily Scripture Readings

Monday		2 Samuel 7:18-29
Tuesday		Romans 4
Wednesday		James 1:1-12
Thursday		2 Peter 1:1-11
Friday		Acts 12:1-11
Saturday		John 17:1-19
Sunday	A.	Exodus 14:19-31; Psalm 106:4-12; Romans 9:1-5; Matthew 14:22-33
	B.	2 Samuel 18:1, 5, 9-15; Psalm 143:1-8; Ephesians 4:25–5:2; John 6:35, 41-51
	C.	Jeremiah 18:1-11; Psalm 14; Hebrews 11:1-3, 8-19; Luke 12:32-40

IV.   Readings for Reflection

V.   Prayers: for the church, for others, for myself

VI.   Reflection: silent and written

VII.   Hymn: "Pass Me Not, O Gentle Savior"

VIII.   Benediction
Lord, allow me, your servant, to go in peace. I have experienced your salvation which you have prepared for everyone. Uphold me as I seek to serve in your name. Amen.

Readings for Reflection

❧ Confirm me, Lord, by the grace of the Holy Spirit, and give me grace to be strong inwardly in soul and to cast out from it all unprofitable business of the world and of the flesh, that it may not be led by unstable desires of earthly things. And grant that I may behold all things in this world as they are—transitory and of short abiding, and I myself also to pass away together with them, for nothing under the sun can long abide, but all in vanity and affliction of spirit.

Therefore, O Lord, give me true heavenly wisdom, that I may learn to seek you and to find you, and above all things to love you, and to understand and know all other things as they are, after the direction of your wisdom, and not otherwise. And give me grace, also, to withdraw myself from those who flatter me, and patiently to tolerate those who grieve me so that the way I have begun will bring me to a good and blessed ending.

—From *The Imitation of Christ* by Thomas à Kempis

❧ My Lord Jesus, I beseech you, do not be far from me, but come quickly and help me, for vain thoughts have risen in my heart and worldly fears have troubled me sorely. How shall I break them down? How shall I go unhurt without your help?

I shall go before you, says our Lord; I shall drive away the pride of your heart; then shall I set open to you the gates of spiritual knowledge and show you the privacy of my secrets.

O Lord, do as you say, and then all wicked imaginings shall flee away from me. Truly, this is my hope and my only comfort—to fly to you in every trouble, to trust steadfastly in you, to call inwardly upon you, and to abide patiently your coming and your heavenly consolations which, I trust, will quickly come to me.

—From *The Imitation of Christ* by Thomas à Kempis

❧ Enlighten me, Lord Jesus, with the clarity of everlasting light, and drive out of my heart all manner of darkness and all vain imaginations and violent temptation. Fight strongly for me and drive away the evil beasts—that is, all my evil and wicked concupiscences—so that peace of conscience may enter and fully rule within me, and that an abundance of glory and praise of your Name may sound continually in the chamber of my soul in a pure and clean conscience. Command the winds and the tempests of pride to cease; bid the sea of worldly covetousness to be at rest; and charge the northern wind—that is, the devil's temptation—not to blow. Then great tranquility and peace will be within me.

Send out your light and your truth of spiritual knowledge, that it may shine upon the earth, barren and dry. Send down your grace from above, and with it anoint my dry heart. Give me the water of inward devotion to moisten the dryness of my soul, that it may bring forth good fruit, agreeable and pleasant to you. Raise up my mind that is sore oppressed by the heavy burden of sin, and lift up my desire to the love of spiritual things, so that by a taste of heavenly joy it may loathe to think on any earthly thing. Take me Lord, and deliver me from the consolation of any earthly creatures which must of necessity shortly perish and fail, for there is nothing created that can fully satisfy my desires. Make me one with you in a sure bond of heavenly love, for you alone are sufficient to your lover, and without you all things are vain and of no substance.

—From *The Imitation of Christ* by Thomas à Kempis

&. Make us worthy, Lord, to serve our fellow men throughout the world who live and die in poverty and hunger. Give them, through our hands, this day their daily bread, and by our understanding love give peace and joy.

Lord, make me a channel of thy peace, that where there is hatred I may bring love; that where there is wrong, I may bring the spirit of forgiveness; that where there is discord, I may bring harmony; that where there is error, I may bring truth; that where there is doubt, I may bring faith; that where there is despair, I may bring hope; that where there are shadows, I may bring light; that where there is sadness, I may bring joy.

Lord, grant that I may seek rather to comfort than to be comforted; to understand than to be understood; to love than to be loved; for it is by forgetting self that one finds; it is by dying that one awakens to eternal life. Amen.

—From *Something Beautiful for God* by Malcolm Muggeridge

꽃 Speak to me low, my Saviour,
From out the hallelujahs, sweet and low,
Lest I should fear and fall, and miss thee so
Who art not missed by any that entreat.
Speak to me as to Mary at thy feet—
And if no precious gums my hands bestow,
Let my tears drop like amber, while I go
In reach of thy divinest voice complete
In humanest affection—thus, in sooth,
To lose the sense of losing! As a child,
Whose song-bird seeks the wood for evermore,
Is sung to in its stead by mother's mouth;
Till, sinking on her breast, love-reconciled,
He sleeps the faster that he wept before.
—Elizabeth Barrett Browning

꽃 O Lord, in whose hands are life and death, by whose power I am sustained, and by whose mercy I am spared, look down upon me with pity. Forgive me, that I have this day neglected the duty which Thou hast assigned to it, and suffered the hours, of which I must give account, to pass away without any endeavour to accomplish thy will, or to promote my own salvation. Make me to remember, O God, that every day is thy gift, and ought to be used according to thy command. Grant me, therefore, so to repent of my negligence, that I may obtain mercy from Thee, and pass the time which Thou shalt yet allow me, in diligent performance of thy commands, through Jesus Christ. *Amen.*
—From *Doctor Johnson's Prayers* edited by Elton Trueblood

꽃 Give God the praise for any well spent day.
—Susanna Wesley

꽃 My Lord Jesus Christ,
two graces I beg you to grant me
before I die:
the first is that in my lifetime
I may feel, in my soul and in my body,
as far as possible,
that sorrow which you, tender Jesus,

underwent in the hour
of your most bitter passion;
the second is that I may feel in my heart,
as far as possible,
that abundance of love with which you,
son of God,
were inflamed, so as willingly to undergo
such a great passion for us sinners.
—From *I, Francis* by Carlo Carretto

ે I do need thee, Lord. I need thee now. I know that I can do without many of the things that once I thought were necessities, but without thee I cannot live, and I dare not die.

I needed thee when sorrow came, when shadows were thrown across the threshold of my life, and thou didst not fail me then. I needed thee when sickness laid a clammy hand upon my family, and I cried to thee, and thou didst hear. I needed thee when perplexity brought me to a parting of the ways, and I knew not how to turn. Thou didst not fail me then, but in many ways, big and little, didst indicate the better way. And though the sun is shining around me today, I know that I need thee even in the sunshine, and shall still need thee tomorrow.

I give thee my gratitude for that constant sense of need that keeps me close to thy side. Help me to keep my hand in thine and my ears open to the wisdom of thy voice.

Speak to me, that I may hear thee giving me courage for hard times and strength for difficult places; giving me determination for challenging tasks. I ask of thee no easy way, but just thy grace that is sufficient for every need, so that no matter how hard the way, how challenging the hour, how dark the sky, I may be enabled to overcome.

In thy strength, who hast overcome the world, I make this prayer. Amen.

—From *The Prayers of Peter Marshall* edited by Catherine Marshall

ે God be in my head, and in my understanding;
God be in my eyes, and in my looking;
God be in my mouth, and in my speaking;

God be in my heart, and in my thinking;
God be at my end, and at my departing.
—*Sarum Primer*

Hymn: Pass Me Not, O Gentle Savior

Pass me not, O gentle Savior,
Hear my humble cry;
While on others thou art calling,
Do not pass me by.

Let me at thy throne of mercy
Find a sweet relief;
Kneeling there in deep contrition,
Help my unbelief.

Trusting only in thy merit,
Would I seek thy face;
Heal my wounded, broken spirit,
Save me by thy grace.

Thou the spring of all my comfort,
More than life for me;
Whom have I on earth beside thee?
Whom in heaven but thee?
—Fanny J. Crosby

42: *The Kingdom Comes*

I. Invocation
    Lord Jesus Christ, hasten the day when all of your
    people may know the joy, peace, and harmony of
    your kingdom. Grant unto me this day the power
    to live within your kingdom. In the name of Christ.
    Amen.

II. Psalm 145

III. Daily Scripture Readings
    Monday   1 Chronicles 29:10-22
    Tuesday   Luke 10:1-12
    Wednesday   Luke 22:14-30
    Thursday   Hebrews 12:18-29
    Friday   Matthew 4:18-25
    Saturday   Revelation 11:15-19
    Sunday   A. Exodus 16:2-15; Psalm 78:1-3, 10-20;
                    Romans 11:13-16, 29-32;
                    Matthew 15:21-28
                B. 2 Samuel 18:24-33; Psalm 102:1-12;
                    Ephesians 5:15-20; John 6:51-58
                C. Jeremiah 20:7-13; Psalm 10:12-18;
                    Hebrews 12:1-2, 12-17;
                    Luke 12:49-56

IV. Readings for Reflection

V. Prayers: for the church, for others, for myself

VI. Reflection: silent and written

VII. Hymn: "Come, Thou Almighty King"

VIII. Benediction
    The Lord bless you and keep you: the Lord make
    his face shine upon you, and be gracious to you; the
    Lord lift up his countenance upon you, and give you
    peace. Amen. —Numbers 6:24-26

Readings for Reflection

     O Christ, my life, possess me utterly.
Take me and make a little Christ of me.
If I am anything but thy Father's son,
'Tis something not yet from the darkness won.
Oh, give me light to live with open eyes.
Oh, give me life to hope above all skies.
Give me thy spirit to haunt the Father with my cries.

'Tis hard for us to rouse our spirits up—
It is the human creative agony,
Though but to hold the heart an empty cup,
Or tighten on the team the rigid rein.
Many will rather lie among the slain
Than creep through narrow ways the light to gain—
Than wake the will, and be born bitterly.

But we who would be born again indeed,
Must wake our souls unnumbered times a day,
And urge ourselves to life with holy greed;
Now ope our bosoms to the wind's free play;
And now, with patience forceful, hard, lie still,
Submiss and ready to the making will,
Athirst and empty, for God's breath to fill.
    —From *Diary of an Old Soul* by George MacDonald

     Only when we have come in touch with our own life experiences and have learned to listen to our inner cravings for liberation and new life can we realize that Jesus did not just speak, but that he reached out to us in our most personal needs. The Gospel doesn't just contain ideas worth remembering. It is a message responding to our individual human condition. The Church is not an institution forcing us to follow its rules. It is a community of people inviting us to still our hunger and thirst at its tables. Doctrines are not alien formulations which we must adhere to but the documentation of the most profound human experiences which, transcending time and place, are handed over from generation to generation as a light in our darkness.
—From *Reaching Out* by Henri J. M. Nouwen

~ *The experience of the race is clear that some things God never can do until he finds a man who prays.* Indeed, Meister Eckhart, the mystic, puts the truth with extreme boldness: "God can as little do without us, as we without him." If at first this seems a wild statement, we may well consider in how many ways God's will depends on man's cooperation. God himself cannot do some things unless men *think*. He never blazons his truth on the sky that men may find it without seeking. Only when men gird the loins of their minds and undiscourageably give themselves to intellectual toil, will God reveal to them the truth, even about the physical world. And God himself cannot do some things unless men *work*. Will a man say that when God wants bridges and tunnels, wants the lightnings harnessed and cathedrals built, he will do the work himself? That is an absurd and idle fatalism. God stores the hills with marble, but he never built a Parthenon; he fills the mountains with ore, but he never made a needle or a locomotive. Only when *men* work can some things be done. Recall the words of Stradivarius, maker of violins, as George Eliot interprets him:

> When any master holds 'twixt chin and hand a violin of mine, he will be glad that Stradivari lived, made violins, and made them of the best. . . . For while God gives them skill I give them instruments to play upon, God choosing me to help him. . . . If my hand slacked I should rob God—since he is fullest good—leaving a blank instead of violins. . . . he could not make Antonio Stradivari's violins without Antonio.

Now if God has left some things contingent on man's *thinking* and *working* why may he not have left some things contingent on man's praying? The testimony of the great souls is a clear affirmative to this: some things never without thinking; some things never without working; some things never without praying! *Prayer is one of the three forms of man's cooperation with God.*
—From *The Meaning of Prayer* by Harry Emerson Fosdick

~ My God, thank you for the physical sight to see both light and darkness around me. Thank you too for insight that comes with the vision to tell the difference. I know that my perception of reality, my vision, determines my ability to respond to life, and that the greater my vision, the more fully alive and fully human I can be.

Still I confess that sometimes the smallness of my vision limits my perception of myself, my neighbors, and the world, so that I treat others as less than human and not fully alive—personally, politically, economically, and socially. . . .

I need the vision that Jesus gives, that sees no difference between sacred and secular, sexual identity and personhood, ethnic group and worth, economic position and dignity, education and value.

I need the vision to ask the hard questions and to change my attitude and the structures of society where I can. Because of the sensitivity of sight you give, enable me to stand in awe and wonder at life and its possibilities. Help me kneel in humility to worship you and not myself. Lord, hear me as I say, "Let my eyes be opened." *Amen.*

—From *Visions of a World Hungry* by Thomas G. Pettepiece

❧   You alone are holy, Lord God, Worker of Wonders.
You are mighty.
You are great.
You are the Most High.
You are omnipotent, our holy Father, King of heaven and earth.
You, Lord God, three and one, are our every good.
You, Lord God, all good, our highest good—Lord God living and true.
You are charity and love.
You are wisdom.
You are humility.
You are patience.
You are security.
You are peace.
You are joy and gladness.
You are justice and temperance.
You are riches altogether sufficient.
You are beauty.
You are meekness.
You are our protector.
You are our strength.

You are our refreshment.
You are our hope.
You are our faith.
You are our most profound sweetness.
You are our eternal life, great and admirable Lord,
    omnipotent God, merciful Savior!
—From *I, Francis* by Carlo Carretto

Hymn: Come, Thou Almighty King

Come, thou almighty King,
Help us thy name to sing,
Help us to praise!
Father all glorious,
O'er all victorious,
Come, and reign over us,
Ancient of Days!

Come, thou incarnate Word,
Gird on thy mighty sword,
Our prayer attend;
Come, and thy people bless,
And give thy Word success;
Spirit of holiness,
On us descend!

Come, holy Comforter,
Thy sacred witness bear,
In this glad hour:
Thou who almighty art,
Now rule in every heart,
And ne'er from us depart,
Spirit of power!

To thee, great One in Three,
Eternal praises be,
Hence, evermore:
Thy sovereign majesty
May we in glory see,
And to eternity
Love and adore! Amen.
—Anonymous

43: Jesus Is the Way

   I.   Invocation
         Almighty God, as you have sent Jesus to be for us light and truth, send now your spirit upon us to grant us grace and strength to follow in his footsteps this day. Amen.

  II.   Psalm 18

 III.   Daily Scripture Readings

Monday	John 14:1-14	
Tuesday	Matthew 11:1-15	
Wednesday	Hebrews 10:19-25	
Thursday	Matthew 8:18-27	
Friday	Luke 5:27-39	
Saturday	John 12:20-36	
Sunday	A.	Exodus 17:1-7; Psalm 95; Romans 11:33-36; Matthew 16:13-20
	B.	2 Samuel 23:1-7; Psalm 67; Ephesians 5:21-33; John 6:55-69
	C.	Jeremiah 28:1-9; Psalm 84; Hebrews 12:18-29; Luke 13:22-30

 IV.   Readings for Reflection

  V.   Prayers: for the church, for others, for myself

 VI.   Reflection: silent and written

 VII.   Hymn: "Jesus, Lover of My Soul"

VIII.   Benediction
         You have been reminded that Jesus Christ is your Lord and that you are God's servant. You are loved; you are forgiven; you are empowered and now you are sent to live as God's faithful one. Amen.

Readings for Reflection

❧ But let us note this, that the dwelling of Jesus in us is the power of the Spirit of God upon us; for "the Lord is the Spirit," and "this comes from the Lord who is the Spirit." *When we think Christ, Christ comes;* when we receive his image into our spiritual mirror, he enters with it.

When our hearts turn to him, that is opening the door to him, that is holding up our mirror to him; then he comes in, not by our thought only, *not in our idea only, but he comes himself, and of his own will.* Thus the Lord, the Spirit, becomes the soul of our souls, becomes spiritually what he always was creatively; and as our spirit informs, gives shape to our bodies, in like manner his soul informs, gives shape to our souls.

In this there is nothing unnatural, nothing at conflict with our being. It is but that the deeper soul that willed and wills our souls, rises up, the infinite Life, into the Self we call *I* and *me*, makes the *I* and *me* more and more his, and himself more and more ours; until at length the glory of our existence flashes upon us, we face full to the sun that enlightens what is sent forth, and know ourselves alive with an infinite life, even the life of the Father. Then indeed we *are;* then indeed we have life; the life of Jesus has, through light, become life in us; the glory of God in the face of Jesus, mirrored in our hearts, has made us alive; we are one with God for ever and ever.

—From *Creation in Christ* by George MacDonald

❧ O God, our Father, we remember at this time . . . how the eternal Word became flesh and dwelt among us.

> We thank you that Jesus took our human body upon him, so that we can never again dare to despise or neglect or misuse the body, since you made it your dwelling-place.

> We thank you that Jesus did a day's work like any working-man, that he knew the problem of living together in a family, that he knew the frustration and irritation of serving the public, that he had to earn a living, and to face all the wearing routine of everyday work and life and living, and so clothed each common task with glory.

We thank you that he shared in all happy social occasions, that he was at home at weddings and at dinners and at festivals in the homes of simple ordinary people like ourselves. Grant that we may ever remember that in his unseen risen presence he is a guest in every home.

We thank you that he knew what friendship means, that he had his own circle of men whom he wanted to be with him, that he knew too what it means to be let down, to suffer from disloyalty and from the failure of love.

We thank you that he too had to bear unfair criticism, prejudiced opposition, malicious and deliberate misunderstanding.

We thank you that whatever happens to us, he has been there before, and that, because he himself has gone through things, he is able to help those who are going through them.

Help us never to forget that he knows life, because he lived life, and that he is with us at all times to enable us to live victoriously.

This we ask for your love's sake. Amen.

—From *Prayers for the Christian Year* by William Barclay

❧ The hour in our life in which we are best employed is the hour in which we best love Jesus.

A soul does good to others not in the measure of its knowledge or intelligence but in that of its holiness.

For me, all men should be enveloped, in God's sight, in the same love and the same indifference. I must no more trouble about health or life than a tree troubles about a failing leaf.

I must remember only Jesus, think only of Jesus, estimating as a gain any loss at the price of which I have more room in myself for thought and knowledge of Jesus, beside whom everything else is nothing.

I must reserve all my strength for Jesus.

—From *Meditations of a Hermit* by Charles de Foucauld

❧ One thing we owe to Our Lord is never to be afraid. To be afraid is doubly an injury to him. Firstly, it means that we forget him; we forget he is with us and is all powerful;

secondly, it means that we are not conformed to his will; for since all that happens is willed or permitted by him, we ought to rejoice in all that happens to us and feel neither anxiety nor fear. Let us then have the faith that banishes fear. Our Lord is at our side, with us, upholding us.

—From *Meditations of a Hermit* by Charles de Foucauld

  ❧ Lord Jesus, I believe that thou art able and willing to deliver me from all the care and unrest and bondage of my Christian life. I believe thou didst die to set me free, not only in the future, but now and here. I believe thou art stronger than sin, and that thou canst keep me, even me, in my extreme of weakness, from falling into its snares or yielding obedience to its commands. And, Lord, I am going to trust thee to keep me. I have tried keeping myself, and have failed, and failed, most grievously. I am absolutely helpless. So now I will trust thee. I give myself to thee. I keep back no reserves. Body, soul, and spirit, I present myself to thee as a piece of clay, to be fashioned into anything thy love and thy wisdom shall choose. And now I *am* thine. I believe thou dost accept that which I present to thee; I believe that this poor, weak, foolish heart has been taken possession of by thee, and that thou hast even at this very moment begun to work in me to will and to do of thy good pleasure. I trust thee *utterly*, and I trust thee *now*.

—From *The Christian's Secret of a Happy Life* by Hannah Whitall Smith

  ❧ Put yourself completely under the influence of Jesus, so that he may think his thoughts in your mind, do his work through your hands, for you will be all-powerful with him to strengthen you.

—From *A Gift for God* by Mother Teresa

Hymn: Jesus, Lover of My Soul

Jesus, lover of my soul,
Let me to thy bosom fly,
While the nearer waters roll,
While the tempest still is high:
Hide me, O my Savior, hide,
Till the storm of life is past;

Safe into the haven guide;
O receive my soul at last!

Other refuge have I none;
Hangs my helpless soul on thee;
Leave, ah! leave me not alone,
Still support and comfort me.
All my trust on thee is stayed;
All my help from thee I bring;
Cover my defenseless head
With the shadow of thy wing.

Thou, O Christ, art all I want;
More than all in thee I find:
Raise the fallen, cheer the faint,
Heal the sick, and lead the blind.
Just and holy is thy name;
I am all unrighteousness;
False and full of sin I am;
Thou art full of truth and grace.

Plenteous grace with thee is found,
Grace to cover all my sin;
Let the healing streams abound;
Make and keep me pure within.
Thou of life the fountain art;
Freely let me take of thee:
Spring thou up within my heart;
Rise to all eternity. Amen.
—Charles Wesley

44: *True Greatness*

I. Invocation
   Almighty God, you have sent Jesus to take our
   nature upon himself and to be for us sign and
   Saviour. Grant that by the power of your spirit
   Christ may be born within us today to the end that
   our ministry may be pleasing to you and helpful
   to your people. We pray in the name and spirit of
   Christ. Amen.

II. Psalm 1

III. Daily Scripture Readings
Monday	Matthew 23:1-36
Tuesday	Matthew 20:20-28
Wednesday	Matthew 6:1-24
Thursday	Matthew 6:25-34
Friday	Matthew 5:1-11
Saturday	Matthew 5:13-20

   Sunday
   A. Exodus 19:1-9; Psalm 114;
      Romans 12:1-13; Matthew 16:21-28
   B. 1 Kings 2:1-4, 10-12; Psalm 121;
      Ephesians 6:10-20; Mark 7:1-8,
      14-15, 21-23
   C. Ezekiel 18:1-9, 25-29; Psalm 15;
      Hebrews 13:1-8; Luke 14:1, 7-14

IV. Readings for Reflection

V. Prayers: for the church, for others, for myself

VI. Reflection: silent and written

VII. Hymn: "O for a Faith That Will Not Shrink"

VIII. Benediction
   And now may the spirit which was in Jesus Christ
   be in me, enabling me to know God's will and
   empowering me to do God's will. Amen.

Readings for Reflection

❧ And you, too, youthful reader, will realize the Vision (not the idle wish) of your heart, be it base or beautiful, or a mixture of both, for you will always gravitate toward that which you, secretly, most love. Into your hands will be placed the exact results of your own thoughts; you will receive that which you earn; no more, no less. Whatever your present environment may be, you will fall, remain, or rise with your thoughts, your Vision, your Ideal. You will become as small as your controlling desire; as great as your dominant aspiration. . . .

In all human affairs there are *efforts*, and there are *results*, and the strength of the effort is the measure of the result. Chance is not. "Gifts," powers, material, intellectual, and spiritual possessions are the fruits of effort; they are thoughts completed, objects accomplished, visions realized.

The Vision that you glorify in your mind, the Ideal that you enthrone in your heart—this you will build your life by, this you will become.

—From *As a Man Thinketh* by James Allen

❧ 'Seek the Kingdom of God and his justice and all these things shall be added unto you.' Be not concerned with how to live, what you will have to eat, nor for your body what to wear. We should rejoice greatly whenever we lack something.

I must divide my time for prayer in two parts. The first, at least equal to the other, I will devote to contemplation and meditation, the second I will give to prayer for all men, for all without exception, and for those with whom I am particularly concerned. I must say my office with great care. It is my daily offering of fresh flowers and roses, symbolical of fresh love offered daily to the Beloved spouse.

I will make frequent spiritual communions, unlimited except by my love, calling upon the beloved Saviour of my soul a hundred thousand times.

'He that heareth you, heareth me. He who humbles himself like a little child will be the greatest in the Kingdom of Heaven,' When in doubt incline always to obedience. Make acts of obedience wherever possible, not only because by so doing you can make sure of doing the will of God, but also in order to imitate Jesus in his submission in Nazareth and to obey his command to be like children. Also so that we may love Jesus in Heaven eternally, having that place reserved for us that is promised to those who put themselves lower than all, under obedience to other men, and practise the humility that this exacts.

I am in the house at Nazareth, between Mary and Joseph, embraced like a little boy, by my elder brother Jesus, who is present night and day in the Blessed Sacrament. So I must act as I ought in such company and in such a place, as I see Jesus act, giving me an example. In the Fraternity I must be always kind and gentle and humble as Jesus, Mary and Joseph were in the house at Nazareth. Gentleness, humility, abjection, charity, and at the service of others.

I must wash the linen of the poor (especially on Holy Thursday) and clean out their rooms myself as much as possible. Do myself, and no one else, all the menial tasks of the house, keeping the parts occupied by the natives clean. I must take upon myself to serve them, so as to resemble Jesus who dwelt amongst his apostles as one who served. I must be very gentle with the poor and with all men: this also is humility. I must cook for the poor when I can, bring them drink and meat, and not leave this task to others.

In the sick I should see not a man but Jesus and feel respect and love and compassion for him, and joy and gratitude at being able to care for him with zeal and tenderness. I must serve the sick as well as the poor, striving to render them the meanest services as Jesus did in washing the Apostles' feet.

I should bear the presence of evil-doers as Jesus bore that of Judas, so long as they do not corrupt others. Do not resist evil. I should accede even to unjust demands upon me out of obedience to God in order, by so condescending, to do good to souls and to do to others as God himself does.
—From *Meditations of a Hermit* by Charles de Foucauld

❧ Our Father, we take our loved ones and all those who need us deeply into our hearts and there we give them completely to thee. May thy peace, the peace which passeth all understanding, rest with them, bringing thy perfect fulfillment to all their needs. Amen.
—From *I Will Lift Up Mine Eyes* by Glenn Clark

❧ Keep open—oh, keep open . . . my eyes, my mind, my heart.
—Hermann Hagedorn

❧ Thou hast made us for thyself, O Lord; and our heart is restless until it rests in thee.
—Saint Augustine

❧ Almighty God, in whose hands are all the powers of man; who givest understanding, and takest it away; who, as it seemeth good unto Thee, enlightenest the thoughts of the simple, and darkenest the meditations of the wise, be present with me in my studies and enquiries.

Grant, O Lord, that I may not lavish away the life which Thou hast given me on useless trifles, nor waste it in vain searches after things which Thou hast hidden from me.

Enable me, by thy Holy Spirit, so to shun sloth and negligence, that every day may discharge part of the task which Thou hast allotted me; and so further with thy help that labour which, without thy help, must be ineffectual, that I may obtain, in all my undertakings, such success as will most promote thy glory, and the salvation of my own soul, for the sake of Jesus Christ. *Amen.*
—From *Doctor Johnson's Prayers* edited by Elton Trueblood

❧ The life of a good religious person should shine in all virtue and be inwardly as it appears outwardly. And it should be the much more inward, for Almighty God beholds the heart and we should always honor and reverence him as if we were always in his bodily presence, and appear before him as angels, clean and pure, shining with all virtue.

We ought every day to renew our purpose in God, and to stir our hearts to fervor and devotion, as though it were the first day of our conversion. And we ought daily to pray and say: Help me, my Lord Jesus, that I may persevere in good purpose and in your holy service unto my death, and that I may now today perfectly begin, for I have done nothing in time past.
—From *The Imitation of Christ* by Thomas à Kempis

Hymn: O for a Faith That Will Not Shrink

O for a faith that will not shrink,
Though pressed by every foe,
That will not tremble on the brink
Of any earthly woe!

That will not murmur nor complain
Beneath the chastening rod,
But, in the hour of grief or pain,
Will lean upon its God;

A faith that shines more bright and clear
When tempest rage without;
That when in danger knows no fear,
In darkness feels no doubt:

Lord, give me such a faith as this;
And then, whate'er may come,
I'll taste, e'en now, the hallowed bliss
Of an eternal home. Amen.
—William H. Bathurst

45: *Forgiveness*

I.   Invocation
     Almighty God, unto whom all hearts are open, all
     desires known, and from whom no secrets are hid:
     Cleanse the thoughts of our hearts by the inspiration
     of thy Holy Spirit, that we may perfectly love thee,
     and worthily magnify thy holy name; through Christ
     our Lord. Amen. —From *The Book of Worship*

II. Psalm 130

III. Daily Scripture Readings
     Monday   Acts 10:34-43
     Tuesday   1 John 2:1-17
     Wednesday   2 Corinthians 3:2-3
     Thursday   Luke 6:27-36
     Friday   Luke 6:37-42
     Saturday   Luke 17:1-6
     Sunday   A. Exodus 19:16-24; Psalm 115:1-11;
                     Romans 13:1-10; Matthew 18:15-20
                 B. Proverbs 2:1-8; Psalm 119:129-136;
                     James 1:17-27; Mark 7:31-37
                 C. Ezekiel 33:1-11; Psalm 94:12-22;
                     Philemon 1-20; Luke 14:25-33

IV. Readings for Reflection

V.   Prayers: for the church, for others, for myself

VI. Reflection: silent and written

VII. Hymn: "Amazing Grace! How Sweet the Sound"

VIII. Benediction
     I commend you to God and to the word of God's
     grace which is able to build you up and to give you
     your inheritance. Amen.

Readings for Reflection

 ❧ "Every sin and blasphemy," the Lord said, "will be forgiven unto men; but the blasphemy against the Spirit will not be forgiven." God speaks, as it were, in this manner: "I forgive you everything. Not a word more shall be said about your sins—only come out of them; come out of the darkness of your exile; come into the light of your home, of your birthright, and do evil no more. Lie no more; cheat no more; oppress no more; slander no more; envy no more; be neither greedy nor vain; love your neighbor as I love you; be my good child; trust in your Father. I am light; come to me, and you shall see things as I see them, and hate the evil thing. I will make you love the thing which now you call good and love not. I forgive all the past."

"I thank you, Lord, for forgiving me, but I prefer staying in the darkness: forgive me that too."

"No; that cannot be. The one thing that cannot be forgiven is the sin of choosing to be evil, of refusing deliverance. It is impossible to forgive that sin. It would be to take part in it. To side with wrong against right, with murder against life, cannot be forgiven. The thing that is past I pass, but he who goes on doing the same, annihilates this my forgiveness, makes it of no effect."

"Let a man have committed any sin whatever, I forgive him; but to choose to go on sinning—how can I forgive that? It would be to nourish and cherish evil! It would be to let my creation go to ruin. Shall I keep you alive to do things hateful in the sight of all true men? If a man refuse to come out of his sin, he must suffer the vengeance of a love that would be no love if it left him there. Shall I allow my creature to be the thing my soul hates?"

There is no excuse for this refusal. If we were punished for every fault, there would be no end, no respite; we should have no quiet wherein to repent; but God passes by all he can. He passes by and forgets a thousand sins, yea, tens of thousands, forgiving them all—only we must begin to be good, begin to do evil no more.

—From *Creation in Christ* by George MacDonald

When I met Peter Böhler again, he consented to put the dispute upon the issue which I desired, namely, Scripture and experience. I first consulted the Scripture. But when I set aside the glosses of men, and simply considered the words of God, comparing them together, endeavouring to illustrate the obscure by the plainer passages; I found they all made against me, and was forced to retreat to my last hold, "that experience would never agree with the *literal interpretation* of those scriptures. Nor could I therefore allow it to be true, till I found some living witnesses of it." He replied, he could show me such at any time; if I desired it, the next day. And accordingly, the next day he came again with three others, all of whom testified, of their own personal experience, that a true living faith in Christ is inseparable from a sense of pardon for all past, and freedom from all present, sins. They added with one mouth, that this faith was the gift, the free gift of God; and that he would surely bestow it upon every soul who earnestly and perseveringly sought it. I was now thoroughly convinced; and, by the grace of God, I resolved to seek it unto the end, 1. By absolutely renouncing all dependence, in whole or in part, upon *my own* works or righteousness; on which I had really grounded my hope of salvation, though I knew it not, from my youth up. 2. By adding to the constant use of all the other means of grace, continual prayer for this very thing, justifying, saving faith, a full reliance on the blood of Christ shed for *me*; a trust in him, as *my* Christ, as my sole justification, sanctification, and redemption.

—John Wesley

There are various kinds and degrees of wrong-doing, which need varying kinds and degrees of forgiveness. An outburst of anger in a child, for instance, scarcely wants forgiveness. The wrong in it may be so small, that the parent has only to influence the child for self-restraint, and the rousing of the will against the wrong. The father will not feel that such a fault has built up any wall between him and his child.

But suppose that he discovered in him a habit of sly cruelty towards his younger brothers, or the animals of the house, how differently would he feel! Could his forgiveness be the same as in the former case? Would not the different evil require a different *form* of forgiveness? I mean, would not the forgiveness have to take the form of that kind of punishment fittest for restraining, in the hope of finally rooting out, the wickedness? Could there be true love in any other kind of forgiveness than this? A passing-by of the offence might spring from a poor human kindness, but never from divine love. It would not be *remission*. Forgiveness can never be indifference. Forgiveness is love towards the unlovely.

—From *Creation in Christ* by George MacDonald

᷍ But there are two sins, not of individual deed, but of spiritual condition, which *cannot be forgiven*; that is, as it seems to me, which cannot be excused, passed by, made little of by the tenderness even of God, inasmuch as they will allow no forgiveness to come into the soul, they will permit no good influence to go on working alongside of them; they shut God out altogether. Therefore the man guilty of these can never receive into himself the holy renewing saving influences of God's forgiveness. God is outside of him in every sense, save that which springs from his creating relation to him, by which, thanks be to God, he yet keeps a hold of him, although against the will of the man who will not be forgiven. The one of these sins is against man; the other against God.

The former is unforgiveness to our neighbor; the shutting of him out from our mercies, from our love—so from the universe, as far as we are a portion of it—the murdering therefore of our neighbor. It may be an infinitely less evil to murder a man than to refuse to forgive him. The former may be the act of a moment of passion: the latter is the heart's choice. It is *spiritual* murder, the worst, to hate, to brood over the feeling that excludes, that kills the image, the idea of the hated.

—From *Creation in Christ* by George MacDonald

᷍ Yes, I too must go beyond justice. To triumph over the sickness of victimisation I must go beyond it. Like Jesus and in imitation of him, I must wearily climb again the slope of my pain, and throw myself courageously in the descent towards my brothers and sisters, above all towards those whom the short-sightedness of my sick eyes sees as the cause of my evils.

There is no other solution. There is no true peace and union with Jesus without it. As long as I waste time defending myself I get nothing done and I am not truly Christian; I do not know the depths of the heart of Jesus.

To forgive, really forgive, means convincing ourselves deep down that we merited the wrong done to us. What is more, it is good to suffer in silence. Jesus taught that the beatitude is reserved for those who are *persecuted* for the sake of justice.

—From *Letters from the Desert* by Carlo Carretto

❧ ALL HAVE SINNED AND COME SHORT OF THE GLORY OF GOD

St. Paul's Letter to the Romans

THE HATRED . . .   which divides nation from nation, race from race, class from class; FATHER, FORGIVE.

THE GREED . . .   which exploits the labours of men and lays waste to earth; FATHER, FORGIVE.

OUR ENVY . . .   of the welfare and happiness of others; FATHER, FORGIVE.

OUR INDIFFERENCE . . . to the plight of the homeless and the refugee; FATHER, FORGIVE.

THE LUST . . .   which uses for ignoble ends, the bodies of men and women; FATHER, FORGIVE.

THE PRIDE . . .   which leads us to trust in ourselves and not in God; FATHER, FORGIVE.

Be kind to one another, tenderhearted, forgiving one another, as God in Christ forgave you (St. Paul to the Ephesians).

—Prayer at the altar of Coventry Cathedral

&. Almighty and most merciful Father, whose clemency I now presume to implore, after a long life of carelessness and wickedness, have mercy upon me. I have committed many trespasses; I have neglected many duties. I have done what Thou hast forbidden, and left undone what Thou hast commanded. Forgive, merciful Lord, my sins, negligences, and ignorances, and enable me, by the Holy Spirit, to amend my life according to thy Holy Word, for Jesus Christ's sake. *Amen.*
—From *Doctor Johnson's Prayers* edited by Elton Trueblood

Hymn: Amazing Grace! How Sweet the Sound

Amazing grace! how sweet the sound
That saved a wretch like me!
I once was lost, but now am found,
Was blind, but now I see.

'Twas grace that taught my heart to fear,
And grace my fears relieved;
How precious did that grace appear
The hour I first believed!

Through many dangers, toils and snares,
I have already come;
'Tis grace hath brought me safe thus far,
And grace will lead me home.

The Lord has promised good to me,
His word my hope secures;
He will my shield and portion be
As long as life endures.

Yea, when this flesh and heart shall fail,
And mortal life shall cease,
I shall possess, within the veil,
A life of joy and peace. Amen.
—John Newton

46: *Beyond Forgiveness*

I   Invocation
Almighty God, from whom every good prayer cometh, and who pourest out on all who desire it the spirit of grace and supplication: Deliver us, when we draw nigh to thee, from coldness of heart and wanderings of mind, that, with steadfast thoughts and kindled affections, we may worship thee in spirit and in truth; through Jesus Christ our Lord. Amen.

II.   Psalm 141

III.   Daily Scripture Readings

Monday	John 5:1-15	
Tuesday	John 8:1-11	
Wednesday	Psalm 25	
Thursday	Ephesians 2	
Friday	Romans 6:1-14	
Saturday	Romans 3:21-31	
Sunday	A.	Exodus 20:1-20; Psalm 19:7-14; Romans 14:5-12; Matthew 18:21-35
	B.	Proverbs 22:1-2, 8-9; Psalm 125; James 2:1-5, 8-10, 14-17; Mark 8:27-38
	C.	Hosea 4:1-3, 5:15–6:6; Psalm 77:11-20; 1 Timothy 1:12-17; Luke 15:1-10

IV.   Readings for Reflection

V.   Prayers: for the church, for others, for myself

VI.   Reflection: silent and written

VII.   Hymn: "O Master, Let Me Walk with Thee"

VIII.   Benediction
The grace of the Lord Jesus Christ and the love of God and the fellowship of the Holy Spirit be with you all. Amen. —2 Corinthians 13:14

Readings for Reflection

❧ Only by a stronger passion can evil passions be expelled, and . . . a soul unoccupied by a positive devotion is sure to be occupied by spiritual demons. *The safety of the Master in the presence of temptation lay in his complete and positive devotion to his mission: there was no unoccupied room in his soul where evil could find a home; he knew what Dr. Chalmers called, "The expulsive Power of a new affection."* When Ulysses passed the Isle of Sirens, he had himself tied to the mast and had his ears stopped with wax, that he might not hear the sirens singing—a picture of many a man's pitiful attempts after negative goodness. But when Orpheus passed the Isle of Sirens, he sat on the deck, indifferent, for he too was a musician and could make melody so much more beautiful than the sirens, that their alluring songs were to him discords. Such is the Master's life of positive goodness, so full, so glad, so triumphant, that it conquered sin by surpassing it. Have you such a saving positiveness of loyal devotion in your life?

—From *The Manhood of the Master* by Harry Emerson Fosdick

❧ And when I thought of the poor I had met in my life, especially in recent years, it was clear that there were poor who were only poor—very sad, often angry, and certainly not blessed.

And then again, I recalled very well, there were poor people who were quite otherwise, poor people who wore their poverty beautifully.

Poor people who had the conviction that they were being guided by God, supported by his Presence.

Poor people who were able to love, in spite of their sudden vexations—poor people who were patient in trial, rich in hope, strong in adversity.

Poor people who were blessed because they could bear witness, every day, that God was present in their lives, and that he provided for them as he did for the sparrows of the sky, which possess no granaries.

Yes, this captivated me.

To bear witness, to testify, to myself and to other human beings, that God alone sufficed for me, and that I did not

have to be concerned about anything, anything at all—
"think of the flowers of the field; they never have to spin or
weave; yet not even Solomon in all his regalia was like one
of these" (Luke 12:27).

The thought of being fed, clothed, and guided by God
himself uplifted me. No power on earth could have persuaded me to change my mind. Putting a little money
aside—keeping a larder—buying a house—for me this
would have meant a lack of trust in my Lord.

Oh, I would not have proposed this manner of life for
everyone. For example, it would not have been the thing for
my father.

That would have been impossible. Society had other
laws. People had different callings.

I was proposing it for myself, as I wished to be a witness of God's love. And I would have proposed it for those
who would follow me.

—From *I, Francis* by Carlo Carretto

ૐ Let us take especial care, sisters, to pray to him for
them, and not be negligent. To pray for those who are in
mortal sin is the best kind of almsgiving—a much better
thing than it would be to loose a Christian whom we saw
with his hands tied behind him, bound with a stout chain,
made fast to a post and dying of hunger, not for lack of
food, since he has beside him the most delicious things to
eat, but because he cannot take them and put them into
his mouth although he is weary to death and actually
knows that he is on the point of dying, and not merely a
death of the body, but one which is eternal. Would it not
be extremely cruel to stand looking at such a man and not
give him this food to eat? And supposing you could loose
his chains by means of your prayers? You see now what I
mean. For the love of God, I beg you always to remember
such souls when you pray.

—From *Interior Castle* by Saint Teresa of Avila

ૐ Lord, I have fallen again—a human clod!
  Selfish I was, and heedless to offend;
  Stood on my rights. Thy own child would not send
Away his shreds of nothing for the whole God!
  Wretched, to thee who savest, low I bend:

Give me the power to let my rag-rights go
In the great wind that from thy gulf doth blow.
—From *Diary of an Old Soul* by George MacDonald

ૐ Keep me from wrath, let it seem ever so right:
My wrath will never work thy righteousness.
Up, up the hill, to the whiter than snow-shine,
Help me to climb, and dwell in pardon's light.
I must be pure as thou, or even less
Than thy design of me—therefore incline
My heart to take man's wrongs as thou tak'st mine.
—From *Diary of an Old Soul* by George MacDonald

ૐ If I should slow diverge, and listless stray
Into some thought, feeling, or dream unright,
O Watcher, my backsliding soul affray;
Let me not perish of the ghastly blight.
Be thou, O Life eternal, in me light;
Then merest approach of selfish or impure
Shall start me up alive, awake, secure.
—From *Diary of an Old Soul* by George MacDonald

ૐ Here we have come back to the compassion that must be formed in one's heart, a compassion that comes out of a deep experience of solidarity, in which one recognizes that the evil, sin and violence which one sees in the world and in the other, are deeply rooted in one's own heart. Only when you want to confess this and want to rely on the merciful God who can bring good out of evil are you in a position to receive forgiveness and also to give it to other men and women who threaten you with violence. Precisely because Merton had discovered this nonviolent compassion in his solitude could he in a real sense be a monk, that is to say, one who unmasks through his criticism the illusions of a violent society and who wants to change the world in spirit and truth.
—From *Thomas Merton: Contemplative Critic* by Henri J. M. Nouwen

ૐ When a man gives up self, his past sins will no longer oppress him. It is enough for the good of life that God lives, that the All-perfect exists, and that we can behold him.

"Father, forgive them, for they know not what they do," said the Divine, making excuse for his murderers, not after it was all over, but at the very moment when he was dying by their hands. Then Jesus had forgiven them already. His prayer the Father must have heard, for he and the Son are one. When the Father succeeded in answering his prayer, then his forgiveness in the hearts of the murderers broke out in sorrow, repentance, and faith. Here was a sin dreadful enough surely—but easy for our Lord to forgive. All that excuse for the misled populace! Lord Christ be thanked for that! That was like thee!

—From *Creation in Christ* by George MacDonald

Hymn: O Master, Let Me Walk with Thee

O Master, let me walk with thee
In lowly paths of service free;
Tell me thy secret; help me bear
The strain of toil, the fret of care.

Help me the slow of heart to move
By some clear, winning word of love;
Teach me the wayward feet to stay,
And guide them in the homeward way.

Teach me thy patience; still with thee
In closer, dearer company,
In work that keeps faith sweet and strong,
In trust that triumphs over wrong;

In hope that sends a shining ray
Far down the future's broadening way;
In peace that only thou canst give,
With thee, O Jesus, let me live. Amen.

—Washington Gladden

47: *Wise Stewards*

I. Invocation
    Almighty God, you who created me and called me
    to ministry, pour out your Holy Spirit on me today
    so that I may be a wise steward of these precious
    gifts. In the name and spirit of Christ. Amen.

II. Psalm 3

III. Daily Scripture Readings
Monday	Ecclesiastes 9:13-18
Tuesday	1 Kings 3:3-28
Wednesday	James 3:13-18
Thursday	Ephesians 3:1-20
Friday	2 Corinthians 6:1-10
Saturday	1 Corinthians 4:1-13

    Sunday   A. Exodus 32:1-14; Psalm 106:7-8,
                 19-23; Philippians 1:21-27;
                 Matthew 20:1-16
              B. Job 28:20-28; Psalm 27:1-6;
                 James 3:13-18; Mark 9:30-37
              C. Hosea 11:1-11; Psalm 107:1-9;
                 1 Timothy 2:1-7; Luke 16:1-13

IV. Readings for Reflection

V.   Prayers: for the church, for others, for myself

VI. Reflection: silent and written

VII. Hymn: "Draw Thou My Soul, O Christ"

VIII. Benediction
     Go forth now as God's servant. Remember God's
     presence often and draw strength from the knowl-
     edge that the One who calls and sends also sustains.
     Amen.

Readings for Reflection

❧ O Lord Jesus Christ, Son of the living God, have mercy on me, a sinner. I am impressed by my own spiritual insights. I probably know more about prayer, meditation, and contemplation than most Christians do. I have read many books about the Christian life, and have even written a few myself. Still, as impressed as I am, I am more impressed by the enormous abyss between my insights and my life.

It seems as if I am standing on one side of a huge canyon and see how I should grow toward you, live in your presence and serve you, but cannot reach the other side of the canyon where you are. I can speak and write, preach and argue about the beauty and goodness of the life I see on the other side, but how, O Lord, can I get there? Sometimes I even have the painful feeling that the clearer the vision, the more aware I am of the depth of the canyon.

Am I doomed to die on the wrong side of the abyss? Am I destined to excite others to reach the promised land while remaining unable to enter there myself? Sometimes I feel imprisoned by my own insights and "spiritual competence." You alone, Lord, can reach out to me and save me. You alone.

I can only keep trying to be faithful, even though I feel faithless most of the time. What else can I do but keep praying to you, even when I feel dark; to keep writing about you, even when I feel numb; to keep speaking in your name, even when I feel alone. Come, Lord Jesus, come. Have mercy on me, a sinner. Amen.

—From *A Cry for Mercy* by Henri J. M. Nouwen

❧ Therefore, be attentive to time and the way you spend it. Nothing is more precious. This is evident when you recall that in one tiny moment heaven may be gained or lost. God, the master of time, never gives the future. He gives only the present, moment by moment, for this is the law of the created order, and God will not contradict himself in his creation. Time is for you, not for time. God, the Lord of nature, will never anticipate your choices which follow one after another in time. You will not be able to excuse yourself at the last judgment, saying to God: "You overwhelmed me with the future when I was only capable of living in the present."

But now I see that you are discouraged and are saying to yourself: "What am I to do? If all he says is true, how shall I justify my past? I am twenty-four years old and until this moment I have scarcely noticed time at all. What is worse, I could not repair the past even if I wanted to, for according to his teaching such a task is impossible to me by nature even with the help of ordinary grace. Besides I know very well that in the future, either through frailty or laziness, I will probably not be any more attentive to the present moment than I have been in the past. I am completely discouraged. Please help me for the love of Jesus."

Well have you said "for the love of Jesus." For it is in his love that you will find help. In love all things are shared and so if you love Jesus, everything of his is yours. As God he is the creator and dispenser of time; as man he consciously mastered time; as God and man he is the rightful judge of you and your use of time. Bind yourself to Jesus, therefore, in faith and love, so that belonging to him you may share all he has and enter the fellowship of those who love him.

—From *The Cloud of Unknowing*

❧ "We are always praying, when we are doing our duty and turning it into work for God." He added that among the things which we should regard as spiritual in this sense are our household or professional work, the social duties of our station, friendly visits, kind actions and small courtesies, and also necessary recreation of body and of mind; so long as we link all these by intention with God and the great movement of his Will.

—From *The Spiritual Life* by Evelyn Underhill

❧ The soul attracts that which it secretly harbors; that which it loves, and also that which it fears; it reaches the height of its cherished aspirations; it falls to the level of its unchastened desires, and circumstances are the means by which the soul receives its own.

Every thought-seed sown or allowed to fall into the mind, and to take root there, produces its own, blossoming sooner or later into act, and bearing its own fruitage of opportunity and circumstance. Good thoughts bear good fruit, bad thoughts bad fruit.

The outer world of circumstance shapes itself to the inner world of thought, and both pleasant and unpleasant external conditions are factors which make for the ultimate good of the individual. As the reaper of his own harvest, man learns both by suffering and bliss.

Following the inmost desires, aspirations, thoughts, by which one allows oneself to be dominated (pursuing the will-o'-the-wisps of impure imagining or steadfastly walking the highway of strong and high endeavor), a person at last arrives at their fruition and fulfillment in the outer condition of life.

The laws of growth and adjustment everywhere obtain.
—From *As a Man Thinketh* by James Allen

&. St. John of the Cross says that every quality or virtue which that Spirit really produces in our souls has three distinguishing characters—as it were a threefold National Mark—Tranquillity, Gentleness, Strength. All our action—and now we are thinking specially of action—must be peaceful, gentle and strong. That suggests, doesn't it, an immense depth, and an invulnerable steadiness as the soul's abiding temper; a depth and a steadiness which come from the fact that our small action is now part of the total action of God, whose Spirit, as another saint has said, "Works always in tranquillity." Fuss and feverishness, anxiety, intensity, intolerance, instability, pessimism and wobble, and every kind of hurry and worry—these, even on the highest levels, are signs of the self-made and self-acting soul; the spiritual parvenu. The saints are never like that. They share the quiet and noble qualities of the great family to which they belong.
—From *The Spiritual Life* by Evelyn Underhill

Hymn: Draw Thou My Soul, O Christ

Draw thou my soul, O Christ,
Closer to thine;
Breathe into every wish
Thy will divine!
Raise my low self above,
Won by thy deathless love;
Ever, O Christ, through mine
Let thy life shine.

Lead forth my soul, O Christ,
One with thine own,
Joyful to follow thee
Through paths unknown!
In thee my strength renew;
Give me my work to do!
Through me thy truth be shown,
Thy love made known.

Not for myself alone
May my prayer be;
Lift thou thy world, O Christ,
Closer to thee!
Cleanse it from guilt and wrong;
Teach it salvation's song,
Till earth, as heaven, fulfill
God's holy will. Amen.
—Lucy Larcom

48: *God Supplies Our Every Need*

I. Invocation
Almighty God, in whom I find life, health, and strength, and through whose mercy I am clothed and fed, grant unto me a thankful and faithful heart. In the name and spirit of Christ. Amen.

II. Psalm 86

III. Daily Scripture Readings

Monday	1 Kings 17
Tuesday	Luke 12:1-21
Wednesday	Luke 12:22-32
Thursday	1 Timothy 6:1-19
Friday	2 Corinthians 10:1-18
Saturday	Philippians 4:10-19
Sunday	A. Exodus 33:12-23; Psalm 99; Philippians 2:1-13; Matthew 21:28-32
	B. Job 42:1-6; Psalm 27:7-14; James 4:13-17, 5:7-11; Mark 9:38-50
	C. Joel 2:23-30; Psalm 107:1, 33-43; 1 Timothy 6:6-19; Luke 16:19-31

IV. Readings for Reflection

V. Prayers: for the church, for others, for myself

VI. Reflection: silent and written

VII. Hymn: "God of the Ages, by Whose Hand"

VIII. Benediction
You have been in communion with your Lord. Go forth now in the strength and assurance that the Lord Jesus Christ goes with you. Amen.

Readings for Reflection

❧ Norman Harrison in *His in a Life of Prayer* tells how Charles Inglis, while making the voyage to America a number of years ago, learned from the devout and godly captain of an experience which he had had but recently with George Müller of Bristol. It seems that they had encountered a very dense fog. Because of it the captain had remained on the bridge continuously for twenty-four hours, when Mr. Müller came to him and said, "Captain, I have come to tell you that I must be in Quebec on Saturday afternoon." When informed that it was impossible, he replied: "Very well. If the ship cannot take me, God will find some other way. I have never broken an engagement for fifty-seven years. Let us go down into the chartroom and pray."

The captain continues the story thus: "I looked at that man of God and thought to myself, What lunatic asylum could that man have come from. I never heard such a thing as this. 'Mr. Müller,' I said, 'do you know how dense this fog is?' 'No,' he replied, 'my eye is not on the density of the fog, but on the living God, who controls every circumstance of my life.' He knelt down and prayed one of those simple prayers, and when he had finished I was going to pray; but he put his hand on my shoulder and told me not to pray. 'Firstly,' he said, 'because you do not believe God will, and secondly, I believe God has, and there is no need whatever for you to pray about it.' I looked at him, and George Müller said, 'Captain, I have known my Lord for fifty-seven years, and there has never been a single day that I have failed to get an audience with the King. Get up and open the door, and you will find that the fog has gone.' I got up and the fog was indeed gone. George Müller was in Quebec Saturday afternoon for his engagement."
—From *I Will Lift Up Mine Eyes* by Glenn Clark

❧ Our Lord is sitting by the Temple watching all the people coming and going, putting their offerings into the box. Some of them were making quite a show of it, no doubt, so that everyone would know how much they had put in. But there, among them all, was a little old lady, rather shabbily dressed, who slipped in her twopence half-penny when no one was looking. But the Lord saw her. And he got terribly excited about it. "She's put in more than all the rest put together!" he exclaims.

This little old lady did not realise that she was doing anything spectacular; nothing could have been further from her mind. She did not want to draw attention to herself, because she knew that what she was giving was not worth very much, it was not going to repair the Temple roof or get them a new organ or even pay for the Boy Scouts' Annual Outing. The Temple authorities might well think it was a confounded nuisance having to count all the small change put in by people like her. But she had given all she had, knowing that it was not much, knowing that she was not going to solve anyone's problems. And surely the Lord recognised in her a kindred spirit. She was doing the same kind of thing that he was doing. He was not solving the world's problems in any sense that the world could understand, he was not reforming society or abolishing poverty—"the poor you will always have with you" was his comment on that (*Mt. 26:11*)—he was not doing any of the things some modern Christians think he should have been doing. And many people considered him a nuisance. But he was giving himself, he was giving all he had got, he was giving his very life.

Blessed are the poor! How easily we take that always to mean somebody else. Yet if we want to be with God, we must learn to hear it as "blessed are we who are poor", we who have not got anything very impressive to give to anybody, whose giving may very well be rather a nuisance, but who still have not given up giving. Who knows? Our giving of ourselves in all our poverty may one day bring some joy to somebody else who is poor, who is not calculating, not trying to repair a church roof. God invites us into this conspiracy of the poor, making himself its head, giving himself in poverty and weakness, knowing that if we will only receive that humble gift of his, it will transform everything. If we are prepared to be poor enough to learn and to appreciate the manner of God's giving, we shall find in that poverty the seed of all perfection.

—From *Prayer* by Simon Tugwell

୬ St. Augustine makes an identical point about miracles in his discussion of the miracle at Cana. "Our Lord's miracle in turning water into wine comes as no surprise to those who know that it is God who did it. At the wedding that day he made wine in the six waterpots he had had filled with water; but he does the same thing every year in the vines. The servants put the water in the jugs, and he turned it into wine. In just the same way the Lord turns into wine the water that the clouds drop. Only that does not amaze us, because it happens every year . . . So the Lord kept back certain unusual things for himself to do, to wake us up with miracles to worship him."

The miracle that breaks the rules reminds us that the rules themselves are miraculous. We need to rediscover and to cherish a basic sense of wonder, of surprise, of the precariousness of actuality. Ecclesiastes, the dismal world-weary preacher of the Old Testament, might grumble that "there is nothing new under the sun" *(Eccles 1:9)*; but the New Testament answers loudly and excitedly, "Look! I am making all things new" *(Apoc 21:5)*. Of course, we may all of us sometimes get Ecclesiastes moods, and if we do, it is comforting to know that they are not utterly debarred from God's domain; but we should not devote our minds and imaginations to prolonging and justifying them. We should aim rather to have minds and imaginations able to respond joyfully to the truth that in Christ everything is given back its youth and at least something of the freshness of the very first days of creation.

> Morning has broken
> Like the first morning,
> Blackbird has spoken
> Like the first bird.
> Praise for the singing!
> Praise for the morning!
> Praise for them, springing
> Fresh from the Word!

To experience the world like this must lead us, however indefinitely, in the direction of prayer, because this kind of appreciation cannot help but include an element of thanksgiving. As Chesterton said: "Children are grateful when Santa Claus puts in their stockings gifts of toys or sweets. Could I not be grateful to Santa Claus when he put in my stockings the gift of two miraculous legs?"

—From *Prayer* by Simon Tugwell

❧ That he [Brother Lawrence] had always been governed by love; without selfish views; and that having resolved to make the love of God the *end* of all his actions, he had found reasons to be well satisfied with his method. That he was pleased when he could take up a straw from the ground for the love of God, seeking him only, and nothing else, not even his gifts.

That he had been long troubled in mind from a certain belief that he should be damned; that all the people in the world could not have persuaded him to the contrary; but that he had thus reasoned with himself about it: *I engaged in a religious life only for the love of God, and I have endeavored to act only for him; whatever becomes of me, whether I be lost or saved, I will always continue to act purely for the love of God. I shall have this good at least, that till death I shall have done all that is in me to love him.* That this trouble of mind had lasted four years, during which time he had suffered much; but that at last he had seen that this trouble arose from want of faith, and that since he had passed his life in perfect liberty and continual joy. That he had placed his sins betwixt him and God, as it were, to tell him that he did not deserve his favors, but that God still continued to bestow them in abundance. . . .

That he expected, after the pleasant days God had given him, he should have his turn of pain and suffering; but that he was not uneasy about it, knowing very well that as he could do nothing of himself, God would not fail to give him the strength to bear it.

That when an occasion of practising some virtue offered, he addressed himself to God, saying, *Lord, I cannot do this unless thou enablest me*; and that then he received strength more than sufficient.

That when he had failed in his duty, he only confessed his fault, saying to God, *I shall never do otherwise if you leave me to myself; it is you who must hinder my falling and mend what is amiss*. That after this he gave himself no further uneasiness about it.

That we ought to act with God in the greatest simplicity, speaking to him frankly and plainly, and imploring his assistance in our affairs, just as they happen. That God never failed to grant it, as he had often experienced.

—From *The Practice of the Presence of God* by Brother Lawrence

  Father, I am beginning to know how much I miss when I fail to talk to thee in prayer, and through prayer to receive into my life the strength and the guidance which only thou canst give. Forgive me for the pride and the presumption that make me continue to struggle to manage my own affairs to the exhaustion of my body, the weariness of my mind, the trial of my faith.

In a moment like this I know that thou couldst have worked thy good in me with so little strain, with so little effort. And then to thee would have been given the praise and the glory. When I neglect to pray, mine is the loss. Forgive me, Lord. Amen.

—From *The Prayers of Peter Marshall* edited by Catherine Marshall

Hymn: God of the Ages, by Whose Hand

God of the ages, by whose hand
Through years long past our lives were led,
Give us new courage now to stand,
New faith to find the paths ahead.

Thou art the thought beyond all thought,
The gift beyond our utmost prayer;
No farthest reach where thou art not,
No height but we may find thee there.

Forgive our wavering trust in thee,
Our wild alarms, our trembling fears;
In thy strong hand eternally
Rests the unfolding of the years.

Though there be dark, uncharted space,
With worlds on worlds beyond our sight,
Still may we trust thy love and grace,
And wait thy word, Let there be light. Amen.
—Elisabeth Burrowes

49: *Faithfulness*

I. Invocation
    Lord Jesus Christ, you demonstrated faithfulness in all of life, even to death on the cross. Grant unto me grace and strength to follow you faithfully all the days of my life. Amen.

II. Psalm 89

III. Daily Scripture Readings
    Monday   1 Samuel 2:27-36
    Tuesday   Hebrews 11:1-31
    Wednesday   Hebrews 11:32–12:2
    Thursday   2 Timothy 2:1-13
    Friday   Revelation 2:8-11
    Saturday   Matthew 25:1-30
    Sunday   A. Numbers 27:12-23; Psalm 81:1-10;
                    Philippians 3:12-21;
                    Matthew 21:33-43
                B. Genesis 2:18-24; Psalm 128;
                    Hebrews 1:1-4, 2:9-11; Mark 10:2-16
                C. Amos 5:6-7, 10-15; Psalm 101;
                    2 Timothy 1:1-14; Luke 17:5-10

IV. Readings for Reflection

V. Prayers: for the church, for others, for myself

VI. Reflection: silent and written

VII. Hymn: "O Jesus, I Have Promised"

VIII. Benediction
    Be bound to Christ for this day and always. Amen.

Readings for Reflection

  Thus, one who makes it a rule to be content in every part and accident of life because it comes from God praises God in a much higher manner than one who has some set time for the singing of psalms.

  The person who dares not say an ill-natured word or do an unreasonable thing because he or she considers God as everywhere present performs a better devotion than the person who dares not miss the church. To live in the world as a stranger and a pilgrim, using all its enjoyments as if we used them not, making all our actions as so many steps toward a better life, is offering a better sacrifice to God than any forms of holy and heavenly prayers.

  To be humble in our actions, to avoid every appearance of pride and vanity, to be meek and lowly in our words, actions, dress, behavior, and designs—all in imitation of our blessed Saviour—is worshiping God in a higher manner than do they who have only stated times to fall low on their knees in devotions. Those who content themselves with necessities that they may give the remainder to those who need it; who dare not spend any money foolishly because they consider it as a talent from God which must be used according to his will, praise God with something that is more glorious than songs of praise.

—From *A Serious Call to a Devout and Holy Life* by William Law

  God gives us the boat and the oars, but then tells us, "It's up to you to row." Making 'positive acts of faith' is like training this faculty; it is developed by training, as the muscles are developed by gymnastics.

—From *Letters from the Desert* by Carlo Carretto

  What is our Lord doing in this last hour before his arrest, before his Passion begins? He goes away alone to pray. So we, when we have a severe trial to undergo, or some danger or some suffering to face, go aside to pray in solitude, and so pass the last hours that separate us from our trial. Let us do this in every serious event in our lives. Let us prepare for it, gather strength, light, grace, to behave well, by praying and praying alone during the last hours before our trial.

—From *Meditations of a Hermit* by Charles de Foucauld

ॐ Never think that in lowering yourself you have less power for good. On the contrary, in thus humbling yourself you are imitating and using the same means that I used. You are walking in my *Way*, and therefore in the *Truth*, and you are in the right state to receive *Life* and impart it to others. The best means for this is always to imitate me. I came down to the level of men by my Incarnation, and to that of sinners by my Circumcision and Baptism. Be lowly, lowly, humble, humble. Let those that are in high places put themselves last in a spirit of lowliness and service, love for men, humility, taking the lowest place so long as the divine will does not call you to another, for in that case you must obey. Obedience first of all—conformity to the will of God. If you are placed high, then keep yourself in humility of soul as though you were the last; occupy your high position as though you were there only to serve others and to lead them to salvation, and as if, though you may command them, you are rather serving them, for you command them only with the purpose of sanctifying them.

—From *Meditations of a Hermit* by Charles de Foucauld

ॐ Don't economize in almsgiving—cut off nothing in charities, rather increase them if anything. 'Give and it shall be given you.' 'In the measure that you do to others so shall it be done to you. What you give to the poor you give to me.' The best way of always having enough is to share generously with the poor, seeing in them the representatives of Jesus himself. And then be full of confidence. 'He who gives life will also give the nourishment. He who gave the body will give the clothing. Seek the Kingdom of God and his Justice (that is to say, perfection) and the rest shall be given unto you.' This is said for all Christians and not only for monks. Be full of confidence. Keep yourself from all anxiety.

—From *Meditations of a Hermit* by Charles de Foucauld

ॐ The more we lack everything the more we resemble Jesus crucified. The more we cling to the cross, the closer do we embrace Jesus who is nailed to it. Every cross is a gain, for every cross unites us to Jesus.

I should possess no more and nothing better than Jesus had at Nazareth, and I should rejoice rather to have less than more. At every moment I should live as though that day I should die a martyr's death.

Only one thing is necessary: that is to do at every moment what is most pleasing to Jesus. I must prepare myself, without ceasing, for martyrdom, and accept it without the smallest attempt to defend myself, like the Divine Lamb, in Jesus, by Jesus, like Jesus and for Jesus.

I should rejoice rather to lack than to have, at failure rather than success, and at penury rather than possessions, for in these I bear the cross and the poverty of Jesus, the greatest blessing the earth can give me.

I must practise *Abjection*, the service of others. I must fix a certain number of menial tasks to be accomplished every day and to do them like Jesus of Nazareth, who 'came to serve.' I must do without the orderly and serve, not be served.

—From *Meditations of a Hermit* by Charles de Foucauld

இ May the Lord give you the blessing of a strong desire to stand inwardly before God. Seek and you will find. *Seek God*: such is the unalterable rule for all spiritual advancement. Nothing comes without effort. The help of God is always ready and always near, but is only given to those who seek and work, and only to those seekers who, after putting all their own powers to the test, then cry out with all their heart: Lord, help us. So long as you hold on to even a little hope of achieving something by your own powers, the Lord does not interfere. It is as though he says: 'You hope to succeed by yourself—Very well, go on trying! But however long you try you will achieve nothing.' May the Lord give you a contrite spirit, a humble and a contrite heart.

—From *The Art of Prayer*

இ O God, immortal, eternal, invisible, I remember with gladness and thanksgiving all that thou hast been to this world of men:

Companion of the brave:
Upholder of the loyal:
Light of the wanderer:
Joy of the pilgrim:
Guide of the pioneer:
Helper of labouring men:
Refuge of the broken-hearted:
Deliverer of the oppressed:
Succour of the tempted:
Strength of the victorious:
Ruler of rulers:
Friend of the poor:
Rescuer of the perishing:
Hope of the dying.

Give me faith now to believe that thou canst be all in all to me, according to my need, if only I renounce all proud self-dependence and put my trust in thee.

Forbid it, O Father, that the difficulty of living well should ever tempt me to fall into any kind of heedlessness or despair. May I keep it ever in mind that this human life was once divinely lived and this world once nobly overcome and this body of flesh, that now so sorely tries me, once made into thy perfect dwelling-place.

Show thy lovingkindness to-night, O Lord, to all who stand in need of thy help. Be with the weak to make them strong and with the strong to make them gentle. Cheer the lonely with thy company and the distracted with thy solitude. Prosper thy Church in the fulfilment of her mighty task, and grant thy blessing to all who have toiled to-day in Christ's name. Amen.

—From *A Diary of Private Prayer* by John Baillie

Hymn: O Jesus, I Have Promised

O Jesus, I have promised
To serve thee to the end;
Be thou forever near me,
My Master and my Friend:
I shall not fear the battle
If thou art by my side,
Nor wander from the pathway
If thou wilt be my guide.

O let me feel thee near me!
The world is ever near;
I see the sights that dazzle,
The tempting sounds I hear;
My foes are ever near me,
Around me and within;
But, Jesus, draw thou nearer,
And shield my soul from sin.

O let me hear thee speaking,
In accents clear and still,
Above the storms of passion,
The murmurs of self-will;
O speak to reassure me,
To hasten or control;
O speak, and make me listen,
Thou guardian of my soul.

O Jesus, thou hast promised
To all who follow thee
That where thou art in glory
There shall thy servant be;
And, Jesus, I have promised
To serve thee to the end;
O give me grace to follow,
My Master and my Friend. Amen.
—John E. Bode

50: A Friend of Souls

I. Invocation
    Almighty God, you who are the source of our life, strength, and ministry. In your presence alone we find help, hope, and life. Send us from this hour as a healing reminder of your love to all whose lives we touch this day. We offer our prayers in the name of Christ. Amen.

II. Psalm 103

III. Daily Scripture Readings
    Monday   Exodus 3:7-22
    Tuesday   Jeremiah 31:23-34
    Wednesday   1 Samuel 18:1-5
    Thursday   Hebrews 8:1-12
    Friday   Hebrews 13:1-21
    Saturday   John 15:1-17
    Sunday   A. Deuteronomy 34:1-12;
                 Psalm 135:1-14; Philippians 4:1-9;
                 Matthew 22:1-14
              B. Genesis 3:8-19; Psalm 90:1-12;
                 Hebrews 4:1-3, 9-13; Mark 10:17-30
              C. Micah 1:2; 2:1-10; Psalm 26;
                 2 Timothy 2:8-15; Luke 17:11-19

IV. Readings for Reflection

V. Prayers: for the church, for others, for myself

VI. Reflection: silent and written

VII. Hymn: "St. Patrick's Breastplate"

VIII. Benediction
    May our Lord Jesus Christ himself, and God our Father, who loved us and in his grace gave us unfailing courage and a firm hope, encourage you and strengthen you to always do and say what is good. Amen. —2 Thessalonians 2:16-17, TEV

Readings for Reflection

      ❧   I stand by the door.
           I neither go too far in, nor stay too far out,
           The door is the most important door in the world—
           It is the door through which men walk when they find
               God.
           There's no use my going way inside, and staying there,
           When so many are still outside and they, as much as I,
           Crave to know where the door is.
           And all that so many ever find
           Is only the wall where a door ought to be.
           They creep along the wall like blind men,
           With outstretched, groping hands.
           Feeling for a door, knowing there must be a door,
           Yet they never find it. . .
           So I stand by the door.

           The most tremendous thing in the world
           Is for men to find that door—the door to God.
           The most important thing any man can do
           Is to take hold of one of those blind, groping hands,
           And put it on the latch—the latch that only clicks
           And opens to the man's own touch.
           Men die outside that door, as starving beggars die
           On cold nights in cruel cities in the dead of winter—
           Die for want of what is within their grasp.
           They live, on the other side of it—live because they
               have not found it,
           Nothing else matters compared to helping them find it,
           And open it, and walk in, and find him . . .
           So I stand by the door.
           Go in, great saints, go all the way in—
           Go way down into the cavernous cellars,
           And way up into the spacious attics—
           It is a vast, roomy house, this house where God is.
           Go into the deepest of hidden casements,
           Of withdrawal, of silence, of sainthood.
           Some must inhabit those inner rooms,
           And know the depth and heights of God,
           And call outside to the rest of us how wonderful it is.

Sometimes I take a deeper look in,
Sometimes venture in a little farther;
But my place seems closer to the opening . . .
So I stand by the door.

There is another reason why I stand there.
Some people get part way in and become afraid
Lest God and the zeal of his house devour them;
For God is so very great, and asks all of us.
And these people feel a cosmic claustrophobia,
And want to get out. "Let me out!" they cry.
And the people way inside only terrify them more.
Somebody must be by the door to tell them that they
    are spoiled
For the old life, they have seen too much:
Once taste God, and nothing but God will do any more.
Somebody must be watching for the frightened
Who seek to sneak out just where they came in,
To tell them how much better it is inside.

The people too far in do not see how near these are
To leaving—preoccupied with the wonder of it all.
Somebody must watch for those who have entered the
    door,
But would like to run away. So for them, too,
I stand by the door.
I admire the people who go way in.
But I wish they would not forget how it was
Before they got in. Then they would be able to help
The people who have not yet even found the door,
Or the people who want to run away again from God.
You can go in too deeply, and stay in too long,
And forget the people outside the door.
As for me, I shall take my old accustomed place,
Near enough to God to hear him, and know he is there,
But not so far from men as not to hear them,
And remember they are there, too.
Where? Outside the door—
Thousands of them, millions of them.
But—more important for me—

One of them, two of them, ten of them,
Whose hands I am intended to put on the latch.
So I shall stand by the door and wait
For those who seek it.
"I had rather be a door-keeper. . . ."
So I stand by the door.
—"I Stand by the Door" by Samuel Moor Shoemaker

❧ I came to a new understanding why Jesus passed up
the religious establishment of his day, the economically
secure, the socially prestigious, and sought out the poor, the
outcast, the sinner, the broken, the sick, the lonely. He felt,
as we so often do not feel, their sorrow. He was acquainted,
as we too seldom are, with their grief. On Calvary he died
of a broken heart. But that heart was broken long before
Black Friday, by the desolation of the common people. "In
all their afflictions he was afflicted."

Most of the time we are not. We seem to have quite a
different conception of life. We avoid as much as possible
the unpleasant. We shun the suffering of others. We shrink
from any burdens except those which life itself inescapably
thrusts upon us. We seek arduously the wealth and power
that will enable us to secure ourselves against the possibility
of being involved with another's affliction. Lazarus sometimes makes his way to our door step. We toss him a coin
and go on our way. We give our charities but we do not
give ourselves. We build our charitable institutions but we
do not build ourselves into other's lives.
—From *The Captivating Presence* by Albert Edward Day

❧ And at the same time, though I am silent, I can make
known to those ignorant brothers of mine the meaning of
our holy religion, and of the Christian spirit, and the Sacred
Heart of Jesus, not by preaching, but by example and charity to all.
—From *Meditations of a Hermit* by Charles de Foucauld

❧ To be a spiritual friend one must have detachment,
discretion, and discernment, with all that prepares for those
gifts. Spiritual companionship is a gentle art, demanding a
willingness to listen as if one had a third ear attuned to the
inner self. It is neither psychotherapy nor is it the sacrament

of reconciliation. Sometimes one needs to confront, but far more often the best intervention of the spiritual guide is in parabolic language, nudging the friend into a new way of seeing. The journey belongs to the other and that person's uniqueness must always be honored.

The friend of the soul is an instrumental image. Such a person is not to be a "buddy," but someone who listens, comforts, and supports. He or she serves as a hermeneut, which means that he or she is a means, not an end. It is important for me not to think too highly of myself in this relationship, but to stand in awe of what God is doing in the life of the other person. Often this requires me to get out of the way. When in ignorance I have nothing to say, I must remain silent.

—From *Spirituality for Ministry* by Urban T. Holmes III

   Inner silence is absence of any sort of inward stirring of thought or emotion, but it is complete alertness, openness to God. We must keep complete silence when we can, but never allow it to degenerate into simple contentment. To prevent this the great writers of Orthodoxy warn us never to abandon completely the normal forms of prayer, because even those who reached this contemplative silence found it necessary, whenever they were in danger of spiritual slackness, to reintroduce words of prayer until prayer had renewed silence.

The Greek Fathers set this silence, which they called *hesychia*, both as the starting-point and the final achievement of a life of prayer. Silence is the state in which all the powers of the soul and all the faculties of the body are completely at peace, quiet and recollected, perfectly alert yet free from any turmoil or agitation. A simile which we find in many writings of the Fathers is that of the waters of a pond. As long as there are ripples on the surface, nothing can be reflected properly, neither the trees nor the sky; when the surface is quite still, the sky is perfectly reflected, the trees on the bank and everything is there as distinct as in reality.

Another simile of the same sort used by the Fathers is that as long as the mud which is at the bottom of a pond has not settled, the water is not clear and one can see nothing through it. These two analogies apply to the state of the human heart. 'Blessed are the pure in heart for they shall see God' (Mt 5:8). As long as the mud is in motion in the water there is no clear vision through it, and again as long as the surface is covered with ripples there can be no adequate reflection of what surrounds the pond.

As long as the soul is not still there can be no vision, but when stillness has brought us into the presence of God, then another sort of silence, much more absolute, intervenes: the silence of a soul that is not only still and recollected but which is overawed in an act of worship by God's presence; a silence in which, as Julian of Norwich puts it, 'Prayer oneth the soul to God.'
—From *Living Prayer* by Anthony Bloom

Hymn: St. Patrick's Breastplate

I bind unto myself today
The strong Name of the Trinity,
By invocation of the same,
The Three in One, and One in Three.

I bind this day to me forever,
By power of faith, Christ's Incarnation;
His baptism in the Jordan river;
His death on the cross for my salvation.
His bursting from the spiced tomb;
His riding up the heav'nly way;
His coming at the day of doom:
I bind unto myself today.

I bind unto myself the power
Of the great love of cherubim;
The sweet "Well done" in judgment hour;
The service of the seraphim:
Confessors' faith, apostles' word,
The patriarchs' prayers, the prophets' scrolls;
All good deeds done unto the Lord,
And purity of virgin souls.

I bind unto myself today
The virtues of the starlit heav'n,
The glorious sun's life-giving ray,
The whiteness of the moon at even,

The flashing of the lightning free,
The whirling wind's tempestuous shocks,
The stable earth, the deep salt sea,
Around the old eternal rocks.

I bind unto myself today
The power of God to hold and lead,
His eye to watch, his might to stay,
His ear to hearken to my need;
The wisdom of my God to teach,
His hand to guide, his shield to ward;
The word of God to give me speech,
His heav'nly host to be my guard.

Christ be with me, Christ within me,
Christ behind me, Christ before me,
Christ beside me, Christ to win me,
Christ to comfort and restore me,
Christ beneath me, Christ above me,
Christ in quiet, Christ in danger,
Christ in hearts of all that love me,
Christ in mouth of friend and stranger.

I bind unto myself the Name,
The strong Name of the Trinity;
By invocation of the same,
The Three in One, and One in Three.
Of whom all nature hath creation;
Eternal Father, Spirit, Word:
Praise to the Lord of my salvation,
Salvation is of Christ the Lord.
Amen.
—Saint Patrick

51: *Servants of Christ*

I.   Invocation
Almighty God, grant that those who worship you this day may present their bodies as a living sacrifice, holy, and acceptable to you. By the power of your holy spirit make us strong to fulfill our ministry this day. In the name of Christ. Amen.

II.   Psalm 71

III.   Daily Scripture Readings

Monday	Matthew 10:1-15	
Tuesday	Matthew 10: 16-23	
Wednesday	Matthew 10:24-42	
Thursday	2 Corinthians 11:7–12:10	
Friday	2 Corinthians 4:1-6	
Saturday	2 Timothy 2:14-26	
Sunday	A.	Ruth 1:1-19a; Psalm 146; 1 Thessalonians 1:1-10; Matthew 22:15-22
	B.	Isaiah 53:7-12; Psalm 35:17-28; Hebrews 4:14-16; Mark 10:35-45
	C.	Habakkuk 1:1-3, 2:1-4; Psalm 119:137-144; 2 Timothy 3:14–4:5; Luke 18:1-8

IV.   Readings for Reflection

V.   Prayers: for the church, for others, for myself

VI.   Reflection: silent and written

VII.   Hymn: "God of Love and God of Power"

VIII.   Benediction
May the Lord make you strong to do the work of ministry. Amen.

Readings for Reflection

❧ Oh, my sisters, how little one should think about resting, and how little one should care about honours, and how far one ought to be from wishing to be esteemed in the very least if the Lord makes his special abode in the soul. For if the soul is much with him, as it is right it should be, it will very seldom think of itself; its whole thought will be concentrated upon finding ways to please him and upon showing him how it loves him. This, my daughters, is the aim of prayer: this is the purpose of the Spiritual Marriage, of which are born good works and good works alone. . . .

Reflect carefully on this, for it is so important that I can hardly lay too much stress on it. Fix your eyes on the Crucified and nothing else will be of much importance to you. If his Majesty revealed his love to us by doing and suffering such amazing things, how can you expect to please him by words alone? Do you know when people really become spiritual? It is when they become the slaves of God and are branded with his sign, which is the sign of the Cross, in token that they have given him their freedom. Then he can sell them as slaves to the whole world, as he himself was sold, and if he does this he will be doing them no wrong but showing them no slight favour. Unless they resolve to do this, they need not expect to make great progress. For the foundation of this whole edifice, as I have said, is humility, and, if you have not true humility, the Lord will not wish it to reach any great height: in fact, it is for your own good that it should not; if it did, it would fall to the ground. Therefore, sisters, if you wish to lay good foundations, each of you must try to be the least of all, and the slave of God, and must seek a way and means to please and serve all your companions. If you do that, it will be of more value to you than to them and your foundation will be so firmly laid that your Castle will not fall.

—From *Interior Castle* by Saint Teresa of Avila

❧ To me it is not possible, O my God, to be rich and at ease and enjoy a prosperous life, when you were poor, struggling, living laboriously. I cannot love thus. 'It is not right that the servant should be above his Master, nor

that the Bride should be rich and the Bridegroom poor,'
especially when he is voluntarily poor. S. Teresa, wearied
with the importunities of those who wished her to accept
endowments for her convent at Avila, was once almost
ready to accept. But when she went to her oratory and saw
the Crucifix she fell at the feet of Jesus, hanging naked on
the Cross, and implored of him the grace never to let her
receive any endowments, but always to be as poor as he
was. . . .

True poverty is poverty of heart, which you said was
'blessed,' my Saviour Jesus, to which all material things
are totally indifferent, for it has broken with them all. As S.
Mary Magdalen broke her vase of spices, the heart empties
itself utterly of all attachment to transitory things, it is left
open wide for God alone. Then God enters in and reigns
alone, filling it entirely, and makes subject for ever to himself, for him and in him, the love of all men, his children.
The heart knows no other than these two loves; nothing
else exists for it and we live on earth as though we were not
there, in perpetual contemplation of the one necessity to our
souls and in intercession for those that the Heart of Jesus
loves.

—From *Meditations of a Hermit* by Charles de Foucauld

ं≜ Their life is tough and austere by worldly standards,
certainly; yet I never met such delightful, happy women, or
such an atmosphere of joy as they create. Mother Teresa, as
she is fond of explaining, attaches the utmost importance
to this joyousness. The poor, she says, deserve not just service and dedication, but also the joy that belongs to human
love. This is what the Sisters give them abundantly. Today,
notoriously, the religious orders are short of vocations.
Nor is the shortage being rectified by permitting nuns to
use lipstick, wear mini-habits, and otherwise participate
in the ways and amenities of contemporary affluence. The
Missionaries of Charity, on the other hand, are multiply-
ing at a fantastic rate. Their Calcutta house is bursting
at the seams, and as each new house is opened there are
volunteers clamouring to go there. As the whole story
of Christendom shows, if everything is asked for, everything—and more—will be accorded; if little, then nothing.
It is curious, when this is so obvious, that nowadays the

contrary proposition should seem the more acceptable, and endeavour be directed towards softening the austerities of the service of Christ and reducing its hazards with a view to attracting people into it. After all, it was in kissing a leper's hideous sores that St. Francis found the gaiety to captivate the world and gather round him some of the most audacious spirits of the age, to whom he offered only the glory of being naked on the naked earth for Christ's sake.

—From *Something Beautiful for God* by Malcolm Muggeridge

ૐ Because we cannot reasonably expect to erect a constantly expanding structure of social activism upon a constantly diminishing foundation of faith, attention to the cultivation of the inner life is our first order of business, even in a period of rapid social change. The Church, if it is to affect the world, must become a center from which new spiritual power emanates. While the Church must be secular in the sense that it operates in the world, if it is only secular it will not have the desired effect upon the secular order which it is called upon to penetrate. With no diminution of concern for people, we can and must give new attention to the production of a trustworthy religious experience.

—From *The New Man for Our Time* by Elton Trueblood

ૐ John Woolman is worth remembering because, more than most Christians, he kept his inner and outer life together. In the happy expression employed by Elizabeth O'Connor, this man of travel engaged, at the same time, in both an inward and an outward journey. The inward journey was marked by an unusual sense of holy obedience. "I have been more and more instructed," he wrote near the end, "as to the necessity of depending, . . . upon the fresh instructions of Christ, the prince of peace, from day to day." The outward journey was marked by an increasing sensitivity to suffering and to an intelligent effort to eliminate as much of this suffering as is humanly possible.

What is most remarkable in Woolman's potent example is the complete bridging of the chasm that so mars our current Christian scene. His devotional experience and his social concern, far from being in conflict, actually required each other. He was acutely conscious of the danger of a social witness that could have become hard and cruel in its

denunciation of others. "Christ knoweth," he said, "when the fruit-bearing branches themselves have need of purging."
—From *The New Man for Our Time* by Elton Trueblood

❧ Our spiritual life is his affair; because, whatever we may think to the contrary, it is really produced by his steady attraction, and our humble and self-forgetful response to it. It consists in being drawn, at his pace and in his way, to the place where he wants us to be; not the place we fancied for ourselves.
—From *The Spiritual Life* by Evelyn Underhill

❧ For a spiritual life is simply a life in which all that we do comes from the centre, where we are anchored in God: a life soaked through and through by a sense of his reality and claim, and self-given to the great movement of his will.

Most of our conflicts and difficulties come from trying to deal with the spiritual and practical aspects of our life separately instead of realising them as parts of one whole. If our practical life is centred on our own interests, cluttered up by possessions, distracted by ambitions, passions, wants and worries, beset by a sense of our own rights and importance, or anxieties for our own future, or longings for our own success, we need not expect that our spiritual life will be a contrast to all this. The soul's house is not built on such a convenient plan: there are few soundproof partitions in it.
—From *The Spiritual Life* by Evelyn Underhill

❧ We cannot see the world as God means it, save in proportion as our souls are meek. In meekness only are we its inheritors. Meekness alone makes the spiritual retina pure to receive God's things as they are, mingling with them neither imperfection nor impurity of its own. A thing so beheld that it conveys to me the divine thought issuing in its form, is mine; by nothing but its mediation between God and my life can anything be mine.
—From *Life Essential* by George MacDonald

Hymn: God of Love and God of Power

God of love and God of power,
Grant us in this burning hour
Grace to ask these gifts of thee,
Daring hearts and spirits free.
God of love and God of power,
Thou hast called us for this hour.

We are not the first to be
Banished by our fears from thee;
Give us courage, let us hear
Heaven's trumpets ringing clear.
God of love and God of power,
Thou hast called us for this hour.

All our lives belong to thee,
Thou our final loyalty;
Slaves are we whene'er we share
That devotion anywhere.
God of love and God of power,
Thou hast called us for this hour.

God of love and God of power,
Make us worthy of this hour;
Offering lives if it's thy will,
Keeping free our spirits still.
God of love and God of power,
Thou hast called us for this hour. Amen.
—Gerald H. Kennedy

52: *True Humility*

I. Invocation
Almighty God, you have sent Jesus to show us how to live. Grant us the power of your Holy Spirit so that we may follow him in faithfulness all the days of our lives. Amen.

II. Psalm 139

III. Daily Scripture Readings
Monday		Isaiah 57:14-21
Tuesday		Zephaniah 3
Wednesday		2 Chronicles 7:11-22
Thursday		Romans 13:1-10
Friday		1 Peter 3:8-12
Saturday		Philippians 2:1-18
Sunday	A.	Ruth 2:1-13; Psalm 128; 1 Thessalonians 2:1-8; Matthew 22:34-46
	B.	Jeremiah 31:7-9; Psalm 126; Hebrews 5:1-6; Mark 10:46-52
	C.	Zephaniah 3:1-9; Psalm 3; 2 Timothy 4:6-8, 16-18; Luke 18:9-14

IV. Readings for Reflection

V. Prayers: for the church, for others, for myself

VI. Reflection: silent and written

VII. Hymn: "Teach Me, O Lord, Thy Holy Way"

VIII. Benediction
Live today in Christ's presence, remembering he is near and will sustain you as you serve in his name. Amen.

Readings for Reflection

&. It has been my observation that all great praying men are simple, relaxed men. Mrs. Thomas A. Edison once said to me, "Mr. Edison's methods are just like yours. He is always perfectly natural and always perfectly relaxed. He feels that all of his discoveries have 'come through him,' that he is but a channel for forces greater than himself."

Always natural, and always relaxed! I do not like to see men work too hard at their prayers. Beware lest the zeal of thy house shall eat thee up. When one strains and labors over his dream he is too often carving ivory and not polishing horn. Don't cut too deeply, don't carve too hard, don't paint the picture too much yourself. Get still awhile, and let God paint it through you. Wrote Gutzon Borglum, "When I carve a statue, it is very simple. I merely cut away the pieces that don't belong there and the statue itself presently comes into view. It was there all the time."

—From *I Will Lift Up Mine Eyes* by Glenn Clark

&. The man who is proud of anything he thinks he has reached, has not reached it. He is but proud of himself and imagining a cause for his pride. If he had reached, he would already have begun to forget. He who delights in contemplating whereto he has attained, is not merely sliding back; he is already in the dirt of self-satisfaction. The gate of the kingdom is closed, and he outside.

The man who does not house self has room to be his real self—God's eternal idea of him. He lives eternally; in virtue of the creative power present in him with momently unimpeded creation, he *is*. How should there be in him one thought of ruling or commanding or surpassing! He can imagine no bliss, no good in being greater than some one else.

He is unable to wish himself other then he is, except more what God made him for, which is indeed the highest willing of the will of God. His brother's well-being is essential to bliss. The thought of standing higher in the favor of God than his brother would make him miserable. He would lift every brother to the embrace of the Father.

Blessed are the poor in spirit, for they are of the same spirit as God, and of nature the kingdom of heaven is theirs.
—From *Life Essential* by George MacDonald

All our merely natural activities will be accepted, if they are offered to God, even the humblest: and all of them, even the noblest, will be sinful if they are not. Christianity does not simply replace our natural life and substitute a new one: it is rather a new organization which exploits, to its own supernatural ends, these natural materials. No doubt, in a given situation, it demands the surrender of some, or of all, our merely human pursuits: it is better to be saved with one eye, than, having two, to be cast into Gehenna. But it does this, in a sense, *per accidens*—because, in those special circumstances, it has ceased to be possible to practise this or that activity to the glory of God. There is no essential quarrel between the spiritual life and the human activities as such. Thus the omnipresence of obedience to God in a Christian's life is, in a way, analogous to the omnipresence of God in space. God does not fill space as a body fills it, in the sense that parts of him are in different parts of space, excluding other objects from them. Yet he is everywhere—totally present at every point of space—according to good theologians.
—From *The Weight of Glory* by C. S. Lewis

In my thoughts, words and actions, whether directed to myself or my neighbour, I must never trouble about worldly position, celebrity, human esteem, but respect the poor equally with the rich. I must take as much trouble about the humblest workman as about a prince, since God appeared as a humble workman. Always, for myself, seek the lowest place, and be as low as my Master, so as to be with him and walk in his steps like a faithful servant and disciple (since in his infinite and incomprehensible goodness he lets me speak so), as a faithful brother, a faithful spouse. Thus I must arrange my life so that I am the lowest and most despised of men, so that I live it beside my Master, my Lord, my Brother, my Spouse, my God who was the outcast of the people, and the reproach of the earth, a worm and no man.

It is my desire to live in poverty, abjection and suffering, in solitude and neglect, so that all my life I may be beside my Master, my Brother, my Spouse, my God, who lived thus all his life, and has given me the example ever since his birth.

—From *Meditations of a Hermit* by Charles de Foucauld

❧ Any spiritual view which focuses attention on ourselves, and puts the human creature with its small ideas and adventures in the centre foreground, is dangerous till we recognise its absurdity. . . .

We mostly spend those lives conjugating three verbs: to Want, to Have, and to Do. Craving, clutching, and fussing, on the material, political, social, emotional, intellectual—even on the religious—plane, we are kept in perpetual unrest: forgetting that none of these verbs have any ultimate significance, except so far as they are transcended by and included in, the fundamental verb, to Be: and that Being, not wanting, having and doing, is the essence of a spiritual life.

—From *The Spiritual Life* by Evelyn Underhill

❧ The old writers call these two activities Mortification and Prayer. These are formidable words, and modern man tends to recoil from them. Yet they only mean, when translated into our own language, that the development of the spiritual life involves both dealing with ourselves, and attending to God. Or, to put it the other way round and in more general terms, first turning to Reality, and then getting our tangled, half-real psychic lives—so tightly coiled about ourselves and our own interests, including our spiritual interests—into harmony with the great movement of Reality. Mortification means killing the very roots of self-love; pride and possessiveness, anger and violence, ambition and greed in all their disguises, however respectable those disguises may be, whatever uniforms they wear. In fact, it really means the entire transformation of our personal, professional and political life into something more consistent with our real situation as small dependent, fugitive creatures; all sharing the same limitations and inheriting the same half-animal past. That may not sound very impressive or unusual; but it is the foundation of all genuine spiritual life, and sets a standard which is not peculiar to orthodox Christianity. Those who are familiar with Blake's poetry will recognise that it is all to be found there. Indeed, wherever we find people whose spiritual life is robust and creative, we find that in one way or another this transformation has been effected and this price has been paid.

Prayer means turning to Reality, taking our part, however humble, tentative and half-understood, in the continual conversation, the communion, of our spirits with the Eternal Spirit; the acknowledgment of our entire dependence, which is yet the partly free dependence of the child. For Prayer is really our whole life toward God: our longing for him, our "incurable God-sickness," as Barth calls it, our whole drive towards him. It is the humble correspondence of the human spirit with the Sum of all Perfection, the Fountain of Life. No narrower definition than this is truly satisfactory, or covers all the ground.

—From *The Spiritual Life* by Evelyn Underhill

&. Basically humility is the attitude of one who stands constantly under the judgement of God. It is the attitude of one who is like the soil. Humility comes from the Latin word *humus*, fertile ground. The fertile ground is there, unnoticed, taken for granted, always there to be trodden upon. It is silent, inconspicuous, dark and yet it is always ready to receive any seed, ready to give it substance and life. The more lowly, the more fruitful, because it becomes really fertile when it accepts all the refuse of the earth. It is so low that nothing can soil it, abase it, humiliate it; it has accepted the last place and cannot go any lower. In that position nothing can shatter the soul's serenity, its peace and joy.

—From *Living Prayer* by Anthony Bloom

&. We often hear the criticism that the Church is afflicted with piety, but the real trouble is that its piety is not deep enough! Since the materials are available, all that is needed is the recognition of where they are, and the will to employ them. An important contribution would be the liberation of the term "piety" from its present damaging connotations, reinstating it as a term of respect. We, indeed, still have a little piety; we say a few hasty prayers; we sing meaningfully a few hymns; we read snatches from the Bible. But all of this is far removed from the massive dose that we sorely need if we are to be the men and women who can perform a healing service in our generation. The seat of our disease, says Helmut Thielicke, "is not in the branches of our nerves at all but rather in our roots which are stunted and starved." The eloquent German points out that Martin Luther prayed four hours each day "not despite his busy life but because only so could he accomplish his gigantic labors." Luther worked so hard that a little desultory praying would not suffice. "To work without praying and without listening," continues Thielicke, "means only to grow and spread oneself upward, without striking roots and without an equivalent in the earth." Trees can grow well in rocky soil, as I can attest by looking out the window of my mountain writing cabin, but they do this only by finding crevices in the rocks where the roots are able to penetrate deeply.

—From *The New Man for Our Time* by Elton Trueblood

Hymn: Teach Me, O Lord, Thy Holy Way

Teach me, O Lord, thy holy way,
And give me an obedient mind,
That in thy service I may find
My soul's delight from day to day.

Help me, O Savior, here to trace
The sacred footsteps thou hast trod;
And, meekly walking with my God,
To grow in goodness, truth, and grace.

Guard me, O Lord, that I may ne'er
Forsake the right or do the wrong;
Against temptation make me strong
And 'round me spread thy shelt'ring care.

Bless me, in every task, O Lord,
Begun, continued, done for thee;
Fulfill thy perfect work in me,
And thine abounding grace afford.

—William Matson

53: *God Can Change Lives*

I. Invocation
    Almighty God, send your transforming power into my life as I seek to serve you this day. Grant unto me wisdom, courage, grace, and strength to faithfully fulfill the ministry to which you have called me. In the name of Christ. Amen.

II. Psalm 19

III. Daily Scripture Readings
    | Monday | | Ezekiel 36:22-32 |
    | Tuesday | | Ephesians 5:1-20 |
    | Wednesday | | John 9 |
    | Thursday | | Luke 19:1-10 |
    | Friday | | Acts 26:2-29 |
    | Saturday | | Colossians 3:1-17 |
    | Sunday | A. | Ruth 4:7-17; Psalm 127; 1 Thessalonians 2:9-13, 17-20; Matthew 23:1-12 |
    | | B. | Deuteronomy 6:1-9; Psalm 119:33-48; Hebrews 7:23-28; Mark 12:28-34 |
    | | C. | Haggai 2:1-9; Psalm 65:1-8; 2 Thessalonians 1:5-12; Luke 19:1-10 |

IV. Readings for Reflection

V. Prayers: for the church, for others, for myself

VI. Reflection: silent and written

VII. Hymn: "Make Me a Captive, Lord"

VIII. Benediction
    May the God of steadfastness and encouragement grant you to live in such harmony with one another, in accord with Christ Jesus, that together you may with one voice glorify the God and Father of our Lord Jesus Christ. Amen. —Romans 15:5-6

Readings for Reflection

❧ In his view, the Fall was essentially a matter of wrong growing up. St. Irenaeus believed, as did many of the early Christians—in marked contrast to the traditional Jewish belief—that Adam was created as a young child. The reason why he was forbidden to eat from the tree of knowledge was simply that he had to grow up first, and that takes time. Unfortunately, Adam was impatient; in trying to anticipate his adulthood, by seizing the fruit before the time was ripe, he thwarted the process of true maturing. St. Irenaeus recognises that one aspect of this is the disorder that afflicts human sexuality, and in fact we might say that his presentation of the Fall is, essentially, as a mishandling of the crisis of puberty. The result is that man can now only grow up properly by a painful dismantling of his false grown-upness. To this end, the Son of God "came to be a child with us," so that we could be led back to childhood and then grow up again, this time in a true way, till we come to the full stature of Christ himself (cf. *Eph 4:13*).
—From *Prayer* by Simon Tugwell

❧ Without solitude it is virtually impossible to live a spiritual life. Solitude begins with a time and place for God, and him alone. If we really believe not only that God exists but also that he is actively present in our lives—healing, teaching, and guiding—we need to set aside a time and space to give him our undivided attention. Jesus says, "Go to your private room and, when you have shut your door, pray to your Father who is in that secret place" (Matthew 6:6).
—From *Making All Things New* by Henri J. M. Nouwen

❧ The spiritual life is not a life before, after, or beyond our everyday existence. No, the spiritual life can only be real when it is lived in the midst of the pains and joys of the here and now. Therefore we need to begin with a careful look at the way we think, speak, feel, and act from hour to hour, day to day, week to week, and year to year, in order to become more fully aware of our hunger for the Spirit. As long as we have only a vague inner feeling of discontent with our present way of living, and only an indefinite desire for "things spiritual," our lives will continue to stagnate in a generalized melancholy. We often say, "I am not very happy. I am not content with the way my life is going. I am not really joyful or peaceful, but I just don't know how things can be different, and I guess I have to be realistic and accept my life as it is." It is this mood of resignation that prevents us from actively searching for the life of the Spirit.

Our first task is to dispel the vague, murky feeling of discontent and to look critically at how we are living our lives. This requires honesty, courage, and trust. We must honestly unmask and courageously confront our many self-deceptive games. We must trust that our honesty and courage will lead us not to despair, but to a new heaven and a new earth.
—From *Making All Things New* by Henri J. M. Nouwen

❧ The words of the Lord are the seed sown by the sower. Into our hearts they must fall that they may grow. Meditation and prayer must water them, and obedience keep them in the sunlight. Thus will they bear fruit for the Lord's gathering.
—From *Life Essential* by George MacDonald

❧ The Lord never came to deliver men from the consequences of their sins while yet those sins remained: that would be to cast out of the window the medicine of cure while yet the man lay sick; to go dead against the very laws of being. Yet men, loving their sins, and feeling nothing of their dread hatefulness, have, consistent with their low condition, constantly taken this word concerning the Lord [Matt. 1:21] to mean that he came to save them from the punishment of their sins. This idea—this miserable fancy, rather—has terribly corrupted the preaching of the gospel. The message of the good news has not been truly delivered.

The mission of Jesus was from the same source and with the same object as the punishment of our sins. He came to work along with our punishment. He came to side with it, and set us free from our sins. No man is safe from hell until he is free from his sins; free of them, hell itself would be endurable to him.
—From *Life Essential* by George MacDonald

❧ Merely to repeat his [Jesus'] words is not to continue his work; we must reproduce his life, passion and death. He desires to live again in each one of his disciples in order that he may continue to suffer, to bestow himself, and to labor in and through them towards the redemption of humanity, until all prodigal and lost children be found and brought back to their Father's house. Thus it is that, instead of being removed far from human history, the life and death of Christ once more take their place in history, setting forth the law that governs it, and, by ceaselessly increasing the power of redemptive sacrifice, transform and govern it, and direct it towards its divine end.

—From "The Atonement" by Auguste Sabatier as quoted in *The Double Search* by Rufus M. Jones

❧ The spiritual life can be lived in as many ways as there are people. What is new is that we have moved from the many things to the kingdom of God. What is new is that we are set free from the compulsions of our world and have set our hearts on the only necessary thing. What is new is that we no longer experience the many things, people, and events as endless causes for worry, but begin to experience them as the rich variety of ways in which God makes his presence known to us.

Indeed, living a spiritual life requires a change of heart, a conversion. Such a conversion may be marked by a sudden inner change, or it can take place through a long, quiet process of transformation. But it always involves an inner experience of oneness.

—From *Making All Things New* by Henri J. M. Nouwen

❧ Some years ago I got up one morning intending to have my hair cut in preparation for a visit to London, and the first letter I opened made it clear I need not go to London. So I decided to put the haircut off too. But then there began the most unaccountable little nagging in my mind, almost like a voice saying, "Get it cut all the same. Go and get it cut." In the end I could stand it no longer. I went.

Now my barber at that time was a fellow Christian and a man of many troubles whom my brother and I had sometimes been able to help. The moment I opened his shop door he said, "Oh, I was praying you might come today."

And, in fact, if I had come a day or so later, I should have been of no use to him.

It awed me; it awes me still. But, of course, one cannot rigorously prove a causal connection between the barber's prayers and my visit. It might be telepathy. It might be accident.

I have stood by the bedside of a woman whose thigh-bone was eaten through with cancer and who had thriving colonies of the disease in many other bones as well. It took three people to move her in bed. The doctors predicted a few months of life; the nurses (who often know better), a few weeks. A good man laid his hands on her and prayed. A year later the patient was walking (uphill, too, through rough woodland) and the man who took the last X-ray photos was saying, "These bones are as solid as rock. It's miraculous."

But once again there is no rigorous proof. Medicine, as all true doctors admit, is not an exact science. We need not invoke the supernatural to explain the falsification of its prophecies. You need not, unless you choose, believe in a causal connection between the prayers and the recovery.

The question then arises, "What sort of evidence *would* prove the efficacy of prayer?" The thing we pray for may happen, but how can you ever know it was not going to happen anyway? Even if the thing were indisputably miraculous, it would not follow that the miracle had occurred because of your prayers. The answer surely is that a compulsive empirical proof such as we have in the sciences can never be attained.

Some things are proved by the unbroken uniformity of our experiences. The law of gravitation is established by the fact that, in our experience, all bodies without exception obey it. Now even if all the things that people prayed for happened, which they do not, this would not prove what Christians mean by the efficacy of prayer. For prayer is request. The essence of request, as distinct from compulsion, is that it may or may not be granted.

—From *The World's Last Night* by C. S. Lewis

Hymn: Make Me a Captive, Lord

Make me a captive, Lord,
And then I shall be free;
Force me to render up my sword,
And I shall conqueror be.
I sink in life's alarms
When by myself I stand;
Imprison me within thine arms,
And strong shall be my hand.

My heart is weak and poor
Until it master find;
It has no spring of action sure,
It varies with the wind.
It cannot freely move
Till thou hast wrought its chain;
Enslave it with thy matchless love,
And deathless it shall reign.

My power is faint and low
Till I have learned to serve;
It wants the needed fire to glow,
It wants the breeze to nerve;
It cannot drive the world,
Until itself be driven;
Its flag can only be unfurled
When thou shalt breathe from heaven.

My will is not my own
Till thou hast made it thine;
If it would reach a monarch's throne,
It must its crown resign;
It only stands unbent,
Amid the clashing strife,
When on thy bosom it has leant
And found in thee its life. Amen.
—George Matheson

54: A Resurrection People

I. Invocation
    O God, the King eternal, who dividest the day from
    the darkness, and turnest the shadow of death into
    the morning: Drive far off from us all wrong desires;
    incline our hearts to keep thy law; and guide our
    feet into the way of peace, that having done thy will
    with cheerfulness while it was day, we may, when
    the night cometh, rejoice to give thee thanks; through
    Jesus Christ our Lord. Amen.
    —From *The Book of Worship*

II. Psalm 90

III. Daily Scripture Readings
    | Monday | Luke 12:35-59 |
    | Tuesday | Hebrews 11:32–12:2 |
    | Wednesday | 1 Peter 1:3-9 |
    | Thursday | Acts 17:16-34 |
    | Friday | John 11:1-44 |
    | Saturday | 1 Corinthians 15:51-58 |

    Sunday   A. Amos 5:18-24; Psalm 50:7-15;
                1 Thessalonians 4:13-18;
                Matthew 25:1-13
             B. Kings 17:8-16; Psalm 146;
                Hebrews 9:24-28; Mark 12:38-44
             C. Zechariah 7:1-10; Psalm 9:11-20;
                2 Thessalonians 2:13–3:5;
                Luke 20:27-38

IV. Readings for Reflection

V. Prayers: for the church, for others, for myself

VI. Reflection: silent and written

VII. Hymn: "Father, I Stretch My Hands to Thee"

VIII. Benediction
    May grace, mercy, love, and peace flow through
    your life and ministry all the day long. Amen.

Readings for Reflection

༄ But light is not enough; light is for the sake of life. We too must have life in ourselves. We too must, like the Life himself, live. We can live in no way but that in which Jesus lived, in which life was made in him. That way is, to give up our life. This is the one supreme action of life possible to us for the making of life in ourselves. Christ did it of himself, and so became light to us, that we might be able to do it in ourselves, after him, and through his originating act.

We must do it ourselves, I say. The help that he has given and gives, the light and the spirit-working of the Lord, the Spirit, in our hearts, is all in order that we may, as we must, do it ourselves. Till then we are not alive; life is not made in us. The whole strife and labour and agony of the Son with every man, is to get him to die as he died. All preaching that aims not at this, is a building with wood and hay and stubble. If I say not with whole heart, "My Father, do with me as you will, only help me against myself and for you," then I have not yet laid hold upon that for which Christ has laid hold upon me.

The faith that a man must put in God reaches above earth and sky, stretches beyond the farthest outlying star of the creatable universe. The question is not at present, however, of removing mountains, a thing that will one day be simple to us, but of waking and rising from the dead now.

When a man truly and perfectly says with Jesus, and as Jesus said it, "Thy will be done," he closes the everlasting life-circle. The life of the Father and the Son flows through him. He is a part of the divine organism. Then is the prayer of the Lord in him fulfilled: "I in them and thou in me, that they may be made perfect in one."

Friends, those of you who know, or suspect, that these things are true, let us arise and live—arise even in the darkest moments of spiritual stupidity, when hope itself sees nothing to hope for. Let us not trouble ourselves about the cause of our earthliness, except we know it to be some unrighteousness in us, but go at once to the Life.

Let us comfort ourselves in the thought of the Father and the Son. So long as there dwells harmony, so long as the Son loves the Father with all the love the Father can welcome, all is well with the little ones. God is all right—why should we mind standing in the dark for a minute outside his window? Of course we miss the *inness*, but there is a bliss of its own in waiting.

What if the rain be falling, and the wind blowing? What if we stand alone, or, more painful still, have some dear one beside us, sharing our *outness*? What even if the window be not shining, because of the curtains of good inscrutable drawn across it? Let us think to ourselves, or say to our friend, "God is; Jesus is not dead. Nothing can be going wrong, however it may look so to hearts unfinished in childness."

—From *Creation in Christ* by George MacDonald

   To struggle used to be
To grab with both hands
     and shake
     and twist
     and turn
     and push
     and shove and not give in
But wrest an answer from it all
As Jacob did a blessing.

But there is another way
To struggle with an issue, a question—
Simply to jump
         off
          into the abyss
          and find ourselves
            floating
              falling
              tumbling
            being led
         slowly and gently
         but surely
         to the answers God has for us—

         to watch the answers unfold
         before our eyes and still
         to be a part of the unfolding.

But, oh! the trust
necessary for this new way!
Not to be always reaching out
For the old hand-holds.
　　—From "A New Way of Struggling" by Susan W. N.
Ruach

❧　There are Christians who have hysterical reactions,
　　　　as if the world would have slipped out of God's hands.
　　They act violently as if they were risking everything.

　　But we believe in history;
　　the world is not a roll of the dice going toward chaos.
　　A new world has begun to happen since Christ has
　　　　risen. . . .

　　Jesus Christ, we rejoice in your definitive triumph. . . .
　　　　with our bodies still in the breach
　　　　and our souls in tension,
　　　　we cry out our first "Hurrah!"
　　　　till eternity unfolds itself.

　　Your sorrow now has passed.
　　Your enemies have failed.
　　You are a definitive smile for humankind.

　　What matter the wait now for us?
　　We accept the struggle and the death;
　　because you, our love, will not die!

　　We march behind you,
　　　　on the road to the future.
　　You are with us
　　　　and you are our immortality!

　　Take away the sadness from our faces.
　　We are not in a game of chance. . . .
　　　　You have the last word!

　　Beyond the crushing of our bones,
　　　　now has begun the eternal "alleluia!"
　　From the thousand openings of our wounded bodies
　　　　and souls there arises now a triumphal song!

　　So, teach us to give voice to your new life throughout
　　　　all the world.

Because you dry the tears from the eyes of the
  oppressed forever. . . .
  and death will disappear. . . .
—Jesuit Father Luis Espinal was assassinated March
22, 1980, in La Paz, Bolivia, by paramilitary forces.
He wrote this meditation shortly before his death.
Reprinted by permission of the *National Catholic
Reporter*.

❧ God became bread in Christ to nourish us with eternal
life. "He who feeds on my flesh and drinks my blood has
eternal life." (John 6:54)

But what is this eternal life Jesus is speaking of? He
has defined it himself: "Eternal life is this: to know you, the
only true God, and him whom you have sent, Jesus Christ."
(John 17:3)

We cannot blame Jesus for any lack of clarity: "Eternal
life is knowledge of God."

It is true authentic knowledge.

That is why I call the God of my faith the "God who
is," not the "God who seems to me to be."
—From *The God Who Comes* by Carlo Carretto

❧ Though I'm but dust, I pray,
  Before God standing,
  Not asking pleasure's way,
  Nor gold demanding;
  But greater things I ask,
  From God requesting
  No less than that he give
  To me that I may live
  Life everlasting.
  My heart now overflows
  . . . .
  With prayers and praises.
  My Heavenly Father knows
  Each sign that raises
  My heart ever nearer his heart
    so tender;
  For there's my joy and peace;
  In thee I've found release,
  My soul's Defender.
  —From *Prayer* by O. Hallesby

❧ Take me aside, O God, and let me be
A little while within thy company.

And speak to me, although no word is spoken
And still the silence closes round, unbroken.

And lead me for my spiritual discerning
Further along thy lonely road of learning.

And let me hold communion, thou and I,
With minds outreaching, and the world put by.
—Hilda M. Orchard as quoted in *Prayers and Thoughts
from World Religions* by Sid G. Hedges

❧ Lord, help me faithfully to journey along my road, hold-
ing my rightful place in the great procession of humanity;
Help me above all to recognize you and to help you in
all my pilgrim brothers.
—Michel Quoist as quoted in *Prayers and Thoughts from
World Religions* by Sid G. Hedges

Hymn: Father, I Stretch My Hands to Thee

Father, I stretch my hands to thee;
No other help I know;
If thou withdraw thyself from me,
Ah! whither shall I go?

What did thine only Son endure,
Before I drew my breath!
What pain, what labor, to secure
My soul from endless death!

Surely thou canst not let me die;
O speak, and I shall live;
And here I will unwearied lie,
Till thou thy Spirit give.

Author of faith! to thee I lift
My weary, longing eyes;
O let me now receive that gift!
My soul without it dies. Amen.
—Charles Wesley

55: See . . . Judge . . . Act

I.   Invocation
     Almighty God, send the light of your Son into our
     lives anew today. Let your presence touch our
     minds and hearts with your mercy, grace, and truth.
     Direct our thoughts, speech, and steps to the end
     that we may walk in your way today and always. In
     the name of Christ. Amen.

II. Psalm 16

III. Daily Scripture Readings
     Monday   Matthew 25:1-13
     Tuesday   Colossians 4:2-18
     Wednesday   1 Thessalonians 5
     Thursday   2 Thessalonians 2
     Friday   2 Thessalonians 3
     Saturday   John 4:31-38
     Sunday   A. Zephaniah 1:7, 12-18; Psalm
                     76; 1 Thessalonians 5:1-11;
                     Matthew 25:14-30
                 B. Daniel 7:9-14; Psalm 145:8-13;
                     Hebrews 10:11-18; Mark 13:24-32
                 C. Malachi 4:1-6; Psalm 82; 2 Thessa-
                     lonians 3:6-13; Luke 21:5-19

IV. Readings for Reflection

V.   Prayers: for the church, for others, for myself

VI. Reflection: silent and written

VII. Hymn: "My Faith Looks Up to Thee"

VIII. Benediction
      Today walk in the power and presence of God,
      Father, Son, and Holy Spirit. Amen.

Readings for Reflection

❧ To believe in God is to believe in the salvation of the world. The paradox of our time is that those who believe in God do not believe in the salvation of the world, and those who believe in the future of the world do not believe in God.

Christians believe in "the end of the world," they expect the final catastrophe, the punishment of others.

Atheists in their turn invent doctrines of salvation, try to give a meaning to life, work, the future of humankind, and refuse to believe in God because Christians believe in him and take no interest in the world.

All ignore the true God: he who has so loved the world! But which is the more culpable ignorance?

To love God is to love the world. To love God passionately is to love the world passionately. To hope in God is to hope for the salvation of the world.

I often say to myself that, in our religion, God must feel very much alone: for is there anyone besides God who believes in the salvation of the world? God seeks among us sons and daughters who resemble him enough, who love the world enough that he could send them into the world to save it.

—From *In the Christian Spirit* by Louis Evely

❧ Likewise, I have already said that we cannot speak with God and the world at the same time. And that is what one does who says her prayers and, at the same time, listens to conversation going on around her or thinks of whatever comes into her mind without checking the thoughts. Sometimes, however, no matter how much a person tries she cannot control these distractions, either because of some indisposition, particularly if she is inclined to be melancholy, or [to have] a weakness of mind. Sometimes, too, God allows his servants to have stormy days for their greater good and, although they are distressed and seek to calm themselves, they are unable to do so. No matter what they do, they cannot pay attention to the words they are saying. Their minds cannot concentrate on anything, but wander so haphazardly as to seem a prey to frenzy. From the pain this causes them, they will know that the fault is not theirs. Let them not be distressed, for that makes matters worse; and let them not tire themselves seeking to infuse sense into an understanding which is, at the moment, incapable of it. But let them pray as well as they can and even not pray at all, but consider the soul to be sick and give it some rest, busying themselves in some other act of virtue.

—From *Way of Perfection* by Saint Teresa of Avila

   Afresh I see thee. Lead me—once more I pray—
Even should it be against my will, thy way.
Let me not feel thee foreign any hour,
Or shrink from thee as an estranged power.
Through doubt, through faith, through bliss, through
     stark dismay,
Through sunshine, wind, or snow, or fog, or shower,
Draw me to thee who art my only day.

I would go near thee—but I cannot press
Into thy presence—it helps not to presume.
Thy doors are deeds; the handles are their doing.
He whose day-life is obedient righteousness,
Who, after failure, or a poor success,
Rises up, stronger effort yet renewing—
He finds thee, Lord, at length, in his own common
     room.

—From *Diary of an Old Soul* by George MacDonald

   The aphorism, "As a man thinketh in his heart so is he," not only embraces the whole of a man's being, but is so comprehensive as to reach out to every condition and circumstance of his life. A man is literally *what he thinks*, his character being the complete sum of all his thoughts.

As the plant springs from, and could not be without, the seed, so every act of a man springs from the hidden seeds of thought, and could not have appeared without them. This applies equally to those acts called "spontaneous" and "unpremeditated" as to those which are deliberately executed.

Act is the blossom of thought, and joy and suffering are its fruits; thus does a man garner in the sweet and bitter fruitage of his own husbandry.

Thought in the mind hath made us. What we are
By thought was wrought and built. If a man's mind
Hath evil thoughts, pain comes on him as comes
The wheel the ox behind. . . . If one endure
In purity of thought, joy follows him
As his own shadow—sure.
—From *As a Man Thinketh* by James Allen

☙ Lord, only one in ten returned to give thanks or so the story goes about the lepers you healed. It is tragic but I confess, Lord, that is probably my percentage compared to the times I ought to be thanking you.

Life has its down turns when I am moved to pray, but it has more joy and therefore more cause to rejoice with thanksgiving. In my life I am discovering deeper thanks, or perhaps understanding more what giving thanks is all about, as I experience life in more profound dimensions.

I've been thinking more too about the countless millions who are more justified than me in keeping their thanksgiving in. Those whose children cry at night from pain, those whose parents die too soon.

When the world seems devoid of hope, it is hard to give thanks. Realistically, I cannot blame them. Yet, I hear of many who faithfully stay together helping one another, who, despite living in the streets and eating the discards of others, sacrifice what they have so others may survive. For these I give thanks.

I hear of others who despite persecution and risk of death stay to minister and serve the poor and hungry in your name, all the while giving thanks for your love and bounty. For these I give thanks.

To the one leper who returned and gave thanks you said, "Your faith has made you well." Your salvation brought healing which restored him to God. Now clean he could find meaningful work and return to a full life.

Oh, the miracle of thanksgiving brought to us in the lessons of life. Praise and majesty be yours, Lord. For the healing of thanksgiving, thank you. *Amen.*
—From *Visions of a World Hungry* by Thomas G. Pettepiece

☙ Not too long ago a priest told me that he cancelled his subscription to the New York *Times* because he felt that the endless stories about war, crime, power games and political manipulation only disturbed his mind and heart and prevented him from meditation and prayer.

That is a sad story because it suggests that only by denying the world can you live in it, that only by surrounding yourself by an artificial, self-induced quietude can you live in a spiritual life. A real spiritual life does exactly the opposite: it makes us so alert and aware of the world around us, that all that is and happens becomes part of our contemplation and meditation and invites us to a free and fearless response.

—From *Reaching Out* by Henri J. M. Nouwen

    All prayer is thus activity, just as all generous activity (mixed motive and all) is a form of prayer. Prayer and action are one. To pray is a form of the verb to do, while to do is a form of the verb to pray. But the identity of prayer and action can be received by us and apprehended only in so far as we also receive and apprehend the tension between the two. Although from the ultimate point of view our being on our knees and, say, our getting a job for a man out of work are both parts of one and the same action, this fact can be recognized only if we also recognize that being on our knees is very different from taking steps to get a man a job. Unless this difference is clearly perceived and admitted, so that we spend time both on our knees and getting the job, our getting the job becomes activism, activity aimed to reassure and benefit myself under the disguise of another.

—From *Tensions* by H. A. Williams

    Grant me, O Lord, to know what I ought to know,
        to love what I ought to love,
        to praise what delights thee most,
        to value what is precious in thy sight,
        to hate what is offensive to thee.
        Do not suffer me to judge according to the sight
            of my eyes,
        nor to pass sentence according to the hearing
            of the ears of ignorant men;
        but to discern with a true judgment between things
            visible and spiritual,

and above all, always to inquire what is the good
   pleasure of thy will.
—Thomas à Kempis

Hymn: My Faith Looks Up to Thee

My faith looks up to thee,
Thou Lamb of Calvary,
Savior divine!
Now hear me while I pray,
Take all my guilt away,
O let me from this day
Be wholly thine!

May thy rich grace impart
Strength to my fainting heart,
My zeal inspire;
As thou hast died for me,
O may my love to thee
Pure, warm, and changeless be,
A living fire!

While life's dark maze I tread,
And griefs around me spread,
Be thou my guide;
Bid darkness turn to day,
Wipe sorrow's tears away,
Nor let me ever stray
From thee aside.

When ends life's transient dream,
When death's cold, sullen stream
Shall o'er me roll;
Blest Savior, then, in love,
Fear and distrust remove;
O bear me safe above,
A ransomed soul! Amen.
—Ray Palmer

Last Sunday after Pentecost
56: Christ the King

I.   Invocation
Almighty God, as you have given Jesus Christ to be Savior and Lord, grant us now grace to accept and rejoice in our salvation and in his lordship. Amen.

II. Psalm 44

III. Daily Scripture Readings
Monday	John 1:43-51
Tuesday	Luke 8:22-56
Wednesday	Acts 17:1-9
Thursday	Luke 19:28-40
Friday	1 Corinthians 15:1-28
Saturday	Matthew 26:1-29
Sunday	A. Ezekiel 34:11-16, 20-24; Psalm 23; 1 Corinthians 15:20-28; Matthew 25:31-46
	B. Jeremiah 23:1-6; Psalm 93; Revelation 1:4b-8; John 18:33-37
	C. 2 Samuel 5:1-5; Psalm 95; Colossians 1:11-20; John 12:9-19

IV. Readings for Reflection

V.   Prayers: for the church, for others, for myself

VI. Reflection: silent and written

VII. Hymn: "I Am Thine, O Lord"

VIII. Benediction
Go forth to serve in the strength, love, and presence of the Lord Jesus Christ. Amen.

Readings for Reflection

❧ Here the purpose and meaning of prayer dawned upon me for the first time. Here I was privileged to see more clearly than ever before the purpose of prayer: to glorify the name of God.

The scales fell from my eyes. I saw in a new light the misuse of prayer and the difficulties connected with prayer as well as the place of our own efforts in prayer.

Prayer life has its own laws, as all the rest of life has. The fundamental law in prayer is this: Prayer is given and ordained for the purpose of glorifying God. Prayer is the appointed way of giving Jesus an opportunity to exercise his supernatural powers of salvation. And in so doing he desires to make use of us.

—From *Prayer* by O. Hallesby

❧ I followed where they led,
　　And in a hovel rude,
With naught to fence the weather from his head
　　The King I sought for meekly stood;
A naked hungry child
　　Clung round his gracious knee,
And a poor hunted slave looked up and smiled
　　To bless the smile that set him free;
New miracles I saw his presence do,
　　No more I knew the hovel bare and poor,
The gathered chips into a woodpile grew
　　The broken morsel swelled to goodly store.
I knelt and wept: my Christ no more I seek.
His throne is with the outcast and the weak.

—"His Throne Is with the Outcast" by James Russell Lowell

❧ *First, then, our own experience suggests that power is always accompanied by the temptation to misuse it, and that the greater the power, the more self-restraint it requires to use it aright.* Great temptations keep company with great powers. The little man fighting his little battles wishes that he were the great man so that the more easily he might overcome them; but when he understands the great man he sees that storms circle around his higher altitudes that make the petty battles of the lower level seem insignificant. The acorn seedling may be impeded by a few dead leaves, but it never will shake in the grip of the tempest until it becomes an oak. The analogy of our experience at once suggests that our Lord was tempted not less but more than we are. Haggard and hungry in the wilderness, as Tintoretto painted him, he was facing temptations that our puny powers can hardly imagine. "If thou art *the Son of God*, command that these stones become bread"; "If thou art *the Son of God*, cast thyself down"; "All the kingdoms of the world . . . if thou wilt worship me." His masterful powers were met by masterful temptations.

—From *The Manhood of the Master* by Harry Emerson Fosdick

❧ When I, Francis, heard the call of the Gospel, I did not set about organizing a political pressure-group in Assisi. What I did, I remember very well, I did for love, without expecting anything in return; I did it for the Gospel, without placing myself at odds with the rich, without squabbling with those who preferred to remain rich. And I certainly did it without any class hatred.

I did not challenge the poor people who came with me to fight for their rights, or win salary increases. I only told them that we would be blessed—if also battered, persecuted, or killed. The Gospel taught me to place the emphasis on the mystery of the human being more than on the duty of the human being.

I did not understand duty very well. But how well I understood—precisely because I had come from a life of pleasure—that when a poor person, a suffering person, a sick person, could smile, that was the perfect sign that God existed, and that he was helping the poor person in his or her difficulties.

The social struggle in my day was very lively and intense, almost, I should say, as much so as in your own times. Everywhere there arose groups of men and women professing poverty and preaching poverty in the Church and the renewal of society. But nothing changed, because these people did not change hearts. . . .

No, brothers and sisters, it is not enough to change laws. You have to change hearts. Otherwise, when you have completed the journey of your social labors you shall find yourselves right back at the beginning—only this time it is you who will be the arrogant, the rich, and the exploiters of the poor.

This is why I took the Gospel path. For me the Gospel was the sign of liberation, yes, but of true liberation, the liberation of hearts. This was the thrust that lifted me out of the middle-class spirit, which is present to every age, and is known as selfishness, arrogance, pride, sensuality, idolatry, and slavery.

I knew something about all that.

I knew what it meant to be rich, I knew the danger flowing from a life of easy pleasure, and when I heard the text in Luke, "Alas for you, who are rich" my flesh crept. I understood. I had run a mortal risk, by according a value to the idols that filled my house, for they would have cast me in irons had I not fled.

It is not that I did not understand the importance of the various tasks that keep a city running. I understood, but I sought to go beyond.

You can reproach me, go ahead. But I saw, in the Gospel, a road beyond, a path that transcended all cultures, all human constructs, all civilization and conventions.

I felt the Gospel to be eternal; I felt politics and culture, including Christian culture, to be in time.

I was made always to go beyond time.
—From *I, Francis* by Carlo Carretto

&& My God, I wish to give myself to thee. Give me the courage to do so.
—François Fénelon

&& If indeed it be necessary, O Lord, to bury the workman that my work may be finished by other hands, help me never to think of myself as indispensable. May I be content to die with my work undone, knowing that my task is to work at the fulfillment of thy purposes, not to work them out.
—Anonymous

&& Govern all by thy wisdom, O Lord, so that my soul may be serving thee as thou dost will, and not as I may choose. Do not punish me, I beseech thee, by granting that which I wish or ask, if it offend thy love, which would

always live in me. Let me die to myself, that I may serve thee, who in thyself art the true life. Amen.
—Saint Teresa of Avila

❧ O Son of God to right my lot,
Naught but thy Presence can avail,
Yet on the road thy wheels are not,
Nor on the sea thy sail!

My "how" or "when" thou wilt not heed,
But come down thine own secret stair,
That thou may'st answer all my need,
Yea, every bygone prayer.
—From "That Holy Thing" by George MacDonald

Hymn: I Am Thine, O Lord

I am thine, O Lord, I have heard thy voice,
And it told thy love to me;
But I long to rise in the arms of faith,
And be closer drawn to thee.

Draw me nearer, nearer, blessed Lord,
To the cross where thou hast died;
Draw me nearer, nearer, nearer, blessed Lord,
To thy precious, bleeding side.

Consecrate me now to thy service, Lord,
By the power of grace divine;
Let my soul look up with a steadfast hope,
And my will be lost in thine.

O the pure delight of a single hour
That before thy throne I spend,
When I kneel in prayer, and with thee, my God,
I commune as friend with friend!

There are depths of love that I cannot know
Till I cross the narrow sea;
There are heights of joy that I may not reach
Till I rest in peace with thee.
—Fanny J. Crosby

Monthly Retreat Models

Retreat Model 1: God's Greatest Gift

Arrival

Thirty Minutes of Silent Listening

Scripture Readings
Luke 1:39-56; Luke 2:22-35; Romans 5:12-21;
Jeremiah 31:1-14; 1 John 1

Readings for Reflection

Reflection

Prayer

Journal Writing

Recreation

Rest

Repeat Cycle of Scripture Readings, Readings for
Reflection, Reflection, Prayer, and Journal Writing

Thirty Minutes of Silent Reflection

Holy Communion

Benediction

Readings for Reflection

🌺 We must learn always to find and procure the advantage of God. For God does not give gifts, nor did he ever give one, so that we might keep it and take satisfaction in it; but all were given—all he ever gave on earth or in heaven— that he might give this one more: himself.... Therefore I say that we must learn to look through every gift and every event to God and never be content with the thing itself. There is no stopping place in this life—no, nor was there ever one, no matter how far along the way a person had gone. This above all, then, be ready at all times for the gifts of God and always for new ones.

—Johannes Eckhart

🌺 For the real good of every gift it is essential, first, that the giver be in the gift—as God always is, for he is love— and next, that the receiver know and receive the giver in the gift. Every gift of God is but a harbinger of his greatest and only sufficing gift—that of himself. No gift unrecognized as coming from God is at its own best; therefore many things that God would gladly give us, things even that we need because we are, must wait until we ask for them, that we may know whence they come. When in all gifts we find him, then in him we shall find all things.

—From *Creation in Christ* by George MacDonald

🌺 I salute you. There is nothing I can give you which you have not; but there is much that, while I cannot give you, you can take.

No Heaven can come to us unless our hearts find rest in it today: take Heaven.

No peace lies in the future which is not hidden in the present: take Peace.

The gloom of the world is but a shadow; behind it, yet within our reach is joy: take Joy.

And so at this Christmas time I greet you, with the prayer that for you, now and forever, the day breaks and the shadows flee away.

—Fra Giovanni

ೞ Clearly Jesus cannot be understood simply as prophet, for that designation, like every other, is inadequate for the historical reality of Jesus. Nonetheless, among his other functions it is clear that Jesus functioned as a prophet. In both his teaching and his very presence Jesus of Nazareth presented the ultimate criticism of the royal consciousness. He has, in fact, dismantled the dominant culture and nullified its claims. The way of his ultimate criticism is his decisive solidarity with marginal people and the accompanying vulnerability required by that solidarity. The only solidarity worth affirming is solidarity characterized by the same helplessness they know and experience. . . .

The birth of Jesus itself represents a decisive criticism of the dominant consciousness. The Lukan account of his solidarity with the poor and the Matthean presentation of his abrasive conflict with the powers that be (seen in the birth narratives) both point to the emergence of an alternative consciousness.

—From *The Prophetic Imagination* by Walter Brueggemann

ೞ It is a wonderfully blessed thing to be privileged to share together the common mood of worship. Miraculous indeed is it to mingle the individual life with its intensely private quality in a transcendent moment of synthesis and fusion—here it is that the uniquely personal is lifted up and seen in a perspective as broad as life, and as profound!

Again and again we are overwhelmed by the littleness of our lives. We are struck by the way in which there seems to close in upon us the intimate need, the demand that often provides no breathing moment sufficient to let us lift up our hearts to take the long look and to sense the ultimate meanings in which our little lives are involved. And yet for those of us who seek it out there is the time of respite and repair when we rest our lives in the Presence of God.

Our needs are so varied and poignant. There are some of us who are in the throes of great and bedeviling temptations which seem to know us by name and face us at the point of our greatest weakness and challenge us where there is no strength and no protection. For some of us anxiety is mounting within so that we are paralyzed by the thought of tomorrow and what awaits us in the coming day. In our desperation we are possessed by panic and are unable to face ourselves even in the Presence of God.

Always there are those of us who are ill in body. In vain we have tried to companion our pain to rob it of its power to eat away the grounds of our peace. If we could know the meaning of what besets us, or at least the effect that it may have upon the length of our days, this would be sustaining. We struggle with an undertone of uneasiness as we sift out the findings of the trained mind and the skilled hand.

We keep a troubled vigil at the bedside of the world. We cannot accept its sickness as unto death but we cannot grasp the meaning and the hope of a cure that will make life all about us hale and well. The contemplation of the destruction of the world at our hands confronts even our little lives and their little part with a guilt too vast to assuage and too overwhelming to manage.

Thus we clutch the moment of intimacy in worship when we become momentarily a part of a larger whole, a fleeting strength, which we pit against all the darkness and the dread of other times.

—From *The Inward Journey* by Howard Thurman

   ❧ It is good to experience the quiet ministry of the living spirit of the living God. Again and again there are the little healings of silent breaches which sustain us in our contacts with the world and with one another. We are stunned by the little word, the unexpected silence, the smile off key; without quite knowing why, the balance is recovered and the rhythm of the hurt is stopped in its place. There is the sense of estrangement which overtakes the happiest human relations and the experience of recovery that makes the heart sing its old song with a new lilt. There are days when everything seems difficult, when the ordinary tasks become major undertakings, when one is sensitive and every moment is threatened by an explosion that does not quite come to pass; then without apparent cause, the whole picture changes and the spirit can breathe again with ease, the spring in the step comes back again. It is good to experience the quiet ministry of the living spirit of the living God.

Sometimes we are catapulted into disaster with a suddenness that paralyzes the mind and leaves the exposure to fear unshielded by courage or by strength. If there had been some warning, some intimation of what was to come, the wisdom of the years could have buttressed the life with a measured protection. But no, this was not the case. Often even before the full awareness of what has taken place can be felt, the realignment of one's powers begins to work and recovery is on the way. There are problems that meet us head-on in our journey. The issue of our spirit and the thing that confronts us is joined—we are engulfed in the great silence of fateful struggle. It seems that nowhere, in no place, can an answer be found. In vain we seek a clue, a key, even a little thing to give a fleeting respite, a second wind. Again and again it is apt to happen: the miracle of relief; a chance word from a casual conversation; a sentiment or a line in a letter; the refrain of an old song; an image from the past; a paragraph from a printed page; a stirring of prayer in the heart—the miracle of relief and we are released. The danger is passed, the conflict is over. It is good, so very good, to experience the quiet ministry of the living spirit of the living God.

—From *The Inward Journey* by Howard Thurman

₰ Loving Father, help us remember the birth of Jesus, that we may share in the song of the angels, the gladness of the shepherds, and the wisdom of the wise men.

Close the door of hate and open the door of love all over the world.

Let kindness come with every gift and good desires with every greeting.

Deliver us from evil by the blessing which Christ brings, and teach us to be merry with clean hearts.

May the Christmas morning make us happy to be thy children, and the Christmas evening bring us to our beds with grateful thoughts, forgiving and forgiven, for Jesus' sake. Amen.

—Robert Louis Stevenson

Retreat Model 2: Called to Serve

Arrival

Thirty Minutes of Silent Listening

Scripture Readings
   Matthew 23:1-12; Acts 9:1-19; Ezekiel 2:1-7; 1 Peter 4

Readings for Reflection

Reflection

Prayer

Journal Writing

Recreation

Rest

Repeat Cycle of Scripture Readings, Readings for
   Reflection, Reflection, Prayer, and Journal Writing

Thirty Minutes of Silent Reflection

Holy Communion

Benediction

Readings for Reflection

&. Such servants of our common Lord as I have named are witnesses to the power of faith. They point beyond themselves to One who is at once the pattern and the object of our faith, and bid us run the race that is set before us, looking unto Jesus. Those words I should wish to take as my motto today. I come as a learner, with no policy to advocate, no plan already formed to follow. But I come with one burning desire; it is that in all our activities, sacred and secular, ecclesiastical and social, we should help each other to fix our eyes on Jesus, making him our only guide. . . . Pray for me, I ask you, not chiefly that I may be wise and strong, or any such thing, though for these things I need your prayers. But pray for me chiefly that I may never let go of the unseen hand of the Lord Jesus and may live in daily fellowship with him. It is so that you will most of all help me to help you. So shall we go forward together—not without stumbling, not without weariness—but always toward the loving welcome that awaits us in our Father's home, where the conflicts which now beset the earth will have vanished, where self-seeking cannot find entrance, where misery gives place to joy and quarreling to peace, because self is either sacrificed or forgotten in the realization of the love of God.

—William Temple as quoted in *William Temple, Archbishop of Canterbury, His Life and Letters* by F. A. Iremonger

&. There is a good saying that comes from Löhe: "Don't be ashamed to do what you are called to do." Even the awkwardly spoken word, if only it comes out of an obedient heart, is better than a word unspoken in disobedience. Even the prayer that seems ineffectual and may perhaps be ridiculed may have left behind a seed of blessing. Indeed, even if no fruit is created in the spiritual sense, so that a soul comes nearer to God, still there is one thing that has happened: a testimony has been given in the biblical sense. And this precisely is our task, a hard task, but a glorious task.

—Erich Schick

&. The idea of *The Servant as Leader* came out of reading Hermann Hesse's *Journey to the East*. In this story we see a

band of men on a mythical journey, probably also Hesse's own journey. The central figure of the story is Leo who accompanies the party as the *servant* who does their menial chores, but who also sustains them with his spirit and his song. He is a person of extraordinary presence. All goes well until Leo disappears. Then the group falls into disarray and the journey is abandoned. They cannot make it without the servant Leo. The narrator, one of the party, after some years of wandering finds Leo and is taken into the Order that had sponsored the journey. There he discovers that Leo, whom he had known first as *servant* was in fact the titular head of the Order, its guiding spirit, a great and noble *leader* . . . this story clearly says that *the great leader is seen as servant first*, and that simple fact is the key to his greatness.
—From *Servant Leadership* by Robert K. Greenleaf

❧ Prophets grow in stature as people respond to their message. If their early attempts are ignored or spurned, their talent may wither away.

It is *seekers*, then, who make prophets, and the initiative of any one of us in searching for and responding to the voice of contemporary prophets may mark the turning point in their growth and service.
—From *Servant Leadership* by Robert K. Greenleaf

❧ The servant-leader *is* servant first—as Leo was portrayed. It begins with the natural feeling that one wants to serve, to serve *first*. Then conscious choice brings one to aspire to lead. That person is sharply different from one who is *leader* first, perhaps because of the need to assuage an unusual power drive or to acquire material possessions. For such it will be a later choice to serve—after leadership is established. The leader-first and the servant-first are two extreme types. Between them there are shadings and blends that are part of the infinite variety of human nature.

The difference manifests itself in the care taken by the servant-first to make sure that other people's highest priority needs are being served. The best test, and difficult to administer, is: Do those served grow as persons? Do they, *while being served*, become healthier, wiser, freer, more autonomous, more likely themselves to become servants?

And, what is the effect on the least privileged in society; will they benefit, or, at least, not be further deprived?
—From *Servant Leadership* by Robert K. Greenleaf

ஐ Teach me, good Lord:
Not to murmur at multitude of business or shortness of time.
Not to magnify undertaken duties by seeming to suffer under them, but to treat all as liberties and gladnesses.
Not to call attention to crowded work, or petty fatigues.
Not to gather encouragement from appreciation by others, lest this should interfere with purity of motive.
Not to seek praise, respect, gratitude, or regard from superiors or equals on account of age or past service.
Not to let myself be placed in favorable contrast with another.
—From *Prayers Public and Private* by Edward White Benson

ஐ Let not thy Word, O Lord, become a judgment upon us, that we hear it and do it not, that we know it and love it not, that we believe it and obey it not; O thou, who with the Father and the Holy Spirit livest and reignest, world without end. Amen.
—Attributed to Thomas à Kempis

ஐ Esteemed ordinands, since I have not the privilege of being a witness of your day of honor and joy, a day that should be a day of joy to the church, I take this means of saying to you what Melanchthon said:
"Christ as High Priest lays his hand upon his own, he chooses them through the voice of the church, he blesses them and anoints them with his gifts."
What riches, but also what responsibility! May both enter deep in your hearts and the church be made glad by your ministry.
I pray for you.
—Hermann Bezzel

ஐ Everyone who has ever occupied a position in life to which tradition and opinion, a long incrusted use and wont and habit of mind attribute a certain rigid pattern of behavior, knows very well the ponderous and incessant pressure of public opinion seeking to force one into the mold. Such types as the statesman, the headmaster, the parson, the poet, are continually subject to this pressure to become what the public expects them to be rather than what they really are. That very expectation becomes the archenemy, the Satan of the soul. If it is not resisted the living person becomes a stylized statue; he is dead. . . . This is murder—murder of spirit—and the murderers are the victim's admirers and friends.

—From *The Kingdom of the Real* by Nicodemus (Melville Chaning-Pierce)

❧ Would-be theologians . . . must be on their guard lest by beginning too soon to preach they rather chatter themselves into Christianity than live themselves into it and find themselves at home there.

—Søren Kierkegaard as recorded in his *Journal*, July 11, 1838

❧ It is our God-appointed office to lead men and women who are weary and wayward, exultant or depressed, eager or indifferent, into "the secret place of the Most High." We are to help the sinful to the fountain of cleansing, the bond slaves to the wonderful songs of deliverance. We are to help the halt and the lame to recover their lost nimbleness. We are to help the broken-winged into the healing light of "the heavenly places in Christ Jesus." We are to help the sad into the sunshine of grace. We are to help the buoyant to clothe themselves with "the garment of praise." We are to help redeem the strong from the atheism of despair. We are to help little children to see the glorious attractiveness of God, and we are to help the aged realize the encompassing care of the Father and the assurance of the eternal home.

—From *The Preacher, His Life and Work* by J. H. Jowett

Retreat Model 3: Principles That Give Life

Arrival

Thirty Minutes of Silent Listening

Scripture Readings
  Matthew 5:1-14; Matthew 7:1-27; Hebrews 12:1-17;
  Colossians 3:5-17

Readings for Reflection

Reflection

Prayer

Journal Writing

Recreation

Rest

Repeat Cycle of Scripture Readings, Readings for
  Reflection, Reflection, Prayer, and Journal Writing

Thirty Minutes of Silent Reflection

Holy Communion

Benediction

Readings for Reflection

&. Say to him "Here, Lord, I abandon myself to thee. I have tried in every way I could think of to manage myself, and to make myself what I know I ought to be, but have always failed. Now I give it up to thee. Do thou take entire possession of me. Work in me all the good pleasure of thy will. Mold and fashion me into such a vessel as seemeth good to thee. I leave myself in thy hands, and I believe thou wilt, according to thy promise, make me into a vessel unto thy own honor, 'sanctified, and meet for the master's use, and prepared unto every good work.'" And here you must rest, trusting yourself thus to Him, continually and absolutely.

Next, you must lay off every other burden,—your health, your reputation, your Christian work, your houses, your children, your business, your servants; everything, in short, that concerns you, whether inward or outward.

It is generally much less difficult for us to commit the keeping of our future to the Lord than it is to commit our present. We know we are helpless as regards the future, but we feel as if the present was in our own hands, and must be carried on our own shoulders; and most of us have an unconfessed idea that it is a great deal to ask the Lord to carry ourselves, and that we cannot think of asking him to carry our burdens too.

—From *The Christian's Secret of a Happy Life* by Hannah Whitall Smith

&. The dreamers are the saviors of the world. As the visible world is sustained by the invisible, so men, through all their trials and sins and sordid vocations, are nourished by the beautiful visions of their solitary dreamers. Humanity cannot forget its dreamers; it cannot let their ideals fade and die; it lives in them; it knows them as the *realities* which it shall one day see and know.

Composer, sculptor, painter, poet, prophet, sage, these are the makers of the after-world, the architects of heaven. The world is beautiful because they have lived; without them, laboring humanity would perish. . . .

Cherish your visions; cherish your ideals; cherish the music that stirs in your heart, the beauty that forms in your mind, the loveliness that drapes your purest thoughts, for out of them will grow all delightful conditions, all heavenly environment; of these, if you but remain true to them, your world will at last be built.

To desire is to obtain; to aspire is to achieve. Shall man's basest desires receive the fullest measure of gratification, and his purest aspirations starve for lack of sustenance? Such is not the law: such a condition of things can never obtain: "Ask and receive."

Dream lofty dreams, and as you dream, so shall you become. Your Vision is the promise of what you shall one day be; your Ideal is the prophecy of what you shall at last unveil.

The greatest achievement was at first and for a time a dream. The oak sleeps in the acorn; the bird waits in the egg; and in the highest vision of the soul a waking angel stirs. Dreams are the seedlings of realities.

—From *As a Man Thinketh* by James Allen

❧ Let no unworthy thought
Enter thy musing mind;
Things which the world hath wrought,
Untrue, unclean, unkind,
Leave these behind.
—Toc-H prayer

❧ There are four ways in which [God] reveals his will to us—through the Scriptures, through providential circumstances, through the convictions of our own higher judgment, and through the inward impressions of the Holy Spirit on our minds. Where these four harmonize, it is safe to say that God speaks.

For I lay it down as a foundation principle. . . . that of course his voice will always be in harmony with itself, no matter in how many different ways he may speak. The voices may be many, the message can be but one. If God tells me in one voice to do or to leave undone anything, he cannot possibly tell me the opposite in another voice. If there is a contradiction in the voices, the speakers cannot be the same. Therefore my rule for distinguishing the voice of God would be to bring it to the test of this harmony.

—From *The Christian's Secret of a Happy Life* by Hannah Whitall Smith

᠕ The Scripture teaches in the history, I think, that when one arrogantly exalts himself he ends by falling even below the earth. And perhaps, if viewed through these events, arrogance might not unreasonably be defined as a downward ascent.
—From *Gregory of Nyssa*

᠕ Do nothing on which you cannot pray for a blessing. Every action of a Christian that is good is sanctified by the Word and prayer. It becomes not a Christian to do anything so trivial that he cannot pray over it.
—John Wesley

᠕ Jacques Ellul puts the matter of prayer in the proper perspective for me. In his stimulating and insightful book *Prayer and Modern Man,* he says, "In the realm of prayer we can make no other claim than to obey." He reveals the hypocrisy of our usual rationale for prayer: to manipulate God and to procure for ourselves, or to produce some psychic peace in our depths.

He then turns us to the words of scripture and Jesus' command to "watch and pray." Prayer has very little to do with words, but rather is the reality of life lived in and through the living God as known in scripture. Ellul's book states that it is a crucial matter of faith to choose that form of life in a doubting and cynical world, and to watch with hope for the coming of Jesus. Prayer rooted in the command and hope of scripture is the only way in which faith is maintained. The life of prayer is commanded for the disciple, not chosen.

Amen! It is exciting to read Ellul's bold statement about the absolute necessity of prayer in this day of vapid and saccharine writing on that subject. My concern is twofold. First, that we have become such activists that most of us have little time for prayer. We have lost the knowledge of the critical nature of prayer—that it is a matter of faith commitment and a demand that God not keep silent in our day.

I am also concerned about the lack of places to pray. Now this may sound strange to some, especially to Protestant ears. Why do we need a "place to pray"? We are comfortable with tossing off prayers as we rush through our current program, or engage in artful oratory before an audience—which we have been known to call "Pastoral prayer."

It is instructive to note the witness of the gospels concerning Jesus and his life of prayer. His reputation continued to grow and large crowds would gather to hear him and to have their sickness cured. But he always went off to some place where he could be alone and pray. (Luke 5:15-16. See also Matthew 14:23 and 26:36, John 6:15, Mark 1:35, Luke 6:12 and Luke 9:28-29.) Jesus felt the need to withdraw to a quiet place for prayer on a regular basis. There was a dialogue in his life between the times of active ministry and the times of prayer filled solitude. The rhythm of the journey inward and the journey outward, as we call it in my own community, is the alternation of prayerful waiting in God's presence, expectantly feeding on the Word, and the outward manifestation of that Word as it becomes a reality in our lives as servant people in the world.

But why speak of a "place to pray"? Can't one pray anywhere? Theoretically and theologically, yes. God is not sequestered at some precise place to which we must go in order to be in touch with the divine presence. However, the point is that *we* need some precise place to go in order to more fully enter into the Presence who enables us to pray. We need this no less, and most certainly more than, Jesus did. Our cramped technological society is constantly bombarding us with noise, sights, smells, and thrills. It insists that we cannot be happy if we are alone or quiet. And to speak of obedience to and communion with a God who was long ago declared dead is to be subjected to ridicule and the most determined assault on our faith's rootedness.

So we go apart to be quiet and expectant in the Lord's presence. We are fed by the scripture, we beg for healing, we struggle for faith, and we wait for the coming of the grace-filled moment of love and hope. In our own homes we can provide space and time for this life of prayer, through what Catherine de Hueck Doherty calls a "poustinia," in her book by the same name. *Poustinia* is the Russian word for desert or wilderness. It is traditional for a Christian in Russia to set aside a room in her house, or a cabin in his woods, to be used for prayer and meditation. One goes there for twenty-four hours, taking only the Bible, bread, water, and a simple straw mattress for sleeping and dreaming.

Perhaps we can create poustinias in our own homes, for ourselves and others, places of silence, prayer, and hospitality with the Lord. If we do this for a period each day—dare we say even an hour?—watching and waiting with the Lord, then we can come to know the poustinia in our hearts where Jesus is always present to us and goes with us into a wounded and doubting world.

I also feel it is critical for Christian communities to set aside places for prayer, meditation, and healing. Traditionally Roman Catholic orders have provided guest houses and retreat centers for the experience of spiritual retreat. Early on in its own life, the Church of the Saviour established its own Dayspring Retreat Farm. Yokefellows (a largely Protestant group sponsoring retreats) has established centers around the country. But in the financial crunch of our day, and because of the demand for therapy *rather* than prayer, many such places for prayer have collapsed. I would suggest that today, more than ever, we need places where persons can go from time to time for solitude, prayer, and reflection on scriptures and on their own lives. They need not be fancy. In fact, simplicity provides the space for the Lord to do his work of healing and vision-giving.

Jesus commands us to "watch and pray." If we are able to be persons of faith, then we will be persons of prayer. If we are to be persons of hope and healing in the world, then we will be persons for whom living is praying, and praying is living. In short, we have no choice but to pray.

—"No Choice but to Pray" by Conrad Hoover in *Sojourners* (June 1977)

Retreat Model 4: The Wounded Healer

Arrival

Thirty Minutes of Silent Listening

Scripture Readings
Psalm 51:1-17; Acts 3:1-16; Romans 8:1-17;
2 Corinthians 4

Readings for Reflection

Reflection

Prayer

Journal Writing

Recreation

Rest

Repeat Cycle of Scripture Readings, Readings for
Reflection, Reflection, Prayer, and Journal Writing

Thirty Minutes of Silent Reflection

Holy Communion

Benediction

Readings for Reflection

‰ When man is no longer able to look beyond his own death and relate himself to what extends beyond the time and space of his life, he loses his desire to create and the excitement of being human. Therefore, I want to look at Peter's problem as that of nuclear man who is searching for new ways of being immortal.

Robert Lifton sees as the core problem of man in the nuclear age the threat to his sense of immortality. This sense of immortality "represents a compelling, universal urge to maintain an inner sense of continuity over time and space, with the various elements of life." It is "man's way of experiencing his connection with all human history" (Lifton, *Boundaries*, p. 22). But for nuclear man the traditional modes of immortality have lost their connective power. Often he says: "I do not want to bring children into this self-destructive world." This means that the desire to live on in his children is extinguished in the face of the possible end of history. And why should he want to live on in the works of his hands when one atomic blitz may reduce them to ashes in a second? Could perhaps an animistic immortality make it possible for man to live on in nature? And how can a belief in a "hereafter" be an answer to the search for immortality when there is hardly any belief in the "here"? A life after death can only be thought of in terms of life before it, and nobody can dream of a new earth when there is no old earth to hold any promises.

No form of immortality—neither the immortality through children nor the immortality through works, neither the immortality through nature nor the immortality in heaven—is able to help nuclear man project himself beyond the limitations of his human existence.

It is therefore certainly not surprising that nuclear man cannot find an adequate expression of his experience in symbols such as Hell, Purgatory, Heaven, Hereafter, Resurrection, Paradise, and the Kingdom of God.

A preaching and teaching still based on the assumption that man is on his way to a new land filled with promises, and that his creative activities in this world are the first signs of what he will see in the hereafter, cannot find a sounding board in a man whose mind is brooding on the suicidal potentials of his own world.

This brings us to the end of our description of nuclear man. Peter was our model. We saw his historical dislocation, his fragmented ideology, and his search for a new mode of immortality. Obviously, the level of awareness and visibility is different in different people, but I hope you will be able to recognize in your own experiences and the experiences of your friends some of the traits which are so visible in Peter's life style. And this recognition might also help you realize that Christianity is not just challenged to adapt itself to a modern age, but it also is challenged to ask itself whether its unarticulated suppositions can still form the basis for its redemptive pretensions.

—From *The Wounded Healer* by Henri J. M. Nouwen

≈ For years it has become increasingly important to me that all our preaching should take place on the verge of prayer. Our preaching should be so near to prayer that it would require only a very slight transposition to turn our words into words of prayer. . . . The center of the congregational sermon is an act of our priesthood, which we share with all believers, but which must first become manifest in us.

Therefore let us help one another to make progress in our praying. What we do in the pulpit is based not only upon the prayers we say during the service; rather it must be the prayers of the whole week that sustain the preacher. They create a spiritual atmosphere which is most in evidence when it is not obvious, and which accordingly makes of our sermon a work of art or a mechanical production.

—Hans Asmussen as quoted in *Minister's Prayerbook* by
  John W. Doberstein

≈ Suffering is the highest action of Christian obedience and I call blessed, not those who have worked, but all who have suffered. Suffering is the greatest work in the discipleship of Jesus.

—Hermann Bezzel as quoted in *Pastoralblätter*, 95 (1955)

❧ God wounds deeply when he wills to heal.
—Hermann Kohlbrügge as quoted in *Pastoralblätter*, 95 (1955)

❧ One of the fruits of solitude is an increased capacity for compassion—the ability "to suffer with" another's pain. It comes about as the result of an increased sense of solidarity with the human family of which we are a part. When Paul talks about "suffering with those who suffer," he is talking about compassion, that supreme gift without which we are less than fully human. It might well be that the greatest threat to human survival now confronting us is not the loss of energy or the increase of pollution, but the loss of compassion. We are confronted daily with the pain of human tragedy—the breakup of a family or the sunken face of a starving child—to such an extent that we soon learn to turn off what we see. In order to cope with our feelings of helplessness, we teach ourselves how *not* to feel. The tragedy in this response, which is probably more widespread than we dare believe, is that we also deaden our capacity for love. For Christians, the cross stands as an ever-present reminder that love and suffering are two sides of the same coin.
—From *Mutual Ministry* by James C. Fenhagen

❧ One can pray everywhere and anywhere, yet there are places where prayer finds its natural climate; those places are churches, fulfilling the promise; 'I will make them joyful in my house of prayer' (Is 56:7).

A church, once consecrated, once set apart, becomes the dwelling-place of God. He is present there in another way than in the rest of the world. In the world he is present as a stranger, as a pilgrim, as one who goes from door to door, who has nowhere to rest his head; he goes as the lord of the world who has been rejected by the world and expelled from his kingdom and who has returned to it to save his people. In church he is at home, it is his place; he is not only the creator and the lord by right but he is recognized as such. Outside it he acts when he can and how he can; inside a church he has all power and all might and it is for us to come to him.

When we build a church or set apart a place of worship we do something which reaches far beyond the obvious significance of the fact.

—From *Living Prayer* by Anthony Bloom

    ❦   When encounter with God gives place to the discovery of my identity with him, what I have to surrender is most of what I am accustomed to call myself: the damaged sick self we all partly are and to which we want to cling because we are obsessively fixated on the damage and sickness; the ego-image self which wants to cut a figure and make a splash even if it be only as a holy and humble man of heart; the self which feels strongly, and since it is religious, likes especially to feel God's love thrilling it through; the self bent on making progress towards spiritual maturity; the self which enjoys the rhythm of rejection and acceptance and calls it sin and repentance; the self aware of its love for God and man—all this is the self which has to be surrendered as we slowly and dimly discover our identity with God, discover the me within me which is greater than me and also authentically me. In the end we find ourselves stripped of everything except that dull, dim, rather remote awareness that we are an articulation of God's own Being, a limb of his body, to use St. Paul's phrase, or to use St. John's, a branch of the vine which is himself.

—From *Tensions* by H. A. Williams

    ❦   Religion is seen in the root meaning of that term— *religio*, to rebind. The thing to be done with religious concern is to rebind humankind to the cosmos, to heal the pervasive alienation.

—From *Servant Leadership* by Robert K. Greenleaf

    ❦   Pray, just as you are led, without reasoning, in all simplicity. Be a little child, hanging on him that loves you.

—John Wesley

    ❦   Always remember the essence of Christian holiness is simplicity and purity: one design, one desire: entire devotion to God.

—John Wesley

Retreat Model 5: *God Cares for Us*

Arrival

Thirty Minutes of Silent Listening

Scripture Readings
    Luke 12:22-34; Psalm 121; John 14:15-31;
    2 Corinthians 1:3-22

Readings for Reflection

Reflection

Prayer

Journal Writing

Recreation

Rest

Repeat Cycle of Scripture Readings, Readings for
    Reflection, Reflection, Prayer, and Journal Writing

Thirty Minutes of Silent Reflection

Holy Communion

Benediction

Readings for Reflection

  ❧   The biggest disease today is not leprosy or tuberculosis, but rather the feeling of being unwanted, uncared for and deserted by everybody. The greatest evil is the lack of love and charity, the terrible indifference towards one's neighbour who lives at the roadside assaulted by exploitation, corruption, poverty and disease.

As each one of this Society is to become a Co-Worker of Christ in the slums, each ought to understand what God and the Society expect from her. Let Christ radiate and live his life in her and through her in the slums. Let the poor seeing her be drawn to Christ and invite him to enter their homes and their lives. Let the sick and suffering find in her a real angel of comfort and consolation, let the little ones of the streets cling to her because she reminds them of him, the friend of the little ones.

Our life of poverty is as necessary as the work itself.

Only in heaven we will see how much we owe to the poor for helping us to love God better because of them.

—From *Something Beautiful for God* by Malcolm Muggeridge

  ❧   All that I ask from you, provided I ask it with faith and confidence, that you will give, that I shall obtain. That is, of course, I must not ask anything that would be harmful, or something mean that, though it seems great in my eyes, is really much less than what you wish to give me. You are a Father, all powerful and infinitely wise and good and tender. You say to us as your children, so frail we are and hardly able to walk except with our hand in yours, 'all that you ask I will give you if only you ask with confidence.' And you do give it, so willingly and easily when our petitions are reasonable and in accord with your desires, and with the feelings that you like to see in our hearts and in conformity with all that you yourself desire, more ardently than we can ever do.

If we ask you for dangerous playthings you refuse them in goodness for us, and you console us by giving us other things for our good. If we ask you to put us where it would be dangerous for us to be you do not give us what is not for our good, but you give us something really for our welfare, something that we would ask for ourselves if our eyes were open. You take us by the hand and lead us, not there where we would wish to go, but there where it is best for us to be.

—From *Meditations of a Hermit* by Charles de Foucauld

• The truth really is that [God's] care is definitely superior to any possibilities of human care; and that he, who counts the very hairs of our heads, and suffers not a sparrow to fall without him, takes note of the minutest matters that can affect the lives of his children, and regulates them all according to his own perfect will, let their origin be what they may.

The instances of this are numberless. Take Joseph. What could have seemed more apparently on the face of it to be the result of sin, and utterly contrary to the will of God, than the action of his brethren in selling him into slavery? And yet Joseph, in speaking of it said, "As for you, ye thought evil against me; but God meant it unto good." "Now therefore be not grieved, nor angry with yourselves, that ye sold me hither: for God did send me before you to preserve life." It was undoubtedly sin in Joseph's brethren, but by the time it had reached Joseph it had become God's will for him, and was, in truth, though he did not see it then, the greatest blessing of his whole life. And thus we see how God can make even "the wrath of man to praise him," and how all things, even the sins of others, "shall work together for good to them that love him."

I learned this lesson practically and experimentally, long years before I knew the scriptural truth concerning it. I was attending a prayer-meeting held in the interests of the life of faith, when a strange lady rose to speak, and I looked at her, wondering who she could be, little thinking she was to bring a message to my soul which would teach me a grand practical lesson. She said she had great difficulty in living the life of faith, on account of the second causes that seemed to her to control nearly everything that concerned her. Her perplexity became so great that at last she began to ask God to teach her the truth about it, whether he really was in everything or not. After praying this for a few days, she had what she described as a vision. She thought she was in a perfectly dark place, and that there advanced toward

her, from a distance, a body of light which gradually surrounded and enveloped her and everything around her. As
it approached, a voice seemed to say, "This is the presence of
God! This is the presence of God!" While surrounded with
this presence, all the great and awful things in life seemed to
pass before her—fighting armies, wicked men, raging beasts,
storms and pestilences, sin and suffering of every kind. She
shrank back at first in terror; but she soon saw that the presence of God so surrounded and enveloped herself and each
one of these things that not a lion could reach out its paw,
nor a bullet fly through the air, except as the presence of
God moved out of the way to permit it. And she saw that
if there were ever so thin a film, as it were, of this glorious
Presence between herself and the most terrible violence, not
a hair of her head could be ruffled nor anything touch her,
except as the Presence divided to let the evil through. Then
all the small and annoying things of life passed before her;
and equally she saw that there also she was so enveloped in
this presence of God that not a cross look, nor a harsh word,
nor petty trial of any kind could affect her, unless God's
encircling presence moved out of the way to let it.

Her difficulty vanished. Her question was answered
forever. God *was* in everything; and to her henceforth there
were no second causes. She saw that her life came to her,
day by day and hour by hour, directly from the hand of
God, let the agencies which should seem to control it be
what they might. And never again had she found any difficulty in an abiding consent to his will and an unwavering
trust in his care.

—From *The Christian's Secret of a Happy Life* by Hannah
   Whitall Smith

ᴥ Nothing else but this seeing God in everything will
make us loving and patient with those who annoy and
trouble us. They will be to us then only the instruments for
accomplishing his tender and wise purposes toward us, and
we shall even find ourselves at last inwardly thanking them
for the blessings they bring.

Nothing else will completely put an end to all murmur-
ing or rebelling thoughts. Christians often feel at liberty
to murmur against people, when they would not dare to
murmur against God. Therefore this way of receiving things

would make it impossible ever to murmur. If our Father permits a trial to come, it must be because the trial is the sweetest and best thing that could happen to us, and we must accept it with thanks from his dear hand. This does not mean, however, that we must like God's will in the trial; and it is not hard to do this when we have learned to know that his will is the will of love, and is therefore always lovely.

—From *The Christian's Secret of a Happy Life* by Hannah Whitall Smith

    It must be possible that the soul made
    Should absolutely meet the soul that makes;
    Then, in that bearing soul, meet every other
    There also born, each sister and each brother.
    Lord, till I meet thee thus, life is delayed;
    I am not I until that morning breaks,
    Not I until my consciousness eternal wakes.
    —From *Diary of an Old Soul* by George MacDonald

    Again I shall behold thee, daughter true;
    The hour will come when I shall hold thee fast
    In God's name, loving thee all through and through.
    Somewhere in his grand thought this waits for us.
    Then shall I see a smile not like thy last—
    For that great thing which came when all was past,
    Was not a smile, but God's peace glorious.
    —From *Diary of an Old Soul* by George MacDonald

    Increasing knowledge is always thus not *extensive* only but *intensive*. The average man returns from seeing the turbines at Niagara, with a vague impression of enormous masses moving at tremendous speed. But the engineer? He knows every bolt and screw, every lever and piston; he knows the particular details of secret bearing and balanced strain; he pokes his wrench around dark corners for hidden bolts that the spectator never guessed were there. The more he knows, as an engineer, the more he sees the details and not the bulk. *Ignorance sees things in mass; knowledge breaks all masses up into units and knows each one; omniscience perfectly understands and cares for every most minute detail.*

Consider then the meaning of God's knowledge of men. When a stranger thinks of China he imagines a vague multitude, with faces that look all alike. When a missionary thinks of China, the vague multitude is shaken loose in one spot, and individuals there stand out, separately known and loved. When God thinks of China, he knows every one of the Chinese by name. He does for humanity what a librarian does for his books, or an engineer for his turbines. We stand, every one, separate in his thought. He lifts us up from the obscurity of our littleness; he picks us out from the multitude of our fellows; he gives to our lives the dignity of his individual care. The Eternal God calls us every one by name. He is not the God of mankind in the mass; he is the God of *Abraham*, of *Isaac*, and of *Jacob*! All great pray-ers have lived in the power of this individual relationship with God.

—From *The Meaning of Prayer* by Harry Emerson Fosdick

    There is probably no image that expresses so well the intimacy with God in prayer as the image of God's breath. We are like asthmatic people who are cured of their anxiety. The Spirit has taken away our narrowness (the Latin word for anxiety is *angustia* = narrowness) and made everything new for us. We receive a new breath, a new freedom, a new life. This new life is the divine life of God himself. Prayer, therefore, is God's breathing in us, by which we become part of the intimacy of God's inner life, and by which we are born anew.

So, the paradox of prayer is that it asks for a serious effort while it can only be received as a gift. We cannot plan, organize or manipulate God; but without a careful discipline, we cannot receive him either.

—From *Reaching Out* by Henri J. M. Nouwen

Retreat Model 6: Prayer and Fasting

Arrival

Thirty Minutes of Silent Listening

Scripture Readings
Matthew 4:1-11; Luke 6:12-49; 1 Timothy 2:1-7;
Isaiah 58:1-12

Readings for Reflection

Reflection

Prayer

Journal Writing

Recreation

Rest

Repeat Cycle of Scripture Readings, Readings for
Reflection, Reflection, Prayer, and Journal Writing

Thirty Minutes of Silent Reflection

Holy Communion

Benediction

Readings for Reflection

❧ If religion requires us sometimes to fast and to deny our natural appetites, it is to lessen that struggle and war that is in our nature. It is to render our bodies fitter instruments of purity and more obedient to the good motions of divine grace. It is to dry up the springs of our passions that war against the soul, to cool the flame of our blood, and to render the mind more capable of divine meditations.

If religion commands us to live wholly unto God and to do all to his glory, it is because every other way is living wholly against ourselves, and will end in our own shame and confusion of face.

How ignorant, therefore, are they of the nature of religion, of the nature of man, and of the nature of God who think a life of strict piety and devotion to God to be a dull, uncomfortable state—when it is so plain and certain that there is neither comfort nor joy to be found in anything else!
—From *A Serious Call to a Devout and Holy Life* by William Law

❧ Prayer is the nearest approach to God and the highest enjoyment of him that we are capable of in this life. It is as much your duty to rise to pray as to pray when you are risen.

And if you are late at your prayers you offer to God the prayers of an idle, slothful worshiper who rises to prayers as idle servants rise to their labor.
—From *A Serious Call to a Devout and Holy Life* by William Law

❧ Is this going to be a period of purification, Lord? Is this going to be the time when you give me insight into the chains that bind me and the courage to throw them off? Is this going to be my chance to see my prison and escape it?

John Eudes said: "This is a time of purification. A time to identify your ambiguous relationships and your ambivalent attitudes, and to make some decisions and choose some directions." Lord, it is you who said this to me. If I believe in your church and the voice of those who speak in her name, in your name, then it was you who pointed out to me the meaning of my stay here: "Identify and choose."

And you also said, "Pray even when you do not feel attracted to it." Yes, Lord, I will try to pray, even when I am afraid to face you and myself, even when I keep falling asleep or feel as though I am going around in circles, even when it seems that nothing is happening.

Yes, Lord, I will pray—not only with others, not only supported by the rhythms of the choir, but also alone with you. I will try not to be afraid. Lord, give me courage and strength. Let me see myself in the light of your mercy and choose you. Amen.

—From *A Cry for Mercy* by Henri J. M. Nouwen

&⃛ Here I would like to mention two things which I have learned from my great master, John of the Cross—one on the method of meditation, and the other on the book to choose.

The Method: Saint John divides it into three parts, and up to this point there's nothing new.

1. Imaginative reflection on the mystery which one wishes to meditate.

2. Intellectual consideration of the mysteries represented. (Here too there's nothing new.)

3. (And this is important.) Loving and attentive repose in God, to make sure we are fully prepared for that moment when the intelligence opens itself up to God's illumination.

This exercise of love, which is deeply human, results in a serene and devout repose before God. It must be meditation clearly directed towards simplicity and interior silence.

The Book to Choose: Above all other books, choose the Bible. If you like, read as many books of meditation as possible, but that isn't essential. It is essential to read and meditate on the Scriptures. Christianity without the Bible is a contradiction in terms. Preaching not anchored in the Scriptures is equally impossible. There is no true religious formation which is not based on the Gospel. The Bible is the letter which God himself wrote to men in the thousands of years of their history. It is the long drawn out sigh for Christ (Old Testament) and the account of his coming among us (New Testament).

When the temple of Jerusalem was burning, the Jews abandoned all its treasures to the flames but saved the

Bible. Paul knew the Bible by heart, and Augustine said, "Ignorance of Scripture is ignorance of Christ."

The Bible is the word of God, the Word made flesh is the Eucharist. I put both of them on the altar and kneel down before them.

—From *Letters from the Desert* by Carlo Carretto

    ↜ When you establish yourself in the inner person by the remembrance of God, then Christ the Lord will enter and dwell within you. The two things go together.

And here is a sign for you, by which you can be certain that this glorious work has begun within you: you will experience a certain feeling of warmth towards the Lord. If you fulfill everything prescribed, then this feeling will soon begin to appear more and more often, and in time will become continuous. This feeling is sweet and beatific, and from its first appearance it stimulates us to desire and seek it, lest it leave the heart: for in it is Paradise.

Do you wish to enter this Paradise as quickly as possible? Here, then, is what you must do. When you pray, do not end your prayer without having aroused in your heart some feeling towards God, whether it be reverence, or devotion, or thanksgiving, or glorification, or humility and contrition, or hope and trust. Also when after prayer you begin to read, do not finish reading without having felt in your heart the truth of what you read. These two feelings—the one inspired by prayer, the other by reading—mutually warm one another; and if you pay attention to yourself, they will keep you under their influence during the whole day. Take pains to practise these two methods exactly and you will see for yourself what will happen.

—Theophan the Recluse

    ↜ If anyone should ask me how to carry out the task of prayer, I would say to him: Accustom yourself to walk in the presence of God, keep remembrance of him, and be reverent. To preserve this remembrance, choose a few short prayers, or simply take the twenty-four short prayers of St. John Chrysostom, and repeat them often with appropriate thoughts and feelings. As you accustom yourself to this, remembrance of God will bring light to your mind and warmth to your heart. And when you attain this state, God's spark, the ray of grace, will fall at last into your heart. There is no way in which you yourself can produce it: it comes forth direct from God. When it comes, dwell in the Jesus Prayer alone, and with this prayer blow the spark of grace into flame. This is the most direct way.

—Theophan the Recluse

    ▪ In our day, as soon as you speak about the mystery of prayer, people cry, "Prayer! There is no time for prayer! All those people to feed, all those real things to organize, how can you still ask us to waste our precious time?

"Why search for a hypothetical relationship with the invisible God, when you can find the immediate and concrete in visible humanity?

"And people are the visible presence of God on earth: serve them, save them, and you've done it all!"

And what can we say when this stand is taken not least by the witnesses of the invisible God, by priests and religious? "Brother Carlo, you are speaking of the desert, of silence, of prayer. But how can you talk like that to us, when we are up to our necks in contemporary civilization, snowed under by thousands and thousands of tasks, caught up from morning to night in contacts with people and the service of the poor?" And you keep silence with a compassionate smile and with the security of a man who continues to believe firmly in past prejudices!

But the fact is that they are not past prejudices!

The fact is that the priest who says he no longer has time to pray will be found on a painful search for his identity after a few years. The busy militants who have so little time that they can't waste time praying, will be found so empty in a few years that you won't know what to do to give them back a little faith in the ideal they have been wanting to serve until now.

No, these are not prejudices.

The first commandment remains the first commandment, and it is the *first*—both under the old law (cf. Deut. 6:5) and under the new (cf. Luke 12:30) that was pronounced by Jesus—"You shall love the Lord your God with all your heart, with all your soul, with all your strength, and with all your mind; and your neighbor as yourself" (Luke 10:27).

Moreover, it is hammered in so forcefully that it leaves no doubts. It would seem that no part of a person has been forgotten on the list—heart, soul, mind, strength—in order to emphasize the necessity of decision in loving God!

And then?

And then the problem. If you don't pray, if you are not searching for a personal relationship with God, if you don't stay with him for long periods in order to know him, study him, understand him, little by little you will start forgetting him, your memory will weaken, you will no longer recognize him. You will not be able to, because you will no longer know how to love.

The proverb "Out of sight, out of mind" is true not only about people; it is terribly true about God, too.

Take an example.

If a fiancé telephones his fiancée to tell her, "I'm sorry, this evening I can't come, I've so much work!", there is nothing wrong. But if it is the thousandth time he has made the same call, he has not been to see her in weeks on the excuse of work or outings with friends, it is more serious—rather, it is quite clear: this is not love.

Because the lover is capable of overcoming all difficulties and discovering all the stratagems necessary to meet his soul's beloved.

So it is better to get clear with ourselves what our relationship with God is.

Have you been not praying, not seeking him personally because you don't love him, or because you have no time?

—From *The God Who Comes* by Carlo Carretto

Retreat Model 7: The Demands of Ministry

Arrival

Thirty Minutes of Silent Listening

Scripture Readings
 1 Corinthians 4; Romans 9:1-27; 2 Corinthians 5;
 2 Peter 3

Readings for Reflection

Reflection

Prayer

Journal Writing

Recreation

Rest

Repeat Cycle of Scripture Readings, Readings for
 Reflection, Reflection, Prayer, and Journal Writing

Thirty Minutes of Silent Reflection

Holy Communion

Benediction

Readings for Reflection

≈ *Resolves*—To try to learn to be thoroughly poor in spirit, meek and to be ready to be silent when others speak.

To learn from everyone.

To try to feel my own insignificance.

To believe in myself, and the powers with which I am intrusted.

To try to make conversation more useful and therefore to store my mind with fact, yet to be on guard against a wish to shine.

To try to despise the principle of the day, 'every man his own trumpeter'; and to feel it a degradation to speak of my own doings, as a poor braggart.

To endeavor to get over the adulterous-generation habit of seeking a sign. . . .

To speak less of self, and think less.

To aim at more concentration of thought.

To try to overcome castle-building.

To be systematic in visiting; and to make myself master of some system of questions for ascertaining the state of the poor.

To listen to conscience, instead of, as Pilate did, to intellect.

To try to fix attention on Christ rather than on the doctrines of Christ.

To preserve inviolable secrecy on all secrets committed to me, especially on any confidential communication of spiritual perplexities.

To take deep interest in the difficulties of others so communicated.

To perform rigorously the examen of conscience.

To fix my thoughts on prayer, without destruction.

To contend, one by one, against evil thought.

To watch over a growing habit of uncharitable judgments.

—Fredrick W. Robertson as quoted in *The Soul of Frederick W. Robertson, the Brighton Preacher* by James R. Blackwood

≈ It may be granted, therefore, that we are called to difficult and costly service. Yet have we abundant cause to

be satisfied with it, from the sustaining support and consolation provided for its emergencies. All, indeed, may be considered to be included in the single promise, "Lo, I am with you always, even to the end of the world." The officers he employs, in every age, are entitled to this treasure, as well as those of the first age. Keep your mind believingly attentive to this "always"—"Lo, I am with you," to qualify and succeed you in whatever work I call you to. "Lo, I am with you, " to comfort you by my presence and Spirit, when your hearts are grieved. "Lo, I am with you," to defend and strengthen you in trials, though all men forsake you. While he stands with you, there can be no just cause for fear or faintness. You need no other encouragement. This you shall never want, if you continue faithful: and thereupon you may conclude, "The Lord shall deliver me from every evil work, and will preserve me unto his heavenly kingdom."
—Daniel Williams as quoted in *On the Ministerial Office*

ᕉ What made George Fox's service to seekers (and their response to him) so exemplary was the significant move to new and more exacting ethical standards, the force of which carries to this day. Fox's major contribution was not his theology, nor even his encouragement to care for suffering, important as these were. Rather it seems to me, what gave durability to the Quaker tradition was the practical result that so many of those who called themselves Friends *behaved more lovingly toward all creatures and assumed an impressive level of responsibility for their society and its institutions*. Perhaps the most innovative result was that, by the effort of those whom Fox inspired, the quality of some contemporary institutions, notably commerce, was markedly improved.

We live in a time that is much more dominated by institutions, both public and private, than was true in Fox's day. And these institutions—all of them, including the very best—are crying out for a new mission to them that would raise their stature as servants of society and drastically reduce their impact as sources of suffering and injustice.
—From *Servant Leadership* by Robert K. Greenleaf

ᕉ What do I want? I want to serve. Whom do I want to serve? The Lord—in the person of his poor suffering children.

And what is my reward? I serve neither for reward nor thanks, but out of gratitude and love; my reward is that I am permitted to serve. And if I perish in doing so? If I perish, I perish, said Esther, who, after all, did not know him who for love of me perished and who will not let me perish. And if I grow old in this service? Then my heart shall flourish like the palm tree, and the Lord will satisfy me with grace and mercy. I walk in peace and am careful for nothing.

—Wilhelm Löhe as quoted in *Der Dienst der Kirche am Menschen, Pastoraltheologie* by Wolfgang Trillhaas

ঌ You were never in your lives in so critical a situation as you are at this time. It is your part to be peacemakers, to be loving and tender to all, but to addict yourselves to no party. In spite of all solicitations, of rough or smooth words, say not one word against one or the other side. Keep yourselves pure, do all you can to help and soften all; but beware how you adopt another's jar.

See that you act in full union with each other; this is of the utmost consequence. Not only let there be no bitterness or anger but no shyness or coldness between you.

—John Wesley

ঌ The Christian journey is a life lived from inside out, a life in which the things we experience within—dreams, memories, images, and symbols, and the presence of him whom we encounter in the deep silence—are in constant tension and dialogue with all that we experience without—people, events, joys, sorrows, and the presence of him whom we encounter in others. Thomas Merton repeats a suggestion of Douglas Steere that the absence of this tension might well produce the most pervasive form of violence present in contemporary society. "To allow one's self to be carried away by a multitude of conflicting concerns," Merton writes, "to surrender to too many demands, to commit one's self to too many projects, to want to help everyone in everything is to succumb to violence. Frenzy destroys our inner capacity for peace. It destroys the fruitfulness of our work, because it kills the root of inner wisdom which makes work fruitful."

One of the most critical tasks of the local church is to enable people to become "journeyers" rather than "wanderers." This suggests that the leadership of a congregation needs to be serious about their own journeys, to the point where they are willing to share their experience with others, not as those who have arrived but as fellow journeyers able to receive as well as to give. . . .

In his *Markings*, Dag Hammarskjöld records some of the often agonizing turning points that were the occasion of the deepening of his remarkable journey. One entry in this journal describes with particular wisdom that sense of creative tension which is the mark of wholeness. "The more faithfully you listen to the voice within you," he writes, "the better you will hear what is sounding outside. And only he who listens can speak. Is this the starting of the road toward the union of your two dreams—to be allowed in clarity of mind to mirror life, and in purity of heart to mold it?" Ultimately, this is the question we all must ask, for it is the question Christ asks of us.
—From *Mutual Ministry* by James C. Fenhagen

❧ What should happen is that our use of the created world becomes related to need, our own and our neighbor's need. I am not suggesting a loss of a certain *joie de vivre* of the kind the pastor I quoted earlier enjoyed. To the contrary, in the freedom that comes from no longer needing to acquire possessions as a measure of our worth we may find a greater pleasure in the material world of things. H. A. Williams comments, "Poverty is the ability to enjoy the world to the full because I am not anxious about losing a bit of it or acquiring a bit of it." He goes on to say, "Poverty also consists of the recognition that I have within my own resources ample enough . . . to meet [life] creatively, so that it builds me up into my own selfhood."
—From *Spirituality for Ministry* by Urban T. Holmes III

❧ We, Protestants, are an undisciplined people. Therein lies the reason for much dearth of spiritual insight and serious lack of moral power. Revolting, as we did, from the legalistic regimens of the medieval church, we have forgotten almost completely the necessity which inspired these regimens, and the faithful practices which have given to Christendom some of its noblest saints.

Without discipline there would have been no Francis of Assisi, no Bernard of Clairvaux, no Teresa of Avila, no

Brother Lawrence, no William Law, no Evelyn Underhill, no Thomas Kelly.

Without discipline there will be no such rich legacy of sainthood bequeathed by us to succeeding generations, or revitalizing the church and redeeming the society of this generation.

The spiritual vitality of the church depends, not on complicated organization or creative administration, important as these are; not on eloquent preaching or adequate theology, valuable as they are; not on unlimited financial resources or cultural maturity, helpful though they be.

What the church primarily needs now, as always, is the presence within it of God-conscious, God-centered souls. Even a few here and there would mean very much to a church confronted by the chaos of this age.

A multitude of men and women, pressing "on to the mark for the prize of the high calling of God in Christ Jesus," would confront the secularism and skepticism of our time with a challenge not easily laughed off or shunted aside.

—From *Discipline and Discovery* by Albert Edward Day

&. I have again and again, with all the plainness I could, declared what our constant doctrines are, whereby we are distinguished only from heathens or nominal Christians, not from any that worship God in spirit and in truth. Our main doctrines, which include all the rest, are three—that of Repentance, of Faith and of Holiness. The first of these we account, as it were, the porch of religion; the next, the door; the third, religion itself.

—John Wesley

&. Woman, remember the faith! In the name of God, set out again, and do the first works. . . . Begin again without delay. The day after you receive this, go and meet a class or a band. Sick or well, go! If you cannot speak a word, go; and God will go with you. You sink under the sin of omission.

—John Wesley

Retreat Model 8: Sent into the World

Arrival

Thirty Minutes of Silent Listening

Scripture Readings
    John 17:1-19; Mark 1:12-28; Luke 24:44-49;
    1 Peter 4:12–5:11

Readings for Reflection

Reflection

Prayer

Journal Writing

Recreation

Rest

Repeat Cycle of Scripture Reading, Readings for
    Reflection, Reflection, Prayer, and Journal Writing

Thirty Minutes of Silent Reflection

Holy Communion

Benediction

Readings for Reflection

❧ Many years ago, when I was at Oxford, in a cold winter's day, a young maid (one of those we kept at school) called upon me. I said: 'You seem half-starved. Have you nothing to cover you but that thin linen gown?' She said: 'Sir, this is all I have!' I put my hand in my pocket, but found I had scarce any money left, having just paid away what I had. It immediately struck me: 'Will thy Master say, "Well done, good and faithful steward? Thou hast adorned thy walls with the money which might have screened this poor creature from the cold!"'
—John Wesley

❧ Evangelism is witness. It is one beggar telling another beggar where to get food. The Christian does not offer out of his bounty. He has no bounty. He is simply guest at his Master's table and, as evangelist, he calls others too.
—From *That They May Have Life* by Daniel T. Niles

❧ One proud, surly, lordly word, one needless contention, one covetous action may cut the throat of many a sermon, and blast the fruit of all that you have been doing.
—From *Gildas Salvanus: The Reformed Pastor* by Richard Baxter

❧ On the contrary, I must say that the desire of most of us was to remain simple brothers, for the dignity of the priesthood was feared as a danger to humility, to unobtrusiveness, to the desire to count for nothing.

Now we were members of the poor class, the lowest class, and the brothers truly wished to remain such.

At first we took up residence in a pair of lean-tos we had discovered down by Twisting Brook, which served as a shelter for donkeys.

But that did not last long.

A farmer soon came with a donkey.

He was unhappy with us, and made us move out because we had taken the animal's space. And perhaps we were bothering him.

So we headed for the woods around Saint Mary of the Angels, the little church, originally called the Portiuncula, right in the middle of the woods, so simple and solitary.

There it was a simple matter to build a few huts for shelter.

We lived like skylarks.

Our real prayer was our gladness. Our rule was the Gospel, and the certainty that it was God who was guiding us. . . .

When I think back on that time I feel uplifted. I would have liked to fasten forever onto that manner of living, for it helped us to break with all our habits, and immersed us in the utopia of the Gospel, which is an explosion of freedom, simplicity of life, love, and the absence of problems.

Unfortunately, things were not always like that. Later on we too knew complications—books, houses . . . houses . . . especially the houses, which we never finished building, and which weighed heavily upon the Gospel.

I had reason to suffer and be uneasy when I saw building in progress.

Once I outright set about to raze to the ground a little house that seemed too large to me, too deluxe for us who wished to be poor.

It was always a drama for me, a thorn planted in my heart.

Besides, in building, we turned aside from our original choice of following Jesus in his poverty, although we did not mean to. Our visible wealth was like a weed, suffocating the delicate shoot that contained the very presence of God.

—From *I, Francis* by Carlo Carretto

❧ Doing something beautiful for God is, for Mother Teresa, what life is about. Everything, in that it is for God, becomes beautiful, whatever it may be; as does every human soul participating in this purpose, whoever he or she may be. In manifesting this, in themselves and in their lives and work, Mother Teresa and the Missionaries of Charity provide a living witness to the power and truth of what Jesus came to proclaim. His light shines in them. When I think of them in Calcutta, as I often do, it is not the bare house in a dark slum that is conjured up in my mind, but a light shining and a joy abounding. I see them diligently and cheerfully constructing something beautiful for God out of the human misery and affliction that lies around them. One of their leper settlements is near a slaughter-house whose stench in the ordinary way might easily make me retch. There, with Mother Teresa, I scarcely noticed it; another fragrance had swallowed it up.

—From *Something Beautiful for God* by Malcolm Muggeridge

ea. Here in Beni-Abbes, during the winter, nomads often arrive with their tents.

They are the poorest of people: they no longer have any camels or goats to sell, no longer the strength to organize caravans. They are seeking some place they can be helped to settle down into a new social reality which has no further need for the nomadic life.

One day a French woman, who was making a retreat here, was walking beside one of these tents. She stopped to pass the time of day and, as she did so, realized that a Tuareg girl, thin as a rake, was trembling with cold.

It is strange, but that is how it is: in the desert it is cold in the sunless dawns.

"Why don't you cover yourself up?", she asked.

"Because I've nothing to cover myself with," replied the girl.

The French woman, without going to the roots of the problem, went—to pray.

She entered the hermitage built by Père de Foucauld himself, where the Blessed Sacrament is exposed.

She prostrated herself in the sand before Jesus, present under the sign of faith, "the Eucharist."

Some time passed, she sought contact with the Eternal One, she tried to pray.

"I couldn't go on," she told me afterwards. "I couldn't pray. I had to go out, back to the tent, and give that child one of my sweaters. Then I returned, and then I was able to pray."

Here is what I should like to say to those who are afraid of personal prayer with God, who don't want to alienate themselves from their suffering brethren.

If you pray, if you pray seriously, if you pray in truth, it will be God himself who will send you out, with greater strength, with greater love, towards your brothers and sisters, so that you may love them more gratuitously and serve them more delicately.

Well then, you will say, why, why in the past have too many Christians scandalized me with their indifference, with the hardness of their bigoted hearts, with the hermetic sealing of themselves against every problem of justice and liberation of the people?

Yet they were praying, they were contemplating!

No, if they were praying, their prayer was just a bit of rhetoric. If they were contemplating, they were contemplating . . . nothing.

They were deceiving you, and they were deceiving the Church.

It is impossible to pray to a personal God—that is, love a personal God—and remain indifferent to those who are suffering.

It is impossible.

Anyone who prays without suffering for his or her suffering brothers and sisters is praying to a pole, a shadow, not to the living God.

—From *The God Who Comes* by Carlo Carretto

&. *The task of prophetic ministry is to nurture, nourish, and evoke a consciousness and perception alternative to the consciousness and perception of the dominant culture around us.* Thus I suggest that prophetic ministry has to do not primarily with addressing specific public crises but with addressing, in season and out of season, the dominant crisis that is enduring and resilient, of having our alternative vocation co-opted and domesticated. It may be, of course, that this enduring crisis manifests itself in any given time around concrete issues, but it concerns the enduring crisis that runs from concrete issue to concrete issue. That point is particularly important to ad hoc liberals who run from issue to issue without discerning the enduring domestication of vision in all of them.

The alternative consciousness to be nurtured, on the one hand, serves to *criticize* in dismantling the dominant consciousness. To that extent, it attempts to do what the liberal tendency has done, engage in a rejection and delegitimatizing of the present ordering of things. On the other hand, that alternative consciousness to be nurtured serves to

energize persons and communities by its promise of another time and situation toward which the community of faith may move. To that extent it attempts to do what the conservative tendency has done, to live in fervent anticipation of the newness that God has promised and will surely give.
—From *The Prophetic Imagination* by Walter Brueggemann

᪵ The disciplined life or obedience is not obsolete for our times, but it takes on a very different meaning than a blind submission to external authority. It turns inward. That inward turning is not so much to our feelings as to our memory, understanding, and will. By memory I mean the images that make up the structures of meaning within us and in terms of which we see the world. Understanding here is the ability to illumine our experience in dialogue with the church so that it has purpose and direction. Will is the courage to act reflectively, not in reaction, but with a vision of the Kingdom.

It is ultimately this vision to which we are called to be obedient, which is why a concern for poverty and peace, traditionally the first evangelical counsel, follows obedience in my ordering.
—From *Spirituality for Ministry* by Urban T. Holmes III

᪵ A simpler life-style is not a panacea. It may be embarked upon for the wrong reasons—out of guilt, as a substitute for political action, or in quest for moral "purity." But it can also be meaningful and significant:

—as an act of *faith* performed for the sake of personal integrity and as an expression of a personal commitment to a more equitable distribution of the world's wealth;

—as an act of *self-defense* against the mind-polluting effects of our overconsumption;

—as an act of *solidarity* with the majority of humankind, which has no choice about life-style;

—as an act of *celebration* of the riches found in creativity, spirituality, and community with others rather than in mindless materialism.
—From *Visions of a World Hungry* by Thomas G. Pettepiece

Retreat Model 9: The Sinner's Friend

Arrival

Thirty Minutes of Silent Listening

Scripture Readings
   Luke 15:1-10; Luke 7:36-50; John 4:7-42;
   Romans 5:1-11

Readings for Reflection

Reflection

Prayer

Journal Writing

Recreation

Rest

Repeat Cycle of Scripture Reading, Readings for
   Reflection, Reflection, Prayer, and Journal Writing

Thirty Minutes of Silent Reflection

Holy Communion

Benediction

Readings for Reflection

❧ Never miss a communion through your own fault; communion is more than life, more than all the wealth of the world, more than the whole universe; it is me, Jesus. How can you prefer something else to me?
—From *Meditations of a Hermit* by Charles de Foucauld

❧ Here is the mystery of the Church of Christ, a true, impenetrable mystery.

She has the power to give me holiness, yet she is made up, all the way through, of sinners—and what sinners!

She has the omnipotent and invincible faith to renew the Eucharist, yet she is made up of weak men groping in the darkness and fighting daily against the temptation of losing their faith.

She carries a message of pure transparence, yet she is incarnate in a mess of dirt, which is the dirt of the world.

She speaks of the sweetness of the Master, of his non-violence, yet in history she has sent armies to disembowel infidels and to torture heretics.

She carries a message of evangelical poverty, yet she often seeks gifts and alliances with the powerful.

We have only to read the Inquisition trial of St. Joan of Arc to convince ourselves that Stalin was not the first to falsify charges and corrupt the judges.

We have only to consider what the innocent Galileo was made to sign under threats to be convinced that the . . . personnel of the Church, although they make up the Church, are often evil and fallible personnel, capable of making errors as great as the earth's path round the sun.

It is useless to want anything else from the Church except this mystery of infallibility and fallibility, sanctity and sin, courage and weakness, credibility and the lack of it.

People who are dreaming of something different from this reality are simply wasting time and keep going back to the beginning again. Moreover, they show they have not understood humankind.

Because that is human, just as the Church shows us to be, in our wickedness and, at the same time, in our invin-

cible courage, which faith in Christ has given us, and the
love of Christ has us live.

—From *The God Who Comes* by Carlo Carretto

&. "For others," I said, "justice is a flowering of charity—
its triumphant realization."

The doctor stared for a long while with a look of surprise and hesitation that was most embarrassing for me.
I think the phrase had annoyed him. It was only a phrase
after all.

"Triumphant! Triumphant! I don't think much of your
triumph, my boy! You'll say the Kingdom is not of this
world. Right. But it wouldn't hurt to give the hands of the
clock a little shove all the same. My grouse against you
people isn't that poverty still exists—oh, no! And I'll even
grant you this much. I'll agree that it's the job of old fools
like me to feed and clothe and look after them and keep
them clean. But since they're really your responsibility I
cannot forgive you for sending them to us so dirty. See
what I mean? Why, damn it all, after twenty centuries of
Christianity, to be poor ought not still to be a disgrace.
Or else you have gone and betrayed that Christ of yours!
There's no getting away from that, good God Almighty!
You have every means of humbling the rich at your disposal, for setting their pace. The rich man wants to be well
thought of, and the richer he is the more he wants it. If you
would only have the pluck to make them take the back seats
in church round the Holy Water stoup, or even out on the
steps—why not? It would have made them think. They'd
all have had one eye on the poor men's seats, I know 'em!
The first everywhere else, but here in the House of God, the
last! Can you see that happening? Oh, of course I know the
thing wouldn't be easy. If the poor man really is the living
image of Jesus—Jesus himself—it's awkward to have him
sitting there in the front row, displaying his obscene misery,
his face from which in two thousand years you haven't yet
been able to wipe the spittle. Because first and foremost the
social problem is a matter of honour; it is the unjust humili-
ation of poor men that makes your pauper. Nobody's asking you to fatten up people who from father to son have in
any case lost the habit of getting fat, who'd probably always
be thin as laths; and at a pinch, to make the thing look a bit

more decent, there's no reason why you shouldn't eliminate freaks, unemployables, drunkards, anything too uncomfortable to look at. The fact remains that a poor man, a real poor man, an honest man, goes of his own accord to what he considers his proper place, the lowest in the house of the Lord. And you've never seen and never will see a beadle dressed up like a hearse come down to look for him, at the very back of the church, to lead him to the altar rails with all the ceremony due to a prince—a prince in the order of Christianity."

—From *The Diary of a Country Priest* by Georges Bernanos

❧ The Church exists, not for the pious and righteous, but for sinners and godless men. It must not judge and condemn, for all the gravity of its message, but heal, forgive, save. Its inevitable warnings must not be an end in themselves, but a reminder of the offer of grace held out by God. It can never, despite all the graces it has received, indeed precisely because of the grace it has received, pretend to be a self-righteous caste or class of pure and holy men. It can never assume, that unholy, godless and evil things exist only outside itself. There is no part of the Church which is perfect, no element which is not endangered, frail, unstable, constantly in need of correction and improvement. The front-line between the world and the reign of God passes directly through the centre of the Church, through the heart of every individual member.

A Church which in these last days does not realize that it is composed of sinful men and exists for sinful men, must grow hardhearted, self-righteous and without compassion, deserving neither the mercy of God nor the confidence of men. But a Church which is genuinely aware that only the perfect reign of God can divide wheat from tares, good fish from bad, will be granted the grace of holiness and righteousness which it cannot create for itself. Such a Church will know that it has no need to affect a high moral tone for the world's benefit, as though everything in it were as good as it possibly could be; it will know that its treasures are stored in very earthly vessels, that its lights are dim and flickering, its faith weak, its knowledge lacking, its confession of faith halting. It knows that there are no sins and omissions to which it cannot be tempted and to which it has not, in one way or another, yielded and that however much it continues to keep sin at a distance, it has no reason to keep the sinner at a distance also. The Church would be unable to enter the kingdom of God justified, if it looked down self-righteously on publicans and sinners. But if the Church, as the fellowship of those who are called to righteousness and holiness, remains aware of its guilt and sin, then it may live in joyful assurance of forgiveness, then in the dawning reign of God its unholy members will be saints, then it need have no fear despite the almost irresistible temptations to which it is exposed and despite its constant failures and mistakes. For the Church has been promised that he who humbles himself shall be exalted.

—From *The Church* by Hans Küng

❧ Do not tell people how they ought to feel toward Christ. It is just what they ought that they cannot do. Preach a Christ that will make them feel as they ought. That is objective preaching. The tendency and fashion of the present moment is all in the direction of subjectivity. People welcome sermons of a more or less psychological kind, which go into the analysis of the soul or of society. They will listen gladly to sermons on character-building, for instance; and in the result they will get to think of nothing else but their own character; which is a fatal thing. Learn to commit your soul and the building of it to One who can keep it and build it as you never can. Attend then to Christ, the Holy Spirit, the kingdom, and the cause, and he will look after your soul.

—From *Positive Preaching and the Modern Mind* by Peter Taylor Forsyth

❧ There is no prayer that ought to be more constantly on your lips than those lines of Charles Wesley, surely the most characteristic he ever wrote:

> O Thou who camest from above
> The pure celestial fire to impart,
> Kindle a flame of sacred love
> On the mean altar of my heart.
> There let it for thy glory burn.

Think of the news you are ordained to declare. That God has invaded history with power and great glory; that in the day of man's terrible need a second Adam has come forth to the fight and to the rescue; that in the cross the supreme triumph of naked evil has been turned once for all to irrevocable defeat; that Christ is alive now and present through his Spirit; that through the risen Christ there has been let loose into the world a force which can transform life beyond recognition—this is the most momentous message human lips were ever charged to speak. It dwarfs all other truths into insignificance. It is electrifying in its power, shattering in its wonder. Surely it is desperately unreal to talk of themes like these in a voice deadened by routine, or in the maddeningly offhand and impassive manner which is all too familiar. It ought not to be possible to conduct a church service in a way which leaves a stranger with the impression that nothing particular is happening and that no important business is on hand. "Went to church today," wrote Robert Louis Stevenson in his journal, "and was not greatly impressed." If that is the best we can do for people, is it worth doing? "Certainly I must confess," cried Sir Philip Sidney, "I never heard the old song of Percy and Doublas, that I found not my heart moved more than with a trumpet." And to you has been committed the infinitely more heartmoving story of the Word made flesh: "that incredible interruption," wrote G. K. Chesterton, "was a blow that broke the very backbone of history." "It were better," he declared, "to rend our robes with a great cry against blasphemy, like Caiaphas in the judgment, rather than to stand stupidly debating fine shades of pantheism in the presence of so catastrophic a claim."

—From *Heralds of God* by James S. Stewart

Retreat Model 10: The Minister as Soul Friend

Arrival

Thirty Minutes of Silent Listening

Scripture Readings
John 10:1-18; Colossians 1:3-29; Philemon;
Ephesians 4:1-16

Readings for Reflection

Reflection

Prayer

Journal Writing

Recreation

Rest

Repeat Cycle of Scripture Readings, Readings for
Reflection, Reflection, Prayer, and Journal Writing

Thirty Minutes of Silent Reflection

Holy Communion

Benediction

Readings for Reflection

❧ That which I am and the way I am, with all my gifts of nature and grace, you have given to me, O Lord, and you are all this. I offer it all to you, principally to praise you and to help my fellow Christians and myself.
—From *The Cloud of Unknowing*

❧ This morning I prayed hard for my parish, my poor parish, my first and perhaps my last, since I ask no better than to die here. My parish! The words can't even be spoken without a kind of soaring love. . . . But as yet the idea behind them is so confused. I know that my parish is a reality, that we belong to each other for all eternity; it is not a mere administrative fiction, but a living call of the everlasting church. But if only the good God would open my eyes and unseal my ears, so that I might behold the face of my parish and hear its voice. Probably that is asking too much. The face of my parish! The look in the eyes. . . . They must be gentle, suffering, patient eyes. I feel they must be rather like mine when I cease struggling and let myself be borne along in the great invisible flux that sweeps us all, helter-skelter, the living and the dead, into the deep waters of Eternity. And those would be the eyes of all Christianity, of all parishes—perhaps of the poor human race itself. Our Lord saw them from the cross. "Forgive them for they know not what they do."
—From *The Diary of a Country Priest* by Georges Bernanos

❧ What makes the tradition from Fox so terribly relevant today is the urgent need, around the world, for leadership by strong ethical persons—those who by nature are disposed to be servants (in the sense of helping others to become healthier, wiser, freer, more autonomous and more likely themselves to be servants) and who therefore can help others to move in constructive directions. Servant-leaders are *healers* in the sense of *making whole* by helping others to a larger and nobler vision and purpose than they would be likely to attain for themselves. This, in essence, is how Fox served—*as a healer*.
—From *Servant Leadership* by Robert K. Greenleaf

❧ I call God to record upon my soul, that I advise no man more than I practise. I do, blessed be God, gain and save and give all I can. And so, I trust in God, I shall do, while the breath of God is in my nostrils.

—John Wesley

❧ Truly this is the unending miracle of love: that one loving person, through his love, can embrace God, whose being fills and transcends the entire creation.

—From *The Cloud of Unknowing*

❧ When the query arises 'Is this it?', make it your rule once and for all mercilessly to drive away all such questions as soon as they appear. They originate from the enemy. If you linger over this question the enemy will pronounce the decision without delay, 'Oh yes, certainly it is—you have done very well!' From then on you stand on stilts and begin to harbour illusions about yourself and to think that others are good for nothing. Grace will vanish: but the enemy will make you think that grace is still with you. This will mean that you think you possess something, when really you have nothing at all. The Holy Fathers wrote, 'Do not measure yourself.' If you think you can decide any question about your progress, it means that you are beginning to measure yourself to see how much you have grown. Please avoid this as you would avoid fire.

—From *The Art of Prayer*

❧ Hospitality, therefore, means primarily the creation of a free space where the stranger can enter and become a friend instead of an enemy. Hospitality is not to change people, but to offer them space where change can take place. It is not to bring men and women over to our side, but to offer freedom not disturbed by dividing lines. It is not to lead our neighbor into a corner where there are no alternatives left, but to open a wide spectrum of options for choice and commitment. It is not an educated intimidation with good books, good stories and good works, but the liberation of fearful hearts so that words can find roots and bear ample fruit. It is not a method of making our God and our way into the criteria of happiness, but the opening of an opportunity to others to find their God and their way. The paradox of hospitality is that it wants to create emptiness, not a fearful emptiness, but a friendly emptiness where strangers can enter and discover themselves as created free; free to sing their own songs, speak their own languages, dance their own dances; free also to leave and follow their own vocations. Hospitality is not a subtle invitation to adopt the life style of the host, but the gift of a chance for the guest to find his own.

—From *Reaching Out* by Henri J. M. Nouwen

ва. The task of prophetic imagination and ministry is to bring to public expression those very hopes and yearnings that have been denied so long and suppressed so deeply that we no longer know they are there. Hope, on the one hand, is an absurdity too embarrassing to speak about, for it flies in the face of all those claims we have been told are facts. Hope is the refusal to accept the reading of reality which is the majority opinion; and one does that only at great political and existential risk. On the other hand, hope is subversive, for it limits the grandiose pretension of the present, daring to announce that the present to which we have all made commitments is now called into question. . . .

The language of hope and the ethos of amazement have been partly forfeited because they are an embarrassment. The language of hope and the ethos of amazement have been partly squelched because they are a threat.

It is mind-boggling to think of the public expression of hope as a way of subverting the dominant royal embrace of despair. I am not talking about optimism or development or evolutionary advances but rather about promises made by one who stands distant from us and over against us before remarkably *for us*. Speech about hope cannot be explanatory and scientifically argumentative; rather, it must be lyrical in the sense that it touches the hopeless person at many different points. More than that, however, speech about hope must be primally theological, which is to say that it must be in the language of covenant between a personal God and a community. Promise belongs to the world of trusting speech and faithful listening.

—From *The Prophetic Imagination* by Walter Brueggemann

꿣 Grant, O Lord, that in all the joys of life we may never forget to be kind. Help us to be unselfish in friendship, thoughtful of those less happy than ourselves, and eager to bear the burdens of others.
—Charles L. Slattery

꿣 All through this day, O Lord, by the power of thy quickening Spirit, let me touch the lives of others for good, whether through the word I speak, the prayer I speak, or the life I live.
—Anonymous

꿣 If I know what I ought to do in a given situation, if I see the action that I should take in order to be true to the deepest thing in me, if I look it steadily in the eye and see not, the light that is in me becomes darkness. If the light becomes darkness, what a darkness!

And you putting out the light? Just think about it. In your own life this past week, did your light become darkness? Think about it without becoming morbid, depressed, or sentimental, but with a chastened spirit. Are you thinking right now about some decision that is waiting; about something that you know that you ought to do? And have you decided that you are not going to do it? When you made that decision, did the lights go out one by one and did you wonder what had happened to you? If the light that is in you be darkness, nothing outside of you can turn the light on again. Only you yourself can do that. Even God can't unless you give him a hand.
—From *The Growing Edge* by Howard Thurman

꿣 It is hard to find words in the language of men to explain the deep things of God. Indeed, there are none that will adequately express what the children of God experience. But perhaps one might say the testimony of the Spirit is an inward impression on the soul, whereby the Spirit of God directly witnesses to my spirit, that I am a child of God; that Jesus Christ hath loved me and given himself for me; and that all my sins are blotted out, and I, even I, am reconciled to God.
—John Wesley

Retreat Model 11: Dark Night of the Soul

Arrival

Thirty Minutes of Silent Listening

Scripture Readings
    Psalm 137; Job 10, 42:1-6; 1 Peter 2:4-10; John 1:1-18

Readings for Reflection

Reflection

Prayer

Journal Writing

Recreation

Rest

Repeat Cycle of Scripture Readings, Readings for
    Reflection, Reflection, Prayer, and Journal Writing

Thirty Minutes of Silent Reflection

Holy Communion

Benediction

Readings for Reflection

≈ Affliction constrained Christ to implore that he might be spared, to seek consolation from man, to believe he was forsaken by the Father. It forced a just man to cry out against God, a just man as perfect as human nature can be, more so, perhaps, if Job is less a historical character than a figure of Christ. "He laughs at the affliction of the innocent!" This is not blasphemy but a genuine cry of anguish. The Book of Job is a pure marvel of truth and authenticity from beginning to end. As regards affliction, all that departs from this model is more or less stained with falsehood.

Affliction makes God appear to be absent for a time, more absent than a dead man, more absent than light in the utter darkness of a cell. A kind of horror submerges the whole soul. During this absence there is nothing to love. What is terrible is that if, in this darkness where there is nothing to love, the soul ceases to love, God's absence becomes final. The soul has to go on loving in the emptiness, or at least to go on wanting to love, though it may only be with an infinitesimal part of itself. Then, one day, God will come to show himself to this soul and to reveal the beauty of the world to it, as in the case of Job. But if the soul stops loving it falls, even in this life, into something almost equivalent to hell.

—From *Waiting for God* by Simone Weil

≈ When we experience God as a meeting with another to whom we are closely linked as to a father or a friend, then the ambivalence of our feelings is inevitable. It is far better to accept that fact honestly and admit it to ourselves than to repress it. There is great wisdom in Mrs. Patrick Campbell's warning not to do it in the street and frighten the horses. But that prudent condition observed, if you want to blaspheme, then for Christ's sake blaspheme. If you want in your prayers to grouse, then for Christ's sake grouse. If you hate God, then for Christ's sake tell him you do and tell him why. He will know that these things are the necessary obverse of your love for him and that he is himself responsible for having made you that way. By having the courage of your aggression you will show greater trust in him and greater love for him than by all that 'resigned submissive meek' stuff which leaves you to take the hell out of other people, and not least out of yourself so that in consequence there is far less of you to give away.

—From *Tensions* by H. A. Williams

❧ Small, seemingly innocent events keep telling us how easily we eternalize ourselves and our world. It takes only a hostile word to make us feel sad and lonely. It takes only a rejecting gesture to plunge us into self-complaint. It takes only a substantial failure in our work to lead us into a self-destructive depression. Although we have learned from parents, teachers, friends and many books, sacred as well as profane, that we are worth more than what the world makes us, we keep giving an eternal value to the things we own, the people we know, the plans we have, and the successes we "collect." Indeed, it takes only a small disruption to lay our illusion of immortality bare and to reveal how much we have become victimized by our surrounding world suggesting to us that we are "in control." Aren't the many feelings of sadness, heaviness of heart and even dark despair, often intimately connected with the exaggerated seriousness with which we have clothed the people we know, the ideas to which we are exposed and the events we are part of? This lack of distance, which excludes the humor in life, can create a suffocating depression which prevents us from lifting our heads above the horizon of our own limited existence.

—From *Reaching Out* by Henri J. M. Nouwen

❧ Now and then, during the time of our prayer, we may get the sense of God thrilling us through. It is something to thank God for and accept gratefully while it lasts. But it must not be clutched at or demanded. We must not try to whip ourselves up to it artificially by psychic effort. Nor must we imagine that something has gone wrong when God no longer thrills us through.

—From *Tensions* by H. A. Williams

❧ The lesson of wisdom is, be not dismayed by soul-trouble. Count it no strange thing, but a part of ordinary ministerial experience. Should the power of depression be more than ordinary, think not that all is over with your usefulness. Cast not away your confidence, for it hath great recompense of reward. Even if the enemy's foot be on your neck, expect to rise and overthrow him. Cast the burden of the present, along with the sin of the past and the fear of the future, upon the Lord, who forsaketh not his saints. Live by the day—aye, by the hour. Put not trust in frames and feelings. Care more for a grain of faith than a ton of excitement. Trust in God alone, and lean not on the reeds of human help. Be not surprised when friends fail you: it is a failing world. Never count upon immutability in man: inconstancy you may reckon upon without fear of disappointment. The disciples of Jesus forsook him; be not amazed if your adherents wander away to other teachers: as they were not your all when with you, all is not gone from you with their departure. Serve God with all your might while the candle is burning, and then when it goes out for a season, you will have the less to regret. Be content to be nothing, for that is what you are. When your own emptiness is painfully forced upon your consciousness, chide yourself that you ever dreamed of being full, except in the Lord. Set small store by present rewards; be grateful for earnests by the way, but look for the recompensing joy hereafter. Continue with double earnestness to serve your Lord when no visible result is before you. Any simpleton can follow the narrow path in the light: faith's rare wisdom enables us to march on in the dark with infallible accuracy, since she places her hand in that of her great Guide. Between this and heaven there may be rougher weather yet, but it is all provided for by our covenant Head. In nothing let us be turned aside from the path which the divine call has urged us to pursue. Come fair or come foul, the pulpit is our watchtower, and the ministry our warfare; be it ours, when we cannot see the face of God, to trust under the shadow of his wings.

—From *Lessons to My Students* by Charles Haddon Spurgeon

&. Contemplatives rarely pray in words but if they do, their words are few. The fewer the better, as a matter of fact; yes, and a word of one syllable is more suited to the spiritual nature of this work than longer ones. . . .

Let me try to illustrate what I mean with an example from real life. A man or woman terrified by sudden disaster is forced by the circumstances to the limits of his personal resources, and marshals all his energy into one great cry for help. In extreme situations, like this, a person is not given to many words nor even to long ones. Instead, summoning all his strength, he expresses his desperate need in one loud cry: "Help!" And with this one little word he effectively arouses the attention and assistance of others.

—From *The Cloud of Unknowing*

෫ O Lord, our heavenly Father, without whom all purposes are frustrate, all efforts are vain, grant me the assistance of thy Holy Spirit, that I may not sorrow as one without hope, but may now return to the duties of my present state with humble confidence in thy protection, and so govern my thoughts and actions, that neither business may withdraw my mind from Thee, nor idleness lay me open to vain imaginations; that neither praise may fill me with pride, nor censure with discontent; but that in the changes of this life, I may fix my heart upon the reward which Thou hast promised to them that serve Thee, and that whatever things are true, whatever are pure, whatever are lovely, whatever are of good report, wherein there is virtue, wherein there is praise, I may think upon and do, and obtain mercy and everlasting happiness. Grant this, O Lord, for the sake of Jesus Christ. *Amen.*

—From *Doctor Johnson's Prayers,* edited by Elton Trueblood

෫ Lord, thou hast said that our Father in heaven notes even the fall of a sparrow to the ground. Help us to believe, O God, that thou art concerned not only with the rolling of the spheres in their orbits, but even with each of us, our doubts, and perplexities.

We remember all too well the bitter discoveries we have made when we have tried to run our lives our own way, when we try to steer our own craft. Wilt thou come aboard, Lord Jesus, and set us a true course, for we grow weary of life's demands, tired of our own blundering ways.

We seek a clear light to shine upon our troubled way.

We ask thee to give us clearer directions.

Where we have missed the way and wandered far, bring us back at whatever cost to our pride.

Take away our stubborn self-will, for we know that in thy will alone is our peace. We seek that peace.

—From *The Prayers of Peter Marshall,* edited by Catherine Marshall

❧ If I have faltered more or less
In my great task of happiness;
If I have moved among my race
And shown no shining morning face;
If beams from happy human eyes
Have moved me not; if morning skies,
Books, and my food, and summer rain,
Knocked on my sullen heart in vain:
Lord, thy most pointed pleasure take
And stab my spirit broad awake.

—From "The Celestial Surgeon" by Robert Louis Stevenson

❧ These troubles and distresses that you go through in these Waters are no sign that God hath forsaken you, but are sent to try you, whether you will call to mind that which heretofore you have received of his goodness, and live upon him in your distresses.

Then I saw in my Dream that Christian was as in a muse a while. To whom also Hopeful added this word, Be of good cheer, Jesus Christ maketh thee whole: and with that Christian brake out with a loud voice, Oh, I see him again, and he tells me, When thou passest through the Waters, I will be with thee; and through the Rivers, they shall not overflow thee. Then they both took courage, and the Enemy was after that as still as a stone, until they were gone over. Christian, therefore, presently found ground to stand upon, and so it followed that the rest of the River was but shallow. Thus they got over.

—From *The Pilgrim's Progress* by John Bunyan

Retreat Model 12: The Servant's Struggle

Arrival

Thirty Minutes of Silent Listening

Scripture Readings
John 15; 2 Corinthians 3; 1 Corinthians 9;
Philippians 3

Readings for Reflection

Reflection

Prayer

Journal Writing

Recreation

Rest

Repeat Cycle of Scripture Readings, Readings for
Reflection, Reflection, Prayer, and Journal Writing

Thirty Minutes of Silent Reflection

Holy Communion

Benediction

Readings for Reflection

❧ Often, in more or less popular literature about prayer, we are told that prayer is an enthralling adventure. It is a commonplace to hear: 'Come on, learn to pray; prayer is so interesting, so thrilling, it is the discovery of a new world; you will meet God, you will find the way to a spiritual life.' In a sense of course this is true; but something very much more far-reaching is being forgotten when such statements are made: it is that prayer is a dangerous adventure and that we cannot enter upon it without risk. As St Paul says, it is a fearful thing to fall into the hands of the living God (Heb 10:31). Therefore to set out deliberately to confront the living God is a dread adventure: every meeting with God is, in a certain sense, a last judgement.

—From *Living Prayer* by Anthony Bloom

❧ Too often prayer has no such importance in our lives that everything else fades away to give it room. Prayer is additional to a great many things; we wish God to be present, not because there is no life without him, not because he is the supreme value, but because it would be so nice, in addition to all the great benefits of God, to have also his presence. He is additional to our needs, and when we seek him in that spirit we do not meet him. Yet notwithstanding all that has just been said, prayer, dangerous as it appears, is the best way to go ahead towards the fulfillment of our calling, to become fully human, which means in full communion with God and, ultimately, what St Peter calls partakers of the divine nature.

Love and friendship do not grow if we are not prepared to sacrifice a great deal for their sake, and in the same way we must be ready to put aside many things in order to give God the first place.

'Thou shalt love the Lord thy God with all thy heart, and with all thy soul, and with all thy strength, and with all thy mind' (Lk 10:27). This seems to be a very simple command, and yet those words contain much more than one sees at a first glance. We all know what it is to love someone with all one's heart; we know the pleasure, not only of meeting but even of thinking of the beloved, the warm comfort it gives. It is in that way that we should try to love God, and whenever his name is mentioned, it should fill our heart and soul with infinite warmth. God should be at all times in our mind, whereas in fact we think of him only occasionally.

As for loving God with all our strength, we can only do it if we cast off deliberately everything that is not God's in us; by an effort of will we must turn ourselves constantly towards God, whether in prayer, which is easier, because in prayer we are already centered on God, or in action, which requires training, because in our actions we are concentrated on some material achievement and have to dedicate it to God by a special effort.

—From *Living Prayer* by Anthony Bloom

❦ Religion can provide a way to avoid the harsh facts of our experience, or it can be a means of living into the unpleasant actuality with reasonable hope. The spiritual life of the pastor or priest necessarily reflects his or her choice between those two alternatives. It is to be regretted that far too frequently the religion of escape characterizes the style of the ordained person, for indeed it is this that often receives the accolades of the powerful and wealthy.

—From *Spirituality for Ministry* by Urban T. Holmes III

❦ "Jesus has so diligently searched for the lowest place that it would be very difficult for anyone to tear it from him."

Nazareth was the lowest place: the place of the poor, the unknown, of those who didn't count, of the mass of workers, of people subjected to work's grim demands just for a scrap of bread.

But there is more. Jesus is the 'Holy One of God.' But the Holy One of God realised his sanctity not in an extraordinary life, but one impregnated with ordinary things: work, family and social life, obscure human activities, simple things shared by all people.

The perfection of God is cast in a material which people almost despise, which they don't consider worth searching for because of its simplicity, its lack of interest, because it is common to all of us.

—From *Letters from the Desert* by Carlo Carretto

❧ God's goodness hath been great to thee;
Let never day or night unhallowed pass,
But still remember what the Lord hath done.
—William Shakespeare

❧ He whom neither humans nor angels can grasp by knowledge can be embraced by love.
—From *The Cloud of Unknowing*

❧ So whenever you feel drawn by grace to the contemplative work and are determined to do it, simply raise your heart to God with a gentle stirring of love. Think only of God, the God who created you, redeemed you, and guided you to this work. Allow no other ideas about God to enter your mind. Yet even this is too much. A naked intent toward God, the desire for him alone, is enough.
—From *The Cloud of Unknowing*

❧ Be sure that if you are occupied with something less than God, you place it above you for the time being and create a barrier between yourself and God. Therefore, firmly reject all clear ideas however pious or delightful. For I tell you this, one loving blind desire for God alone is more valuable in itself, more pleasing to God and to the saints, more beneficial to your own growth, and more helpful to your friends, both living and dead, than anything else you could do.
—From *The Cloud of Unknowing*

❧ As you hear the wind, and feel it too, while it strikes upon your bodily organs, you will know you are under the guidance of God's Spirit the same way, namely, by feeling it in your soul; by the present peace, joy and love which you feel within, as well as by its outward and more distant effects.
—John Wesley

❧ To have a cure of souls . . . is the highest task to which any minister can be called. To stand in the pulpit on Sunday and see the eager and expectant faces of the people turned toward you, and know they have come for worship and for the bit of bread that you have been preparing for them in the week; to feel as you look at them: "These are my people";

to know that in all the great hours of their life, when they want to be wed, when a child is born into their home, when trouble comes, when the doctor is going in and out, when bereavement robs them of every scrap of joy—to know that in that hour the door is open, and you not only may go but you must go; that the cry of their heart then is for their minister . . . to dwell upon that is to know a joy which, to my mind, not even the unquestioned delights of scholarly research can surpass. To receive the confidence of people, to know the secrets they have told to no other living soul; to blush with them over their sins and exult with them when the sin is flung under the table; to know their private affairs and to be the sharer of their highest ideals, is to have a joy of which not one of us is really worthy.

—From *The Approach to Preaching* by W. E. Sangster

   O Lord, I have been talking to the people;
      Thought's wheels have round me whirled a fiery zone,
      And the recoil of my word's airy ripple
      My heart unheedful has puffed up and blown.
      Therefore I cast myself before thee prone:
      Lay cool hands on my burning brain and press
      From my heart the swelling emptiness.
      —From *Diary of an Old Soul* by George MacDonald

   We must make sure that we do not decide that we shall succeed. If we decide to succeed then we may succeed without succeeding in God's way. But if we go on from day to day seeking to do his will, then we shall be prepared to receive success from him if he wills it; and if he does not, then humbly to say—It is God's decision that David shall not build the temple, but he will raise up Solomon.

—W. A. Visser't Hooft as quoted in *That They May Have Life* by Daniel T. Niles

   Teach us, our Father, that if we nourish within ourselves those things that turn us away from the light, we shall spend our years stumbling through the darkness. Teach us, our Father, that if we be true to the light that is within us, we shall become like thee, and to become like thee is the be-all and end-all of our desiring.

—From *The Growing Edge* by Howard Thurman

❧ Holy God, to whose service I long ago dedicated my soul and life, I grieve and lament before thee that I am still so prone to sin and so little inclined to obedience:

So much attached to the pleasure of sense, so negligent of things spiritual:

So prompt to gratify my body, so slow to nourish my soul:

So greedy for present delight, so indifferent to lasting blessedness:

So fond of idleness, so indisposed for labour:

So soon at play, so late at prayer:

So brisk in the service of self, so slack in the service of others:

So eager to get, so reluctant to give:

So lofty in my profession, so low in my practice:

So full of good intentions, so backward to fulfil them:

So severe with my neighbours, so indulgent with myself:

So eager to find fault, so resentful at being found fault with:

So little able for great tasks, so discontented with small ones;

So weak in adversity, so swollen and self-satisfied in prosperity:

So helpless apart from thee, and yet so little willing to be bound to thee.

O merciful heart of God, grant me yet again thy forgiveness. Hear my sorrowful tale and in thy great mercy blot it out from the book of thy remembrance. Give me faith so to lay hold of thine own holiness and so to rejoice in the righteousness of Christ my Saviour that, resting on his merits rather than on my own, I may more and more become conformed to his likeness, my will becoming one with his in obedience to thine. All this I ask for his holy name's sake. Amen.

—From *A Diary of Private Prayer* by John Baillie

Index